WEIMAR GERMANY'S LEFT-WING INTELLECTUALS
A POLITICAL HISTORY OF THE WELTBÜHNE AND
ITS CIRCLE

WEIMAR GERMANY'S LEFT-WING INTELLECTUALS

A Political History of the *Weltbühne* and Its Circle

by ISTVAN DEAK

UNIVERSITY OF CALIFORNIA PRESS
Berkeley and Los Angeles, 1968

University of California Press
Berkeley and Los Angeles, California
Cambridge University Press
London, England
Copyright © 1968, by
The Regents of the University of California
Library of Congress Catalog Card Number: 68–9271
Printed in the United States of America

TO GLORIA AND EVA

PREFACE

This book is due to a youthful fascination with the writers, poets, and dramatists of my native Hungary, some of whom made political history. Ever since the late eighteenth century, Hungarian intellectuals molded public opinion, launched new political movements, and alternately bolstered and undermined the existing government. All this was taken for granted by Hungarians: if the country's professional politicians were traditionally short-sighted and ruthless, true leadership rightfully belonged to the more imaginative and graceful literati. Even the avowedly anti-intellectual regime of Admiral Nicholas Horthy could not prevent the literati from dazzling the nation with magnificent revolutionary programs. And the intellectuals were taken so seriously that in 1945 several were given leading political positions.

As an adult, I came to recognize the heavy debt that Hungarian literati owed to the men of ideas abroad. Just as the previous generation had looked to Paris for inspiration, the Hungarian intellectuals of the interwar period, whether Communists, democrats, populists, conservative revolutionaries, or fascists, looked to Berlin. But the German intellectuals, to whom I inevitably turned, proved to have had neither power nor influence in their political world. In twentieth-century Hungary the literati were at least partly responsible for two revolutions, those of 1918–1919 and 1956, and for the political and social ferment of other years. Their brilliant German counterparts achieved almost nothing. My first attempt to understand why led to a doctoral dissertation, written at Columbia University, on Carl von Ossietzky, a martyr among the German left-wing literati. More comprehensive attempts led to the present work.

I wish to thank the many friends and acquaintances who let me share their knowledge of Weimar Germany; some gave me valuable information and I would like to record their names. Heinz Pol, Kurt R. Grossmann, Kurt Hiller, Walther Karsch, Hilde Walter, and the late Manfred George, all former writers of the *Weltbühne,* told me of the journal and of their own Weimar experiences. Raimund Koplin and Norbert Muhlen, writers, and Hellmut Jaesrich, editor of the Berlin *Der Monat,* permitted me to draw on their expert knowledge of German affairs. Ferdinand Fried, Giselher Wirsing, and the late Hans Zehrer, all former writers of the *Tat,* and the late Rudolf Pechel, editor of the *Deutsche Rundschau,* described to me their days as conservatives and conservative revolutionaries of Weimar and their polemics with the left-wing intellectuals. Reverend Hanno Stapel in Hamburg opened to me the literary *Nachlass* of his father, Wilhelm Stapel; Mary Gerold-Tucholsky put documents at my disposal from the rich Tucholsky archives in Rottach-Egern, Bavaria.

The government of the German Federal Republic provided a fellowship which permitted me to spend the year 1960–1961 in Heidelberg garnering material; the Columbia University Council for Research in the Social Sciences gave me a grant for the summer of 1966 to aid in the writing of the manuscript; the European Institute of Columbia University (Director Professor Philip E. Mosely) helped cover the costs of typing the manuscript. My heartfelt thanks to these benefactors.

I would like to thank Professor Werner Conze and Dr. Wolfgang Schieder of the University of Heidelberg for their valuable advice. Of my American friends and advisers, special gratitude is due to Professors Peter Gay of Columbia University; Robert A. Kann and Harold L. Poor of Rutgers University; Klemens von Klemperer and Allan Mitchell of Smith College; Henry L. Roberts of Dartmouth College; Helmut Gruber of the Brooklyn Polytechnic Institute, and Werner T. Angress of the State University of New York at Stony Brook. Some of them spent many hours trying to argue me out of false conceptions; others read and corrected the manuscript in one or all its forms. Of Professor Fritz Stern, my friend, colleague, and master at Columbia University, I can say only that without him I would be neither a writer nor a teacher.

Mr. Max Knight of the University of California Press helped me immeasurably. His assistance I can only interpret as love for the profession and for the subject matter of which he is in any case a foremost expert.

I received valuable assistance from several Ph.D. candidates at

Columbia University. Miss Manuela Dobos-Schleicher did extensive research for me and wrote an outline for some sections; more importantly, through the brilliant mind of this young left-wing intellectual, I came to a closer understanding of her spiritual antecedents. Miss Ingrun Lafleur, Miss Sophia Sluzar, and Mr. Trevor Hope did valuable research for me and read parts of my manuscript.

Mrs. Florence Aranov, Miss Ene Sirvet, and Mrs. Hilda McArthur typed the manuscript, the first two out of generosity, the third professionally, but all three with expert care and great forbearance.

My wife—herself a writer—edited, reedited, and again reedited the manuscript. She also raised a child while I was writing. And our three-year-old daughter viewed my manuscript as so many more sheets to be scribbled on: I am indebted to her for this new perspective of my work.

I.D.

CONTENTS

INTRODUCTION

There was in Weimar Germany a band of journalists, writers, poets, and philosophers whom it was customary to call *linke Intellektuelle,* "left-wing intellectuals." Politically, they stood somewhere between Social Democracy and Communism but it is awkward to classify those who relentlessly criticized every political movement. They appointed themselves the conscience of Germany and as such, in the period leading to the National Socialist takeover, they were singularly unsuccessful. But they were a vibrant part of the Weimar scene and it is surprising that, until now, their politics have been given so little scholarly attention. Historians have concentrated largely on the ideologies and behavior of the Right in Weimar; the studies that have been made of the Left have been confined to individual political parties. The most vociferous and consistent opposition to the nationalists, however, came not from the hesitant liberals or Social Democrats, nor from the supremely inconsistent and suicidal Communists, but from the left-wing intellectuals. Moreover, these literati, and such Communists as Bertolt Brecht, Ludwig Renn, Erwin Piscator, and Anna Seghers, to whom they stood very close, were responsible for much of the cultural brilliance and vitality of the Weimar period. *Die Weltbühne,* a weekly journal which printed the views of most of these literati, is the subject of this study.

There were various terms used to designate this band of intellectuals. Some called them "radical democrats," some "radical humanists," and others "radical leftists." Thomas Mann spoke of "the left

---

Notes indicated by arabic numerals follow the text in the back of the book.

side of social philosophy," and Heinrich Mann of "revolutionary democracy."[1] "Left-wing intellectual" is adopted here because it was the term most familiar to the politically articulate of that period. *Linker Intellektuelle* in the Weimar days evoked images in the public mind which varied from the lone defender of justice or humanity— Prometheus or Don Quixote?—to the offensive *Asphaltliterat*, a despicable product of big-city immorality engaged in the subversion of sacred German values. Their enemies also called the left-wing intellectuals *Kulturbolschewisten*. Carl von Ossietzky, an editor of the *Weltbühne*, showed that the latter term was most elastic. The *Kulturbolschewist*, he wrote in 1931,[2] was the latest version of the eternal subversive: in the Middle Ages he was called a witch; under Bismarck "he wore royal Hannoverian Junker boots, a worker's beret, a red shirt and a black cassock. In his inner pocket he carried the statutes of a freemasonic lodge and a freshly printed copy of the *Vossische Zeitung*."[a] In the twentieth century, the eternal subversive became a *Kulturbolschewist*.

Kulturbolschewismus is when Conductor Klemperer takes tempi different from his colleague Furtwängler, when a painter sweeps a color into his sunset not seen in Lower Pomerania; when one favors birth control; when one builds a house with a flat roof; when a Caesarean birth is shown on the screen; when one admires the performance of Charlie Chaplin and the mathematical wizardry of Albert Einstein. This is called cultural Bolshevism and a personal favor rendered to Herr Stalin. It is also the democratic mentality of the brothers Mann, a piece of music by Hindemith or Weill, and is to be identified with the hysterical insistence of a madman for a law giving him the permission to marry his own grandmother.[3]

The camp of cultural Bolshevism's enemies is large, wrote Ossietzky. It includes the "two Josephs": Joseph Goebbels and Joseph Wirth,[b] P. N. Cossmann,[c] and the entire bourgeois press. It includes the Social

---

[a] *Die Vossische Zeitung*, the oldest daily newspaper in Berlin (founded in 1704) opposed Bismarck on progressive liberal grounds.

[b] Joseph Wirth (1879–1956), leader of the democratic wing of the Catholic Center Party ("Zentrum"), was Reich Chancellor from October 1921 to November 1922. After World War II, Wirth headed a small political movement for the reunification of Germany through East-West reconciliation. In 1955, he was awarded the Stalin Prize for Peace. The coupling of this staunch republican with Goebbels was certainly not accidental. Ossietzky was suspicious of Wirth and his "black" party.

[c] Paul Nikolaus Cossmann (1869–1942), a Catholic conservative, was the editor from 1905 to 1933 of the *Süddeutsche Monatshefte*. During World War I, Cossmann demanded total victory. In 1922, he was instrumental in staging the anti-Versailles "War Guilt Trial," yet he was also an opponent of the "Stab in the Back" legend. In 1930, he opened the pages of his journal to both Jews and

Democrats whose press avoids this term in print but echoes it in spirit. And the Communists? Well, "when one reads what feelings certain Communist papers express towards the writers of the *Weltbühne*, one often feels like offering the Communists a helping hand and urging them to go ahead: 'But children, say it! You too would love to call us cultural Bolshevists. Say it, at last!' " [4]

The left-wing intellectual could often overcome the isolation traditionally imposed on the free publicist by thinking of himself as a better sort of German who belonged to *das andere Deutschland*, "the other Germany." [d] On the occasion of the twenty-fifth anniversary of the *Weltbühne*, Kurt Tucholsky, another editor of the journal, wrote: "As long as *Die Weltbühne* will be *Die Weltbühne*, we will give it our utmost. And this utmost will serve a good cause . . . that of transforming this *Teutschland* [•] into a *Deutschland*, of proving to all that, besides Hitler, Hugenberg, and those fish-eyed academicians of the year 1930, there are also other Germans in Germany." [5]

The left-wing intellectuals continually haggled over their identity as well as their purpose. Yet perhaps the best, because the most characteristic, formulation of their views comes not from a Weimar manifesto but from a recent autobiographical novel by Leonhard Frank, an expressionist writer and a collaborator of the *Weltbühne*. The title of the work itself, *Links wo das Herz ist* ("Heart on the Left") aptly describes the tenor of the left-wing intellectual's beliefs. Frank says about his hero:

He believes that under a capitalist economy . . . human virtues, both in the rich and the poor, are unable to develop. It says much for men and women that in an economic order of extreme inequality they are as good as they are. He believes that history is moving, impelled by its own laws, towards a Socialist economy; that the oppressed, whether individuals or nations, act in their forward drive as executive organs of history, as grains of sand in the wheels of what is at present the established system. He proclaims to all, whether they wish to hear or not, that the grains of sand

---

anti-Semites in a debate on the Jewish question in Germany. Cossmann loathed the *Asphaltliteratur* of the period and hailed Hans Grimm (*Volk ohne Raum*) and other *völkisch* authors. Of Jewish descent, Cossmann died in the ghetto of Theresienstadt.

[d] The expression "the other Germany" probably originates from the title of the pacifist journal, *Das andere Deutschland*, founded in January 1920 by Friedrich Küster in Hagen, Westphalia. In Hitler's era it was used extensively by the German emigrés and the Western press in a careful attempt to differentiate between "good" and "bad" Germans. See, for instance, Erika and Klaus Mann, *The Other Germany* (New York, 1940).

[•] *Teutschland* is an archaic form occasionally used both by the conservatives and their opponents to designate traditional, historic Germany.

will triumph, for the movement towards the Socialist economy cannot be stayed. . . . He believes that the acquisitive economic system [*Haben-haben-haben Wirtschaftsordnung*] will be replaced, even without an atomic war, before the dawn of a new century, by a Socialist economic order. He believes that our children's grandchildren may have greater happiness than we have ever been allowed to know. . . . He believes that man can and will become humane only when nothing compels him to be inhumane. He believes in mankind for he accepts what he sees in the eyes of innocent children.[6]

Socialism, democracy, and a belief in the inherent goodness of man were the main tenets of the left-wing intellectual creed. A child of the Enlightenment and of the French Revolution, the left-wing intellectual dreamed of a world where the heretofore impossible combination of peace, individual liberty, and social equality would prevail. He fondly wished to "debarbarize" society and "unromanticize" war if by no other means than by his burlesque assaults upon solemnity and cruelty. He believed that society could and should be changed, that it is the inherent right of man to be happy, and that world solidarity was far from being a hopeless proposition.

Such views were obviously compatible with the platforms of the great democratic and socialist parties, and some left-wing intellectuals gave these parties their allegiance. But those who did so invariably felt uneasy. Had the Independent Socialist Party,[f] a product of the Great War, survived the troubled postwar years, it would probably have attracted most of these intellectuals. But the USPD disappeared in 1922. So it was that the left-wing intellectual in the SPD[g] reproached his leaders for betraying the cause of the German workers to the bourgeoisie; that his counterpart in the KPD[h] resented his leaders for sacrificing the interest of the German workers to that of the party apparatus, and that the left-wing intellectual in the DDP[i] imputed to his leaders the surrender of free thought to bigotry and the betrayal of the educated man's foremost task: the defense of the lower classes. In every instance, the left-wing intellectuals reproached their parties for ignoring the literati and entrusting leadership to dull-witted functionaries. Most of them were not so unrealistic as the phi-

---

[f] "Unabhängige sozialdemokratische Partei Deutschlands" (USPD). Its members were often called the "Independents."

[g] "Sozialdemokratische Partei Deutschlands," the Social Democratic Party of Germany. Its members were also often called Majority Socialists.

[h] "Kommunistische Partei Deutschlands," the Communist Party of Germany. It originated from the war-time "Spartakus" movement.

[i] "Deutsche Demokratische Partei," the German Democratic Party—the organization of the liberal and republican German bourgeoisie.

losopher Kurt Hiller who pleaded for a *Logokratie,* a government of philosopher-kings where "the morally and intellectually superior would reign." [7] What all of them did demand was a *Vergeistigung,* an "intellectualization" of the political life of Germany.

There was a great deal of naïveté in these aspirations. Far removed from political power, even from its illegitimate or revolutionary variety, the left-wing intellectuals often eschewed considerations of means and spun out lovely visions of what might be. In political terms, their dedication to the good of mankind was insufficient, their claims often impossible. Yet perhaps what Germany needed was to tackle the impossible. The republican moderate who preached compromise with the Right masked his fear of forceful action, as did the Communist militant who, because he was preparing for the "final struggle," refused to work honestly with the republicans, not to speak of non-Communist workers. In the final analysis, both paved the way for the triumph of Hitler. The revolution for which the left-wing intellectuals clamored in the pages of the *Weltbühne,* however imprecisely defined, was meant to revitalize both republicans and Communists, and to bring them together on a common platform of antifascist action.

"Die Weltbühne!" wrote Kurt Hiller in his recent reminiscences, "It wasn't a journal. It was an institution! It wasn't the journal of the so-called homeless Left alone; it belonged to those who had a home but weren't quite satisfied. . . . Around 1930 . . . it was considered uncouth not to have read the latest issue of the *Weltbühne.*" [8] Hiller was one of the journal's main contributors, but other writers, much less rhapsodic about *Die Weltbühne,* had no hesitation either in giving it its due: "The majority of its [*Die Weltbühne's*] readers were recruited from among coffeehouse intellectuals (*Literaten*), bohemian types, students, agnostics, sceptics," writes Hermann Behr, a liberal critic of the left-wing intellectuals, "yet thanks to the sharp and masterly style of its articles, it came to be regarded as the best-written journal in Germany and its influence extended far beyond the circle of its main readers." [9] Nor were the *Weltbühne's* rightist enemies unappreciative of its influence and significance. When, on the night of May 11, 1933, on the Opera Square in Berlin, Nationalist [J] and National-Socialist stu-

---

[J] The term "nationalist" had a dual meaning in Weimar politics designating (1) all right-wing enemies of the republic, (2) members of the "Deutschnationale Volkspartei" or DNVP (German Nationalist Party), the major conservative political movement which concluded a tactical alliance in the early 1930's with Hitler's "Nationalsozialistische Deutsche Arbeiterpartei" or NSDAP (National

dents and professors ceremoniously burned piles of books, student "callers" enumerated the particular sins of the authors. Of the fifteen they named, thirteen had, at one time or another, made contributions to the *Weltbühne*. Of the two others, one, Theodor Wolff,[k] editor of the *Berliner Tageblatt*, was a close friend of the *Weltbühne*. The other was Karl Marx.[10]

Established in 1905 in Berlin as *Die Schaubühne* ("The Theatrical Stage"), this weekly organ of the performing arts began to dabble in politics in the years immediately preceding World War I. Thereafter, columns dealing with political issues multiplied, and with the change of the journal's name in 1918 to *Die Weltbühne* (The World Stage), politics dominated its pages. This publication attracted hundreds of contributors, German and foreign. They delighted in the journal's self-sufficiency—it was independent of sponsors and advertisers—in its casual and free atmosphere, its courage, the sarcastic violence of its style, in its "causes" and its campaigns, and in the talents of its three successive editors, Jacobsohn, Tucholsky, and Ossietzky. Siegfried Jacobsohn, the journal's founder, and its editor until 1926, was a formidable theater critic and a demanding stylist; he also had a remarkable political flair. Kurt Tucholsky's editorship was brief (1926–1927), but as the journal's star contributor, he issued a torrent of polemical writings marked by extraordinary insight. He was, in turn, exasperatingly arrogant, jocularly kind, and naïve; today, he is one of the prophets of German youth. Carl von Ossietzky, editor in chief between 1927 and 1933, and a more enigmatic personality, was a first-class journalist and a man of great courage. Later he achieved world fame as a prisoner of the Gestapo and as the recipient—while still a prisoner—of the Nobel Prize for Peace. He died in 1938, still in the hands of the Nazis.

We must not, however, exaggerate the importance of the *Weltbühne*. There were other left-wing intellectual publications. *Das Tage-Buch*, a weekly journal founded in 1920, resembled *Die Weltbühne* in style, in format, in its manifold preoccupations, and often in its political message. Led by two able journalists, Stefan Grossmann and Leopold Schwarzschild, it was often more successful

---

Socialist Party). Members of the DNVP are often referred to in English as "Nationalists" (with a capital "N") in an attempt to distinguish them from other members of the rightist or "nationalist" camp.

[k] A brief resumé on Theodor Wolff, as well as on some other individuals, journals, and political organizations frequently mentioned in the pages of the *Weltbühne* is included in Appendix II. This Appendix contains information on some of the "Friends and Enemies" of the *Weltbühne*.

in attracting famous names, especially from abroad. *Das Tage-Buch* appealed to the same audience as did *Die Weltbühne* and employed almost the same writers (Ossietzky, for instance, came from the *Tage-Buch* to the *Weltbühne*)—with little love lost between the pugnacious Jacobsohn and the editors of the rival paper. If *Die Weltbühne* and not *Das Tage-Buch* was chosen here for examination, it is because *Das Tage-Buch* was less radical and, as years went by, became increasingly friendly to the failing republic, whereas *Die Weltbühne* stepped up its attacks.[1] *Das Tage-Buch* had no revolutionary message while *Die Weltbühne* was commonly accepted as the principal paper of the radical writers. A certain magic surrounded the name of the *Weltbühne* which the rival paper never enjoyed. Ultimately, the journal and its circle were chosen for this study as an example: a start on the very difficult problem of left-wing intellectual politics in the Weimar era.

There were at least two other noteworthy journals: *Die Zukunft*, edited by Maximilian Harden, and *Die Fackel*, edited by the brilliant Karl Kraus. Both were highly controversial and their editors fiercely hated. More will be said about them later. What is significant here is that in the Weimar era the importance of these journals had begun to decline. Disillusionment—and a brutal beating by "patriotic" assailants—forced Harden, this unique political critic of the Wilhelmian era, to put an end to *Die Zukunft*. As for the Viennese Karl Kraus, his savage political and social commentaries were relished by the sophisticated reader but *Die Fackel* was little more than a private mouthpiece. Whether Kraus was truly of the Left is at least doubtful. Moreover, what had sounded like welcome nonconformity on the part of Kraus in the old regime became plain viciousness in the republican era. A maniacal hatred for the liberal press and politicians eventually distorted Kraus's vision of the dangers from the Right and—in the words of Arnold Zweig—he "abandoned his struggle against tyranny at the very moment when it was most needed, namely in 1933." [11]

The left-wing intellectuals did not write for the *Weltbühne* alone. Those who were members of political parties contributed to the party organs; others wrote for the officially nonaffiliated Münzenberg concern. This curious private chain of newspapers and journals, cleverly directed by Willi Münzenberg, a functionary of the Comintern in Germany, succeeded in attracting many who might otherwise have

---

[1] After 1933, the exile editions of the two papers no longer resembled each other: *Die Weltbühne* was gradually taken over by Communists and *Das Tage-Buch* became more and more critical of Communists tactics.

never written for the Communist press. In addition, many in the *Weltbühne* worked for the big liberal and democratic dailies. The *Berliner Tageblatt* owned by the great Mosse concern and also the newspapers of the more prestigious House of Ullstein were open to the left-wing intellectuals and published some of their best pieces. There was undoubtedly some opportunism in this willingness to be in print on opposite sides, but the attraction of the good life in Berlin was irresistible and asceticism unknown to these writers. Mass-circulation papers paid far better than *Die Weltbühne*. What motivated this literary proliferation, however, was more likely the fact that the left-wing intellectuals, justifiably convinced they had something to say, were prepared to say it anywhere in the corridors of Left or Center. There was also a certain *hauteur* in their feeling that they would remain unsullied. Weren't they, after all, the uncrowned rulers of the Berlin stage and of literary life? Weren't many in the *Weltbühne* circle —Heinrich Mann, Alfred Polgar, Erich Kästner, Alfred Döblin, Leonhard Frank, Theodor Plievier, Carl Zuckmayer, René Schickele, Lion Feuchtwanger, Fritz von Unruh, Ernst Toller, Arnold Zweig—among the great novelists, essayists, and dramatists of Weimar?

It is hard and perhaps unjust to attribute uniformity of any kind to men of this caliber, to intellectuals who held so tenaciously to the sovereignty of their minds. But this particular brand of stubbornness and the things they did share in common—their utopias, their ambivalences, their ideals, their passions, and their radicalism—clearly bind them. And these intellectuals were united further, in a more significant way, by their certainty that revolution alone could save Weimar Germany. In the attempt by others to bind them, they have been characterized as "homeless," an oft-repeated political epithet that has a much wider meaning. Although very German in some of their characteristics—idealism, sentimentality, undialectical either-or-ness, unwillingness to accept halfway measures like the republic—they were out of place in Germany. In a country where society's ideal was the functionary, where everybody wished to belong, they generally shied away from affiliation. In a country where the bourgeois flaunted his idealism and the apolitical nature of his existence—and then voted the nationalist ticket—they threw themselves into politics with the enthusiasm of converts. In a culture generally characterized by provincialism, bigotry, and narrow nationalism, they believed themselves the first true cosmopolitans since the lonely giants Marx, Engels, Nietzsche, and Burckhardt.

Furthermore, the writers of the *Weltbühne* were the archetypes of a Central European phenomenon: the journalist who was also a literary figure, an intellectual, a social critic, a reformer, and a revolutionary. They combined within themselves features of the bourgeois, the artist-intellectual, and the revolutionist—a volatile blend of personality ingredients which accounts for much of their personal and artistic ambiguity. In an age of specialization, it is refreshing, and sometimes exasperating, to reckon with those who thought themselves protean. They considered themselves "tribunes of the German people"—guardians and innovators who, because they were not covered with dust as were the *Bonzen* (the bosses) of political parties, knew better how society ought to be run than Germany's tired bureaucrats.

Finally, left-wing intellectual politics in Weimar Germany has its parallels in the efforts of Western European literati in the late 1930's. The British poet or French writer in the Spanish republican trenches had his precursor in the Weimar man of letters who, like his counterpart in the International Brigade, fought militarism, intolerance, and social injustice, and believed that international Communism was an ally in this struggle. Because of the unique character of Weimar, the writers of the *Weltbühne* were confronted, well before their Western counterparts, with fascism, popular ennui, political disengagement, and the collapse of republican and democratic ideas. Their unsuccessful call for a unity of antifascists was a tragic rehearsal for the Popular Front appeals in the late 1930's when Western literati belatedly tried to avert the catastrophe which had engulfed Germany in 1933.

Part One

THE "OTHER GERMANS"

Chapter I
THE WRITERS OF THE *WELTBÜHNE*

BERLIN

"Travel across the world from the North Pole to the South Pole"— wrote Kurt Tucholsky—"you will find that everything takes place among two hundred people." [1] So it must have seemed to the buoyant literary establishment of the 1920's in Berlin where Döblin wrote *Berlin Alexanderplatz* and Brecht *Die Dreigroschenoper;* where Erwin Piscator crowded the stage with mechanical devices and Leopold Jessner used only a stairway; where Fritz Lang produced *Dr. Mabuse* and Werner Krauss frightened his audience in the "Cabinet of Dr. Caligari"; where Emil Jannings acted, Lotte Lenya sang, and Kurt Weill composed. It was the *Weltbühne's* achievement to capture the moods of this particular world and to recruit most of Berlin's intellectual elite as collaborators. Only extreme—and fairly rare—political commitment, orthodox Communist or conservative, stopped a Berlin writer from contributing to the journal.

The cultural eminence of Berlin was of relatively recent date, for Germany had traditionally been without a cultural center as well as without a political capital. Even after its elevation in 1871 to the rank of Imperial capital, Berlin, for a while, bore the marks of its original designation as a garrison town. But now it was gripped by the fever of real-estate speculation and its expansion in the 1870's, unguided by any architectural tradition, gave it the aspect of a Teutonic Chicago. Twenty years later it was culturally still overshadowed by Munich and the more gracious capitals of Germany's lesser princes.[a] What gradu-

---

[a] "In implicit opposition to Berlin the southern capital of Munich seemed raffish and Bohemian. It was known as a city of painters and creative writers, of French influence, and of a teasing *esprit frondeur.* In the prevailing humorlessness

13

ally invigorated its cultural life was the formation of the big newspaper concerns which had followed in the footsteps of big business, and the many new theaters where the newly affluent were invited to spend their money and to receive their weekly fare of shock and provocation in the form of theatrical "realism" and "naturalism." By the early 1900's, Berlin was an important gathering place for artists who casually defied Imperial and bourgeois cultural standards, and cultivated everything that was artistically modern. Even so, it was only after 1918 that Berlin truly became Germany's cultural capital. The reason for this was political. While Munich turned savagely reactionary and most of the other great German cities remained conservative, Berlin suddenly became progressive. Not only was it now the seat of a republican Reich administration, but also that of democratic Prussia, and of two clashing, but active working-class parties. Of course, even in the Weimar era, Germany remained culturally decentralized to some degree. Leipzig continued to be the headquarters of Germany's book trade and of a radical and intelligent regional socialist movement; Frankfurt had a democratic university and the illustrious *Frankfurter Zeitung;* Cologne was the seat of German Catholicism, and Hamburg was always regarded as the window to Britain. Theaters flourished in these and dozens of smaller urban centers. But the small towns gradually fell into a cultural blight reflected in the decline of provincial journalism and its gradual submission to the big syndicated press of the nationalist-conservative Hugenberg variety. A victim of this blight was the *Bauhaus* school of Hugo Gropius and Wassily Kandinsky: in 1925, the citizens of Weimar expelled the *Bauhaus* artists from their town.

Berlin harbored those who elsewhere might have been subjected to ridicule or persecution. Comintern agents, Dadaist poets, expressionist painters, anarchist philosophers, *Sexualwissenschaftler,* vegetarian and Esperantist prophets of a new humanity, *Schnorrer* ("freeloaders" —artists of coffeehouse indolence), courtesans, homosexuals, drug addicts, naked dancers, and apostles of nudist self-liberation, black marketeers, embezzlers, and professional criminals flourished in a city which was hungry for the new, the sensational, and the extreme. Moreover, Berlin became the cultural center of Central and Eastern

---

of Wilhelmian Germany, the Munich review *Simplizissimus* was almost the only voice of irony and satire. . . . It was no accident that the young Thomas Mann— like many other refugees from the unsympathetic north—just after the turn of the century should have settled in Munich and associated himself with *Simplizissimus.*" H. Stuart Hughes, *Consciousness and Society* (New York, 1958), 46.

Europe as well. Those who now dictated public taste and morals, who enlightened, entertained, or corrupted their customers were not only Germans but Russian refugees from the Red and Hungarian refugees from the White terror, voluntary exiles from what was now a withering and poverty-stricken Vienna, Balkan revolutionaries, and Jewish victims of Ukrainian pograms.[b] There was nothing degrading about being a newcomer to the city; it wasn't even important to have been born a Prussian.[c] Of Tucholsky's two-hundred elite—or rather seventy-five, the appropriate figure for the story of the *Weltbühne*— more than three-fourths were not natives of Berlin. Some were not even Germans but came from Austria, Hungary, the Ukraine, and Poland.[d] The famous "Berlin style" of the 1920's was largely a product of these non-Berliners who forged new traditions in the theater, in art, in literature, and in journalism. The city's native inhabitants, speaking a delightful dialect and capable of a biting wit (immortalized, among others, by Tucholsky), were a world unto themselves. The talented outsiders who now peopled hospitable Berlin transformed the city from a political capital to a genuine nerve center of the nation, creating in the process a cosmopolitan audience for their cosmopolitan ideas.

THREE GENERATIONS

In the Weimar era alone *Die Weltbühne* attracted about three hundred contributors. To be sure, most of them wrote only a few articles but there were at least seventy-five who could be termed assiduous and important collaborators. Who they were, and the nature of their political message, will form the basis of the collective image of the *Weltbühne* circle attempted in this study.[e] The oldest member of the

---

[b] The Hungarian Marxist philosopher György Lukács, the Austrian theater director Max Reinhardt, the Prague journalist Egon Erwin Kisch, the phenomenal operetta singer from Budapest, Gitta Alpár, and the Polish embezzlers Leo and Willy Sklarek were some of these famous "Berliners."

[c] This was not the case in Munich, for instance, where Bavarian particularism and xenophobia were rampant in the 1920's.

[d] There was, among others, an astonishingly large number of Hungarian writers at the *Weltbühne*, all Communists or left-wing Social Democrats, whom Tucholsky half jestingly accused of incurable nostalgia and chauvinism.

[e] The choice of these seventy-five writers is, of necessity, arbitrary. For instance, such prolific contributors as Bernhard Citron, Adolf Weissman, Ossip Kalenter, Bruno Manuel, Frank Warschauer, Wolf Zucker, Hanns-Erich Kaminski had to be omitted because too little is known about them. In fact, the many literary and political "Who is Who's" of the period are of no great help to the researcher for they list mainly the officially honored luminaries of the time. Information on many of the writers was culled from contemporary accounts, autobiographies

Weltbühne circle, Georg Ledebour, an independent socialist politician and the Eugene Debs of German socialism, was born in 1850; the youngest, Walther Karsch, last editor of the journal in Weimar Germany, was born in 1906. Between these two extremes lay the three generations of the *Weltbühne:* the oldest, which knew Bismarck and the aging William I; the middle generation, which achieved maturity under William II; and the youngest, which grew up during World War I.

The oldest generation of the *Weltbühne* was the most "respectable," not only because of the advanced age of its members in the Weimar era, but because of their conviction that only moral means lead to moral ends. Having grown up in the atmosphere of confidence and bureaucratic probity which had characterized the Bismarckian era, and still firmly anchored in the upper-middle class milieu of their youth,[*] they were the least "alienated" of all *Weltbühne* writers. Characteristically, most of them had traveled a long political road before they became radical democrats or socialists. The democrat and pacifist Hellmut von Gerlach began his political career as an anti-Semite;[2] the pacifist Lothar Persius as a nationalist naval officer.[3] It was in the Wilhelmian period that most of these men went into opposition. They were, of course, not alone among the intellectuals in opposing the Wilhelmian regime: some of the greatest lights of German culture—Max Weber, Friedrich Meinecke, Ernst Troeltsch, Thomas Mann, and Lujo Brentano—strongly objected to the philistinism of the German bourgeoisie and the coarseness of the Imperial court. But unquestioning patriotism moderated their opposition.[4] Not so their counterparts among the *Weltbühne* writers. The historian Ludwig Quidde risked imprisonment with a satire on the Kaiser;[5] Hellmut von Gerlach resigned as a civil servant and Lothar Persius as a naval officer; Heinrich Mann wrote *Der Untertan* ("The Patrioteer"), his derision of Germany's ruling classes, shortly before the

---

(very rare), and the personal reminiscences of the survivors. For brief individual resumés on the "seventy-five," see Appendix I.

[*] Heinrich Mann, the brother of Thomas, was a Lübeck patrician; the theater critics Oskar Bie and Arthur Eloesser, and the writer Arthur Holitscher were sons of rich businessmen; Dr. Magnus Hirschfeld, the founder of "sexology," was the son of a *Sanitätsrat* (a physician decorated by the government); the democratic journalist Hellmut von Gerlach was a Junker; the pacifist General von Schoenaich the son of a landowning aristocrat; the historian Ludwig Quidde descended from a long line of civil servants and so did the pacifist Captain Persius whose father sat in the Prussian Upper House; the satirical writer Alexander Roda Roda (Sándor Friedrich Rosenfeld) was the son of a bailiff who had been a career officer in the Austro-Hungarian army.

war.[6] Furthermore, when the war broke out and Weber, Troeltsch, Meinecke, Brentano, and Thomas Mann threw their reservations to the four winds, the members of the *Weltbühne's* elder generation were among the first ones to join the antiwar organizations. After 1918, when Meinecke and the other giants of German culture became *Vernunftsrepublikaner*—republicans not by conviction but by reason —the members of the old *Weltbühne* generation were enthusiastic republicans.

The middle generation constituted the great majority of the *Weltbühne* writers. Siegfried Jacobsohn, Kurt Tucholsky, and Carl von Ossietzky, the three successive editors of the journal, belonged to this generation, as did Alfred Polgar, Walter Mehring, Kurt Hiller, Ernst Toller, Rudolf Leonhard, Arnold Zweig, Walter Hasenclever, Leonhard Frank, Erich Mühsam, and a host of other famous collaborators. Turning into adults in the Wilhelmian age, this middle generation had experienced none of the political triumphs of the Bismarckian period. On the other hand they initiated, or participated in, the cultural awakening that marked the turn of the century. For them, Imperial Germany was an age of intellectual excitement, a prelude to some great cataclysm. They were the "war generation" who, as H. Stuart Hughes explains in his study of the conflict of generations in Western culture, doubted the wisdom of their elders and searched for a faith and an ideal. Their intellectual imagination had been aroused by the Russian revolution of 1905 and the first Moroccan crisis, the consequences of which they—"the generation of 1905" as Hughes terms them—had personal reasons to fear. "It was this prospect of war service," writes Hughes, "which most sharply marked off the new generation from those who had reached intellectual maturity in the 1890's."[7] During World War I, this generation began to turn its cultural rebellion into a political crusade. The republic was to be its responsibility. The members of this generation demanded a new beginning but could not help making constant references to the Wilhelmian past. They called in the *Weltbühne* for a republic unencumbered by the remnants of Imperial Germany but were nostalgic for an age which suddenly seemed invested with an aura of decency. To give only one example, these writers often compared postwar with prewar Social Democracy, and they could find in the postwar leaders none of the qualities of courage, honesty, and purposefulness of the old leadership. Little did it matter that the prewar leaders of the SPD had prepared the way for the post-1918 policy of that party. It was difficult for this generation not to fight the battles of the old, and even more difficult to detect, behind the figure of the authoritarian opponent, the shadow of the totalitarian enemy.

As to the young "postwar" generation, it knew nothing of Imperial Germany. For them, the Kaiser meant war, in which some were called up to serve.[g] Others were in school and were constantly hungry. "The war, that's our parents," exclaimed the hero of Ernst Glaeser's popular novel, *Jahrgang 1902*.[8] They viewed the Weimar Republic not as an answer to Wilhelmian decadence (the concept of the old generation), nor as a perpetrator of the worst in Imperial Germany (the general opinion of the middle generation), but as a true beginning. Again, unlike their elders, they were immune to nostalgia and looked beyond the republic for a political solution.

Composed mainly of journalists, the postwar generation of the *Weltbühne* circle was more dynamic, more versatile, and more radical than their elders; their youth had been less secure and their world more agitated. Some changed their politics in a bewildering fashion. Unlike the oldest generation which moved gradually from a conservative to a democratic progressive position, they often started out on the extreme Left and changed later to an apolitical or strongly anti-Communist position. Arthur Koestler, Ernst Glaeser, Bruno Frei, Heinz Pol, Ödön von Horvath, Gerhart Pohl were Communists or Communist-sympathizers in the 1920's. Of these, only the Austrian journalist Bruno Frei is today an avowed Communist. Koestler's break with the Communist Party became a matter of world renown.[9] Ernst Glaeser, whose books were burned by the National Socialists on their first pyre, and who had to flee Germany, returned to his homeland in 1939 to become the editor of a German army newspaper. Glaeser, incidentally, was the only writer of the *Weltbühne* to make his peace with Nazi Germany. The others of the young generation mostly went into exile; if they stayed in Germany, they either remained in opposition, or, at least, abstained from political writing.[h]

HERITAGE AND EDUCATION

Communists and Social Democrats were right in asserting that the writers of the *Weltbühne* were bourgeois who had no contact with the

---

[g] At least three of these writers were soldiers in World War I. Four were too young for front line duty in that war, and two served in World War II (Walter Kiaulehn in the German and Arthur Koestler in the British army).

[h] Gerhart Pohl, Walther Karsch, Walter Kiaulehn, and Erich Kästner chose to remain in National Socialist Germany. Axel Eggebrecht was put in concentration camp and, after his release, became an office worker. The rest of the young generation: Bruno Frei, Ödön von Horvath, Hermann Kesten, Arthur Koestler, and Heinz Pol fled abroad.

masses: even those among them who belonged to the Communist Party seldom addressed the workers directly. Moreover, some of them showed distinctly upper-middle-class inclinations. Wasn't, after all, their intellectual and political idol the renegade Communist Paul Levi, a successful and wealthy lawyer, a connoisseur of antiques, and of beautiful women? And of Kurt Tucholsky, an admirer wrote: "There was nothing conspicuous about his appearance. He was always soberly and meticulously dressed. He put great emphasis on cleanliness and he had inordinately good manners. He was an accomplished gentleman; nay an aristocrat." [10] Or as Kurt Hiller described his encounter in 1919 with Carl von Ossietzky: "Ossietzky visited me. I recall it well. He came wearing a frockcoat and gave me frightfully stiff bows." [11]

The members of the *Weltbühne* circle were born into upper-middle-class or middle-class families. Their fathers were physicians, professors, music teachers, civil servants, landowners, wholesale merchants, or manufacturers. Even among these "better people," members of the commercial, financial, and professional bourgeoisie formed the vast majority. None of them was a proletarian, and there were only a few artisans and shopkeepers, as well as two fairly well-to-do peasants.[1] There is nothing surprising about the professional distribution of the fathers (have not most socialist intellectuals been of bourgeois background?), but it certainly distinguishes the collaborators of the *Weltbühne* from the writers of the conservative revolutionary *Die Tat*, whose fathers were mainly Protestant ministers, officers, or civil servants; or of the Communist *Die Linkskurve*, where bourgeois offspring were colleagues of genuine proletarians.[12] Most of the *Weltbühne* writers had received an excellent education. Only two, Leonhard Frank and the sailor-poet Joachim Ringelnatz were *bona fide* self-taught men. The others had attended a *Gymnasium*[1] or a university, with the latter group forming a very large majority. Only the fact that about one-third of the "academics" did not care to acquire the coveted title of "Herr Doktor" shows that, at least for some of these intellectuals, creativity was a primary urge. There were among these publicists some practicing lawyers and physicians, two

---

[1] The father of the pacifist expressionist writer René Schickele was a winegrower in Alsatia, the father of the left-radical journalist Kurt Kersten was an *Urbauer*, the owner of an ancestral holding in the Rhineland.

[1] The *Gymnasium* was equivalent to the French *lycée* and therefore more exclusive and demanding than the American high school. Its graduates were full-fledged gentlemen as they qualified both for officer's school in the army and for dueling.

career officers (both retired), and nine professors.[k] The others drew a regular income as journalists, reporters, theater critics, editors, readers for publishing houses, or as unattached novelists, dramatists, and song writers.

These writers were no Bohemians, not even of the coffeehouse variety.[l] Although they traveled more and changed domiciles more often than the average *Bürger,* most of them lived "respectably." Only in their personal relations with women did they violate convention: several lived in common-law relationships (a popular practice in intellectual circles); some proudly exhibited a series of girl friends, and many were married at least twice. But here again most members of the first generation must be excepted.

It was customary for the Right to call the left-wing intellectuals shirkers who, in "characteristic un-German" fashion, had evaded military service in wartime. This was a deliberate confusion of left-wing intellectual antimilitarist ideology with personal conduct. In fact, the left-wing intellectuals contributed to the creation of this malevolent legend by their campaign against the German practice of sizing up a civilian in terms of his military service. Nothing exasperated them more than the customary question: *Haben Sie gedient?* (Did you serve?). "It is no business of the court of the republic, whether or not I served in the army of the former Kaiser," Ossietzky snapped at the examining judge in the course of one of his trials. Ossietzky, in fact, had served during the war. The enthusiasm with which some of these young intellectuals marched off into the war in 1914 has been written about a good deal. Ernst Toller, for instance, volunteered for the front in a mood which he later described as an "emotional delirium." [13] Almost one-third of the "war generation" saw front-line service and several were wounded. (Arnold Zweig was almost blinded at Ver-

---

[k] The historians Ludwig Quidde and Veit Valentin, the architect and city planner Werner Hegemann, the jurist Max Alsberg, the economist Alfons Goldschmidt, the mathematical statistician Emil J. Gumbel (he taught, until his death in 1966, at Columbia University in New York City), the philosopher Ludwig Marcuse (later at the University of California in Los Angeles), the musicologist Oskar Bie, and the international jurist Hans Wehberg (later at the Institut Universitaire des Hautes Études Internationales in Geneva).

[l] There were, however, a few jacks-of-all-trades among these writers. Joachim Ringelnatz, originally a sailor, was also a painter and a cabaret singer and tried —according to his own boastful admission—at least thirty other professions before he became a successful poet and writer. Axel Eggebrecht began his career as a clerk and a traveling salesman, but by 1925 he already had a good income as a radio and screen writer. Egon Erwin Kisch was a magician, choir singer, busboy, sailor, film extra in Algiers, etc., mostly in performance of his duty as *rasender Reporter* for a number of well-paying journals.

dun.) Of course, some had opposed the war from the beginning; others turned against it because of their front experiences. Leonhard Frank, René Schickele, and Max Brod went to Switzerland early in the war and wrote pacifist articles. Rudolf Leonhard, who had volunteered in 1914, was later court-martialed for pacifist agitation. Ernst Toller, who received a medical discharge after two years of front-line service, was imprisoned in 1918 for incitement to revolution. Erich Mühsam, a revolutionary anarchist from the prewar days, declined to perform even labor service during the war and was put under surveillance. Although none of the "old" generation went into exile, almost all joined the antiwar organizations. This too demanded courage and brought about a good deal of police harassment and social ostracism.

Clearly, little of what has been said until now explains why these writers were in opposition. They did not share in the miseries of the workers and salaried employees, nor in the fears and frustrations of the upper classes. They had, as it must seem, no personal grounds for opposing a state and a society that allowed them freedom of expression and economic comfort. Nor did they share in the general *Weltschmerz* or "cultural despair" of the conservative intellectuals. They were philosophical and social optimists whose hopes often survived the National Socialist oppression. Was their opposition then an act of will due to compassion and to premonition? This is undoubtedly true to some degree. They were genuine humanitarians, horrified by social injustice and the suffering of the poor; they were also prophets who foresaw the coming triumph of nihilism. But there were other considerations: their historical heritage as unattached, free German intellectuals, and the Jewish background of most of these writers.

The role of the free writer in German society was never an easy one; the craft of writing was not respected unless the writer was a recognized scholar. Men of letters who hoped to gain a following for their ideas generally sought to do so within a university or learned society. This is borne out by a random listing of the outstanding intellectuals in nineteenth-century Germany who were, for the most part, academicians. Fichte, Hegel, and Schelling held university posts, as did a very large number of the German savants who came after them: Niebuhr, Ranke, Dahlmann, Treitschke, Harnack, Weber, and Meinecke, to name a few. The university professor commanded, and still does, a prestige very near the top of the country's social scale. Schopenhauer's unsuccessful attempt to become a lecturer at one of the great German universities made him bitter for the rest of his life. The professor, with his traditional role, his central place in the history of his country and his acknowledgment of authority, enjoyed almost a monopoly of respectability in the intellectual world. Even the radical poet Heine, with all his unruliness, sought a university post and went abroad when he failed to find a niche for himself in the official life of Germany.

This situation changed somewhat late in the nineteenth century, but even when successful the independent writer never gained that respect which the public reserved for academics.[m] More often than not he was regarded by the public with suspicion: he had no "official" identity; he moved outside of authority within an urbane and frivolous society, and he was arrogant enough to venture into political criticism. If his political views inclined to the Left, he was regarded as that obnoxious *Literat* whose disrespect for German traditions bordered on treason. Academicians knew well enough, especially after 1848, to leave politics to the politicians; Hermann Baumgarten, who taught at the technical academy of Karlsruhe in Baden and who played a part in the political life of that state, made this point very clear not only on behalf of himself and his fellow academicians, but all educated Germans: "It is one of the most ruinous errors to believe that a good scholar, lawyer, merchant, or civil servant, who is interested in public affairs and reads the newspapers assiduously, is able to participate actually in political life." [14]

In Britain and in France, the man of letters had an honored place in society, and he often outshone the scholar. In Germany, a high-school teacher of pedestrian talent (actually there were many brilliant Germans who taught in the *Gymnasiums*) was apt to feel himself superior —because he was a respected servant of the state—to a celebrated journalist or writer. Heine, the successful *Literat* who left Germany at the age of thirty-four and never returned, was something of an enigma to his countrymen. To live such a scandalous existence as Heine did, to criticize harshly one's country, and to glorify the German language while consorting in Paris with French revolutionary rabble violated all the criteria for respectability. Although Heine had considered himself a German patriot, these circumstances complicated his relations with his fatherland: he had a French *esprit* which serious-minded Germans interpreted as a lack of depth or sincerity, and he was a Jew. Maxi-

---

[m] Golo Mann, "The Intellectuals," *Encounter*, June 1955, p. 43. Mann reports that a public-opinion poll conducted in Western Germany in 1954 on the prestige of professions in that country brought the unequivocal response that the university professor ranked above the parliamentarian, the industrialist, and the trade-union leader. No profession ranked above that of the academician. The writer was ranked far below the teacher in an elementary school.

milian Harden had similar difficulties; he began his career as a Prussian conservative but in the end, his rebelliousness and his Jewishness caused him to repudiate his conservative past and to be repudiated by German society in turn.

There was still another aspect of the writing of the free publicist which the "true" German found irritating: its frequent Western orientation. A bitterness toward the West, its political institutions and modes of life had taken root in German thought after the Napoleonic invasion. The alleged materialism and rationalism of the West was considered a threat to all that was uniquely German. Beginning in the second half of the nineteenth century, this reaction in Germany led in some intellectual quarters to an intense preoccupation with a "Germanic" ideology.[n] The proponents of this ideology regarded Germany's historical destiny as a thing apart because, it was said, the German personality recoiled from the hollow values trumpeted by the West, values which would drag Germany down from her spiritual heights in the leveling process of democracy. Such philosophical patriotism was to be repudiated by the Weimar literary radical who sincerely believed, as did Heine, that Germany's greatest contributions could only be made within the mainstream of Western traditions. Because of the conflict between these two schools of thought, the so-called Westerner among German intellectuals easily passed for subversive. A very high percentage of the Weimar left-wing intellectuals combined all the characteristics repugnant to the Germanic ideologists: Francophile, Jewish, Western, rebellious, progressive, democratic, rationalist, socialist, liberal, and cosmopolitan. Heine's contrast of French and German patriotism was as much pertinent for the Weimar period as it was in his own day:

The patriotism of the Frenchman consists in the fact that his heart is warmed by it . . . it expands and spreads. . . . The patriotism of the German . . . makes his heart narrower, so that it contracts like leather in the cold—he hates whatever is foreign, and does not wish to be a citizen of the world, or of Europe, but only a cabined and cribbed German.[15]

It was because of their sense of isolation that the unattached German intellectuals, not only of the Left, but also of the Right, tended to show an intolerance, an extremism generally missing from their French, British, or American contemporaries. Zola could pride himself

---

[n] Fritz Stern, *The Politics of Cultural Despair* (Berkeley and Los Angeles, 1961) , p. xiii, shows that the principal goals of Germanic ideology were "the revival of a mythical *Deutschtum* and the creation of political institutions that would embody and preserve the peculiar character of the Germans."

at the time of the Dreyfus affair for having shaken the French nation from the bottom; German writers never had such power. As a consequence, they wanted a fundamentally altered society that would listen to their exhortations. When accused of demagogy, they countered with heightened criticism.

Their criticism became even more radical, or at least more conspicuous, if they suffered from the additional burden of being Jewish. This was true of most *Weltbühne* collaborators. Of the sixty-eight writers whose religious origin could be established—and this, admittedly, was a difficult and delicate task—forty-two were found to be of Jewish descent, two were half-Jews and only twenty-four were non-Jews. Of the latter, three were married to Jewish women.°

The term "Jewish origin" is being used here in full consciousness of its ambiguities. The criterion for "Jew" and "non-Jew" used in this study actually bears some resemblance to the stipulations of the Nuremberg laws because "Jewishness" was generally defined in Germany in the spirit of these laws well before their enactment in 1935. Not only the Rightists, but many liberals and Jewish writers on Jewish accomplishments in Germany (such books were at that time very popular) diligently qualified anyone a Jew who had at least one Jewish parent. Even less did it occur to anyone to treat such converts as Karl Marx and the conservative theoretician Friedrich Julius Stahl, or the anti-Semitic Jew Walther Rathenau as non-Jews.ᵖ This German usage must be accepted here if our examination is to make sense. For it must be borne in mind that "Jewishness" in Weimar Germany was a publicly imposed condition. A significant minority of those whom the German public considered Jews were not aware of their Jewishness or, rather, denied this awareness. Even smaller was the number of those who practiced the Jewish religion. Only a few of the *Weltbühne* circle

---

° It might be more than a coincidence that in the middle or "war generation" of the *Weltbühne* the Jews outnumbered the non-Jews by more than two to one. In the two other generations the ratio was about one to one. It was around the turn of the century that Jews predominated in the German press. By the 1920's, the non-Jews were in a stronger position and by 1930 "Aryanization" was proceeding at a high speed in the big Berlin press, especially in the Jewish House of Ullstein and in the Christian Scherl (Hugenberg) concern.

It might also be of interest to note that all foreign-born collaborators of the *Weltbühne* (or at least those who are under consideration here) were of Jewish descent—a reflection on the great Western migration (or, re-migration) of the Jews in the twentieth century.

ᵖ See, for instance, Rudolf Schay, *Juden in der deutschen Politik* (Berlin, 1929). The author, definitely philo-Semitic, devotes a separate chapter to each one of these political thinkers.

openly acknowledged that they were Jews and hardly anyone (Jew or non-Jew) was a believer. Yet, as the years passed, what had been avoided as a delicate question in liberal circles began to be openly discussed. And the references to Jewishness were all the more painful when they came from liberal friends. Alfred Kerr, the drama critic, wrote:

Even people of sensitive nature could put up with such things as when, on the Day of Atonement, a boor would call a gentleman with a prayer book "damned Jewish dung!" Or when a major of the "Eleventh" [regiment] would publicly declare on the streetcar: "There are so many pregnant Jewish women—makes you want to vomit!" These things did not hurt. But when enlightened, well-meaning, and considerate friends said "The Jewish gentlemen"—that hurt.[16]

Jewishness indeed was determined not so much by one's enemies as by one's friends; and it was a source of humiliation, for—all the hypocritical assertions of the courts of the Weimar Republic to the contrary— "Jew" was a pejorative term.

The Jewish writers of the *Weltbühne* grew up, for the most part, in a bourgeois milieu where religion was seldom taken seriously, but where certain family practices and the circle of friends made Jewishness a foregone conclusion. The rebellion of these intellectuals against their bourgeois heritage included their rejection of the formal Judaism of their parents. It involved a tacit recognition that Judaism and unquestioning German patriotism were mutually exclusive propositions and that assimilation, heralded since the days of Moses Mendelssohn, had failed in the face of German middle- and upper-class opposition. Thus some converted to Lutheranism (if the conversion was only for the sake of convenience), others to Catholicism (if they had some interest in religion).[q] The rest generally proclaimed themselves to be agnostics or atheists. In a way, these intellectuals proposed their complete assimilation, not into Germandom, but into a community of progressive Europeans. There was, however, no such community; therefore they felt themselves "homeless." "Homelessness" might become an advantage if it allowed the individual the freedom of unemotional and uncommitted observation. But these intellectuals

---

[q] Oskar Bie, the essayist Egon Friedell, and Kurt Tucholsky were Lutheran converts. The novelist Alfred Döblin renounced Judaism in 1917 and twenty-four years later converted to Catholicism. In his old age Döblin published several religious essays. (See the similar case of Franz Werfel, another *Die Weltbühne* contributor.)

were neither unemotional nor uncommitted; nor were they allowed to
be impartial observers. On the contrary, they were urged to alternately
identify themselves as Jews and as Germans—being alternately
chided, when they tried, for clannishness or for "infiltration." They
were told that not even their style was their own but an expression of
"Jewish agony." A moderation of zeal brought accusations of subterfuge; a heightening of zeal was damned as Jewish arrogance.
Consequently, the Jewish intellectuals labored under the impression
that their ideologies were less a product of intellectual conviction than
of an imposed alienation, that anything they said or wrote would be
interpreted as abject self-justification. In the words of Jakob Wassermann, himself an occasional contributor to the *Weltbühne:*

Vain to adjure the nation of poets and thinkers in the name of its poets and
thinkers. Every prejudice one thinks disposed of breeds a thousand others,
as carrion breeds maggots.—Vain to present the right cheek after the left
has been struck. It does not move them to the slightest thoughtfulness; it
neither touches nor disarms them; they strike the right cheek too. They
say: He dares to open his mouth? Gag him!—Vain to act in exemplary
fashion. They say: We know nothing, we have seen nothing, we have heard
nothing.—Vain to seek obscurity. They say: The coward! He is creeping
into hiding, driven by his evil conscience.—Vain to go among them and
offer them one's hand. They say: Why does he take such liberties, with his
Jewish obtrusiveness?—Vain to keep faith with them, as a comrade-in-arms
or a fellow citizen. They say: He is Proteus, he can assume any shape or
form.—Vain to help them strip off the chains of slavery. They say: No
doubt he found it profitable.—Vain to counteract the poison. They brew
fresh venom.—Vain to live for them and die for them. They say: He is a
Jew.[17]

There is no attempt here to imply that this too was the attitude of
the non-Jewish writers of the *Weltbühne:* there is no trace of anti-
Semitism among them and they risked their lives in defense of the
Jewish community. Yet, even they expected from their Jewish colleagues in the *Weltbühne* that they show solidarity with their har-
assed and ridiculed former coreligionaries. This, of course, contradicted a very basic belief of the left-wing intellectuals: that they
should not be looked upon as Jews, but as Europeans.

From all this the Jewish left-wing intellectual could deduce only
one thing: that his Jewishness enslaved him. "The Jews are proletarians," wrote Arnold Zweig in 1933.[18] "They are proletarians, despite
their luxury, their ten-room apartments, their university education,
and their intellectual professions. The essence of proletarian existence

is also symptomatic of their lives: they have no way of securing their present or their future, because they possess neither political guarantees, the right to participate in political decisions, nor do they possess the instruments of production." The Jew in Germany, Zweig argued, was a proletarian even at a time when he was granted a privileged position. These privileges were always revokable. Consequently, there were only two sorts of Jews in Germany: those who persisted in their dream of equality and assimilation, and those who, recognizing their true condition, joined the working-class movement or at least aligned themselves with the proletariat.

There is no reason for disagreement with Zweig's argument to this extent: the Jew in Germany always bore a stigma. And the only way to rid himself of it was to conclude a "silent contract," in Zweig's words, with that group—the workers—which had no interest in being anti-Semitic. Many Jews took this step, from the founders of the socialist movement to such twentieth-century figures as Rosa Luxemburg, Paul Levi, or Hugo Haase; the Jews in the *Weltbühne* were proud to be their followers, short of an unconditional submission to either of the two parties which claimed these socialist leaders. The enthusiasm of the *Weltbühne* writers for revolutionary socialist propositions was to a great part due to the recognition of their inescapable Jewish condition. With this recognition came a growing pride in particular Jewish accomplishments. Or, if it did not come, there was always the consolation of that "characteristic Jewish humor": "A Jew has said once"— wrote Kurt Tucholsky—" 'I am proud to be a Jew. Were I not proud, I would still be a Jew—then I might as well be proud!' " [19]

In the years after the National Socialist assumption of power, German exile literature gradually abandoned what had initially been one of its favorite occupations: the documenting of Jewish accomplishments in science and culture. In the growing Popular Front atmosphere where Communist and anti-Communist emigrés referred to each other as "antifascist patriots," specific Jewish contributions to German life were passed over in silence to make common cause with the non-Jewish political emigrés. It was considered indelicate, and even suspicious, to mention that most of those "other Germans" who had represented German democratic culture, were in fact Jews. Indeed not the emigrés, but the National Socialists (and a few Jewish nationalist organizations) were the Jewish intellectuals' best propagandists with their many accounts of Jewish accomplishments in pre-1933 Germany. Inaccurate as these accounts were, they generously granted the title of

"Jew" to many outstanding non-Jews.[r] On the other hand, Western liberal historians generally underplay the cultural significance of the German Jews while the Communist historians do not mention it at all. Yet there is no reason why it should not be acknowledged that, in twentieth-century Germany where the Jews formed less than one percent of the nation's population,[20] Jews were responsible for a great part of German culture. The owners of three of Germany's greatest newspaper publishing houses; the editors of the *Vossische Zeitung* and the *Berliner Tageblatt;* most book publishers; the owners and editors of the *Neue Rundschau* and other distinguished literary magazines; the owners of Germany's greatest art galleries were all Jews. Jews played a major part in theater and in the film industry as producers, directors, and actors. Many of Germany's best composers, musicians, artists, sculptors, and architects were Jews. Their participation in literary criticism and in literature was enormous: practically all the great critics and many novelists, poets, dramatists, essayists of Weimar Germany were Jews. A recent American study has shown that thirty-one of the sixty-five leading German "expressionists" and "neo-objectivists"[s] were Jews.[21] It is well known what fatal damage the emigration of Jewish physicists and other scientists caused to Germany after 1933.

If cultural contributions by Jews were far out of proportion to their numerical strength, their participation in left-wing intellectual activities was even more disproportionate. Apart from orthodox Communist literature where there were a majority of non-Jews, Jews were responsible for a great part of leftist literature in Germany. *Die Weltbühne* was in this respect not unique; Jews published, edited, and to a great part wrote the other left-wing intellectual magazines. Jews played a decisive role in the pacifist and feminist movements, and in the campaigns for sexual enlightenment.

---

[r] See, for instance, such standard anti-Semitic diatribes as Theodor Fritsch, *Handbuch der Judenfrage* (Leipzig, 1937) or Adolf Bartels, *Jüdische Herkunft und Literaturwissenschaft* (Leipzig, 1926). Not only do these "manuals" list the names of thousands of eminent Jewish Germans, but they qualify as Jews such people as Karl Liebknecht (whose mother was Jewish), the Mann brothers (who had Jewish wives), Willi Münzenberg, Bertolt Brecht, and the *Weltbühne* writers Leonhard Frank, Annette Kolb, and Friedrich Wolf, none of whom was Jewish. The same excess of zeal characterizes some Jewish publications as, for instance, S. Winninger, ed., *Grosse jüdische Nationalbiographie* (1925–1936). For a rectification of these common errors, see Siegmund Kaznelson, ed., *Juden im deutschen Kulturbereich* (Berlin, 1962), 1043 ff.

[s] "Neo-objectivism" or *Neue Sachlichkeit* was a major literary movement in the second half of the 1920's in Germany.

The left-wing intellectuals did not simply "happen to be mostly Jews" as some pious historiography would have us believe,[22] but Jews created the left-wing intellectual movement in Germany. The extraordinary Jewish participation in German culture is to be explained by the peculiarities of the Central European Jewish intellectual tradition and by the Jews' historic exclusion from the more "respectable" professions as the civil service, the army, the judiciary, or university teaching. The even higher Jewish participation in leftist culture, however, is due to a specific development: their recognition of the fact that business, artistic, or scientific careers do not help solve the Jewish problem, and that Weimar Germany had to undergo dire transformation if German anti-Semitism was to end.

In summary, the "typical" *Weltbühne* writer in the Weimar era—with due respect to significant exceptions—was born into the "war generation"; he was the son of bourgeois parents; he belonged to the educational elite, and he was more likely to be of Jewish than of non-Jewish origin. As a Jew, as a man of the Left and as an intellectual, he undoubtedly belonged to a very small minority of Germans. Hence the frequent reference by historians to the "small group" around the *Weltbühne*.[t] But the group was not small, nor was the *Weltbühne* archetype as isolated from the mainstream of German life as he felt he was, or as he is often depicted as being. For one thing, he was obviously at home in Berlin. For another, as a member of the "war generation," he—as many other German intellectuals—had gnawing doubts about the purpose and justification of Imperial Germany, of German society, and of his own life. As a patriot in 1914 and as a soldier in the war, he experienced the same exaltations and the same disillusionments as did the other Germans. As a revolutionary in 1918 he voiced the hopes of millions of Germans. Finally, as a disaffected German in the Weimar era, he showed the discontent of most of his compatriots. These experiences, particularly the militant role he played, made him a part of German history.

---

[t] For instance, Koppel S. Pinson writes in his *Modern Germany* (New York, 1954), 459: "A small group of pacifist, antimilitarist, and antinationalist humanitarians gathered around the *Weltbühne*, edited by Carl von Ossietzky, were dedicated to the cause of deflating the pompous façade of the still flourishing Prussianism and of exposing the secret machinations of the old order of officers and Reichswehr."

Chapter II
DIE *WELTBÜHNE* AND ITS EDITORS

SIEGFRIED JACOBSOHN

When Prussian police and the SA seized the editorial offices of the *Weltbühne* on March 7, 1933, and forbade further publication, the journal was precisely twenty-seven and a half years old.[1] The first issue of the *Schaubühne* appeared on September 7, 1905, in Berlin, and immediately created a stir through the quality of its contents. In it appeared a scene from Hugo von Hofmannsthal's until then unpublished *Ödipus und die Sphinx;* a remarkable essay on Maximilian Harden, and a spirited jibe at contemporary German drama by Julius Bab, a young critic, who spared only Frank Wedekind and Hugo von Hofmannsthal. The Berlin theater, into which *Die Schaubühne* entered with such lusty energy, was a battlefield where naturalists, realists, symbolists, neoromantics, and the advocates of *Stildrama*[a] relentlessly slaughtered each other. Through the audacity and talent of its editor, *Die Schaubühne* soon rose to the front rank among the theatrical journals.

When he founded the journal, Siegfried Jacobsohn[2] was only twenty-four years old but already an authority in a field dominated by such devastating critics as Alfred Kerr, Fritz Mauthner, Arthur Eloesser, and Oscar Blumenthal (one of Jacobsohn's relatives). Jacobsohn's family history reflected the profound effect of nineteenth-century legal emancipation on German Jews—indeed it is an example of the radical transformation achieved within three generations. Jacobsohn's grandfather was devout and orthodox; he spoke Yiddish. Jacobsohn's father,

---

[a] Writers who insisted on the primacy of form and rejected both the rigidity and drabness of naturalism and the unbridled emotionalism of neoromantic theater.

a wholesale merchant in Berlin, was a liberal in politics and religion who gave the son a Teutonic name and a good secular education. The son turned against his father when he was sixteen. He quit the *Gymnasium* to become a *Theatromane* (a "theater maniac"), and a professional critic.[3] In 1901, a Hamburg newspaper printed his first theater critique and in the same year he was given charge of the drama section of the *Welt am Montag,* a Berlin newspaper. Three years later Jacobsohn published a learned study of the Berlin theater which he liked to call his "unrequested doctoral dissertation."[4] The book brought him fame as well as serious trouble. On November 12, 1904, the *Berliner Tageblatt* accused him of plagiarism for having borrowed a few lines from someone else's critique. It needed the cultural ferment of Berlin for the mushrooming of such a petty crime into a major *affaire*. Almost all Berlin newspapers gave it prominent coverage and well-known writers (Maximilian Harden, Arthur Schnitzler, and others) as well as psychologists (C. G. Jung!) came out in Jacobsohn's defense. He himself wrote a book on the subject.[b] The fact that twenty years later Bertolt Brecht could borrow with casual elegance, and with relative impunity, reflects, if not the extent of the moral revolution that had meanwhile taken place, then at least the wide conquests made by the concept of artistic freedom. Jacobsohn had less luck. He lost his position at the *Welt am Montag* and decided to found his own theatrical journal. *Die Schaubühne,* after some initial difficulties with financial backers, soon became a successful enterprise.[c]

When Jacobsohn left the *Gymnasium,* the idea of becoming a critic was for him not so much a profession as an exalted avocation. The

---

[b] S. J. [Siegfried Jacobsohn], *Der Fall Jacobsohn* (Charlottenburg, 1913). Jacobsohn argued that the plagiarism had not been a conscious act of pirating but was due to his extraordinary memory which retained—often word for word—everything of value that he read.

[c] During the first few years of its existence *Die Schaubühne* was published by various businessmen but in October 1912, Jacobsohn set up his own publishing house, the Verlag der Schaubühne. Besides printing the journal, the Verlag also published about half a dozen books, mostly collections of articles which had appeared in the journal. The latter experiment was unsuccessful and cost Jacobsohn a good deal of money. Following Jacobsohn's death, his successors abandoned the book-publishing business. Jacobsohn was anything but a financial wizard and he barely eked out a living from his very successful journal. (See, for instance, Tucholsky's letter to Fräulein Hünicke, administrative secretary of the *Weltbühne,* June 19, 1925, Kurt Tucholsky, *Ausgewählte Briefe,* 106 ff.) Jacobsohn's wife, Edith, a translator, also engaged in the publishing business as owner of "Williams and Co." This too was a financial debacle, but then Mrs. Jacobsohn, who was related to Eugen Schiffer, vice-chancellor of the Weimar Republic from 1919 to 1921, was independently wealthy. (See Kurt Hiller, "Aufstieg, Glanz und Verfall der Weltbühne," *Konkret,* June 1962.)

Berlin theater critic at the turn of the century was not simply a frustrated playwright and professional grumbler; he was a priest assisting the dramatist and the theater director in the performance of a sacred function. That function was to inculcate culture and progress in the heart of the Wilhelmian *Bürger*. Through the ruthless presentation on the stage of "truth, nothing but the truth,"—the creed of the "naturalists"—the *Bürger*, by definition servile, materialistic, pompous, bigoted, and conventional, was to be persuaded to become a modern and, therefore, better man. He was to stop prostrating himself before the higher orders and through a moral and aesthetic regeneration become a self-respecting bourgeois.[d] Clearly, this metamorphosis could not be accomplished through the medium of the officially sponsored theaters of the "Hoftheater" variety, nor through the other established theaters whose directors rejected "naturalism" as an unaesthetic aberration. New society had to be molded by new, free theaters. This, at least, was the concept behind the "Freie Bühne," a club founded in 1889 at the instigation of Maximilian Harden. The leader of the Freie Bühne, which issued its own journal, called *Freie Bühne*, and organized theatrical presentations, was Otto Brahm, who in the "Deutsches Theater" introduced Hauptmann, Shaw, Strindberg, Ibsen, and Wilde to the Berlin audience. The crucial piece in Brahm's repertory was Gerhart Hauptmann's "Weavers," a drama shocking in its stark naturalism and in its social-revolutionary implications. As a theatrical trend, "naturalism" was in vogue for only a few years; by the time *Die Schaubühne* was founded, it was already outmoded. But many succeeding movements—and succession occurred at an amazing pace—were also understood to perform a revolutionary function.

Missionary theater did produce some masterpieces, but the intellectuals' attempt to lead the *Bürgertum* through the medium of the stage proved a failure. It gradually dawned on the Freie Bühne circle that its influence was limited to the hours the audience spent in the theater, and it was particularly disheartening that not only the *Bürger* but the working class itself proved to be immune to the call for an ethico-aesthetic upheaval. One year after the founding of the Freie Bühne club, Bruno Wille founded the "Freie Volksbühne," an association expressly designed to attract the masses. "Art shall belong to the people and not

---

[d] The German word *Bürger* is not equivalent to the French *bourgeois*, at least not in the modern German usage of these words, for the first has a feudal connotation and denotes an estate (*Bürgerstand*) to which one belongs by birth or by one's profession, the second has a French revolutionary and Marxist meaning and denotes membership in the capitalist or entrepreneurial class.

be the privilege of one class," Wille announced in his first speech to the members of his association. The new experiment was not without promise, for many workers trained and educated by Social Democracy were ready for the theater. But as it turned out rapidly, it was education through the classics they were interested in and not the revolutionizing of their consciences. According to Erwin Piscator, the great Communist theater director of the 1920's, the workers at the turn of the century were not ready for the political theater.[5] For them, the theater remained a *Feiertagskunst,* a holiday affair, for which they wore their Sunday best and were shocked to discover their week-day worst paraded on stage. It was not until the Freie Volksbühne was taken over by the trade unions that it became a powerful instrument of popular education. By then the Freie Volksbühne's original revolutionary purpose was forgotten. Whether Piscator was right in asserting that "naturalism" and the Freie Volksbühne, being typically *bürgerlich,* were bound to remain ineffective because of their indirect appeal[6] is too complicated a question to examine here. (Piscator's own grandiose experiment with political theater in the 1920's, although very "in" among snobs, did not have a demonstrably greater impact upon the proletariat.) The fact remains that in the first decade of the twentieth century both social drama and socially conscious directors tended to disappear from the great Berlin stage. Social rebelliousness fled to the small theaters of the new expressionist literature. The great theater gradually succumbed to the genius of Max Reinhardt, whose scenes combined the festive with the fantastic, the spiritual with the sensual. The founders of the Freie Bühne either retired, as did Otto Brahm, or turned to politics, especially to political journalism (Theodor Wolff, one of the founders of the Freie Bühne, became a crusader of political democracy as editor of the *Berliner Tageblatt*). More and more the former drama critic waxed political, enlarging his sphere of influence through a combination as yet unheard of: culture and politics. The changing names of the intellectual journals reflected this new direction. Thus the *Freie Bühne,* the journal of Brahm's club, changed its name with successive shifts in editorial emphasis: it became the *Freie Bühne für modernes Leben* (Free Stage for Modern Living), then the *Freie Bühne für den Entwicklungskampf der Zeit* (Free Stage for the Evolutionary Struggle for Our Time), and, finally, in 1904, it became the all-encompassing *Die Neue Rundschau.*

Die Schaubühne was relatively slow in going over to politics. As Enseling points out, Jacobsohn, who was a member of the Freie Bühne club, insisted with a perseverance bounding on "monomania,"[7] that the theater alone was called upon to regenerate society. The primary preoccupation of the journal remained the theater almost until World War I, yet *Die Schaubühne* was by no means the most progressive review of its kind. Because it refused to accept much of the real avant-garde literature, it was ultimately less successful than such small magazines as *Der Sturm, Die Aktion,* or *Pan* in exploiting new ideas or in appreciating the revolutionary significance of the newest literary trend, expressionism.*

When the journal began to make the shift from theater to politics, it was not Siegfried Jacobsohn but some of his collaborators—especially young Kurt Tucholsky—who provided the impetus. And it was Tucholsky's phrase, coined in April 1914, "We dislike our radicals precisely because they aren't radical"[8] that might have served henceforth as the motto of the journal. With its commitment to political agitation, *Die Schaubühne* now energetically sought the commitment of others. "We have a hundred dogmas on meditation but hardly one on action," complained Tucholsky.[9] Taking up Heinrich Mann's demand for the bridging of *Macht* and *Geist,* of political and intellectual power, he let loose his agile aliases Peter Panter, Theobald Tiger, and Ignaz Wrobel (his fourth alter ego, Kaspar Hauser, made his début only after World War I) against the German *Bürger.*

Tucholsky and *Die Schaubühne* were at the beginning of their political campaign when they were interrupted by World War I.

Because they had not yet set themselves a definite political course, most writers of the *Schaubühne* threw themselves into the August war enthusiasm. Julius Bab proclaimed that he himself would "stand or fall with Germany." The Viennese essayist Egon Friedell, an habitué of the Café Central, who had mocked patriots, politicians, journalists, Zionists, Jewish assimilationists, left-wing and right-wing radicals, and all other conceivable ideas and organizations,[10] asserted that it was Germany's task to colonize France culturally "so as to raise those crude Celtic tribes [the French] at least half-way to the level of Central European civilization."[11] He declared in the same article that the English were a "nation of dumb criminals" and that Prussian militarism was equivalent to "self-sacrifice, dutifulness, fear of God, humanitarianism, knowledge, and progress."[12] It is enough to know to what paroxysms of exaltation avant-garde writers rose in those days to

---

* Julius Bab pointed to fundamental shortcoming of "expressionism" when he questioned in the *Schaubühne* the feasibility of a fusion between "brotherly love and aristocratic seclusion." See Alf Enseling, *Die Weltbühne* (Münster, Westf., 1962), 48.

be quite confident that Friedell meant what he said and that he, like so many of his Jewish fellow intellectuals, was now certain to find a warm place in the bosom of the fatherland. Jacobsohn was sober enough to protest against the gushy patriotic plays and operettas that had invaded the German stage and to ask for serious drama in serious days but, in the first years of the war, *Die Schaubühne* had no radical message. Political commentaries were written by Robert Breuer (he signed his name as Germanicus), an experienced socialist politician, who followed the patriotic line of the Majority Socialists.[*]

In 1917, a literary revolution transformed *Die Schaubühne*. Now, as prowar idealism gave way to antiwar idealism, the writers of the journal began to talk of the "triumph of morality over narrow nationalism." They no longer spoke of Germany but of humanity, and shortly before the end of the war, Alfred Polgar called the war "God's great antagonist." [13] In April 1918, Jacobsohn changed the journal's name to *Die Weltbühne*. The following years brought contributions by Germany's best leftist writers and sensational revelations in the journal about the "Black Reichswehr," illegal rearmament, and the antirepublican judiciary. The political image of the *Weltbühne* for all later years was molded by Jacobsohn who now found in politics his true vocation. He was a man in whom everything exuded passion: he was enthusiastic, fanatical, obstinate, often ruthless, and unduly suspicious. "This man was full of extremes of emotion," wrote a Danish friend [14] after Jacobsohn's death, "yet his extremism was genuine. Genuineness attracts and repels at the same time. So does *Die Weltbühne* . . . because it is Siegfried Jacobsohn's soul and his truth." Many of Jacobsohn's writers developed a deep affection for him. "There was abundant goodness and sensitiveness in this man; much leniency and understanding," wrote Walther Victor.[15] Enseling writes of Jacobsohn's "Old Testament fanaticism," [16] of his obstinate search for truth relieved by an occasional lightheartedness. Jacobsohn was an unyielding pedant with regard to linguistic purity but he did not refrain from colorful Yiddish or Berlin jargon. He was a dictator of style: "His almost automatic stylistic mechanism permitted no wild innovations," wrote Tucholsky,[17] "no violent punctuation signs, no dash following a period (a mortal sin) . . . he was always on the alert. And so our contributions were really letters addressed to him; written for him,

---

[*] In a postwar apology Jacobsohn explained to Kurt Hiller how he had been presented, in 1914, with a choice between military service or lending the pages of his journal to war propaganda. He chose the latter. See Hiller, "Aufstieg, Glanz und Verfall der Weltbühne," *Konkret*, March 1962, p. 7.

with our mind on him. We hoped to meet with his approval, his agreement—his pleasure."

Jacobsohn was a model editor because he allowed his collaborators a maximum in thematical freedom and a minimum in stylistic extravagance, but his passionate nature helped to give the journal the epithet "hysterical." He transplanted into the political *Weltbühne* the petty professional squabbles of a theatrical magazine. He hated with a passion Alfred Kerr, Maximilian Harden, and Karl Kraus. Stefan Grossmann, his competitor from the *Tage-Buch* and *Montag Morgen,* he accused—not quite unjustly—of having taken bribes from a dramatist and of being a plagiarist.[18] The result of all this was a good number of libel suits. In the spring of one year alone (1925), Jacobsohn fought simultaneous legal battles with the radical socialist writer Wilhelm Herzog (whom he had accused of having pocketed the money of the workers), Gustav Stresemann (whom Jacobsohn had accused of currency manipulations), the German Nationalists (because the *Weltbühne* had asserted that the international smuggler Honnef was a prime force in that party), and, of course, Stefan Grossmann. Jacobsohn seems to have been in the wrong in most of these cases.[19] These disputes were characterized by great vulgarity in which "dung" was a common epithet. When Tucholsky and, later, Ossietzky assumed leadership of the *Weltbühne,* personal attacks on fellow left-wing intellectuals disappeared from the journal. But as long as Jacobsohn was its editor, Arnold Zweig's generalized judgment applied to the *Weltbühne:* "They were Heine's successors . . . these founders and publishers of the small, courageous weeklies, who hated each other as Heine hated Börne, as the several schools of Greek Sophists or the French philosophes of the eighteenth century hated each other." [20]

On December 3, 1926, Jacobsohn suddenly died in an epileptic fit. A few months earlier he had won Ossietzky over to the *Weltbühne.* Now it was agreed that Tucholsky should become editor with Ossietzky as his deputy. At this time Tucholsky was living in voluntary exile in France; he now reluctantly agreed to return.[21]

KURT TUCHOLSKY

Kurt Tucholsky was born in 1890 in Berlin.[22] Like Jacobsohn, he was a member of the "war generation," and he too was the son of a prosperous and assimilated Jewish merchant. But there was nothing rebellious, passionate, or dedicated in the young Tucholsky. His father, to whom he was devoted, was sensitive, warm-hearted, melancholy, with a considerable gift for music; his mother, whom he apparently loathed, was cold, calculating, and something of a tyrant.ᵍ After the death of his father in 1905, Tucholsky left home, but he never broke away from his family and remained profoundly attached to his brother and sister. He attended the French *Gymnasium* in Berlin, founded in the seventeenth century for Huguenot emigrés, which was considered liberal and progressive and attracted the richest offsprings of the old and the new aristocracy. At his best Tucholsky was an indifferent, at his worst a failing student. Writing many years later, he attributed his low marks to the shortcomings of his teachers:

Our school wasn't so nationalistically stirred up as today's. Our teachers weren't any more unintelligent, lazy, industrious, or smarter than other teachers. . . . And what did we learn?

German: A ridiculous dismembering of the classics; fatuous essays, sloppily and injudiciously corrected; Middle High German poetry was learned by heart; no one had an inkling of its beauty.

History: A senseless, incoherent complication of dynastic dates. We never had history instruction.

Geography: Tributaries. Government districts. Names of cities.

. . . .

I don't think back to my schooling with hatred—it has become a matter of complete indifference to me. We never had any tragedies in school, nor terrible grievances. Bad teaching is what we did have.²³

Indifferent or not, Tucholsky did not forego those diplomas which would qualify him for privileged treatment in the army and for admission to a university. He completed his studies, after much coaxing by hired tutors, at a less fashionable *Gymnasium.* He then registered at the faculty of law of the University of Jena but again he made a poor student; his doctoral dissertation was at first rejected. Again he appealed to the assistance of tutors and in 1915 finally became "Herr Doktor." By then, he was a celebrated writer; he also had a private income. In the same year, he was drafted into the army. As manager of a barbed-wire depot at a quiet sector of the Eastern Front, as a librarian at a school for aviators, and, finally, as a police commissioner in occupied Rumania, he never fired a weapon nor was ever in serious danger. Later he claimed that his war experience had taught him to hate the war and the military. This is possible, and certainly he was

---

ᵍ So Tucholsky relates in a theater critique where the target of his attacks is not the fictitious heroine of a play by Strindberg but unmistakably his own mother. See Kurt Tucholsky, "Rosa Bertens," *Die Schaubühne*, May 7, 1914, p. 520. Also in *Gesammelte Werke*, I, 190 f, and Kurt Tucholsky, "Letter to Mary Gerold-Tucholsky" (September 4, 1918), *Ausgewählte Briefe*, 339.

never a war enthusiast, not even in 1914, but his wartime letters betray
no antiwar emotions. His behavior as a soldier met with the approval
of his superiors, and he did not begin writing antiwar articles until the
summer of 1918.

Reminiscing twelve years after the revolution of 1918, Tucholsky
saw himself then as having been engaged in relentless revolutionary
activity, "hitting, first softly, then harder, always harder." [24] His private
correspondence in 1918, recently published, tells another story: [25] it
speaks of bewilderment, of anxiety, of career worries; everything is
there but a conscious approval of the revolution. "As far as conditions
here in Berlin are concerned," he wrote in a letter dated December 19,
1918, to his future wife, [26] "they are more than rotten [*oberfaul*]. What
will become of us, no one can tell. For a while, I expected the entry
into Berlin of the Entente troops. What with the unreasonableness of
the Berliners, this would have been only natural. They don't work;
they hold meetings instead and rampage about. . . . The city resembles a small town, a fourth-class waiting room. It is unrecognizable.
Well, we must wait patiently to see what the future holds." Only the
brutality of the counterrevolutionary soldiers in 1919 brought Tucholsky to a realization of what Germany had lost by not carrying the
revolution to its conclusion. He then began his phenomenal career as a
political critic and an agitator. For the only time in his life, he took
grave risks; it was now that he was "hitting harder, always harder." As
one of the most hated *Kulturbolschewisten* in Germany, his life was
often in danger. In 1924, however, he left Germany and thereafter
returned only for short visits. After 1929, he never again set foot on
German soil.

Assuredly, Tucholsky did not always have the courage of his convictions; he ruthlessly abused and ridiculed the liberal bourgeois press
while drawing a substantial income from the *Vossische Zeitung* of
which he was for many years the Paris literary correspondent. Yet
there was no trace of malevolence in him. In his personal relations he
was both kind and straightforward. Even when he took up his pen he
never indulged in the *ad hominem* attacks that characterized the style
of Jacobsohn. He loathed the Social Democratic leader Friedrich
Ebert for his politics, for example, but he was ready to defend him
against slander because he found Ebert personally honest.

Tucholsky, whose collected (and by no means complete) works fill
three bulky volumes totaling 5,000 pages, never wrote a major work. A
delightful travelogue, *Ein Pyrenäenbuch* [27] and two delicately erotic
stories, *Rheinsberg: Ein Bilderbuch für Verliebte* and *Schloss*

Gripsholm [28] are his longest pieces. None exceeds a hundred and fifty pages. The rest are short pieces, essays, feuilletons, political commentaries, manifestoes, monologues, reportages, poems, glosses, an unsuccessful comedy, drama and book critiques, aphorisms and chansons, to the order of at least two and a half thousand. They can be read successively without boredom, despite the author's insistence on the same themes. They are Tucholsky's "Magic Mountain," a kaleidoscopic picture of his life and times and of the ethos of his period. Perhaps he had neither the talent nor the patience for a *magnum opus,* but each of his short pieces aimed at perfection, written and rewritten with pedantic care. In the words of Erich Kästner:

That man who perspired, typed and smoked his pipe in an attic, toiled for five people. At his little typewriter he dealt out foil thrusts, sabre blows, deft punches. Because even then the gentlemen of the Third Reich, arm in arm with the gentlemen of the Reichswehr and heavy industry, were knocking rather audibly at Germany's gates. He tweaked their noses, kicked them in the shins, knocked some of them out—. A little fat Berliner tried to stop a catastrophe with his typewriter.[29]

Tucholsky called his passion for writing under five names "gay schizophrenia." Indeed, his four aliases, with their distinct personalities, were symbolic of his intellectual restlessness and the diversity of his thought.[30] The "sour and bespectacled" Ignaz Wrobel was an angry political and social critic; the "round and agile" Peter Panter dealt mainly with literature and was rather tolerant and kind; Theobald Tiger wrote poems and songs; Kaspar Hauser was "always slightly bewildered," and wrote mainly thoughtful musings and narratives.[31] The name Kurt Tucholsky was reserved for major political pronouncements. This playful split of personality was sometimes carried to an extreme: in 1919, for instance, it was not Kurt Tucholsky but "Sergeant Ignaz Wrobel" who mounted the tribune at the first meeting of the "Peace League of War Veterans" in Berlin and almost got himself killed in the process.[h] Of course, everybody knew who hid behind the many pseudonyms. Tucholsky's later publication *Mit 5 PS* could be rendered both as "Under Five Pseudonyms," and in a play on words, as "With Five Horsepower." To avoid all misunderstanding, the cover page sported not only the names but also the imaginary portraits of

---

[h] When Tucholsky-Wrobel declared at the meeting that German officers, during the war, "had cared more for their whores than for their men," revolvers were drawn; it required the intervention of a sergeant of the republican Security Service to disarm the Free Corps officers who had invaded the meeting hall and to bundle their weapons into the cloakroom. See "Die Feldgrauen gegen die O.H.L. [Army High Command]," *Berliner Volks-Zeitung,* December 15, 1919.

Tucholsky's five identities. There was a practical reason for the pseudonyms: Tucholsky often contributed as many as three pieces to an issue of the *Weltbühne*.[1]

His penetrating and irreverent voice was heard in a variety of other literary media. Between 1918 and 1920, Tucholsky was editor in chief of *Ulk*, a satirical supplement to the *Berliner Tageblatt;* he wrote, among others, for the *Vossische Zeitung,* the *Berliner Illustrirte* [1] *Zeitung, Uhu, Tempo,* and *Die Dame*—all products of the mildly liberal Ullstein Verlag; the democratic *Berliner Volks-Zeitung* and *Prager Tagblatt;* the radical democratic *Die Welt am Montag* and *8 Uhr-Abendblatt;* the revolutionary pacifist *Die Menschheit* and *Das andere Deutschland;* the Social Democratic *Vorwärts* (only before the war) and the left-wing Social Democratic *Dresdner Volkszeitung;* the Independent Socialist *Die Freiheit,* and the crypto-Communist *Welt am Abend* and *Arbeiter Illustrierte Zeitung* of the Münzenberg concern. If this meant writing for the newspapers of three political parties (DDP, SPD, USPD) and for so-called independent newspapers whose political allegiance ranged from liberal to Communist, Tucholsky could, however, draw a line. Thus he rarely wrote for an official Communist publication, and to the *Vossische Zeitung* he contributed only nonpolitical articles (nor was he asked to do otherwise). His standard of measurement was quality; he would never have thought of working for the main Communist newspaper, *Die Rote Fahne*—"unfortunately, it is not a newspaper"—nor did he ever write for the *Berliner Tageblatt* which he, surprisingly, considered journalistically unacceptable.[32]

Most Berliners never heard of Tucholsky the serious critic; he entered their lives as a cabaret lyricist, writing songs for some of the famous singers of his day and often setting his songs to music. His talent was one of the principal lights of "Schall und Rauch," Trude Hesterberg's "Wilde Bühne," Rosa Valetti's "Grössenwahn," and other

---

[1] Tucholsky's performance at the *Weltbühne* was not quite even. In 1923, for instance, when the inflation forced him for a while to take a job as bank clerk (an experience that drove him to despair) he wrote only 21 contributions for the journal. But almost every other year he turned in at least a hundred signed contributions and many unsigned shorter pieces. Thus, in 1922, there were 4 articles by Tucholsky, 4 by Kaspar Hauser, 40 by Peter Panter, 39 by Theobald Tiger and 31 by Ignaz Wrobel, a total of 118. In 1929, *Die Weltbühne* printed 113 of his poems and articles. In the first half of 1932 there were 62 contributions, but in the second half only 6, and none of these was political.

[1] Because of an early mistake, the masthead of the *Berliner Illustrirte Zeitung* was printed with a spelling error all through the fifty years of its existence.

popular night spots.[33] "Even today, 25 years after his death"—writes Fritz Raddatz—

these chansons are very much alive. There is no cabaret performance, no radio program, without lyrics by Tucholsky. . . . None of these chansons is really "funny"; the humorist Kurt Tucholsky—where is he? . . . Once, in an article on Roda Roda, Tucholsky called humor "the highest form of comicality weighed down by melancholy." [34]

Because he often wrote in untranslatable Berlin jargon, Tucholsky is only moderately well-known in countries outside of Germany despite the increasing number of translations of his works. In Germany, his works have been sold in close to two million copies.[k] Wilhelm Stapel, Tucholsky's most articulate enemy on the Right wrote in 1937, that "of all the Jewish literati, who, between 1918 and 1933, molded public political opinion in Germany, none could equal the effectiveness, in breadth and depth, of Kurt Tucholsky." [35] Success Tucholsky undoubtedly had, but was he effective? Tucholsky was the first to doubt the force of his political thrust. More realistic and more pessimistic than his friends, he was haunted by a sense of futility which was relieved occasionally by the tentative conviction that *Die Weltbühne* was exercising a salutary influence "through a thousand little channels," [36] and that "a long line of intelligent and courageous provincial editors as, for instance, Walther Victor in Zwickau, pick up the ball thrown by the *Weltbühne* and with considerable risk hurl it even further." [37] In 1931, Tucholsky wrote:

What worries me most is the problem of effectiveness. Does my work have any? (I don't mean success; that leaves me indifferent.) It sometimes seems to me so terribly ineffective. I write and write—and what effect does it have on the conduct of the country? Did I get a single one of those foul, perverted, tormented and tormenting female wardens dismissed? Or a single sadist? Or a bureaucrat . . . . This often depresses me.[38]

Especially painful was the accusation that his, and the *Weltbühne's*, political impotence was due to "negativism." "Wir Negativen" ("We Negatives") was the indignant answer to his accusers: [39] "We, the writers of the *Weltbühne* are being reproached for always saying 'No,' for not being sufficiently constructive. We are being accused of reject-

---

[k] Up to 1958, *Rheinsberg* was published in 233,000 copies and *Schloss Gripsholm* in 258,000 copies. *Mit 5 PS*, a collection of his articles written for the *Weltbühne* between 1913 and 1927, reached the publication figure of 25,000 by 1932; by the same year his *Deutschland, Deutschland über alles* had sold 50,000. For a statistical compilation of Tucholsky's popularity, see Klaus-Peter Schulz, *Kurt Tucholsky* (Hamburg, 1959), 173.

ing, of criticizing everything, of dirtying our own German nest. And what is worse—we fight hate with hate, force with force, fist with fist." But how could it be otherwise, Tucholsky added, in a country where the revolution had collapsed; where the bourgeois—as nowhere in Europe—was profoundly antidemocratic and extremist; where the civil servant counted far more than his function; where the politician's credo was the prosperity of the well-to-do; where the intellectual could plan a revolution, proclaim that God was dead, propagate the most dangerous ideas, but always and only on paper. His influence on legislation was nil. What else was there to do but to shake this system from the very bottom?

If we others—who have looked behind the scenes, who believe that the present state of affairs can not be the final goal of mankind—cannot find a way to implement our visions, then we will be damned to live forever, and even longer, among butcherboys. Nothing would be left for us but to play with books, ink, and paper. . . . They tell us that we should make positive proposals. But these are worthless without a nation-wide epidemic of candor. . . . No, we cannot say "Yes." Not yet. We know only one thing: that we must sweep away with an iron broom all that is rotten in Germany. We will get nowhere if we wrap our heads in a black-white-and-red rag and whisper anxiously, "later, my good fellow, later!" . . . No, we want it now! . . . We want to fight with love and hatred.[40]

Realism and irrationality, puritanism and self-indulgence, sympathy and intolerance mixed incongruously in Tucholsky. He could show an inordinate depth of sympathy for an individual weakness; for the country at large his tolerance was easily exhausted. "Tucholsky's attitude towards Germany was a *Hassliebe*,"—writes Harry Zohn—"a mixture of hatred and love; the crux of his problems and the motivation of his writings was the painful discrepancy between the real and the ideal German. It was love which made Tucholsky scourge Germany and the Germans; when he foretold its doom, he did so in an agonizing attempt to avert it." [41] This is the view of all of Tucholsky's sympathetic biographers. Yet it would be better to say that it was a love *in abstracto*, a love for "Germany" but not for her people. He punctuated his *Deutschland, Deutschland über alles* with attacks unparalleled in their ferocity on Weimar Germany. Then he added at the end:

For 225 pages, we have said no—no, because of pity; no, because of love, no, because of hate and no, because of passion. Now we want to say yes. Yes to the landscape and to the countryside of Germany.[42]

It was, to be precise, the landscape of Northern Germany. While in the Baltics during the war, Tucholsky was delighted to discover there a topographical similarity with the region of Germany from which he came, describing it in terms of its cool beauty, its puritanical elegance, its "divine clarity." Tucholsky himself was a mixture of the Nordic and the Mediterranean and, like so many other Jewish Germans—and non-Nordic Christian Germans—he perhaps wished to be identified with the Nordic ideal. What emerged, however, was a denunciation of all Germans unmatched in bitterness by any of the left-wing intellectuals. He was obsessed by the idea that the Germans "deserved" a tyranny, in punishment for the political morass they had created—a tyranny which he foresaw well before Hitler's coming to power. In 1933, he refused to raise his voice in public because "one can struggle in the name of a majority oppressed by a tyrannical minority, but one cannot preach to a people the contrary of that which they desire in their majority." [43] Or, as he wrote more than a year later: "What is taking place there [in Germany] partly reflects the deepest instincts of the German people." [44] Even if we dismiss these statements as expressions of despair, some simple statistics would show that Tucholsky abominated the majority of his fellow citizens. Princes, barons, Junkers, officers, policemen, judges, officials, clergymen, academicians, teachers, capitalists, *Bürger*, university students, peasants, and all Bavarians he condemned collectively. These people, he felt, were too deeply committed to their estates and institutions to be viewed individualistically. They were, for him, members of tightly knit, and inherently evil, groups which molded their personalities and even determined their facial characteristics. He wrote in an article, "Face of a German":

A rather thick-set head, a none too high forehead; cold, small eyes; a nose that likes to lower itself into a drinking glass; a disagreeable toothbrush-like moustache. . . .
Company commander in the war. Implacable, cold. Cold toward the office attendants who couldn't defend themselves, cold toward the young clerks.—"Had to go through this myself once!"—cold toward the world, cold toward God. . . .
Plays the part. Advances his career. Will probably soon be some big-shot ambassador, head of a ministry, secretary of state, or what-have you.
Germany? Germany.[45]

Tucholsky's literary caricatures are akin to those of the painter George Grosz (to whom, incidentally, he dedicated this article). Both created disagreeable prototypes for some social groups in Germany and then forced all members into the molds. Worse even, Tucholsky—and Grosz—saw all these prototypes uniformly as Prussian drill sergeants. For the period of the monarchy this might have been true. But it left the public unprepared for the emergence of the Nazi leader who was too multifaceted—or faceless—to fit any description. The Prussian drill sergeant, although still the favorite Nazi figure of popular literature, was indeed only one, and not the most sinister, of the Nazi characters. There was, also, the soft-spoken dandy (Dr. Mengele), the cunning and rapacious operator (Goering), the histrionic demagogue (Goebbels), the modest bureaucrat (Eichmann), and the petty bourgeois of everyday appearance (Hitler or Himmler).

It was not *Hassliebe* but intolerance, mixed with wit and iconoclasm, that provoked Tucholsky's characterization of the Germans as *Ein Volk der Richter und Henker* (A People of Judges and Executioners) in a provocative play of words on the popular *Ein Volk der Dichter und Denker* (A People of Poets and Thinkers). In Tucholsky's time at least, the victims of these judges and executioners were themselves Germans, and he felt a good deal of sympathy for them. He was devoted to the German workers for whom he wrote sentimental songs and poems. But he was attracted to the workers because he thought of them as internationalists and therefore uncharacteristic Germans. He was also devoted to the poor, "to the inarticulate masses who lived lives of quiet desperation," [46] but although he fought for these people when, as individuals, they got into trouble, he never knew a poor man. Moreover, he was only too well aware that some of the most ardent followers of the right-wing demagogues came from the ranks of the desperately poor. He alone of all the left-wing intellectuals was never to entertain the hope that the German proletariat would rise against Hitler. Only by dismissing the sympathetic argument that Tucholsky was a suffering patriot can we appreciate the significance of his "treasonous" statements:

I proclaim, fully aware of the meaning of my words, that there is no secret of the Germany Army which I would not hand over readily to a foreign power, if this were warranted by the preservation of peace. . . . We [revolutionary pacifists] hold that the war of national states is a crime, and we fight it wherever and whenever we can, with whatever methods. We are traitors. But we betray a state that we disavow [*verneinen*] in favor of a land that we love, for peace and for our true fatherland: Europe.[47]

Or as he wrote in another place:

The moral condemnation we receive from the patriots [*durch die Vaterländischen*] is for us sometimes an honor, but mostly it leaves us indifferent. This country which I am allegedly betraying, is not my country; this state is not my state; this legal system is not my legal system. Its different banners [the republican "black, red, and gold" or the monarchist "black, white, and red"] are to me as meaningless as are its provincial ideals. I have nothing to betray here, because I have not been entrusted with anything.[48]

It was his lack of German patriotism which permitted Tucholsky to be a true European and to be a better prophet than were his fellow pacifists and fellow literati whom, in the same article, he scolded for their patriotic scruples and illusions. Tucholsky, a Jew and an intellectual, had little choice but to become a leftist writer. His decision to abominate his fellow Germans was, however, his own, and it was a lonely, and therefore courageous, decision.

There was also a great deal of *Hassliebe* in Tucholsky which he reserved for the German Jews and for himself. Was he capable of love pure and simple? "I know what I regret most: our unlived life"—he wrote shortly before his suicide to his wife Mary, whom he had divorced two years earlier—

Your loving patience made you go along with this mad joke. The unrest, the patience to live with a man who was always hunted, who was possessed of a fear, no—an anxiety—that anxiety which has no basis and which no one can explain. . . . If love is when one becomes turned around and every thread of being goes crazy, then it is nothing unusual. That can be found almost anywhere. But if we speak of true love, that which endures, that which returns again, again, and yet again—: then I loved only once in my life. You.[49]

Tucholsky had a few close male companions; he was uncritically devoted to Siegfried Jacobsohn as well as to his "household gods," Sigmund Freud and Knut Hamsun, the rebellious Norwegian writer. He admired James Joyce, Franz Kafka, Sinclair Lewis, Alfred Polgar, Alfred Döblin, Arnold Zweig, and the poet of the absurd, Christian Morgenstern. Finally, he genuinely admired the French as a people. In 1924, he fled to Paris to "take a rest from the fatherland"; his periodic returns to France he celebrated as "homecoming." In 1926, he wrote in his "Parisian Thanksgiving":

How nice it is to live here, without those faces that are none; without rowdies and bowlers—without that dusty Berlin wind. Ten years too late! And yet I can't complain. It is so good to say "yes" once again.[1]

---

[1] This poem which is replete with such statements as "here [in Paris] no one steps on my toes; here people are kind and polite"; "here the cars travel smoothly and fast"; "here clouds are still clouds and stones are still stones; here it still makes sense to be alive," was too much for Siegfried Jacobsohn who printed a preface to the poem in which Tucholsky promised to moderate his Parisian zeal in the future. See Theobald Tiger [Kurt Tucholsky], "Pariser Dankgebet," *Die Weltbühne*, May 25, 1926, p. 811. Also in *Gesammelte Werke*, II, 448.

But even his Francophilism was not unwavering. While he never lost his affection for the French way of life, he later became more critical of French politics. In his last years he took up residence in Sweden and it was to Swedish—not to French—citizenship that he aspired, although he spoke little Swedish. It was again his Nordic nostalgia that triumphed and perhaps it is fitting that, in 1935, he killed himself in a little village in Sweden.

Categorical judgments permitted Tucholsky to operate with the stylistic device of utter simplicity. His sentences were usually short; his message easily understandable. He was never afraid of the vernacular, of slang, and even—occasionally—of coarse expressions. He avoided and ridiculed circumlocution, pomposity, and verbiage which he held for faults inherent in the bureaucratic style of life in Germany. He campaigned relentlessly against stylistic prudery. His very first book *Rheinsberg*, which is an idyllic account of the erotic escapade of a young Berlin couple, brought about a "revolution of naturalness *[Natürlichkeit]*." [50] Published in 1912, when eroticism was still either taboo or projected in the dramas of Strindberg and Wedekind as a lurid but irrepressible passion, *Rheinsberg* first presented eroticism as a healthy and delightful experience. [51]

Tucholsky was a genius in giving new uses to conventional expressions, in spinning out *bons mots*, and in the ironical rephrasing of citations. Peter Panter's famous *Schnipsel*, these shortest of Tucholsky's satirical jibes, contain some of the best examples of his epigrammatic style:

On account of bad weather, the German revolution took place in music.

The rumor that, should Hindenburg decide to resign, the SPD will nominate Ludendorff for President does not, as yet, correspond to facts.

KPD. A pity that you are not a Party member—so that you could now be expelled.

Was it a coincidence that the apostles of the wildest theories of violence, Nietzsche, Barrès, Sorel, were unable to perform twenty kneebends? No, it couldn't be a coincidence.

There are people who prefer standing room in the first class to seats in the third. They are not attractive people.

Everything is true; also the opposite of that. Only "well yes . . . but" is never true. [52]

Tucholsky had mastered that requirement of a short, epigrammatic style: an unexpected, rousing, devastating last sentence. At times the punch line summed up the argument in a wild exclamation; at other times the reader, having been led through a long-winded story of impeccable respectability, is suddenly put to shame for his joyful acceptance of conventionality. Another of Tucholsky's popular artistic devices was the monologue, construed in the form of endless chatter. Two of his best-known heroes, the Jewish businessman *Herr Wendriner* and the scatterbrained Berlin girl *Lottchen,* were such babblers. They quarreled, gossiped, argued, joked, complained, nagged without ever waiting for an answer. It was a technique which familiarized the reader with Tucholsky's characters to the point of greatest intimacy; it also brought home his oft-repeated argument that people, especially big-city people, do not talk to one another but "next to one another." Although it is impossible to reproduce from "Herr Wendriner Gets a Haircut" either Herr Wendriner's Berlin Jewish jargon, or his attempt to imitate the clipped, harsh language of the upper-class Prussian, the buffoonery is not entirely lost in translation:

Pardon me, but I was first! In any case, I've been waiting here longer than you have, Mister! But certainly—! Haircut, quite short in the back. As usual. And less grease than the last time; you ruined my whole hat-lining! Just a second—let me undo my collar first . . . So, good now. Well, let's see, what do you have—a picture magazine or any newspaper—makes no difference. Tja—the *Lokalanzeiger* [m]—Give it to me. No—I didn't read it yet. Oh, that? That's an old story, I read it in the *B.Z.*[n] No—I don't think so—the French can't impress me at all. A band of phoneys. Paris is not to be trusted. Your machine is pulling at my hair. In my opinion it would be wrong to sign a trade agreement with these people—let them come to us first. They will come when they need us. . . .

Nu, Herr Welsch, what's new. Thanks, I'm alive. And how is your mother? Still sick? Well, an old woman . . . We once had a great-aunt living with us; she stayed with us till she died, she used to say when there was trouble, "Who knows, how long you'll have me—!" Well, we had her long enough . . . I'm just telling Lauch: We should enter into an alliance with [Soviet] Russia. Aren't you of the same opinion? No! Right? But of course. Absolutely out of the question. What, another wage raise? These people must be out of their minds. You are quite right: not enough of them were put against the wall. Sure, I'm socially conscious myself: I mean, these people should be given their wages. But they shouldn't blackmail us. They are ruining the whole middle-class. Of course, the industry too. Where should

[m] A nationalist newspaper that *Die Weltbühne* never ceased to refer to as the *Idiotenblatt der Reichshauptstadt.*
[n] The *B.Z. am Mittag* was an Ullstein publication, the most successful boulevard paper in Berlin.

all this money come from. Hey you, don't let your soap drip on my shoes. And after the shampoo something sharp. Bah . . . aah . . . that feels good. Look at the pretty girl there! . . .[53]

In time, Tucholsky found many critics, not only political but literary. He was reproached by his friends for his chronic absenteeism from the political stage and, again and again, for his negativism. Others found him of limited literary talent. When, in 1958, in Berlin's *Der Monat*, Hermann Kesten ranked Tucholsky low in the literary hierarchy, there followed a stormy debate which lasted for several months.[54] Interestingly, both Kesten who was his friend and Wilhelm Stapel[55] who was his enemy came to similar conclusions. Both argued that Tucholsky's greatness was limited to "Berlin realism," that his genius lay in the description of the lives of little men, in "written mimicry," best represented by the Wendriner stories.[56] Kesten called Tucholsky a *Volkskomiker* and a *Volksschriftsteller* whose enemies were those of the little people: "the high court of justice and the great lords, the higher estates and the ruling classes, the officers and their cheap ladies and expensive girl friends, the false poets, and false pretensions."[57] Worse even, Kesten writes, Tucholsky was a bad prophet for although he foresaw the Third Reich, he foresaw it as a continuation of the old monarchy° just as a second world war would be a continuation of the first.[58]

Perhaps Kesten is right when he says that there was—and still is—too much hulabaloo about Tucholsky. A lot of bad stuff issued with the good from Tucholsky's typewriter: cheap jokes, revolutionary songs full of pathos (the workers loved them), sentimental idylls, abject Francophilism. His great talent was to prod, to sneer, to applaud, and to satirize. His only attempt at a small, center role was a failure: Tucholsky's editorship of the *Weltbühne* had lasted eleven months. Being no organizer, and feeling uncomfortable in the Berlin chair of his former mentor, he fled back to Paris.

Beginning October 11, 1927, Ossietzky signed as editor in chief of the *Weltbühne*. To reassure Tucholsky's admirers, his name was kept on the cover as the journal's principal writer.

° What Kesten is referring to is undoubtedly Tucholsky's famous "Herr Wendriner Under the Dictatorship" where this Jewish bourgeois finds that life is not at all unbearable under the Nazis as long as one keeps one's mouth shut and attends to one's own business. (See Kaspar Hauser, "Herr Wendriner steht unter der Diktatur," *Gesammelte Werke*, III, 547–550. For an English translation of this article, see Harry Zohn, ed., *The World Is a Comedy* (Cambridge, Mass., 1957), 117 ff.)

CARL VON OSSIETZKY

If Jacobsohn and Tucholsky had wide open personalities and aired their individual likes and dislikes in public, Ossietzky was, to say the least, enigmatic. Colleagues who later tried to reminisce about him were embarrassed to realize how little they knew.[59] They remembered mainly the appearances: his exceeding modesty, his pedantic working habits and his seeming lethargy. Alfred Kantorowicz described Ossietzky's "fine, dark blond hair, combed to the back, which left uncovered his high, powerfully arched and noble forehead. His rather flat, evenly shaped face was unusually pale. His dark blue eyes lay deeply imbedded. Rarely did they light up. . . . He was a man of modest appearance; a man turned inward: a dreamer, rather than a fighter." [60] Axel Eggebrecht found him "a modest, quiet man. He dressed like a correct civil servant with a gold watchchain stretched across the front of his black vest. He fought his battles against power and the abuse of power at his desk, at night, with coffee and cigarettes." [61] His apparent impassiveness estranged even his admirers: "This superior stylist, this man with the unequaled courage of his convictions," wrote Tucholsky in 1933, "displayed a singular lethargy that I could never understand." [62]

Ossietzky was born in Hamburg in 1889 (in the same year as Hitler). He was the son of a stenographer.[63] His father was Catholic, his mother Lutheran; his own religion, if any, remains unknown. On his father's side, Ossietzky was of Silesian Polish descent. The origin of the *von* in his name is uncertain.[ᵖ] He referred to it only in jest: he told his friends that in the seventeenth century the Great Elector of Brandenburg, with his war chest empty, once made nobles out of two entire regiments of his Polish lancers because he could not pay them; an ancestor of his, he said, was a soldier in one of these regiments.[64] Of

---

[ᵖ] The hesitation of friends about Ossietzky's background might be responsible for the confusion reigning in non-German historical sources with regard to Ossietzky. It is, for instance, generally assumed that Ossietzky was an aristocrat, if not a career officer, who became a convert to pacifism because of his war experience. For example, John W. Wheeler-Bennett, *The Nemesis of Power* (London, 1954), 94 n. writes that Ossietzky was "a member of an aristocratic Prussian Catholic family," and that "his experiences as an officer in the First World War rendered him a convinced and ardent pacifist." The mistake is understandable for there were a number of active officers (Generals von Schoenaich and von Deimling, Captains von Richthofen, Paasche, Meyer, Persius, and others) who converted to pacifism during World War I. On the other hand, it was rare for a man of lower-middle-class background, such as Ossietzky, to become a militant pacifist.

his mother, who ran a small canteen, Ossietzky remarked only that she was an anti-Semitic petty bourgeois who would have been horrified by her son's circle of friends.[65] His father died when Ossietzky was two years old, and he grew up in modest circumstances. Like Tucholsky, he was an indifferent student and never finished high school. Between 1907 and 1914 he was a less than diligent clerk in the Hamburg provincial administration.

The crucial change in Ossietzky's life occurred in 1913 when he married Maud Woods, the orphaned daughter of a lieutenant in His British Majesty's 1st Dragoon Guards Regiment. This aristocratic woman who, on her mother's side was partly East Indian, partly British, but in both cases of exalted lineage, had been active in the English pacifist and feminist movements. Her education and her money (the latter incidentally lasted only until the outbreak of the war when the couple faced extreme poverty) gave Ossietzky the necessary impetus to a writing career.[66]

Despite his uninspiring background, Ossietzky became remarkably erudite and cosmopolitan. He knew history, the arts, the stage, and the English poets: he spoke English well and admired English tradition. He shared in the German predilection for citing Shakespeare and the other classics. "Carl von Ossietzky's erudition was enormous and well cemented," wrote Walther Karsch, one of his assistants at the *Weltbühne;* "he had read Mommsen, Treitschke, Sybel, Ranke, Carlyle, Marx. . . ."[q] His intellectual curiosity was not restricted to politics alone. A noble soul, he felt great responsibility for the future of his nation, and was therefore driven to engage in political activity. But secretly he longed for the arts. His book reviews, written under the name of Celsus, made delightful reading; his drama critiques were well documented as well as humorous, pointed, and revealing."[67] Some of Ossietzky's biographers maintain that it was his stepfather Gustav Robert Walther, a sculptor and a devoted Social Democrat, who introduced Ossietzky to progressive thought.[68] This is possible but young Ossietzky did not become a Social Democrat. Instead, around 1912, he almost simultaneously joined three organizations of the progressive upper bourgeoisie, the "Demokratische Vereinigung" (Democratic Alliance), the "Deutsche Friedensgesellschaft" (German Peace Association), and the "Deutscher Monistenbund" (German

---

[q] This last is at least doubtful as Ossietzky's writings reveal great unfamiliarity with Marxist teachings.

Monistic League). There must have been a certain amount of snob-
bishness and *arrivisme* in his entering these intellectually refined associations of professors, journalists, and Jewish businessmen. But whatever his reasons for joining, Ossietzky remained faithful to the end to
the philosophies of these movements: social justice, peace through
international disarmament, free thought, and militant anticlericalism.
To these beliefs he added a strong sympathy for socialism and for
militant socialist organizations. His political convictions were formed
at an early date and underwent no substantial changes.

The Demokratische Vereinigung was founded in 1908 by a group of
dissenters from the Progressive Liberal Party in Wilhelmian
Germany.[69] The new splinter party repudiated the Progressives' tactical alliance with the National Liberals and the Conservatives, and
vowed to fight for a system of international arbitration, social equality,
and political freedom. More important, alone of all liberal parties, the
Demokratische Vereinigung advocated a permanent alliance between
the progressive bourgeoisie and the Social Democratic Party.[70]

The Demokratische Vereinigung failed pitifully. At the January
1912 election, it won 28,000 votes but not a single seat in the Reichstag.[71] Of its founders, Theodor Barth had died earlier, Rudolf Breitscheid joined the Social Democrats, and Wilhelm Herzog became a
radical left-wing writer who later entered the Independent Socialist
Party. Ossietzky, who in 1913 became the secretary of the Hamburg
chapter of the Demokratische Vereinigung, assisted in the gradual
liquidation of this once buoyant undertaking. As one of the main
writers of *Das freie Volk*, the party's weekly, he faithfully contributed
to this failing journal—of course, without pay—until its collapse early
in the war.

Ossietzky's editorials in *Das freie Volk* showed him the full-fledged
left-wing intellectual for whom nothing seemed impossible: any
change in the political or social structure could be brought about by
propaganda and education. Society in its existing form was bad because the majority of the population, the producers, were unaware of
their true interests and made themselves prisoners of their narrow
ideologies. The bourgeois who clung to the notion of profit and the
proletarian who saw everything in terms of class struggle, behaved not
only selfishly but suicidally because they did not see their true task:
cooperation. There was, in fact, no inevitable antagonism between the
capitalist and the worker, but only between these two and feudalism.
Accordingly, there was only one genuine conflict, that between the

forces of the old and the forces of the new, the one represented by the German state, the churches, the army, and the landowners, and the other by the mass of producers.[72]

The reconciliation of the German workers with the liberal bourgeoisie had been advocated earlier by such men as Court Preacher Adolf Stöcker, the sociologist Lujo Brentano, and the founder of the "National Socialist League," Friedrich Naumann. Yet, in each case, reconciliation was understood as an integration of the workers into the middle class, a winning over of the proletariat for German national interests. The Demokratische Vereinigung inaugurated a new—if hopeless—program: the aligning of the bourgeoisie alongside the proletariat, with both sides making some concessions. The stubborn bourgeoisie of course had to be criticized more sharply than the socialist workers. Failing to see the growing political and economic power of the German bourgeoisie, and its aggressive imperialism, Ossietzky bemoaned in his editorials the enslavement of the *Bürger* by the aristocracy and called to the barricades those who had more to lose than to gain by a revolution.

Ossietzky turned with fervor to the struggle for social justice. This he considered man's supreme task, his ethical obligation. He spoke of a new religious feeling sweeping over Europe, a "religion of hopefulness, of untiring labor, but also of sacrifice and bitter tears." [73] This quasi-religious approach to social problems reflected his early association with the then fairly popular "monistic League." Ossietzky cared little for the involved argumentation of the German monists on the essential unity of matter and energy as the manifestation of a single (*monos*) reality or substance; he saw only the practical aspects of their teaching, the advocacy of a secular, materialistic education and militant anticlericalism.[74] In his editorials he called for a separation of church and state and a mass withdrawal from the Prussian Protestant *Landeskirche*. A weak, and possibly separated, Church would—he hoped—deprive the Prussian government of its strongest support and force the latter to abolish the archaic three-class electoral system on which the power of the Junker aristocracy rested.[75] In his enthusiasm, young Ossietzky saw an epic struggle developing between Progress and Reaction, between the forces of "this-worldliness" in one camp, and of "other-worldliness" in the other. His "this-worldliness" was Godless: the state of the future was to be based on unconditional atheism.

If the churches were the spiritual arm of the aristocracy, the army was its secular arm. Consequently, the military establishment had to be abolished. What might have been useful in the age of feudalism, was now only an obstacle to progress and a corrupter of society.

Here in Germany the military is enormously overestimated. Mars, this rabid god of war, lives his golden age. Nowhere does he receive richer offerings, nowhere is his authority greater. . . . Militarism has been turned into a Moloch; we admire it with gloomy stupefaction while it is about to devour one victim after another! . . . Yes, silly and spineless is the flattery and incense-burning that the bourgeoisie offers to militarism.[76]

Inspired by the then popular work, *The Great Illusion* (1911), of the British pacifist Norman Angell, Ossietzky asserted that economic interdependence among the great powers made wars unprofitable and therefore unlikely. Who then needed an army? The threat of war in the summer of 1914 came as a great shock to Ossietzky, and for the first but not the last time in his life he expressed enthusiasm for radical socialism by praising Rosa Luxemburg's efforts to prevent war by every method available.[77] On one occasion at least, at a meeting of the Demokratische Vereinigung in Hamburg, he suggested a general strike as a last resort against war.[78] But precisely because war seemed so pointless among industrialized nations, Ossietzky attributed it when it finally came to the forces of the old—not to international capitalism —and he blamed Russian reactionary barbarism. Thus, having been on the extreme Left in the question of militarism, but not in questions of politics, he now involuntarily reversed himself, and voiced the patriotic rationalizations of the Social Democratic Party. "Germany must become a country imbued with the spirit of freedom," he wrote on the eve of war. "Democracy has the same effect on tsarism that the crucifix has on the devil. A feudal, capitalistic Germany may well dread the Slavic onslaught. A free Germany has nothing to fear. Let the tsar hurry his Hunnish hordes across Europe. They will crack their skulls against the wall of our superior democratic *Kultur* . . ."[79] His conditional approval of the war reflected no change of sentiments. It was entirely in agreement with his concept of the battle of two titans, modern man versus the ancient. When he saw that Social Democracy was unable or unwilling to wrench democratic concessions from the government in exchange for its support of the war effort, Ossietzky immediately denounced the war. In surprisingly Marxist language he called the war "a manifestation of imperialism and of predatory capitalism"[80] at a meeting of the German Peace Association held in March 1915.

Because of his weak constitution, Ossietzky was drafted in the army only in 1916. He then served on the Western Front as a private.[81] Having been a radical democrat before 1914, he was not unduly influenced by the war experience: it only strengthened his pacifism and injected in him a mood of elation for the coming golden age of peaceful humanity. While still a soldier he became an enthusiastic "activist," one who demanded that the intellectuals become political. His wartime articles, published in a pamphlet in 1919,[82] were replete with statements on the ivory-tower attitude of the intellectuals in the past, on the need to end the fateful dualism of art and power, and on the coming conquest of politics by ethics. The revolution of November 1918 brought him to paroxysms of enthusiasm, and although he immediately repudiated the Spartacus League (the far Left of German socialism), he called for a struggle with no comprises:

No! It is better to be like the erring Faust on the Blocksberg, swaying between remorse and desire in the midst of the infernal chaos of the witches' sabbath; better to be like the wandering knight, alone in the horrible wilderness, threatened by devil and death, than to conclude a pact with that Philistine adroitness of emotions and thought, that greasy correctness, that dull and flat single-mindedness which sees only the next step but is unable to grasp the essence of things. Thus must be the Man of our days: the Man who builds the house in which the generations of the future will live.[83]

These lines, taken from his pamphlet, were initially written for a monistic journal and must have had a bewildering effect on Ossietzky's gentle monist readers. They also smacked of bombastic provincial journalism. Yet neither their tone nor their message was unusual; they faithfully mirrored the prevailing expressionist-activist trend in political literature. Of course, Ossietzky also hoped for the triumph of socialism: an expectation shared by almost all German intellectuals of the period. When the German revolution failed, Ossietzky blamed both Mr. Average (*Herr Durchschnittsmensch*) and the followers of Liebknecht (*Revolutionshysteriker*).[84]

For two years Ossietzky continued his collaboration with the monistic journal, the *Monistische Monatshefte*, but he had less and less interest in the monists, most of whom refused to become political. Invited by Ludwig Quidde, the president of the German Peace Association, and by Hellmut von Gerlach to act as the association's secretary, Ossietzky moved to Berlin in 1919. He was then thirty and for the first time in his life was to be paid for his journalistic and political activity.[r] He began his new vocation with great expectations, and he was never to lose his loyalty to the pacifist cause though he soon found the pacifists exasperating. They were, he often recounted afterward, much too scholarly, naïve, and inefficient. Still worse, they were belligerent—but only toward each other; in July 1920, Ossietzky resigned as secretary of the Peace Association. Having joined, seven months earlier, the staff of the *Berliner Volks-Zeitung*, he was now a full-fledged Berlin journalist and no longer unknown.

The *Volks-Zeitung* for which Ossietzky worked during the next four years was an old newspaper, acquired in 1904 by the Mosse Verlag. Although it appeared twice daily and had an average circulation of 150,000,[85] it was overshadowed by Mosse's prestige publication, the *Berliner Tageblatt*, edited by Theodor Wolff. Unlike the *Tageblatt*, it aimed at the average reader, but since it insisted on rather high cultural and ethical standards, it was no match for the mass-circulation newspapers of the Ullstein variety. Like the *Tageblatt*, the *Volks-Zeitung* was consistently democratic, and its editor in chief, Otto Nuschke, was a member of the German Democratic Party's presidium. Actual direction was left to a team of young radicals composed of, among others, Karl Vetter, Manfred George, and Berthold Jacob, the last two collaborators of the *Weltbühne*.[s] They were ardent "activists" and ventured outside the field of journalism in their attempts to form revolutionary mass organizations. Vetter, their leader, had come from the Youth Movement; the war turned him into a pacifist, and, in

---

[r] Besides serving as secretary of the Peace Association, Ossietzky also signed as the editor of the *Völker-Friede*, the association's journal. When financial distress forced the liquidation of this rather ambitious journal in December 1919—"much too wise children seldom live long," Ossietzky commented (Der *Völker-Friede*, December 1919)—he signed as the editor of the more modest *Mitteilungen der Deutschen Friedensgesellschaft*.

[s] The fate of the leading members of the *Berliner Volks-Zeitung* is worth noting. They were close friends, yet each of them went in different directions. Nuschke, who in 1931 resigned the editorship of the *Volks-Zeitung*, remained in Germany after Hitler's seizure of power but was forbidden to exercise his profession. In 1945, he was cofounder of the Christian Democratic Union, an East-German fellow-traveling political organization. He later became Vice-Chancellor of the German Democratic Republic. Vetter, who in 1924 was to experiment with his own "Republican Party," later became a businessman, and then again engaged in journalism. In April 1933, as manager of the "streamlined" *Berliner Tageblatt*, he declared his loyalty to Hitler. (See Hiller, *Koepfe und Troepfe*, 344.) Manfred George died in 1965 in New York as editor of the *Aufbau*, the prestigious publication of the German-Jewish emigré intellectuals. Berthold Jacob generally considered the top antimilitarist reporter of the period, died in 1944 in Gestapo captivity.

November 1918, he sat in the Council of Workers in Berlin.[86] Less than a year later, he founded a veterans' organization, the "Friedensbund der Kriegsteilnehmer" (Peace League of War Veterans), under the slogan, "Veterans of the World—Unite!" [87] The new organization was (avowedly) formed in answer to the inefficacy of the Peace Association. It was hoped that the war veterans would be more dynamic than the professorial types of the official peace movement. In cooperation with foreign veterans' organizations, the German League launched the campaign "Nie wieder Krieg" (No More War) and held impressive mass demonstrations.[t] But the "No More War" movement, ridiculed by Communists and snubbed by official Social Democracy, had popular support only as long as it was espoused by the Independent Socialists. When this party dissolved itself in 1922, the "No More War" movement gradually declined. Nor was the Friedensbund a match for the nationalist and Social Democratic veterans' associations. Karl Vetter tried to inject some vitality into the League by combining a call for a socialist state with a strong appeal to *grossdeutsch* patriotism (one of his manifestoes called for a "German unitary state from the Meuse to the Memel, and from the Adige [South Tyrol] to the [Great] Belt"),[88] but without political party support the Friedensbund was also doomed.

In all these activities, Ossietzky was an enthusiastic participant. Late in 1921, he became editor of *Nie wieder Krieg*, the League's erratic journal; [89] he also participated, as a member of the action committee, in the "No More War" demonstrations. Again and again the shy Ossietzky would make public speeches, overcoming his persistent stage fright for what seemed to him worthwhile causes. Like a fair number of the left-wing intellectuals he was not loath to enter a political movement, yet there was something almost comical in his repeated support of luckless undertakings. In 1924, Ossietzky would again directly involve himself in political activity; for the time being he settled down to political journalism. Of this he was now a more sober practitioner. There was to be less dabbling in *Weltanschauung*, fewer Faustian scenes, and fewer sweeping proclamations. Not long before,[90] he had been bitterly complaining that the *weisse Sekunde*, the triumph of love and universal reconciliation, so ardently expected by

---

[t] In August 1921 and 1922, at the demonstrations held in the Berlin Lustgarten, leading German and French pacifists spoke to an estimated crowd of between 50,000 and 100,000 people. See Otto Lehmann-Russbüldt, *Der Kampf der Deutschen Liga für Menschenrechte, 1914–1927* (Berlin, 1927), 103, and Frederick J. Libby, *War on War* (Washington, D.C., 1923), 29 f.

the wartime activists, had not been realized. Imploring the Germans to tear down the accursed frontiers, he concluded his article: "Only when this happens [the frontiers crumble], will the bell of reconciliation sound, and the last warrior bury his sword under a heap of roses." [91] Between 1920 and 1924, Ossietzky was writing in much more measured tones.

The editorials that Ossietzky contributed to the *Volks-Zeitung* between January 1920 and March 1922 [u] show that he saw enemies both on the Right (nationalists, conservative bourgeoisie) and on the Left (Leninists), and he saw in both groups the repositories of Prussian *Kadavergehorsam* (unconditional obedience), of the "spirit of Potsdam." [92]

Ossietzky called on the leaders of the republic to combat simultaneously both threats to democracy, and he expected of them reforms which would reconcile at least the Left extremists to the republic. The pattern was clear: the extreme Left was dangerous but not unredeemable; it was up to the republic to make constructive left-wing Social Democrats of the destructive Communists. [93] As far as Ossietzky was concerned, the republic was on probation during this period and, therefore, despite the catastrophic incidents of the Rathenau murder and the Ruhr crisis, it deserved good will and support. The breaking point came at the end of 1923 after the Beerhall putsch and the bloody suppression of a stillborn Communist revolt. Not only was the Weimar Coalition guilty of fighting the Left more violently than it fought the Right, but in entering in a Great Coalition with the monarchist and reactionary "People's Party" under Stresemann, it surrendered republican purity. Even worse, the Vetter group felt, the republican parties, floundering in one cabinet crisis after another and with hopeless ancients for leaders, had failed to create a republican *mystique*. On January 6, 1924, Vetter, Ossietzky, Manfred George, Berthold Jacob, the astrophysicist Professor Wilhelm Westphal, and others, founded the "Republican Party of Germany." [94] For party leader they invited the pacifist-expressionist writer Fritz von Unruh, the son of a general and himself a retired career officer.

The Republican Party of Germany was an insignificant venture; if its story is briefly related here, it is because it shows how weak the

---

[u] Ossietzky continued as editor of the *Berliner Volks-Zeitung* until 1924, but copies of the newspaper for the years 1922–1924 are not available. In the East-Berlin Stadtbibliothek, the only repository of the *Volks-Zeitung*, the issues for these years were destroyed by fire. See Raimund Koplin, *Carl von Ossietzky* (Berlin, 1964), 45.

parliamentary tradition was among some left-wing intellectuals. The founders of the party were out to get votes and to build a mass following. In order to achieve this, they were willing to be quite realistic. They secured the financial support of at least one great industrialist, Robert Bosch in Stuttgart.[95] According to one reputable source, Vetter and his party also received substantial sums from the Soviet embassy in Berlin.[v] Their first manifesto distinctly appealed to popular political sentiments.[96] The abolition of monopolies, the protection of the economically weak, the reconciliation of *Arbeiter* and *Bürger* were demands common to almost all parties. The establishment of a unitary Reich and the replacement of the army by a people's militia were radical democratic postulates. But the demand for an "active" foreign policy, leading to the "banding of all brothers of the German tongue in a unitary Reich," even if couched in democratic *grossdeutsch* language, were unmistakable concessions to German nationalism. So were the many references to an "indivisible German *Volkstum*," to the "leadership idea," or to the "fateful deterioration of parliamentarism." The party's emphasis on the conflict of generations, and its appeal to the "war generation" was another concession to antidemocratic sentiments. This "Party of the Thirty-Year Old for the Thirty-Year Old" promised, in case of victory, to force every party to give half of its administrative positions to young people. Vetter and Ossietzky gave campaign lectures entitled "Fort mit den Bonzen" (Cast Out the Bosses); others, such as Professor Westphal and Manfred George, entitled their speeches, "Youth and Veterans into the Parliament!"[97] Berthold Jacob voiced clearly antiparliamentary sentiments: "We have declared openly and often that we will hail the day when we can dissolve the Republican Party of Germany and join the great State Party (*Staatspartei*) of the German Republic."[98]

This was poor performance. Writing twenty-five years after the event, Kurt Hiller angrily rebuked "these so-called left democratic *frondeurs* who infamously fraternized with the spirit of gradually rising nationalism."[99]

The Reichstag elections of May 4, 1924, in which Ossietzky was one of the candidates, brought less than 50,000 votes to the party and not a single seat in the parliament.[100] Shortly after the elections, Vetter, Westphal, Ossietzky, and others left the party; its chairmanship was thereupon entrusted to Manfred George,[101] but it never again participated in elections.

---

[v] For further details, see p. 162.

Earlier, Vetter and Ossietzky had resigned their positions at the *Volks-Zeitung* [102] which would not have tolerated the venture of its staff members into politics hostile to the German Democratic Party (DDP). At the end of May 1924, Ossietzky joined *Das Tage-Buch* whose editor in chief Stefan Grossmann had shown some sympathy for the experiment of the "republicans." For the next two years, he signed as responsible editor of this journal.[103] He was by no means replacing either Leopold Schwarzschild or Grossmann as chief editorial writer; he was rather expected to perform the time-honored function of the *Sitzredakteur,* the dummy editor willing to "sit" in prison for articles written by his superiors. His numerous commentaries written for *Das Tage-Buch* betray Ossietzky's growing impatience with the republic and the republican leaders. Earlier, he had begged the republican leaders to show force and determination; to have confidence in their own cause; to be militant. Now his judgment of the republic amounted to a proclamation, later to become famous, of despair:

It is no cheap pessimism but a cogent recognition of facts to say at last in public: There is no republic in Germany! One hears people say that this republic is without republicans. Unluckily, the situation is just the reverse: The republicans are without a republic. And there is no republic because there is no [republican] Left in the country. Because the great morass of the "Center" absorbs everything. Because people prefer "balance" to "struggle." [104]

Under such conditions, he continued in the same article, written in 1924, to be a republican is no more than a "private indulgence." It resembles a hopeless love affair—but without a lover.[105]

From that time on Ossietzky gradually developed his revolutionary program for direct action, no longer in support of but against the republic. It was to bring him to a political position which often paralleled that of the Communists and provoked his active participation in Communist-inspired undertakings. The obvious forum for such an activity was not the relatively moderate *Das Tage-Buch,* but the more abrasive and exasperated *Die Weltbühne.* His initial contribution to the *Weltbühne* appeared in 1926; in October 1927, the widow of Siegfried Jacobsohn made him editor in chief of the journal.

The journal was in healthy condition when Ossietzky inherited it. Its circulation had increased from 1,200 copies in 1917 to 12,600 in January 1926.[106] It eventually reached 20,000 under his editorship, providing Jacobsohn's widow with a secure income. Ossietzky was to write a few years later: "*Die Weltbühne,* when I took it over . . . was a wonderful receptacle in which were assembled many beautiful things, and they shone so seductively in the sunset of the bourgeois age! . . . Today, in 1932, all is crammed full with politics and economics, and this refuge of beauty has become a depot of all anxieties."[107] This was nostalgia on the part of an artist *raté;* in fact, *Die Weltbühne* was as full of politics and economics in 1926 as it was six years later. And as for anxiety, it will be shown that it could not have been worse in the middle of the Locarno period.

Did Ossietzky as editor in chief effect any significant changes? His only outspoken critic on the Left, Kurt Hiller, answers the question negatively. "Ossietzky lacked entirely the passion for editing," he writes in his reminiscences;[108] "he had no new ideas, he did not inspire, he was not a director; he merely published from the incoming leftist contributions what seemed to him stylistically acceptable." Or as Hiller writes in another place: "Ossietzky did not edit the *Weltbühne:* under him the review edited itself."[109] Ossietzky was undoubtedly too distant and retiring to inspire: his unsatisfactory relationship with Tucholsky and Hiller is a proof of this. Tucholsky, whose articles had been "letters addressed to Jacobsohn," exchanged hopelessly stiff letters with his new superior or would wait in vain for a reply to his suggestions.[110] But Hiller goes even further. He accuses Ossietzky of being essentially negative,[111] of being a political impressionist, an artist who had no basis for judgment. He was, Hiller asserts, unable to decide whether or not he was a socialist; disgusted by the systematic and the methodical, he never bothered to study or reconstruct Marxism. He didn't know whether he preferred capitalism or nationalization, parliamentary democracy, or the dictatorship of the proletariat. Even as a pacifist he failed, because he refused to give his pacifism a socialist-revolutionary interpretation (Hiller's own creed). His worst failure was that Ossietzky saw no point in carrying on Jacobsohn's tradition in organizing debates on the question of "Red unity." All in all, Hiller argues, this "natural politician" lacked political foresight, whereas Jacobsohn, a politician *malgré lui* with the instinct and enthusiasm of a theater director succeeded in giving his journal a positive content.[112]

There was between Hiller and Ossietzky an enormous difference in temperament; this might account for Hiller's negative opinion. In reality, it was under Ossietzky that *Die Weltbühne* achieved world fame—partly, of course, because of the treason trial of its editor. But under him the journal also became more gracious and respectable, in the moral if not in the political sense. There were to be no more quarrels, no libel. Ossietzky broke with the tradition of "individualistic journalism" that had characterized the literary efforts of Maximilian Harden, Karl Kraus, and Jacobsohn.[113] He was no egoist, and although the inflated "I" pronouncements of his predecessors were perhaps more amusing, the journal gained in seriousness and universality. Unlike the "individualistic journalists," Ossietzky did not claim to have special inspiration; his own words did not inebriate him, and he did not write for eternity. Although a frustrated artist, he did not act as though he were stooping to the lower level of journalism. He took his *métier* seriously and in so doing developed a skill that made him one of the best in his profession. He wrote with elegance but also simply and understandably; his sources of information were unimpeachable —a rarity in German journalism—and, above all, he had the courage of his convictions. With Ossietzky as editor of the *Weltbühne,* the interested reader could every week stake out the battle positions between "progress" and "reaction." When the journal declined in quality shortly before Hitler's triumph, it was because the entire Left disintegrated and because the writers of the *Weltbühne,* threatened by the state prosecutor and the SA, began to tire of dancing on a tightrope.[114] "Ossietzky was a fanatic of truth and a born martyr, a type not unknown in German history," said his friend, Manfred George. "He was always ready to sacrifice himself, for his idol was Florian Geyer, the poor German noble of the sixteenth-century peasant revolution, who aspired to the leadership of the oppressed." [115]

Part Two

CAUSES AND CAMPAIGNS

Chapter III

FOR UNIVERSAL FRATERNITY
DURING THE WAR

The outbreak of the war in 1914 and the defeat of the German army in 1918 were the occasions for two impressive manifestations of German solidarity. Both events were marked by a surge of optimism because the majority of the German people saw in the declaration of war, and again in the armistice, the portents of a great and new era. Yet neither occurrence brought about a truly fresh beginning. The Weimar Republic inherited the problems of the prewar years and, in turn, failed to solve them. Most of the social and political crises of the postwar years had their roots in the pre-1914 philosophical idealism, practical opportunism, and aggressive imperialism of the bourgeoisie; in the utopian socialism, opportunism, patriotism, and pacifism of the workers; and in the intolerant authoritarianism of the aristocracy, especially of the officers. Germany's fundamental problem, the inability of her tradition-bound society to cope with the machine age, also preceded World War I. What mainly differentiated these two periods from each other was the self-confidence of the Wilhelmian Germans and the pessimism of Weimar society. Only a few intellectuals, more of the Right than of the Left, and a significant sector of the educated youth, felt before 1914 that Germany was foundering. Most Germans were satisfied in their belief that theirs was a relatively decent and law-abiding state which, "compared with its sinister Eastern neighbors, loomed like a heaven of human rights and freedom." [1] They were also aware that their country "with its yearly population increase of almost a million, with an industry surpassed only by that of the United States, with an army of incomparable striking power, constituted one of the world's great energy centers." [2]

No wonder that the war was seen by the Germans as a conspiracy by Germany's envious neighbors and that, in August 1914, the nation was united in its will to victory.[3] The Kaiser's slogan "I know no more parties, I know only Germans" was readily accepted by a population that had always looked with suspicion at the squabbles of party politics. "When the war broke out, it seemed that a generous angel might once more lead the German people," wrote Friedrich Meinecke thirty years later. "All the rifts which had hitherto existed among the German people, both among the bourgeoisie themselves and between the bourgeoisie and the working class, were suddenly healed in the face of the common danger." [4]

Almost all Europe was gripped by war enthusiasm. But only the Germans were to insist then, and later, that theirs was a special kind of exuberance: the revival of their country's proud military traditions and the expectation of a resplendent German future. There was a blissfulness in the climate of 1914 which permitted the liberal scholar Ernst Troeltsch, to speak of a "new religiosity," [5] a religiosity not denominational, but emotional and all-embracing. It led Thomas Mann to talk of the war as a "heroic festivity" [6] and to place his talent at the service of the nation, his *Zeitdienst* as he called it later.[7] The jubilation of 1914 "has been wrongly interpreted," writes the American historian Fritz Stern, "as proving Germany's militarism or chauvinism; actually it was the response of a nation that had for decades searched for 'the moral equivalent to war' and now had found in war the equivalent of morality. The heroism and the national unity it had sought for so long had at last been attained." [8] Or as Golo Mann has recently written: "How beautiful it was to be there as a soldier, or at least as a patriot in civilian attire. How sad it was to be excluded. . . . This was the mood of August 1914." [9]

If this is how things stood in 1914, if it is true that orthodox Social Democrats and liberal university professors joined the masses in singing the "Song of Hate," the "Gott strafe England," [a] if the eternal rebel Karl Kraus could suggest no better than "all those who today have something to say should step forward and remain silent," [10] then it is certainly no wonder that *Die Schaubühne* fell in step with the rest of

---

[a] One stanza of this poem, written in 1914 by Ernst Lissauer, a Viennese *Literat*, reads:

> Hate by water and hate by land,
> Hate of heart and hate of the hand;
> We love as one and hate as one;
> We have but one foe alone—England.

Translation by Pinson, p. 315.

the Germans. But it is remarkable how many of those who contributed to the journal after 1918 belonged to the handful who voluntarily excluded themselves from the national delirium. Hellmut von Gerlach, Arthur Holitscher, Otto Lehmann-Russbüldt, Heinrich Mann, Lothar Persius, Ludwig Quidde, Helene Stöcker, Hans Wehberg, Leonhard Frank, Kurt Hiller, Rudolf Leonhard, Walter Hasenclever, Erich Mühsam, and René Schickele took an antiwar position if not from the beginning then after the first months of the war. They were later to exercise a decisive influence on the politics of Jacobsohn, Tucholsky, and Ossietzky, and were to set the tone of the *Weltbühne*. Their condemnation of the war had little to do with their earlier political involvement; many of them had had no previous interest in politics. They opposed the war because their humanity revolted against the senseless slaughter. Reaching out for the company of those who shared their views they, together with a handful of other intellectuals, soon formed two separate groups. The first, consisting mainly of the older generation, sought to oppose the war through political agitation. The other group, made up of the "war generation," used literature as a weapon.

The "Bund Neues Vaterland," to which the older generation belonged, was organized on November 16, 1914, by Captain Kurt von Tepper-Laski, a noted equestrian.[11] It derived from an *ad hoc* committee for Franco-German understanding founded in 1913. In the first years of the war, the Bund became the refuge of those who felt that the war was a fatal mistake. This motley organization of orthodox and revisionist Social Democrats (for instance, Eduard Bernstein, Hugo Haase, Karl Kautsky, Ernst Reuter, and Kurt Eisner), pacifist professors (Albert Einstein, Friedrich Wilhelm Foerster, Walter Schücking, and the pacifists of the later *Weltbühne*), militant feminists, democratic journalists (Theodor Wolff), and a number of diplomats (Prince Lichnowsky) as well as other aristocrats (Count Georg von Arco), was not supported by any political party and had only one newspaper, Gerlach's *Die Welt am Montag*, at its disposal. In February 1916, their organization was suppressed. Their greatest achievements had been the publication of some pamphlets and participation in a fruitless negotiation with like-minded politicians of the Entente powers in Holland in 1915. Still, the Bund was not an insignificant venture because, for the first and almost only time, it gathered intellectuals of many political views into one group. Friedrich Meinecke wrote of them later: "They were the men in whom the synthesis of classical liberalism was still working and in whom the classical idea of humanity and the feeling for the community of Western culture and for moderation in victory were still alive."[12] Their collective efforts filled the Bund's members with pride. It led to the illusion that intellectuals as a collective group were destined to play a role in the postwar metamorphosis of Germany.

On the negative side, their experience left behind a deep resentment among these intellectuals. In taking their antiwar stand when so few others did, members of the Bund were confronted by the hostility of the majority of Germans and by official harassment. Gerlach relates in his autobiography how, in 1914, his friends in the Demokratische Vereinigung and in the Friedrich Naumann Club threatened to denounce him to the Army Command for defeatism. "They believed in every pronouncement, be it the most absurd, of that imperial regime and of those generals whom, a few weeks earlier, they had fought most sharply. . . . They too believed in the spies in nun's attire . . . in the poisoned flour, in the hoard of gold being transported by car from France to Russia."[13] Those who had braved public contempt in the early years of the war never really forgave the chauvinists of 1914 and looked with suspicion at the turncoats who, like Maximilian Harden or Georg Bernhard, the editor of the *Vossische Zeitung*, changed their opinion when Germany's defeat appeared inevitable. Much of the later dissension among the left-wing intellectuals was due to the frequently posed question: "Where did he stand in 1914?" The same resentment marked these intellectuals in their attitude toward the politicians of the Weimar Republic, especially toward the Majority Socialists. The foreign minister of the Weimar Republic, Gustav Stresemann could be forgiven for his rabid wartime annexationism—the gradual turn of this conservative-nationalist statesman to a policy of international cooperation was rather remarkable—; the wartime betrayal of principle on the part of the Majority Socialists Ebert, Noske, and Scheidemann was inexcusable.

The Bund Neues Vaterland inspired the belief of the postwar *Weltbühne* in international arbitration, legalistic pacifism, and a cultural community of the West European nations. The antiwar movement of some young writers and poets inspired optimism with regard to the feasibility of humanity's ethical and social regeneration. Shortly after the outbreak of the war the Alsatian poet René Schickele, the novelist Leonhard Frank, the literary historian Max Brod, the Austrian writer Andreas Latzko—all later collaborators of the *Weltbühne*—established themselves in Switzerland.[14] Their journal, *Die weissen Blätter*, which was first published in Leipzig, followed them in 1916 into exile.[15] Yet it was still on German soil that *Die weissen Blätter* printed Heinrich Mann's study on Zola—a categorical denial of both the war and the imperialistic state—and also Johannes R. Becher's hymns to universal fraternity. From the very start this journal found nothing appealing about the war, nothing elevating. Its writers abhorred the war precisely because it debased man to a cipher and deprived him of his most essential quality: his personal dignity. They compared war to an orgy of self-destruction where—in the words of Henri Barbusse—"two armies fight each other like one great army about to commit suicide." [b] War was "no longer a tournament" (Schickele) but collective folly where the two camps became indistinguishable. But the war's massive uniformity—the same atrocities, the same crimes, the same heroism—also offered the first ray of hope. If on both sides identical little men were thrown into the battle, if neither camp had a valid ideal, then perhaps the two opposing armies were the generators of some new collective ideal. "Europe has never been more strongly united,"—wrote Schickele in 1916. "The solidarity of nations has never been greater than at this moment when they are trying to destroy each other." [16] It was the mission of the literati to recognize this curious synthesis and to propagate the idea of humanity born from inhumanity.

The first step toward this collective recognition was self-examination and confession. All men—not only the war lords—were guilty of the war because all men sinned by indifference, gullibility, selfishness, and ill-concealed sadism. "Not the English, not the Russians are our real enemies," cried the hero, a melancholy waiter, in Leonhard Frank's antiwar novel, *Der Mensch ist gut,* "the enemy is in ourselves. The real enemy is something we cannot see: it is the lack of love in our souls. . . . We must love, and then cannons will be fired no longer." [71]

The language of these manifestoes was vague and emotional; it was punctuated by ecstatic exclamations, impassioned outbursts, and endless soliloquies. Characteristically, despite the appeals to mankind and the anonymous heroes (the Waiter, the Widow, Man, Woman, the Son), the tone was intensely personal and the hero always identical with the author. This was the style of expressionism, the major German literary trend of that period.

The expressionist movement was the literary creation of the German "war generation." It began, around 1910, in answer to both the natur-

---

[b] The journal printed excerpts from the antiwar novel, *Le feu,* of the French writer, Barbusse. (See Henry Barbusse, "Das Frühlicht," *Die weissen Blätter,* May 1917, p. 130.)

alist and the neo-romantic or symbolist theater.[e] It soon turned into a social protest against bourgeois society. In the endlessly repeated thematic conflict between sons and fathers, the sons strove not only for the destruction of the fathers, but also for the annihilation of everything that the fathers represented: conventional order, dull philistinism, materialism, and the capitalistic world order. During the war father and fatherland became interchangeable terms in expressionist literature. Fatherland, just as father, was guilty of having overdisciplined, oppressed, misled, and betrayed the young generation. But a belief in the inviolability of the intellect offered hope, and to the condemnation of father and fatherland was added a call for spiritual regeneration and universal reconciliation.

Well before the war, expressionist writers like Georg Heym, Carl Hauptmann (*Krieg*, 1912) Franz Werfel (*Der Weltfreund*, 1911), had demanded "a revolution of brotherly love, of the heart, of gentle persuasion, and of serenity" (Schickele). Now antiwar literature took up with eagerness the belief in the fundamental goodness of men. In Walter Hasenclever's *Antigone* (1917), the masses surge forward to establish the new world of peace and freedom. Their leader, identified as "A Man of the People," exclaims:

> Palaces totter. Power is at an end.
> Those who are great fall into the abyss. . . .
> Those who have owned lose everything.
> The slave in the sweat of his hands
> Is richer than they.
> Follow me! I shall lead you.
> The wind rises from the ruins,
> The new world dawns.[18]

It was precisely this terrible vagueness—a socialism innocent of any dogma or program—which appealed to the war-weary German intellectuals. *Die weissen Blätter* was initially kept out of Germany by the censor, but beginning in 1916, a turning point in the war when general disillusionment set in, the literature of the expressionist exiles began to spread rapidly. *Der Mensch ist gut*, at first smuggled into Germany, was printed in half a million copies on newsprint by the Independent Socialists[19] and was eagerly read in the trenches. "Man is good!"

---

[e] Expressionism is a favorite topic in German literary history. The reader is referred to the following essential works in English: Walter H. Sokel, *The Writer in Extremis* (Stanford, Calif., 1959) and *An Anthology of German Expressionist Drama* (Garden City, N.J., 1963), edited by the same writer.

explained the soldier Ossietzky, "A novel, no: more than a novel, a document of our times. . . . Man is rediscovering Man. . . . Man will no longer be Man's devil and desolator, but his brother and helper. 'Man is good.' . . . Like Dante in his dreams, mankind, led by Vergil, leaves the inferno of the present to enter the spheres of purification." [20]

Some writers were not satisfied merely with these lofty pronouncements and attempted to give concrete political meaning to expressionist pacifism. Back in 1910, Heinrich Mann had urged the union of *Geist* and *Tat*, of the intellect and political action. Mann argued that historical greatness was solely the claim of nations where the masses acted as faithful soldiers of the intellectuals. The French were such soldiers during the Great Revolution because they willingly sacrificed their lives for an idea outlined by the intellectuals. (His subsequent enthusiasm for Soviet Russia had its roots in this conviction.) It was the task of the German literati to transform the selfish and indolent German masses into soldiers of the revolution.[21] Five years later Heinrich Mann again appealed to the intellectuals to repudiate existing authority and to form a new power elite: "The man of authority and of the fist is our enemy. The intellectual who caters to the lordly estate betrays the intellectuals." [22] In the same year, Kurt Hiller formulated his revolutionary program. *Aktivismus,* as he called it, would put an end to the intellectuals' splendid isolation and mobilize their talents in the service of humane goals. The intellectuals were to demand the outlawing of the war; the promotion of the process of natural selection by an equal distribution of all "superficial" or "external" goods; a guaranteed minimum wage to all, even to nonworkers; free love; eugenics; governmental protection of the psychiatric profession; an end to the teaching of philosophic positivism and utilitarianism at the universities, and the creation of a true *Universitas Litterarum;* the suppression of parliaments if they oppose the will of the intellect; a House of Lords composed of intellectuals, and *Logokratie,* the rule of philosopher-kings.[23] In human history, Hiller wrote, "Paradise was followed by hell and hell by the state . . . from the state the intellect will lead us back to Paradise." [24] *Logokratie* was amazingly popular among the German literati (and among such non-Germans as H. G. Wells) especially because of its call for the "dictatorship of the intellectuals." Alfred Kerr wrote in the same year:

I want a *Kratie* of the *Aristoi.* I want that in the future the will of the best be imposed on the worst among us—unlike today when the will of the worst is imposed on the best. . . . I want that we, the raped become the rapers. I want that the real *Kratie* of the *Aristoi* be inaugurated; whereas today in the warring camps of Europe . . . an *Oligo-Ochlokratie* still holds sway.[25]

Hiller's program, with its mixture of the feasible and the Quixotic, and with its complete disregard of the revolutionary means to power, foreshadowed the troubles of 1918–1919. Those intellectuals who had expressed only a vague yearning for a revolution were entirely unprepared, and could not find their place in the revolutionary ranks, when the forces which toppled the old regime divided into parliamentarians and advocates of soviet dictatorship. Those, who like Hiller or Heinrich Mann had what they believed were precise aims, found themselves ridiculed by the politicians. For the time being, they entered a world of wonders: they saluted the collapse of the Imperial regime, and the proclamation of the democratic socialist republic as the greatest event in their lives.

Chapter IV

FOR AN INTELLECTUALIZED SOCIALIST REPUBLIC DURING THE REVOLUTION 1918–1919

Agitation for peace, once the doubtful privilege of some individuals in Germany, had become a major parliamentary issue in 1917. The aim of an early and equitable peace was pursued, with varying degrees of conviction, by the leaders of the parties that were later to form the Weimar coalition. In October 1918, these parties came within sight of their aim when the Kaiser, driven by military defeat, formed a parliamentary government from the parties that had signed the 1917 Peace Resolution. At the desperate prompting of the German High Command, the new government communicated with President Wilson in the hope of obtaining a negotiated armistice and an honorable peace. But the government reckoned neither with the determination of the Allies to impose an armistice reflecting the measure of Germany's military defeat, nor with the hesitation and maneuverings of the Kaiser and of the German High Command. Finally, early in November 1918, the revolt of the German workers and soldiers forced the abdication of the Kaiser and the signing of the long overdue armistice. The Majority Socialists, anxious lest the radical socialists establish a Bolshevist republic, proclaimed Germany a democratic and socialist republic.

November 1918 brought about "das Traumland der Waffenstillstandsperiode" (the dreamland of the armistice period), so aptly termed by Ernst Troeltsch.[1] It was a brief period of euphoria when no one in Germany was willing to shed blood—or tears—for the defunct monarchy, when the proclamation of the republic was generally cele-

73

brated as the decisive step to set defeated Germany on an equal footing with the victors, when the literati from the far Right to the far Left confidently expected the birth of a unitary and socialist state.[a] "Now, now, finally, now!"—wrote René Schickele.

The new world has begun. It is here: the liberated mankind! A face appears in the atmospheric maelstrom of anxiety and lies: the face of Man. The face of a creature bathed in heavenly light. . . . He finally sets himself to task. The Man. Finally. . . . Now! Let us begin afresh, freed from the burden of the Middle Ages. Let us create the Man of Modern Times. Forward![2]

The communion of the intellectuals with the nation, once tried in 1914, was now again attempted. Let us quote Schickele again:

The ninth of November was the most beautiful day of my life. On the ninth of November I was a believer; I would say even that I was positively in Heaven. I felt that from that day on I would never again be alone. Never again would I be forced to despair for myself and for others. For the first time I lay, well protected, on the bosom of Germany.[3]

The exaltation, however, was of even shorter duration than in 1914. Revolutionary harmony ended within a few weeks, and civil war began when Karl Liebknecht, Richard Mueller, Georg Ledebour, and other radical socialists in the Spartacus League, in the Independent Socialist Party, and in the group known as Revolutionary Shop Stewards ("Revolutionäre Obleute"), moved to force the establishment of a proletarian dictatorship. In their desire to have Germany follow the example of the Bolshevik Revolution of the previous year, many of these leaders mistook the popular uprising against the old regime and against the war for a conscious revolutionary socialist movement. The aim of the majority of German workers was not a Soviet republic; they followed the moderate Social Democrats whom they elected to their councils. It was therefore a badly armed minority of workers who were hurled against the Free Corps [b] troops led by army generals who had quickly offered their services to the Majority Socialist government

---

[a] Contrary to a general assumption even the most conservative intellectuals placed themselves in 1918–1919 on the *Boden der Tatsachen* (the platform of realities); that is, they accepted the new political situation. Some actually outdid the Left in clamoring for a "socialist" Germany of their own imagination. For a brief but masterly analysis of this short period of truce between left-wing and right-wing intellectuals in Germany, see Klemens von Klemperer, *Germany's New Conservatism* (Princeton, N.J., 1957), 76 ff.

[b] Free Corps ("Freikorps") were irregular units of volunteers recruited throughout this period by the High Army Command at the behest of the Social Democratic leaders for all sorts of patriotic duty. See Robert G. L. Waite, *Vanguard of Nazism* (Cambridge, Mass., 1952).

for the suppression of the uprising. The attempt at a "Second Revolution" thus not only ended in bloody defeat in January 1919, but the radicals' mistake led to the murder of their two most capable leaders, Karl Liebknecht and Rosa Luxemburg, by the government's troops.

For years the expressionist prophets had preached that the Great Day of Mankind would come without bloodshed. "No one should kill another for any cause whatsoever," wrote Ernst Toller. "We want a revolution with no other force but that of the heart, of persuasion, and of the happy example," wrote Schickele. The civil war brought a painful awakening to the intellectuals and divided their ranks. A few writers in the *Weltbühne*, Rudolf Leonhard for instance, cast their lot with the Spartacus League; others supported the moderate wing of the Independent Socialists; again others, mainly of the old generation, opted for the emerging parliamentarian and anti-Bolshevist republic. Jacobsohn himself embraced the idea of radical socialism without, however, accepting the Spartacus League, which he deemed violent, uncivilized, and barbarian. He dismissed his wartime chief editorialist, the Majority Social Democrat Robert Breuer, and replaced him with the Independent Socialist Heinrich Ströbel. Under Ströbel the journal demanded a complete break with the past, an immediate peace treaty at any cost, and a recognition of Germany's responsibility for the war.[4] It insisted that Richard Grelling, a wartime exile in Switzerland, whose tract, *J'accuse*,[5] was bought up by the French and distributed among the German soldiers across the front lines, be co-opted by the newly formed Kautsky Commission on the War Guilt Question and that the commission's findings be immediately published. No sooner did the conservatives concoct the legend that the hinterland had stabbed the undefeated German army in the back, than *Die Weltbühne* began a campaign against this legend[6] and availed itself of the services of a democratic army officer to show that Germany had lost the war well before the revolution.[7]

All this was mere talk, however, and worthless from the point of view of those writers who during the war had urged the intellectuals not only to herald, but to make a revolution. Their attempt to live up to their own expectations provided the events of 1918–1919 with two side shows: the Bavarian Soviet Republic which ended in tragedy, and the Council of Intellectual Workers which ended nowhere.

The proclamation of the Bavarian Soviet Republic, in April 1919, was preceded by a democratic revolution in Munich under the leadership of Kurt Eisner. An Independent Socialist, Eisner nevertheless bore all the marks of a nonparty left-wing intellectual. During the war he was a member of the Bund Neues Vaterland; his Marxist socialism was overshadowed by ethical and aesthetic considerations. He was first and foremost a pacifist, imbued with Kant's idea of eternal peace. His revolution shed no blood, and while he was prime minister from November 1918 to February 1919 he sought to introduce scores of humanitarian reforms. Shortly before his assassination, Eisner projected his marvelous vision of the future:

> We swear to hear the call of freedom.
> We shield the holy weald from storms.
> Let mankind recover in common endeavor.
> The new Reich arises. O world, rejoice! [8]

Unpopularity soon dampened Eisner's ambitions. Heavily defeated in the Bavarian Landtag elections of January 1919, he was about to surrender power to the Majority Socialists when he was murdered. There was, after his death, a period of turmoil, and then, on April 7, 1919, two anarchists (the philosopher Gustav Landauer and the poet Erich Mühsam), as well as some Independent Socialists (such as Ernst Toller), proclaimed in Munich the Bavarian Soviet Republic. This was a misnomer, for there were in Bavaria no true soviets, nor did this regime emulate the dictatorial Russian Soviet Republic. It amounted to a private undertaking by a few gentle souls, one of whom, the commissar of foreign affairs, Franz Lipp, was probably insane. The soviet republic was denounced by the Reich government, the Bavarian Communists, and the Social Democrats as well. Because no one else was willing, Ernst Toller, then 26, accepted the chairmanship of the soviet republic's Central Council.[9] By the time he "came to power," the Spartacist uprisings had been crushed by the Majority Socialists and the Free Corps in all other parts of the Reich. Within a few days the soviet of the intellectuals collapsed and the Communists seized power in Munich, but even then Toller refused "to leave the masses in the lurch." He led a Red brigade at Dachau against the counterrevolutionary troops. At the same time, he tried to prevent the extermination of Communism's enemies. He went around "wringing his hands and tearing up execution orders." Toller's failure to save a group of hostages from the Communist execution squad, the horrible revenge of the Whites, the murder of Landauer and hundreds of others, his and Mühsam's imprisonment, marked the end of this chapter in revolutionary idealism.

"I had always believed that socialists, despising force, should never employ it for their own ends," Toller wrote in his autobiography.

And now I myself had used force and appealed to force; I who hated bloodshed had caused blood to be shed. . . . I meditated on the position of men who try to mould the destiny of this world, who enter politics and try to realize their ideas in face of the masses. Was Max Weber right after all when he said that the only logical way of life for those who were determined never to overcome evil by force was the way of St. Francis? Must the man of action always be dogged by guilt? Always? [10]

In his expressionist drama, *Masse Mensch* ("Man and the Masses"), written in prison during 1919, Toller expounded the dilemma of the revolutionary idealist. Here, Man as an individual was confronted with Man as a member of the community. Man as a part of the Mass alternately yielded to and repudiated the common impulses, the mob emotions of the Mass.[11] The drama was built around three characters: Man who represented the state, the unquestioned faith in government; Woman who symbolized radical humanitarianism; and the Nameless One who stood for the Spartacus League or the ruthless revolution. At the drama's end, Woman was killed because she refused to defend herself at the cost of the death of a single hostile guard: "A leader has the right to sacrifice no one but himself" is her final warning.

The Bavarian literati had, at least, understood that revolutions could not be made without masses. The founders of the "Rat geistiger Arbeiter" (Council of Intellectual Workers), being pure "activists," relied solely upon the magic power of the word pronounced in what they thought was the proper historical moment. On November 7–8, 1918, the Rat geistiger Arbeiter held its first congress in Berlin.[12] The council's first manifesto began with a vigorous affirmation of the "sanctity of human life." It indicted compulsory military service as the worst form of slavery and called for a League of Nations and for universal disarmament. It demanded, further, the transformation of capitalistic enterprises into workers' owned cooperatives; complete educational reform including the supervision of education by international committees; a rewriting of history textbooks; equality of teachers and students; abolition of the *Abitur* (final high-school examination), and so on. The manifesto of the council advocated the freedom of the press (with, however, a purge of the degraders of the press); the separation of church and state; the abolition of the teaching of religion in schools; an end to capital punishment; the right of the individual to use his body as he chooses, and to kill himself. Finally, the manifesto urged the creation of an all-German socialist republic. The government of the new republic was to be made up of delegates of the Reichstag and of the council; the president of the republic would be elected by the Reichstag from among candidates selected by the council. As for the council itself, its members would not be elected democratically nor appointed, but the council was to "regenerate itself spontaneously." This remarkable program was supported, among others, by Otto Flake, A. H. Fried, Manfred George, Alfons Goldschmidt, Wilhem Herzog, the writer Lou Andreas-Salomé, Annette Kolb, Kurt Hiller, the Austrian novelist Robert Musil, Magnus Hirschfeld, Arthur Holitscher, Rudolf Leonhard, the young Social Democrat Carlo Mierendorff, Hans Natonek, Helene Stöcker, and Siegfried Jacobsohn. The sociologist Lujo Brentano and Heinrich Mann were chairman of two separate *Räte geistiger Arbeiter* in Bavaria.[c] René Schickele represented the council in Switzerland.[13]

The council's proposals were subsequently submitted to the Weimar National Assembly. Nothing, of course, came of these proposals, and most of the founding members soon left the council.[d] Yet it is remarkable how many literati had been ready to endorse a movement which demanded the immediate transfer of power to the intellectuals.

Following the early demise of the council—Hiller, the council's driving spirit, admitted readily that they had made grave mistakes—some activists held a second congress in Berlin in June 1919. Here, in the wake of some spirited clashes,[e] the participants set up a new program. This time, they stressed aristocratic concepts even more. Their new manifesto [14] called for the establishment of a dual dictatorship, "the economic dictatorship of those who, by their labor, create the material goods, and the cultural dictatorship of those who, by their revolutionary creativity, produce the cultural values." [15] Whether these dictatorships expressed the will of the majority was irrelevant. The

---

[c] In Bavaria, where the revolution in November 1918 was further "left" than in Berlin, one of two *Räte geistiger Arbeiter* seems to have played a more conservative role. Founded by some professors at the University of Munich, it attempted to moderate Kurt Eisner's alleged dictatorial tendencies. Sending thirty delegates to the Council of Workers and Soldiers, this *Rat* participated in the first revolutionary government, although the delegates felt rather neglected by the proletarian leaders. Eisner attempted to make the chairman of the *Rat*, Professor Brentano, a member of his cabinet, an honor which caused this cautious liberal no little embarrassment. See Lujo Brentano, *Mein Leben um die soziale Entwicklung Deutschlands* (Jena, 1931), 353 ff.

[d] A month after he had published the activist manifesto and had agreed to be one of the council's founders, Jacobsohn withdrew from the movement which he now termed "idealistic, confused, and childish." See, "Antworten," *Die Weltbühne*, December 12, 1918, pp. 566 ff.

[e] In his memoirs, Brentano complained that it "could not have been more difficult to preside over a meeting of anarchists" than over the meetings of the *Rat geistiger Arbeiter*. Brentano, 362.

signers of the manifesto were still opposed to the use of force for any purpose whatsoever: "The congress . . . salutes all methods that lead to a change without contradicting our absolute postulate for the sanctity of human life." [16]

The "elitism" of the council was the first but not the last flirtation of a few left-wing intellectuals with rightist concepts. It stemmed from the general arrogance of German *Kultur*, the Youth Movement experience of some of these writers, their hidden admiration for the aristocratic way of life, and their devotion to Kant and Nietzsche. Many *Weltbühne* writers had only limited patience with elitist ideas. Ernst Toller turned against Hiller in a letter written in 1923 from his prison cell in Bavaria:

You assume that every intellectual [*Geistige*] is endowed with a higher faculty of judgment. . . . Remember what sort of judgment the "intellectuals" showed during the war! You wish to set up a *Logokratie:* the reign of the intellect. But where would you take your power from? You know well that without a social metamorphosis your *Logokratie* would mean nothing. Yet, if you want power, you must fight. . . . Do you know Napoleon's dictum? "Men who changed the world did not get results by securing the support of the leaders but by setting the masses in motion." [17]

Hiller remained undaunted. This indefatigable champion of human rights, of socialism, of radical pacifism, and of Red unity discovered, in the 1920's, a temporary sympathy for Mussolini.[18] But he never gave up his belief in the historical role of the literati. Back in 1915 he had argued that even among the intellectuals, the *Literat*, that is, the free writer alone, was entitled to world leadership. Describing the philosopher as lacking in will, the artist as lacking in universality, Hiller designated the *Literat* as "the builder of the future."

The Literat of tomorrow will bear great responsibility . . . he is a thinker yet he is unburdened by theories; he is profound, yet worldly. Not only will he not be hampered by dogmas, but his instinct will push him toward action. . . . He exists already in a few specimens; it is up to us to rally these few people.[19]

Thirty-two years later Hiller still felt himself undefeated and renewed his elitist *Ziel-Philosophie* for the benefit of a Germany now in ruins and divided.[20]

The revolutionary period of the new German republic brought immense joy to the German left-wing intellectuals; it also brought them profound disappointment. Their active role had been at best peripheral, at worst ludicrous. Yet even after their disappointment with the outcome of the revolution, some of them continued to analyze events largely in the manner of their wartime idealism. Those who had assumed that man was good and that, given the opportunity, he would spontaneously create a peaceful socialist society, now indicted both the Spartacus League and the Majority Socialists for failing to preserve revolutionary harmony. Presented with the reality of a completely divided society, René Schickele fell back on the only explanation he knew for this division: the clash between generations. Writing in 1919, he argued that a magnificent opportunity had been lost during the "fourteen days" of November. Had elections been held in November 1918 rather than in January 1919, and had the war industry been nationalized, then, perhaps, the revolution could have been successful. Schickele indicted the generation of the fathers for the vanishing of his dreams. "This had been the hour of the German youth, and German youth was equal to the task." [21] Intellectuals, students, journeymen, young workers, typists, returning soldiers—in brief, the entire "young proletariat" had been ready to create the young republic. But the ancients betrayed the youth "to maintain themselves for another quarter hour." Social Democracy had been brought to power by the youth but Social Democracy abandoned the young generation. There had been a few true leaders, a few "renovators" among the politicians, and here Schickele pointed to the heroes of the expressionist-activist [f] literati: the Independent Socialists Kautsky, Dittmann, Breitscheid, Bernstein, and Eisner, and the Bund Neues Vaterland members Gerlach, Simon, and Count Arco. These men, however, had been pushed aside by the mean old men of the Reichstag parties. Yet, Schickele insisted, the sounds of November would still ring in the ears of German youth. Youth will defeat the fathers. [22]

The events of 1918–1919 had shown anything but a clash between generations. The line was drawn through the generations: counter-revolutionary middle-class youth in the Free Corps opposed the proletarian youth in the Communist ranks. Germany's class lines were drawn much more sharply than they had been before the war, and the socialist movement was itself profoundly split. The majority of the socialists believed that the laws of history, which moved beyond human control, had placed bourgeois democracy on the European agenda. Telescoping this process by struggling for socialist dictatorship was unrealistic. The moderate socialists therefore found themselves directly or indirectly aiding in the suppression of those other

---

[f] It is questionable whether these terms are rightfully combined. For a valuable attempt at distinguishing between genuine expressionists and political activists, see Wolfgang Paulsen, *Aktivismus und Expressionismus* (Bern, 1935).

socialists who believed that reality could only be changed, that is, socialism achieved, by conscious human intervention for the most progressive aims possible. The heroes of the wartime idealists fell into both camps: Kautsky and Bernstein in one, Luxemburg, Liebknecht and Ledebour in the other. It was this split which was to loom increasingly important for the left-wing intellectuals, and which now rendered them perplexed and powerless. Their idealistic and pacifist conceptions did not place them fully in either camp.

Chapter V
FOR FRIENDSHIP WITH FRANCE AND
A EUROPEAN FEDERATION

The defeat of the extreme Left in 1919 resulted in neither the unification of the socialist movement nor the strengthening of democracy in Germany. The Social Democrats, heading a so-called Weimar coalition with Democrats and the Catholic Center after the January 1919 elections, carried out none of the socialist reforms for which they had campaigned—they concentrated on defending the government against the threat of Bolshevism. Adopting no measures to undermine the social and economic bastions of the Right, and too few measures to satisfy the demands of the workers, the Weimar coalition placed itself in a dangerous position. The Communists, more sobered with regard to their minority position among the German workers, now sought to win the working class away from the Social Democrats. But their goal remained the seizure of power.[1] With the Left front split and polarized, the nationalist Right quickly regained confidence and, in March 1920 in the Kapp putsch, it temporarily seized power. The "Kappists" (so named after the nationalist politician Wolfgang Kapp whom some army officers had proclaimed chancellor of Germany) were defeated by a general strike in a few days, but this impressive show of working-class determination did not succeed in bridging the gap between the revolutionary and reformist camps of socialism.[2] A reflection of this disunity was the dilemma of the Independent Socialists, a mass party which had broken away from the Social Democrats in 1916 over the issue of peace. By 1919 the Independents were hopelessly divided. Their moderate wing could conceive of taking power only with a clear mandate given by the masses throughout Germany; since this mandate

82

was not forthcoming, the moderates in the USPD had no idea what to do. Their left wing, on the other hand, surpassed even the Communists in demanding that the offensive be taken against the bourgeois republic with or without the support of the masses. Like the *Weltbühne* intellectuals who generally favored the Independents, this party attempted to straddle the gap between the two socialist camps. It failed: in October 1920 the majority of the USPD voted to join the Comintern, and eventually united with the Communist Party, while the rest returned to the SPD two years later.[a]

The left intellectuals of the *Weltbühne* reacted to the failure of the socialists to create even a relatively democratized Germany by looking beyond the country's borders for a possible solution. There was in their overriding involvement with Germany's foreign policy in the early 1920's a holdover of the left-wing intellectuals' wartime idealism. It now manifested itself in a postwar version of "universal fraternity": a belief in an international community of Western nations as the only hope for peace and justice in Germany. This was the basis for their faith in the ultimate wisdom of the Versailles treaty. And if they were mistaken in their hope that the great Western powers, especially France, would succeed in reeducating Germany and guiding her along the path of peace and democracy, there was considerable wisdom in their argument that sincere cooperation with the Allies was a *sine qua non* in preventing the resurgence of German imperialism.

If Europe was to take charge of the German republic, it had first to be pacified. The pacification of Europe in turn depended on Germany; therefore the first objective was to prevent the remilitarization of Germany. For the moment Germany was in a unique position, for she alone of all the great powers had achieved the precondition for a peaceful foreign policy: almost complete disarmament and the inability to defend herself. Free from all resentment and from revanchist hysteria, unarmed Germany could, if she wished, take the lead in international diplomacy. This was the *Macht in Ohnmacht* (Power in Impotence) theme, a favorite among the pacifists and other left-wing intellectuals. The slogan was not entirely new: many intellectuals of all political shades had argued since 1918 that undefeated German

---

[a] For instance, *Die Weltbühne* writers Heinrich Ströbel and Kurt Rosenfeld. Even more significant from the point of view of the *Weltbühne* was the decision of Paul Levi, former leader of the Communist Party, to enter the united Social Democratic Party in 1922. On the other hand, Georg Ledebour refused to join "the party of Noske" and for several years continued as head of a splinter Independent Socialist group. See Richard N. Hunt, *German Social Democracy, 1918–1933* (New Haven, 1964), 204 ff.

Kultur—and Germany's economic potential—were the keys to Germany's future greatness. In the "Dreamland of the Armistice" period it was common even among rightist intellectuals to have visions of German greatness derived from Germany's defeat and humiliation. "We lost the war but nothing is lost; our economic and intellectual forces are healthy. . . . This is death and rebirth at the same time. Germany is dead; long live Germany," wrote *Die Tat* in November 1918.[3] But only the left-wing intellectuals insisted then, as they did later, that Germany's unimpaired economic potential should benefit all of Europe and not be used for rebuilding German military and political power. Military weakness was to be perpetrated as Germany's greatest blessing. "Sixty million producers and sixty million consumers" no longer need waste their production on the maintenance of a large army.[4]

Of course, the elimination of all Germany military forces—for not even the 100,000-man army allowed by the Versailles treaty was needed in the view of the *Weltbühne*—meant that Germany could no longer resort to the instruments of traditional power politics. There were to be no secret negotiations, no bilateral treaties. An *Anschluss* with Austria, however desirable, was impossible as was a separate agreement with Soviet Russia, for such moves would be interpreted abroad as manifestations of German revanchism. Only by unconditionally accepting her role as a victim could Germany regain the confidence of the other nations and lead them toward peace and international disarmament.

The trouble was, as *Die Weltbühne* saw it, that the Germans would not accept the consequences of their defeat. Not long before, even the left-wing intellectuals had permitted themselves the illusion that universal fraternity—that is, equal treatment for defeated Germany— would emerge from the lost war. A bit wiser, they now urged the acceptance of the Versailles treaty. Heinrich Ströbel found in the general German opposition to the treaty a clear case of German nihilism, an expression of the suicidal German desire to pull all Europe into the abyss of eternal warfare.[5] Well before the German government made its first modest move toward a "fulfillment policy" in 1921, the writers of the *Weltbühne* had argued in favor of immediate reparations payments. For a while they hoped—together with pacifists everywhere—that reparations would be limited to the reconstruction of areas destroyed in the war. Only this did they recognize as Germany's moral obligation. They insisted that such reconstruction be financed by the German upper classes and carried out by French and German workers.[6] Others, like Carl von Ossietzky (at that time still writing for the *Berliner Volks-Zeitung*) put their hope in the reparations program of the Vienna or "Two and a Half" International, which was convened in February 1921. This abortive congregation of French, English, and German left-wing socialists proposed the "internationalization" of all war debts and recommended that countries spared by the war contribute their share to the reconstruction of devastated areas.[7] Again Ossietzky subscribed enthusiastically to the project of the pacifist Count Harry Kessler for the creation of an International Institute on Reparations staffed by economic experts and trade-union representatives.[8] The institute was to become an integral part of a new League of Nations composed not of politicians, but of the national representatives of workers, employers, consumers, financiers, ethical and religious organizations. Kessler's League of Nations, which was to act as a world-wide socialist economic planning board, enchanted the left-wing intellectuals and was a favorite subject of their discussions.[9] Yet when it became clear that nothing would come of these projects and that the Allies wanted much more than reparations in kind and in labor, *Die Weltbühne* recommended that honest efforts be made toward meeting these requirements. Only after German good will had been demonstrated could the country ask for an easing of the truly unbearable reparations burden.

To counter the seeming naïveté of their proposals, which would have made Germany lastingly defenseless among heavily armed and cynical powers, the *Weltbühne* writers argued that Germany had no enemies intent upon aggression. For the next twelve years, while the bourgeois political parties (and the Communists) alternately conjured up the threat of Polish, Russian, French, or English aggression, the *Weltbühne* insisted that no foreign power threatened German territorial integrity. Moreover, although they themselves were outspoken in their criticism of foreign governments, they remained convinced that once the peoples of the great powers were reassured of Germany's peaceful intentions, they would coerce their governments to embark on the road to reconciliation.

The crucial point in the left-wing intellectuals' foreign political program was reconciliation with France. On this issue they differed sharply from both the Social Democrats and the Communists. As far as the Communists were concerned, the Versailles treaty was the product of an imperialist victory. The French capitalists were now conducting an offensive against German capitalists which, at the same time, threatened the national and physical existence of the German people, particularly its lower classes. Ultimately, too, the treaty, by structuring Europe into one block under Anglo-French tutelage, was a threat to the Soviet Union. The Communist Party therefore decisively opposed the acceptance of the Versailles treaty.[10] On the other hand the Social Democratic leaders [11] saw in France a chauvinistic power whose aggressiveness could be tempered only by German reliance on Great Britain, the one great power interested in weakening French preponderance in Europe.[b] Most German left-wing intellectuals—and the German pacifists in general—were unshakable in their belief that aggressive French nationalism was a passing phase and that the eventual victory of the French Left would bring about an easing of the Franco-German tension.

The French policy of the *Weltbühne* was therefore simple: "fulfillment," not to achieve Allied evacuation of the Rhineland, or the entry of Germany into the League of Nations as an equal and equally dangerous partner, but to end all continental antagonisms. Moreover, friendship with France was sought for the beneficial effects that French culture might have on the Germans. With a nostalgia, envy, and admiration so characteristic of the Central European literati, the writers of the *Weltbühne* looked to Paris for salvation. They envied in the French their civil liberties, Latinity, *savoir vivre*, gaiety, and humanism; they admired the French for their artfulness in juxtaposing pedantry and disorder; they saw in France the mirror of democracy, intelligence, anticonformism, good taste, artistic refinement, and progressive literature—in short, they admired the French for all that they felt the Germans lacked. The left-wing intellectuals deemed their western neighbors more tolerant, flexible and yet stronger than the Germans. They rejoiced over the fact that even the most militaristic French general was unable to circumvent the democratic safeguards built into France's political structure. One writer noted with relish in the *Weltbühne* that the École de Saint Cyr had difficulties in recruiting cadets and that contemporary French literature savagely attacked militarism and the war.[12]

---

[b] A small coterie of young Social Democratic intellectuals took a foreign policy stand similar to that of the *Weltbühne:* Carlo Mierendorff, Theodor Haubach, and Julius Leber advocated a European federation based on Franco-German cooperation. Mierendorff, who had launched the slogan "Transcend Versailles by Europe!" argued as late as 1932 that the depression and the danger of fascism could be combatted only by an immediate understanding with France and the resumption of German reparations payments in kind. See Wolfgang von Manowski, "Carlo Mierendorff and the Iron Front" (unpublished Master's thesis, New York: Columbia University, 1967), 31 ff.

The question can be rightfully raised how these writers were able to reconcile their violent anticapitalism with their advocacy of unconditional Franco-German reconciliation. Even the least dogmatic anticapitalist was expected to argue that the post-Versailles offensive of French capitalism on German capitalism could not be terminated by mere political agreements. Was it not an illusion to think of Germany as a community of interests which would benefit if it rid itself of nasty German nationalism and submit to superior French power? How could such submission benefit the German worker? The anticapitalism of the left-wing intellectuals was not only determined by their socialism, but by undogmatic ethical and cultural considerations. These intellectuals loathed the capitalist for his ruthlessness, his arrogant self-confidence, and his social callousness, but they held that even a capitalist was the product of his national environment; in France, not even an armaments manufacturer could wholly escape the civilizing effects of a superior culture. Moreover, the left-wing intellectuals were confident that France, able to restrain her generals, would eventually curb her capitalists as well. In Germany, they argued, capitalism was more securely established because it had entered into an alliance with the still viable forces of feudalism; it had acquired a monopoly on patriotism, and it had caused the German people to transfer their submissive loyalty from princes to robber barons. In the Anglo-Saxon countries the situation was not much more encouraging; there capitalism had become the life and blood of large segments of the population. The French bourgeois did not entirely lose his appreciation of higher cultural values; the case of the British was more doubtful; the American bourgeois seemed beyond redemption. The United States was the capitalist country par excellence: money-mad, barbarian, vulgar, philistine, sanctimonious, bigoted, and sentimental. Egon Erwin Kisch presented the United States as a giant mail-order house: a charge account in this august institution alone qualified its holder to full citizenship. Those who held no such account, wrote Kisch, "had their homes built by architects and not by mail-order firms; bought their books in a bookstore and their paintings in an art gallery . . . and by these very acts turned themselves into Bolsheviks who ceased to be free Americans and individualists." [13]

Admittedly, there was little in Harding's and Coolidge's America that a progressive European man of letters could find to his liking. Nor is it surprising to see them protest against lynch justice, the monkey trial, the filthy stockyards in Chicago, the execution of Sacco and Vanzetti, prohibition, and corruption. What made these protestations tasteless was their indictment of a way of life which these writers so little understood.[c]

And yet, *Die Weltbühne* made some efforts to keep itself informed on developments in the United States by soliciting contributions from democratic German-Americans.[d] It also gladly risked the accusation of "cultural bolshevism" by propagating American jazz, the films of Chaplin,[e] and the writings of Jack London, Upton Sinclair, Theodore Dreiser, F. Scott Fitzgerald, and Sinclair Lewis. At one point in his commentaries, Tucholsky discovered the not entirely unattractive personality of the American *Bürger*. In an enthusiastic appraisal of Sinclair Lewis's *Babbitt*, Tucholsky pointed to the essential youthfulness, energy, playfulness, and frustrated longing for goodness of this American equivalent to the German Herr Wendriner.[14] But Tucholsky could never warm up to the English-speaking peoples. In the words of Harry Zohn:

> Tucholsky rejected the Anglo-Saxon world, especially America, which he considered cold and reactionary, repeating Heine's dictum: "I am firmly convinced that a cursing Frenchman is a more pleasing sign in the eyes of God than a praying Englishman." He especially lampooned what he considered typical American advertising copy: "Why does Mona Lisa smile? Because she has taken Hitkinson's Digestion Tablets and thus has been permanently cured of troublesome constipation. You, too, can smile if you . . ."[15]

The general hostility of the *Weltbühne* writers toward America might have stemmed from their uncertainty about the future of capi-

---

[c] "What objections did I have to the United States? . . . What, indeed, was there to say about a state that had not even fought Germany? We studied a good deal of Greek and a good deal of Latin, and even a little French; at home we had a 'Bonne' and a 'Mademoiselle': we never had a 'Miss.' Pericles and Augustus were our friends; the French we knew too because of the battle of Sedan and the Moulin Rouge—the English-speaking nations were only earning money. . . . I knew nothing of Pitt; less even of Jefferson. When, as a student, I saw the title of a book which compared the ideas of 1789 with those of 1776, I learned to my great surprise that there had been something like a French Revolution on the other side of the ocean. . . . New York and the neighboring colonies were farther away than Africa. . . . This then was my image of America: skyscrapers, and far-down, in the narrow sunless canyons, an infinite mass of humanity crawling around in the eternal quest for money." Ludwig Marcuse, *Mein zwanzigstes Jahrhundert* (Munich, 1960), 248 f.

[d] For instance, Eduard Goldbeck, the editor of the German *Wochenblatt* in Chicago.

[e] *Die Weltbühne* prided itself justly for having introduced Chaplin to the educated German public. "Chaplin is an oasis" in a drab, stupid, and pompous world, wrote Tucholsky, and praised the artist for his ability to illustrate the deepest human misery in a seemingly carefree manner. See Peter Panter, "Oase," *Die Weltbühne*, May 3, 1923, pp. 522–523. Also in *Gesammelte Werke*, II, 1093–1094.

talism. As the Soviet experiment was clearly a matter for the Russians and could not be exported, there was danger that the world would ultimately belong to the United States. Perhaps the United States was the land of the future; definitely it was not the Promised Land. There was a world of difference between the left-wing intellectuals' rejection of the United States and their criticism of the Soviet Union. The United States, and perhaps even Great Britain, were dangerous powers. The union of France and Germany in a European socialist and democratic federation was meant to avert this danger to European culture.

The slogan of Franco-German reconciliation gave the *Weltbühne* writers a concrete program. They were to help close the terrible gap in understanding that separated the two countries, if not to unite French and Germans "as two halves of one human soul" (Ernest Renan). In the early 1920's, *Die Weltbühne* printed scores of informative articles and travelogues on France, gaining the collaboration of such French writers as Romain Rolland, Henri Barbusse, and the pacifist Victor Basch. When three of its writers—Tucholsky, Morus, and Walter Mehring—set out for Paris, it was with the intention of explaining France to the Germans. Surveying the scene in 1925, Tucholsky found the situation still exasperating: the two nations were purposefully ignorant of each other, though the French were infinitely better informed than the Germans.[16] Tucholsky found both pacifists and artists, the only Germans sincerely interested in working for Franco-German friendship, ineffectual. The artists were bickering among themselves; the pacifists took themselves too seriously. Both groups abroad gave the impression—illusory, of course—that they had some influence at home. Meanwhile, the Paris correspondents of the big German press behaved like wide-eyed tourists in search of erotic scandals. As for the German government, it was unable to get any point across to the French people. Consequently, the Germans considered the French decadent and dangerous madmen, while the French tended to overestimate the strength and aggressive intentions of the German army, instead of appreciating the long-range threat of German domestic militarism. The businessmen alone showed themselves to be *Realpolitiker*, Tucholsky argued in a surprising reversal of his usual anticapitalism. They did more to effect a Franco-German understanding than the "hysterical old maids" of the pacifist movement.[17] Exasperated, Tucholsky predicted a Franco-German war for 1939, brought about not by the monarchists, but by the German democrats.

The francophile campaign of the left-wing intellectuals met with its severest test in 1923 during the Ruhr crisis. Reproaching the Germans with the sabotage of reparations payments, the government of Poincaré in January of that year ordered its troops to seize two-thirds of the Ruhr area "to secure the rights and claims of France." The German answer was a "scream of indignation." [18] The conservative Cuno government ordered the workers of the Ruhr to strike, and proclaimed "passive resistance" against the aggressors. The consequences were the devaluation of the German mark, the ruin of the middle class and of the workers, large-scale strike movements in the Reich, separatist agitation in Bavaria and the Rhineland, the rise of political extremism, and numerous political murders. During these terrible months the German pacifists and left-wing intellectuals were again almost alone in denouncing resistance to the French occupying forces. The Communists who saw in France the greatest enemy of Soviet Russia,[†] ordered all-out workers' resistance to the troops of the French bourgeoisie. Karl Radek, the principal agent of the Comintern in Germany, appealed to the German Right to form a common front of Communists and Nationalists.[19] True, the Communists also proclaimed a simultaneous proletarian struggle against the German bourgeoisie, but their slogan "Beat Poincaré on the Ruhr and Cuno on the Spree" was an implicit approval of the German government's resistance policy.[20]

As for the Social Democrats, they were bewildered. Fearing the rise of a new stab-in-the-back legend were they to refuse to join in the national resistance, they contented themselves with polite criticism of the government.[21] Only the small reviews of the left-wing intellectuals and of the revisionist Social Democratic opposition insisted that resistance on the Ruhr was national suicide and that reconciliation with France was mandatory, be it in the presence of the French army of occupation. There were defections in their ranks, a few writers having again succumbed to the call for national unity, but the majority remained undaunted. Germany could have fulfilled her obligations in the past, Morus wrote in the *Weltbühne* during the first days of the Ruhr occupation, if only she had worked harder and placed her wares on the world market. To satisfy France would have been both a moral obligation and a good strategy. It would have allowed the creation of a Franco-German economic alliance against British industry. France erred morally by ordering a violent measure; it was up to the Germans to score a point by showing more generosity.[22] Passive resistance is

---

[†] As late as 1930 Stalin still considered the French his most dangerous opponents. He called France "the most aggressive and militarist of all aggressive and militarist countries." See E. H. Carr, *German-Soviet Relations Between the Two World Wars, 1919–1939* (New York, 1966), 102.

senseless, Morus exclaimed a few weeks later. What is the point in bleeding to death heroically when the creditor is in firm possession of the collateral, the Ruhr area? Only the debtor suffered. There was still time for payments but the government must bring itself to tax the industry which had drawn enormous profits from the inflation.[23]

There was no issue of the *Weltbühne* at that time which would not have argued, with more or less economic expertise, the possibility of paying reparations. Not only Germany, the whole world will suffer, so the journal's argument ran, because the Reichstag lives in mortal fear of being called unpatriotic and chooses to submit to the industrialists, the true profiteers of the Ruhr occupation.[24]

In another article Morus spelled out the conditions of German surrender. There must be an armistice, he insisted; French evacuation of the Ruhr should follow upon the termination of German resistance. It is not true that the situation resembles that of October 1918. Then Germany had risked losing her weapons; now she had nothing to lose. The French and Belgian troops must consent to return to their barracks and end all controlling operations. They must also suspend the state of siege and abandon arrests and expulsions. In exchange, the Germans must resume work in the mines and the factories. Negotiations on reparations can begin after the conclusion of an armistice.[25] This was written in May 1923. Three months later the Cuno government fell and in September, the new chancellor, Gustav Stresemann, liquidated passive resistance in the Ruhr area.

Although *Die Weltbühne* weathered rather well the emotional stresses of the Ruhr crisis, some of its writers adopted a more traditional stand in matters of foreign policy when they began to advocate a Continental Bloc directed against the Anglo-Saxon powers. Their aim, however, remained the same: to foster German democracy and European peace through close Franco-German cooperation. Back in 1920, *Die Weltbühne* had suggested that a bloc of European debtor states be created against Great Britain, and ultimately against the chief creditor, the United States. After 1923, the chief advocate in the *Weltbühne* of an anti-British "Continental Policy" was Felix Stössinger, a revisionist Social Democrat and contributor to Joseph Bloch's *Sozialistische Monatshefte*.[26] Bloch and his friends abhorred the constant German, and especially Social Democratic, flirtation with Great Britain, the purpose of which was the weakening of French power. They saw the balance of power policy of England as an excuse for English imperialism and they judged Germany's position vis-à-vis England as that of a flunky. England, they said, was encouraging an aggressive German *Ostpolitik* which threatened the French policy of international security and was bound to lead Europe to a new war. Characteristically, it was in 1925, during the preparation for the Locarno treaty between Germany and the Western powers that Stössinger detected the rising threat of an international conflict. For the Locarno Pact, although it guaranteed France's own boundaries, left the question of Polish-German settlement open, and encouraged German, British, and Soviet maneuvering in this vital area.[27] In the Eastern question *Die Weltbühne* again took an unusual stand and thoroughly repudiated the politics of all leftist political parties.

Chapter VI
FOR PEACE WITH POLAND AND AGAINST SOVIET-GERMAN COLLABORATION

German-Soviet relations presented the Weimar political parties with an immediate postwar dilemma. Obviously, there had to be some contacts and even some cooperation between the two great victims of the World War but, no less obviously, there were serious ideological and practical obstacles in the way of a *rapprochement*.[1] The most vociferous opponent in Germany of Russo-German cooperation had been the Social Democratic Party. Following the Bolshevik assumption of power, the Social Democrats exchanged ther traditional hostility to reactionary and obscurantist tsarist Russia for a no less intense ideological dislike of Soviet Communism. They also opposed German-Soviet cooperation because it threatened the chances of Germany's eventual reconciliation with the Western powers. The Social Democratic position was widely shared by the other republican parties. Even the Nationalists, steeped as they were in the tradition of Junker sympathy for Russia, and of violent anti-Western sentiments, could initially conceive only of an alliance with a counterrevolutionary, "White" Russia.

Yet it was on the Right that the first break occurred in the front of common hostility to Bolshevist Russia. In 1919, a number of conservative intellectuals came out for a Soviet-German alliance and some even advocated the Bolshevization of Germany. There was a good bit of masochism and fantasy in the *Tat's* advocacy of a German form of Bolshevism as the only avenue of escape for future generations of Germans from Western imperialism.[2] Only through the sacrifice of the present generation of Germans, *Die Tat* contended, could the union of all Germans be realized and the greatest threat of all averted: the

93

appropriation by Anglo-American capital of all of Germany's productive forces. "Without Bolshevism, the wealth of our capitalists would inevitably fall into the hands of foreign countries; Bolshevism would turn this wealth over to the German people." [3] Despair over the terms of the Versailles treaty and hatred for Wilson, that "high priest of Mammon," that "servant of the Antichrist," [4] caused the arch-conservative *Der Türmer* to argue that inasmuch as "the German people will be plundered in any case, there is only one solution: immediate understanding with Russia, and our transformation on Bolshevist grounds, but according to German ideals." [5]

Even after the passing of the first wave of conservative disorientation, rightist intellectuals continued to toy with the thought of an alliance among the "young" or "have-not" nations—by which they meant Germany and, alternately, Russia, Japan, or sometimes the United States—against the old "haves," the capitalist, materialist, individualist, and liberal Western powers. [6] A small but fashionable group of conservative intellectuals went even further in developing the concept of German "National Bolshevism," based on the union of all anticapitalist forces within and outside Germany. [7]

These intellectual rantings would have been of little consequence had a handful of conservative German diplomats and officers not embraced similar ideas. [a] As early as December 1918, General Hans von Seeckt, who was to become the chief of the Reichswehr less than a year later, mentioned the possibility of a Russo-German alliance directed against Poland and the Western powers. [8] In the following year, two officers, Colonel Max Bauer and Admiral Paul von Hintze, approached the Comintern agent Karl Radek, then in a Berlin prison, to offer him an alliance between the German working class and the "officer class." The German socialist revolution, the officers argued, should be led by professional soldiers. [9] Undoubtedly, Seeckt did not share the exalted views of these officers; his concept was that of a conventional Russo-German military alliance directed against the Versailles powers. Seeckt had to proceed slowly because the Soviet leaders were divided between those who confidently expected a Com-

---

[a] Needless to say, the German Communists also advocated close German-Soviet cooperation, but they did not make clear whether this alliance was to be an outcome of the triumph of the German revolutionary proletariat or whether a close cooperation between bourgeois Germany and Soviet Russia was also desirable. But as the German Communists vehemently denounced any *rapprochement* between Germany and the Western powers, while they never raised their voice against German-Soviet contacts, they indirectly supported the conservative advocates of an exclusively pro-Russian foreign policy.

munist revolution in Germany and those who believed that since the world revolution was not forthcoming, at least one bourgeois power, Germany, should be accommodated. Only after the defeat of the Red Army at the gates of Warsaw in the fall of 1920, did Lenin conclude that an understanding with the Weimar republic was desirable. On April 26, 1922, a Soviet-German treaty was signed in Rapallo, ostensibly normalizing relations between the two countries. This would have been a perfectly acceptable move on the part of Germany, had it not taken place during an international conference, held in Genoa, where Germany appeared for the first time as an equal partner.

The Rapallo treaty came as a surprise to the assembled diplomats and was recognized as an open challenge to the Western powers. It was suspected by everybody that secret military clauses lurked behind the seemingly harmless official agreement.[10] There were, in fact, no such clauses because they were no longer needed. Following secret military conversations, German officers had gone to Russia early in 1922 to train with forbidden weapons, and German industrialists had set up factories in Russia for the manufacture of tanks, airplanes, poison gas, and ammunition. These ventures were mostly unsuccessful because of Russian incompetence, but Germany continued for the next ten years to undertake similar military experiments in Russia. Strategically negligible, Soviet-German military cooperation proved to have important political consequences.[11] Not only did the fairly well-known and usually exaggerated facts of this secret collaboration irritate Western public opinion, but military cooperation contributed to the ruin of democracy in Germany. No matter how hostile some German politicians were to these military contacts, they considered it their patriotic duty to remain silent. Worse than that, many cabinet members were simply not informed by the army command and consequently knew less, or pretended to know less, than some astute journalists. On the other hand, Seeckt was allowed to pursue his own foreign policy, as unrealistic as it was aggressive. Fancying himself a "global" politician, Seeckt greatly exaggerated the occasional tensions between France and Great Britain. In September 1922, for instance, he argued in a memorandum to Chancellor Wirth that a Franco-British war was inevitable and that Britain would soon seek an alliance with Germany. As a price for this alliance, Britain would then allow Germany to pursue an independent Eastern policy. What Seeckt meant by the latter was simply that Germany, and possibly Russia, should occupy Poland. Poland was Seeckt's *bête noire*, a mortal threat to Germany which had to be eliminated.[12]

The worst sufferers of Seeckt's *Ostpolitik* were the Social Democrats who were so afraid to appear unpatriotic that they usually refrained from even mentioning the Russo-German military collaboration. When they finally broke their silence, as Scheidemann did in the Reichstag in December 1926, it was too late, and their revelations failed to move public opinion.[13] The fact was that Rapallo proved to be popular among the German middle and upper classes. Untutored as these people generally were in international affairs, they shared Seeckt's "global" political thinking and his predilection for an apocalyptic view of history. The curious situation arose in which the majority of the workers condemned the ties that linked Germany to the country of socialism, whereas the bourgeoisie hailed the alliance. Tucholsky's Herr Wendriner typified the bourgeois view of the Soviet alliance:

[Herr Wendriner sits in a barber's chair and reads the *Berliner Lokalanzeiger:*] "The New Russia. Unveiling of the Worker's Monument." The foul gangsters! These people are in power today—so they are having a ball. Of course, one should conclude an alliance with Russia. You see, England will soon march against Russia because of India; then Germany will have to help Russia. Let France burst with envy. And after that? After that, we will give it to the Russians too.[14]

Of all the German political groups only the left-wing intellectuals remained forever outspokenly hostile to the Soviet-German alliance. Nothing alienated them more from the two working-class parties than the left-wing intellectuals' knowledge that the Social Democrats tolerated and the Communists indirectly fostered close contacts between the two powers.

No sooner did the "bombshell" explode in Rapallo than *Die Weltbühne* denounced what it called a "conspiracy" and an open provocation of the Western powers. Its first commentary on the subject exempted Foreign Minister Rathenau from direct responsibility in this move and correctly indicted Baron von Maltzan, a Foreign Ministry official, for having masterminded the Rapallo agreement.[15] The writer of the article, Moritz Heimann, indicated rightly that Rathenau had signed the agreement only reluctantly, but he erred when he thought that Chancellor Wirth had also been tricked by von Maltzan into accepting the treaty. In reality, Wirth, a progressive Catholic politician and the first champion in Germany of a fulfillment policy, was much in favor of the Soviet treaty.[16] Why Wirth chose to follow in the footsteps of Bismarck by keeping the line open to Moscow is still a mystery.[17] In any case, *Die Weltbühne* found the situation exasperating. Rapallo has reopened the Eastern question—Heimann argued—

and it has upset the painfully established international order. The German Foreign Ministry, by shrouding the preparation for the treaty in mystery, had reverted to the prewar practice of secret diplomacy.[18] Rapallo is a tragedy, wrote Morus: "it is a special treaty directed openly against Europe. And this at the very moment when the European powers, having lived through four years of war and three years of postwar confusion, were meeting for the first time to discuss their common future." [19] Again Germany parades as Europe's chief trouble-maker, Morus lamented. In another article Morus became more judicious in reviewing the failure of the Genoa conference. He called Poincaré's obstructionist tactics a crime, but labeled Germany's and Russia's actions worse than a crime: a mistake.[20] The Russian Foreign Commissar Chicherin acted not as a statesman but as a ghetto merchant—Soviet Russia generally suffered from a ghetto mentality—and Rathenau acted the fool by throwing away Germany's best chance of becoming an equal among the European powers. We went to Genoa as equals, Morus complained, we returned as defendants: again the Germans have become international outcasts.[21] *Die Weltbühne* knew nothing at that time of the secret Russo-German military contacts. Morus first mentioned the rumor in August 1922, refusing at the same time to believe it because "it would be too terrible." [22] Soon thereafter the evidence became overwhelming and *Die Weltbühne* made it one of its principal missions to air the secret military contacts. Its military experts were thereupon dragged from one treason trial to another.

German-Soviet relations took a new turn after the liquidation of the Ruhr crisis in the summer of 1923. In the slowly developing international *détente*, the Germans found themselves in a central position in European diplomacy. Courted from all sides, they could now take the initiative in foreign affairs. In 1924, Foreign Minister Stresemann began an active *rapprochement* with the Western powers, a program for which he now received the support of General von Seeckt. But throughout, Stresemann—and Seeckt—remained intent on keeping the door open to an independent German Eastern policy. In this, they were greatly aided by both domestic and foreign developments. In October 1923 the German Communists made their last unsuccessful attempt to overthrow the bourgeois republic. Thereafter the German Communist Party became a parliamentary party.[23] As for the Russians, they became increasingly convinced that France and Great Britain were their most dangerous enemies. Weimar Germany seemed by far the lesser evil unless she was drawn into a capitalist coalition directed against Soviet Russia. It seemed incredible to the Russians, writes

E. H. Carr, "that the capitalists should be too short-sighted to form such a combination."[24] In 1925 the situation seemed indeed frightening to the Russians. Having signed the Dawes Plan on reparations payments and on foreign loans to be provided to Germany, Stresemann signed the Locarno treaty on October 16, 1925, according to which Germany promised to respect the sanctity of the Franco-German and Belgo-German frontiers. This ended the short-term possibility of a Franco-German conflict. But the treaty also made clear that Germany had not surrendered her claims on the rectification of her Eastern boundaries. Although Germany signed arbitration treaties with Poland and Czechoslovakia, it was generally understood that she would not specifically bind herself to refrain from aggression in the East.[25] Since this was the case, the Russians wanted to keep on the good side of the Germans. Long before the signing of the Locarno treaty, Russia had given several indications of her dissatisfaction with German policy by arranging friendly Russian visits to Warsaw and Paris. The Germans understood the hint, and new German-Soviet negotiations began in Berlin in December 1925, the month that the Locarno treaty was ratified by the Reichstag. On April 24, 1926, while Germany was actively seeking admission to the League of Nations, Germany and Russia signed a treaty of neutrality in Berlin.[26]

Locarno and Berlin expressed two realities in German life, writes E. H. Carr: Germany's financial dependence on the West, and especially on the United States," and her "military dependence on Soviet Russia."[27] Indeed, the Berlin treaty included secret clauses on the manufacture of ammunitions for Germany and the training of German officers in Soviet Russia.[28] It was typical of conditions in Germany that while the Locarno treaty was wildly denounced by the Communists and the Nationalists in the Reichstag, the Berlin treaty was ratified unanimously with only three opposing votes cast by dissident Communist deputies.[29]

The "spirits" of Locarno and Berlin were mutually exclusive. The Locarno treaty was based on the understanding that Germany would join the status quo powers, harbor no more resentment against France, and fully collaborate with the Western powers in building a peaceful but anti-Bolshevist Europe. The secret military clauses of the Berlin treaty cast grave doubts on the sincerity of the Germans. In 1927, when Anglo-Soviet relations appeared to reach the breaking point and Germany was unofficially asked by both Great Britain and Russia to take sides, the incompatibility of the two treaties became apparent.[30] Although the Germans gave elusive answers to both powers, they really had no choice but to side with Great Britain, and thereafter Soviet-German relations were kept within more cautious limits. But even then Stresemann, and the German diplomats in general, were ready to use the threat of an intimate Russian alliance to put pressure on the Western powers. Furthermore, they understood friendship with Russia to mean the first step toward an anti-Polish *Machtpolitik* in Eastern Europe.[31]

The writers of the *Weltbühne* found no redeeming grace in Stresemann's "two-faced" policy. They were distressed to see Germany revert to the secret diplomatic maneuvering which had served her so poorly in the decades before the war. What was Germany to gain from all this? Why the Soviet alliance if not for a new war? Tucholsky addressed an "open letter" to Stresemann from Paris.[32] He accused the foreign minister of "having recognized at Locarno only half of the Versailles treaty." And even that half was of doubtful value. For the military road to Paris did not necessarily lead through Belfort—there was also a road leading through Warsaw. Stresemann was clever to recognize that Poland represented a vacuum through which Europe could again be infiltrated by German power. He was clever but, Tucholsky asked, was he also wise? For a while everything would go well for Germany, Tucholsky predicted. The *Anschluss* of Austria will be an easy matter; Czechoslovakia will be a harder nut to crack, but because of the nationality struggle in that country, Germany will succeed there as well. There remains only Poland where Stresemann counts on the support of Russia. But the Russians—and here, only, Tucholsky's vision is faulty—will not go along with the bargain. Stresemann will also try to protect his back by winning over England for his Polish campaign. And this is where his calculation will fail. For he is wrong to believe that the Germans are popular in Great Britain. In fact, there is less sympathy for Germany in that country than there is in France. If not provoked, France might be willing to cooperate with Germany. Not so the English. What Stresemann does not realize, but the English do, is that this is one world, and that a brawl started in one corner of the great hall of assembled nations will upset the entire gathering. If Germany attacks Poland, the whole world will fight Germany. "You might be betting well in the first half hour"—Tucholsky wrote to Stresemann—"but in the end you are going to lose the race."[33]

All of the *Weltbühne* circle found Stresemann's policy wanting. Felix Stössinger interpreted Locarno as a threat to France and Poland, and a stupid submission to British imperialist ambitions.[34] Hans

Schwann saw no hope for peace as long as Stresemann was directing German foreign policy.[34a] Morus violently attacked the German attempt to conclude a "reinsurance treaty" with Russia. Where Caprivi failed in the 1890's, Stresemann could not be more successful. Whoever wants to follow a realistic policy, Morus argued, must ignore the Rapallo treaty.[35] In April 1926, when the Berlin treaty was about to be signed, Ossietzky turned against Stresemann whom he had otherwise admired. In his first editorial for the *Weltbühne*, entitled "The Sealed Railroad Car,"[36] Ossietzky derided the notion that the Soviet Russians were brilliant foreign politicians. Ever since Rapallo, where, to the general surprise of the Germans, the Russians had appeared not as wild barbarians or as slovenly Bohemians but as polished gentlemen, the Germans had developed the impression of an incomparably cunning Soviet diplomacy. Yet what in reality had Soviet diplomacy accomplished since the "surprise" of Rapallo? Nothing but a series of failures, and this because the plotter and the agitator had always followed in the wake of the diplomat. The genius of Soviet foreign policy, Ossietzky wrote, consists in providing the world with an export article called revolution:

Revolution in all sizes and qualities: heavy pieces of equipment for China and India; delicate little traveling cases for the Nomadic tribes of Arabia; Marx theory and pastoral letters for Germany; wild apocalyptic prophecies for the pious Anglo-Saxons.[37]

The effect of this export trade was the isolation of Soviet Russia. Only the Germans, Ossietzky continued, take Soviet diplomacy seriously.[b] Here every flag-waving reactionary casts an expectant eye on Russia. Not that these Germans are socialists. Far from it. They are friends of crises and of international catastrophies. "They think from one catastrophe to another." They want revenge against Poland and, to achieve this, they are ready to send new "sealed railroad cars" with new Lenins into a peaceful world. That the dilettantes of the Wilhelmstrasse are no better than the average conservative *Katastrophenpolitiker* is understandable. But Stresemann is above these considerations: he is the first Weimar politician with a realistic view. Stresemann alone understands that Germany's road must lead to an understanding with France and to the League of Nations. Why then this flirtation with the Soviets? Because Stresemann fancies himself a

---

[b] It is small wonder that of all of Ossietzky's pieces, this commentary is most seriously criticized in the highly laudatory East German account of his life. Bruno Frei, *Carl v. Ossietzky* (Berlin [East], 1966), 91 ff.

great tactician. Because for him Locarno is not a step toward the creation of a new supranational order, but toward "pacifist maneuvering." Yet "pacifism is an absolute requirement. . . . One cannot play up peace as a threat the way war was played up earlier." [38]

Then and later Ossietzky made clear his conception of Germany's new role: strict neutrality and the surrender of her great power status: "Our boot-licking neutrality will not do. It must become a conscious neutrality. . . . Here [in Germany] must crystallize all that still remains on this earth of reasonableness and of the will for peace." [39]

The withdrawal of the Allied Control Commission from Germany in January, 1927, all but restored Germany's military independence [40] and increased the domestic political activity of the German army command, especially as it now professed to be certain of the imminence of a Polish attack. This alleged danger was exploited—as it would be again and again—by conservative politicians and by the military to silence criticism of the army and to push new military appropriations through the Reichstag. In 1928, Minister of Defense General Groener convinced the German government to proceed with the controversial armored-cruiser program because of "Poland's hunger for German territory in East Prussia and Upper Silesia, and the general aggressiveness of her policy." [41] In 1932, the military used the argument of the Polish war to obtain from the government the prohibition of the SA. Subsequently, when the generals reversed their views on the probable behavior of the SA in the event of a Polish invasion, they obtained from the government the lifting of the prohibition. [42]

The unsatisfactory course of German foreign policy, and the ability of the German generals to mould policy both abroad and at home, decisively influenced the *Weltbühne's* views on the republic. In domestic affairs, they set themselves four main tasks: (1) to impress on the politicians the need to concentrate all political power in civilian hands and to make a "revolution from above"; (2) to weaken by every means the prestige of the army; (3) to bring about the reform of the judiciary, that other enforcer of public servility, and, (4) to help revive prewar working-class unity. When the passivity of the republican leadership toward the officers became unmistakably clear, they saw "Red unity" or the Left Front as the last hope for the complete overhaul of the republic.

Chapter VII

FOR A MILITANT REPUBLIC AFTER THE KAPP PUTSCH AND THE RATHENAU MURDER

In 1928, when the Weimar republic congratulated itself for having weathered ten stormy years, Kurt Tucholsky asked:

> Happier now, you worker's wife?
> You, the miner down there?
> And for all of you in the prison block
> Has the republic sweetened the air?
> Ah, but we are a republic
> All black and white and red.
> Doing our best to run the shop
> Just like the founder said.
>
> We have judges worse than the Kaiser's
> Industrialists now rob with a sting
> The Junkers—they're hard to get rid of
> The Church still rides Victory's wing.[1]

What mattered, indeed, was not the individual fate of the miner or of the prisoner—certainly no worse than in most other countries—but the indestructibility of the forces of reaction. That there had been opportunities to suppress them, and that the republican parties had not been equal to the challenge, earned for Weimar the epithet "the republic of missed opportunities." Perhaps the best of these opportunities presented itself in January 1919 immediately after the elections to the National Assembly, which had secured an enormous majority to parties that stood—at least in theory—for a democratic and socialist republic.[2] No doubt, the winners were divided. Their strongest group,

102

the Majority Social Democrats, polled a disappointing 38 percent of the total vote, not enough to form a government. A new coalition with the Independent Socialists being out of the question, the Social Democrats formed a coalition government with two bourgeois republican parties, the German Democrats and the Catholic Center. Even this coalition held an unmistakable mandate for sweeping reforms. These parties together polled more than three-fourths of the total vote; their electoral platforms had been almost identical in demanding such measures as the socialization of certain industries and mines, drastic financial reform based, above all, on taxation of property and capital, a far-reaching welfare program, and the democratization of such old Imperial institutions as the army, the judiciary, and the administration. Furthermore, since the Spartacus League had boycotted the elections, the Weimar coalition shared the benches of the left in the National Assembly with only the Independent Socialists whose moderate wing favored the reform legislation of the Weimar coalition. As if this were not enough, the program of the new government enjoyed the theoretical support of the Right opposition whose electoral platforms had echoed a few socialist reform proposals.[3] The Weimar Constitution, subsequently ratified by the National Assembly, embodied the achievements of the November revolution: a republican government, political equality, human rights. But it did not provide for institutions encouraging social and economic equality, such as the state ownership of basic industries. In the words of Evelyn Anderson:

All these [socialistic] measures could have been carried out even by the coalition Government which was formed with the Social Democrat, Philipp Scheidemann, as Premier. It would not have been Socialism, but these measures would have provided some elementary safeguards for German democracy. Moreover, they would have had an immensely popular appeal not only to Socialists but equally to the vast number of people who had voted for the Democratic and Catholic Parties. However, nothing of that sort was done.[4]

Many reasons were advanced for the failure of Social Democracy, for it was the Social Democratic Party that failed above all: a general lack of self-confidence in Social Democratic ranks; fear of economic sabotage by the capitalists and the landowners;[5] an unwillingness to displease the Allied Powers; above all, anxiety over the possible resurgence of Communist agitation.[6] But for the overriding reason, it is necessary to go further back. Well before the First World War, the SPD had developed a semi-autocratic party machinery committed to an unimaginative kind of trade-union reformism and the suppression of revolutionary elements in the party. The great historian of German Social Democracy, Carl Schorske, goes so far as to argue that the prewar SPD had a vested interest in the preservation of capitalism.[7] Whether or not Schorske is correct, the fact remains that the SPD's electoral platform in 1919 promised the introduction of socialist measures and that, after the elections, the party did not even try to live up to its promises. Never again would the SPD receive such electoral support. Nor would the combined votes of the working-class parties—and these parties remained forever divided—come close to the figures of that year. Nor would, finally, the Weimar coalition again command a majority in the Reischstag. After 1919 no parliamentary combination could muster sufficient electoral support for effective reform legislation: Weimar history came to be characterized by the stagnation of the political parties, a pattern broken only in 1930 with the phenomenal rise of National Socialism and the parallel decline of the bourgeois political parties.[a]

But if the opportunity for sweeping but orderly reform was lost in 1919, there still remained other avenues for energetic political action. On several occasions a sudden political consensus and the pressure of mass demonstrations put the democratic minority in a position to impose its will on its divided opponents. It was the kind of action that the left-wing intellectuals harped on with maddening monotony. Even Tucholsky, who had repudiated the bourgeois republic almost as it was created, repeatedly called for republican dynamism. In his biography of Tucholsky, Harold Poor has commented:

He [Tucholsky] spoke in the enthusiastic, but generally vague language of revolution. Party programs, parliamentary resolutions, political speeches seemed to have little to do with the exciting business of sweeping away the old order and creating the new. . . . He struck a pose of despair before a hopeless society, using such words as "spirit," "sensibility," and "atmosphere." . . . In the early years, he predicted disaster while hoping for, and half-believing in, salvation.[8]

For the majority of the *Weltbühne* writers, separation from the parties that made up the republic was a much slower process. It will be shown later that in the early years of the republic they consistently

---

[a] There are good surveys of the voting patterns of the Weimar era in Evelyn Anderson, *Hammer or Anvil* (London, 1945), pp. 140 f., and Hunt, 111 ff. Both authors demonstrate convincingly the stagnation of all political combinations in the post-1919 era, be it of the working class parties or of the "Weimar Coalition." They also show that the combined strength of the bourgeois parties (excluding the Center) remained stable only until 1930, when the voters deserted these parties for National Socialism.

adopted a Social Democratic position, that they considered the Weimar Constitution the basis for further political action. The old, Imperial Constitution had interested no one, Ossietzky wrote on the second anniversary of the constitution's adoption.[9] The passions stirred up for and against the Weimar Constitution show, he wrote, that it represents force. True, it is no work of art; it has little appeal and does not aim at man's soul as does the French constitution; it has no inner music. But it represents an element of unity in a divided country. The Weimar Constitution "is an attempt," he affirmed, "to translate into terse sentences the loftiest socio-ethical tendencies of modern society." [10] But the success of the constitution depends on the conversion of the Germans' exaggerated individualism into a feeling of solidarity.

The trouble was that "democratic solidarity," although not entirely lacking, came to the fore only in extreme emergencies as, for example, during the reactionary coup d'état of March 1920. The Kapp putsch had been met by an impressive show of democratic solidarity and a grave threat to the republic was thereby averted. But the republic proved incapable of exploiting the fruits of its victory. Although the Social Democratic minister of defense, Noske, was dismissed for having overlooked the threat of counterrevolution, his place was given to Otto Gessler, a Bavarian member of the Democratic Party whose republican loyalty was at least doubtful. The decidedly antirepublican Seeckt was rewarded with the command of the Reichswehr for his "neutrality" during the Kapp putsch. The putschists themselves were either allowed to escape or were soon amnestied. Finally, the government of the Weimar coalition failed to suppress the putsch in Bavaria where a Social Democratic government had been replaced by a reactionary regime under von Kahr. Thereafter, this government—openly hostile to the Reich—harbored all the counterrevolutionary elements.

The net result of the Kapp putsch was disheartening. Immediately after the suppression of the counterrevolution, the triumphant trade-union leaders demanded the formation of a labor government supported by both socialist parties and the socialist and Christian trade unions. Almost inconceivably, the offer was snubbed by the socialist parties, whereupon the trade unions acquiesced in the return of the Weimar coalition. This was a turning point in the history of the German trade unions. A decisive force in the republic, the trade unions subsequently concentrated on economic problems, developing the republic's already impressive welfare institutions but repeatedly compromising with the ruling powers. On the other hand, the second decisive force in the republic, the army, was allowed to be built by

Seeckt into a "state withing the state." [11] Temporarily loyal, it proved
in the long run to be fatal to the republic.

The *Weltbühne's* only cessation of activity during the entire history
of the Weimar republic occurred during the Kapp putsch. Two consecutive issues could not be published in Berlin while the soldiers of
Lüttwitz and Ehrhardt patrolled the streets. When it reappeared on
March 25, 1920, *Die Weltbühne* launched an immediate appeal for the
long overdue "German revolution." In his first post-Kapp article,[12]
Tucholsky offered concrete suggestions to the republican leaders. He
demanded the ousting of all the "conservative Prussian" officers from
the Reichswehr; the suppression of military jurisdiction; the transformation of the army into a "reliable people's militia," the disbanding of
all paramilitary units; drastic "enlightenment" of the population on the
past and present crimes of the nationalists, and, finally, the complete
overhaul of education in a democratic, antimonarchical and pacifist
spirit:

If the German republic, awakened by the military coup, now makes up for
the passivity which has dogged it since November 1918, then this [coup]
has not been in vain.

No one will raise his voice against the reform of the great public
institutions; the resistance of small communities and interest groups, down
to family units, will be considerable. Break that resistance! We have had no
revolution. Make one! [13]

Two years later Tucholsky repeated his recommendations to the
republic, adding such other proposals as the demilitarization of the
"Schutzpolizei," that mobile police force in which the number of
officers in relation to enlisted men has come to resemble the situation
in Liberia; a thorough purge of the judiciary, especially of the state
prosecutor's office; the strengthening of the Reich against the *Länder;*
immediate amnesty to all except rightist political prisoners (which
would have meant no amnesty to the Kapp conspirator Herr von
Jagow, the republic's only rightist political prisoner), and, finally,
permission for all citizens to display medals and to claim honorific
titles, including titles of nobility, whether or not they had ever been
officially bestowed.[14] This charming frivolous demand, inspired by the
French model, was characteristic of Tucholsky's approach. No less
characteristic was his omission of a recommendation that the republic,
again following the French model, finally begin to hand out medals
and titles of its own. Yet, according to Erich Eyck, the republic's
puritanical refusal to engage in such activity contributed greatly to its
unpopularity.[15]

What Tucholsky recommended was, in essence, the fulfillment of the traditional Social Democratic demands but it was unlikely that the demands would be met. How could substantial educational reforms get under way as long as even the Social Democrats insisted on fostering "patriotic values"? Or a purge of the judiciary as long as the government saw the radical Left, and not the Right, as its main enemy? And as for a "people's militia"—an army of organized workers under socialist officers—this extraordinary feat was nearly accomplished in Austria where the old army had evaporated at the end of the war; in Germany it was all but hopeless because of the pact that the Social Democrats had concluded with the military in November 1918 for the suppression of Bolshevism, and because of the pacifist mood of the workers who had no interest in playing soldiers.

But perhaps the workers' reluctance to bear arms for the bourgeois republic was only temporary, a direct consequence of their disillusionment. Perhaps these writers were correct in asserting that the workers would respond if rallied at the proper time. Leo Lania wrote in a retrospective article:

What was the duty of Social Democracy after Kahr had formally taken over command in Bavaria? To sound the alarm. There was not a minute to lose. . . . It should have mobilized the masses—everybody who stood for the republic! The Kapp Putsch, one thought at that time, had shown them the way. What happened instead? "Social Democracy kept its cool and waited. . . ." Its main worry was how to maintain the parliamentary-democratic façade in all its beauty.[16]

The republican parties could not find their way out of the impasse: distrusting the masses, they did not dare take energetic measures, above all the purge of the army. But without such energetic measures they could not win the active support of the masses and consequently did not dare purge the army.

Two years after the Kapp putsch an unmistakable opportunity for "a revolution from above" presented itself following the assassination of Foreign Minister Rathenau. Rathenau's tragedy—he was murdered by a group of young men for no other apparent reason than that he was a Jew accorded cabinet rank—was only one in a long series of attempts on the lives of democratic politicians. But while previous murders had grieved only the victim's political friends (not even the assassination of the Center politician Erzberger in 1921 had met with widespread indignation), there was now an immediate and vehement public reaction. In the words of Erich Eyck:

Rathenau's murder caused greater and more general excitement than had Erzberger's. This time no normal man could say that the victim had deserved his dreadful end. Republican elements of the nation were the most disturbed, for they regarded the assassination as a crime against the state. Rathenau had been murdered because he had served the Republic; indeed, because his remarkable talents lent the new state a certain prestige. . . . . Gigantic mass demonstrations filled the streets. Labor protested with a twenty-four hour strike. A few unfortunate incidents occurred, as was to be expected at a time of such tension. But in general a sober discipline was maintained. And everywhere it became apparent that some thorough, radical step had to be taken for the protection of the Republic and of republicans.[17]

Chancellor Wirth voiced the feelings of a majority of Germans when, a few days after the murder, he declared war on the nationalists in the Reichstag:

There stands the enemy, where Mephisto drips his poison into the nation's wounds; there stands the enemy and there can be no doubt about it: the enemy stands on the Right.[18]

Die Weltbühne had had little sympathy for Rathenau, this exotic businessman who mixed socialist theories with mystical philosophy, cosmopolitan cynicism, German chauvinism, democratic convictions, and anti-Semitic racial ideologies. Now the journal joined in the general indignation and, in clear allusion to the fact that the enemy was isolated, demanded that the "insane adventurers" be eradicated from "the universities, army barracks, and sports associations." [19] Even Tucholsky felt that he was speaking for the majority of Germans:

In thousands of beer halls toasts are being drunk to celebrate the bloody occurrence. But we other Germans, we hundreds of thousands and millions, refuse to wait any longer. We declare that if the republic does not help us then we will help ourselves! . . . All that has been neglected since November 9, 1918, since the Kapp putsch, since the murder of Erzberger, must be accomplished here and now. Out with the thousands of civil servants who conspire against the republic! Out with the unreliable generals! Dissolve the nationalist leagues! Tear down from the buildings the monarchist flags! Rathenau must not have died in vain. It is up to you to create a republic at his bier.[20]

Again, *Die Weltbühne* was not short of concrete reform proposals. The most interesting was a call for the abolition of proportional representation. Back in 1921, Morus had bemoaned the multiparty system and asked for *klare Fronten* in the Reichstag with a republican front facing the nationalists. He discerned the main difficulty in the existence of the Center which gathered Catholic votes all the way from extreme reactionaries to democratic socialists. Such unpolitical interest groups should not be tolerated, Morus declared: the Center was to be cut into democratic and conservative groups.[21] After the Rathenau murder, Otto Flake, one of the moderates in the *Weltbühne*, took up the cry for a two-party parliament of republicans and nationalists.[22] Proclaiming himself a pacifist, Flake nevertheless insisted on the use of force against the Right and repeated Voltaire's slogan: *Écrasez l'infâme!* Only by the application of force could the republic provide its citizens with a republican temperament and the spirit of adventure. "A nation without political temperament has no right to political existence. . . . Beasts must be slain; reconciliation leads us nowhere." [23]

Again almost nothing came out of the general clamor for action. An emergency presidential decree for the "Protection of the Republic" ordered the *Länder* to suppress the antirepublican leagues and to prosecute the vicious slanderers of the republic but, despite its subsequent ratification by the Reichstag, it was openly and unconstitutionally rejected by Bavaria, and even in the rest of the Reich it was not put into effect except against the Communists.

There would be periods of republican resurgence even after the Rathenau affair. In the summer of 1923, a general strike helped to put an end to the conservative Cuno government and to "national resistance" on the Ruhr. The December 1924 elections reestablished the balance of power in the Reichstag, so badly shaken by the rightist electoral victory in May of the same year. There was, as will be shown later, an impressive democratic mass movement in 1926 and a leftist electoral victory in 1928. But those events interested the left-wing intellectuals only because they manifested popular dissatisfaction with the republic. After the election of Hindenburg to the presidency, no one could doubt the judgment of Tucholsky that this was a "republic until further notice." It was a regime that merited no consideration. And why? Because it was ashamed of the upheaval that had brought it to power—instead of commemorating the November days, it celebrated the Day of the Constitution (and celebrated it unctuously and without emotion); because it was afraid to criticize its main opponents for fear of alienating the already alienated; because it did nothing to combat the very agencies whose intent to overthrow the republic, the international situation permitting, had never been masked. The left-wing intellectuals found Weimar hopelessly philistine, without a republican mystique, and therefore not viable. But Weimar was still better than the nationalist regime to which it was bound to cede power and, therefore, worth rejuvenating. This, however, became inconceivable without a revolution. What Germany needed was another, more successful November 1918, this time directed not against the Kaiser but against the Kaiser's successors.

Ossietzky saw the murder of Rathenau as the turning point in the fortunes of the republic:

[In June 1922] the Germans were confronted with a vision of the republic that was always before French eyes: a militant republic, a daughter of freedom wearing a Phrygian cap—not that bonnet crocheted by the old maids of the Weimar National Assembly. . . . Then, and only then, the German republic could have acquired an essence, an idea.[24]

The French republican revolutionaries had been able to win, Ossietzky wrote in another article, because they had aimed for conquest, not only survival; they had been ready to behead their unsuccessful generals. "The republic here does not appeal to the *citoyen;* it appeals to the *bourgeois.* Never would it be capable of symbolizing the Goddess of Reason in a harlot." [25] Ossietzky, who personally abhorred the pompous and the theatrical, longed for Germany to imitate the theatrical verve of the French. For the benefit of the socialists he recalled the personality of Lassalle, "this most independent and profound thinker of German democracy . . . this first champion of the industrial proletariat, who had died the death of a Byronic hero." [26] Lassalle, he wrote, had brought the German workers' associations out from behind the shelter of the hot house into the arena of world events. When he died,[b] the German socialists—this "brotherhood of skittle players"—were left orphaned. Never again could they find a true leader. Marx was a mighty man of action, he wrote elsewhere; his German followers, with their blind belief in the ultimate success of his philosophy, lacked the spark that alone could have led them to success.[27]

Whoever saw the picture of President Ebert, dressed in a cutaway and striped pants, marching past the iron wall of an honors' guard of the Reichswehr, must agree with the *Weltbühne* that this "me-too" approach was not the way to deal with the aristocratic and bourgeois enemies of the republic. Try as he might, this former saddler's apprentice could not earn the respect of those he imitated. True, Ebert had been a party functionary for several decades before he assumed the presidency of the republic: his masquerading as a worker would have been only slightly less preposterous than his masquerading as a gentleman. And yet, this was the disguise that he and his Social Democratic

---

[b] Ferdinand Lassalle (1825–1864), founder of the "Allgemeiner Deutscher Arbeiterverein" (General German Labor Union), was killed in a duel over the honor of a lady.

companions should have assumed. In the 1920's, the German upper classes lived in profound fear of the "Worker." A persistent play on this fear, and an occasional show of working-class force, would have achieved more than all the sober Social Democratic appeals to national unity and interclass cooperation. In a society where the figures of the Worker, the Peasant, the Officer, the Jew, the Bolshevist loomed large in popular imagination, it was a grave mistake not to exploit these simplistic concepts. In a society where force was highly respected, it was wrong to dismiss force, or at least a threat of force, as a tactical weapon. How could Ebert and his companions overlook the fact that prewar Social Democracy had thrived on its ability to conjure the giant figure of the Worker who could, if he wished, cast away the empire! These were tactics that *Die Weltbühne* urged Social Democracy to employ; today, forty years after these events, it is still hard to see why so few of these tactics were adopted.

Unfortunately, not even *Die Weltbühne* writers could remain consistent in their call for leftist militancy. These writers were not only republicans and socialists but also pacifists, and they could never quite overcome their abhorrence of violence in any form. At one occasion, Ossietzky greeted the creation of the "Reichsbanner Schwarz Rot Gold," a Social Democratic veterans' organization, as both "necessary and useful." He acknowledged with only slight sarcasm that "apparently some people now wished to defend the republic." [28] But suspicion got the better of him, and he foresaw the Reichsbanner units as future "henchmen of the *Bonzokratie*," the party bigwigs, and he derided as signs of militarism the Reichsbanner's predilection for uniform windjackets, caps, canteens, haversacks, and marching music. Contradicting his own theory on the advantages of republican pageantry, he deplored the fanfaronade of the Reichsbanner.[29]

Ossietzky was of course right in his recognition of the unrevolutionary character of the Reichsbanner. Nor was he far off the mark when he argued that many members of these organizations were only frustrated soldiers. But such extremely popular institutions (the Reichsbanner alone had three and a half million members) [30] nevertheless acted as powerful deterrents to rightist conspirators. Only in the early 1930's, when there was no republic to speak of, and no pacifist movement, did the writers of the *Weltbühne* advocate the creation of armed antifascist units in the factories and the trade unions. Until then not only the republic, they themselves faced an impasse: the extreme Right could be fought only by armed workers. But the arming of the workers threatened to undermine the democratic mentality of the workers, and therefore it was better not to arm them.

Chapter VIII

AGAINST THE REGULAR AND THE SECRET REICHSWEHR

Die Weltbühne was justly regarded as a forum, if not of organized pacifism, then of all pacifist sentiments. Its collaborators were at the head of various peace organizations and practically every well-known German and foreign pacifist contributed to the *Weltbühne*.[a] Ludwig Quidde was, for many years, the chairman of the German Peace Cartel, an attempted coordinating organization of all German peace associations; Quidde and General von Schoenaich were successive chairmen of the "Deutsche Friedensgesellschaft" (German Peace Association), the largest single pacifist group; Otto Lehmann-Russbüldt, Hellmut von Gerlach, Rudolf Olden, Robert Kuczynski, E. J. Gumbel, Ossietzky, Tucholsky, Lothar Persius, Heinrich Mann, Alfons Goldschmidt, Arthur Holitscher, Ernst Toller were, at one time or another, board members of the "Deutsche Liga für Menschenrechte" (German League for Human Rights), perhaps the most dynamic pacifist organization. Hans Wehberg edited the *Friedenswarte*, one of the more durable pacifist publications; Berthold Jacob was an editor of the "radical pacifist" journal, *Das andere Deutschland;* Lothar Persius, Veit Valentin, Erich Mühsam, and Ossietzky edited various short-lived pacifist publications. Helene Stöcker founded the women's peace association and Kurt Hiller headed his own "Gruppe revolutionärer Pazifisten" (Revolutionary Pacifist Group) of which Tucholsky was a surprisingly devoted member. During its heyday in the early 1920's,

---

[a] For example the founder of "Pan-Europa," Count Coudenhove-Kalergi; also Romain Rolland, the French pacifist leader Victor Basch, and the British pacifists Norman Angell and Arthur Ponsonby.

the German Peace Cartel counted 100,000 members,[1] a figure undoubtedly inflated by the multiple membership of the more dedicated peacefighters.

A product of late nineteenth-century agnostic liberalism, German pacifism lacked entirely the nonconforming religious fervor of its older Anglo-Saxon counterparts. There were but a handful of clergymen in the German peace movement. Again unlike its Anglo-Saxon counterparts, early German pacifism had no labor contacts; it was categorically rejected by the orthodox Marxist German workers' movement. International Pacifists held their first conference in London in 1843, but not until 1874 did German opponents of war form their initial "peace committee."[2] The first Universal Peace Congress, held in 1889, did not include a single German delegate among its ninety-seven participants.[3] Then, growing international tension, general rearmament, and a piece of sentimental fiction, Bertha von Suttner's [b] *Die Waffen nieder* (Lay Down Your Arms) turned German attention to the peace movement.[4] In the words of Ossietzky:

The point of departure [of German pacifism] was the sniveling novel of a very sensitive and very unworldly woman. . . . She [Suttner] fought guns with holy water; she adored, with touching innocence, all treaties and institutions; she was a priestess of emotion. She addressed her appeals to

---

[b] Born Countess Kinsky in 1843, Suttner was the daughter of an Austrian general and of a *bürgerliche* mother. The *mésalliance* of her parents beclouded her life as did poverty. Never admitted to the Austrian "first society" she had an errant youth that brought her into close contact with Ekaterina Dadiani, a beauty from the Caucasus who bore the unlikely title of Princess of Mingrelia; in her company, the young countess experienced the thrills of the court of Empress Eugénie. Later, she took employment as a governess in Vienna. At 33, she married the son of her employer, a Baron von Suttner, over the violent objections of the bridegroom's family. Appropriately, the young couple spent their honeymoon in Mingrelia in the Caucasus where they stayed for nine years, witnessing the Russo-Turkish war of 1878. Following their return to Austria in 1885, she developed a passion for peace through international arbitration. When already a celebrated author, she persuaded her long-time admirer, Alfred Nobel, to found a peace prize, to be awarded every year by the Norwegian *Storting*. She was president of the Austrian Peace Association and official representative of her government at several international peace conferences. In 1905 she was awarded the Nobel Peace Prize, and subsequently prevailed upon Andrew Carnegie to donate ten million dollars to the cause of international peace. Fortunately for the old lady, she died a few days before the Sarajevo murder. See Ann Tizia Leitich, "Bertha von Suttner," *Grosse Österreicher* (Vienna, 1957), X, 66–75. Also E. Reut-Nicolussi, "Drei österreichische Rufer zum Frieden" (B. v. Suttner, A. H. Fried, and H. Lammasch), *Gemeinschaft des Geistes* ("Schriftenreihe der Österreichischen Unesco-Kommission," 14, 1957); Beatrix Kempf, *Bertha von Suttner* (Vienna, 1964), and Bertha von Suttner, *Memoiren* (Stuttgart, 1909).

kings and statesmen, and considered her task accomplished when she met with friendly approval. . . . There floated around the Peace Bertha [*Friedensbertha*] a gentle perfume of absurdity; that perfume has unfortunately stayed with the German peace movement.[5]

A year after *Die Waffen nieder* appeared, the Austrian Alfred Hermann Fried formed an "Austrian Peace Association," and in 1892 a German Peace Association.[c] By 1900, there were in Germany alone about one hundred different peace clubs.[6] Several members of the Reichstag attended the conferences of the "Interparliamentary Union," and German pacifist clubs sent their delegates to the "International Peace Bureau," a coordinating organization. But the imperial government participated only out of politeness at the two Hague peace congresses initiated by the tsar;[d] at home, the title *Leutnant der Reserve* on one's calling card remained the key to social success. A pacifist, although held in less contempt than a Social Democrat, could not aspire to a public career in Wilhelmian Germany.

During the war the peace movement experienced the usual tribulations. Some clubs enthusiastically dissolved themselves, others launched appeals to their foreign comrades affirming Germany's innocence. Only a few prewar pacifists dared to "betray" Germany: "I had no intention of surrendering my belief in humanity," wrote Hans Wehberg in retrospect, "therefore I could not possibly desire the momentary triumph of my fatherland."[7]

Inevitably, the end of the war and the defeat of Germany enhanced the cause of organized pacifism. On November 2, 1918, under the banner of the Bund Neues Vaterland, 100,000 people demonstrated in

---

[c] Alfred Hermann Fried (1864–1921), who was of Hungarian-Jewish middle-class background, worked for the *Neue Freie Presse* in Vienna. As leader of both the Austrian and German Peace Associations, he edited a monthly pacifist bulletin and in 1899 founded *Die Friedenswarte*, the pacifists' leading publication. In 1911, he received the Nobel Peace Prize. His *Handbuch der Deutschen Friedensbewegung* (1905; new extended edition 1911–13) became the bible of German pacifism. Fried was one of the few professional pacifists who combined zeal with journalistic talent. He spent the war years in Switzerland, and returned to Germany in 1919. When he died in 1921, *Die Friedenswarte* came under the direction of Ludwig Quidde, Walter Schücking, and Hans Wehberg. Its last editor in chief in Germany, Hans Wehberg, took *Die Friedenswarte* in 1934 to Geneva. For a reliable account, see Hans Wehberg on Fried in *Neue Deutsche Biographie*, V, 441 f.; also E. Reut-Nicolussi, "Drei Österreichische Rufer zum Frieden," 121 ff. On *Die Friedenswarte*, see K. F. Reichel, *Die pazifistische Presse* (Würzburg, 1938), 7 ff.

[d] It was on the occasion of the first Hague Peace Conference in 1899 that the Kaiser wrote his famous marginal note on a report of the conference: "I . . . on all these resolutions and prefer to trust my sharp sword." Quoted in Richard Barkeley, *Die deutsche Friedensbewegung, 1870–1933* (Hamburg, 1948), 14.

Berlin for universal disarmament.[8] Now labor also discovered the attractions of organized pacifism and entire socialist locals, especially those of the Independent Socialists, joined the Peace Association. This, in turn, made the split between socialist or "young," and bourgeois or "old" pacifists inevitable. The old pacifists stood for international arbitration and for the League of Nations; the young pacifists argued that war could be prevented only by categorical conscientious objection, a general strike, and a socialist revolution.[*][9] Their foremost spokesman was Kurt Hiller, and he at the same time called for civil war and insisted on the "sanctity of life" and on the obligation of the pacifist not to shed blood even in self-defense.[10] Yet Hiller was not without followers. His Revolutionary Pacifist Group was supported at one time or another by Rudolf Leonhard, Tucholsky, Erich Kästner, Count Harry Kessler, the philosopher Theodor Lessing, Klaus Mann (the son of Thomas Mann), Helene Stöcker, and others.[11]

The notion that the individual had the right, if not an obligation, to refuse military service, and that he had to prepare a revolution to prevent war, proved to be enormously popular among educated youth in the Anglo-Saxon countries. This amalgamation of Tolstoyan religious pacifism with elements of Marxism was to culminate in 1933 in the famous resolution of the Oxford Union in England "that this House refuses to fight for King and country." In Weimar Germany very few students joined organized pacifism. Comparing the German pacifists with their Western counterparts, Ossietzky found the Germans unrealistic, dogmatic, and overenthusiastic. He wrote about the annual congresses of the peace movement:

The main purpose of these events seems to be the physical training of its participants. . . . As a consequence, these congresses are dominated by the most turbulent instincts. They resemble an enormous bloodbath, accompanied by a massive chopping off of leading heads. . . . Herr Hiller swings his tomahawk, dripping with ink. . . . He says "humanity" but means "bludgeon"![12]

Or as he complained in the same article:

This movement is inundated by fanatics and sectarians of every conceivable denomination. Project makers with wonder drugs for all the ills of

---

[*] While the call of the socialist pacifists for the prevention of war through a general strike and a revolution was similar to Karl Liebknecht's and Rosa Luxemburg's prewar platform, it contradicted the Third International's call for the infiltration of the armies at war by Communist agitators and the revolutionary overthrow of the capitalist system not at the beginning, but at the end of the war. Hiller never ceased to point to this essential difference between his and the Communists' program. See, for instance, Kurt Hiller, "Kriegsdienstverweigerung," *Die Weltbühne*, May 7, 1929, pp. 694–696.

society; universal reformers who hate meat. . . . These people produce children only because they see no other solution, but they do it with a pronounced dislike. They would be happy only if they were allowed to prescribe a diet of kohlrabi for the entire human race.[13]

The pacifists are pure and courageous, Ossietzky commented, but utterly without talent. It is dreary enough to go through life as a peaceable man; the affair becomes hopeless if one is also stupid into the bargain.[14]

Nonetheless, German officialdom took the organized pacifists seriously. General Freiherr von Schoenaich and several other pacifist leaders were tried for treason.[15] Writing in 1958, the former Reichswehr minister of the republic, Otto Gessler, called the pacifists of the Weimar era "rootless *Literaten* of test-tube purity," "doctrinaire fanatics," or "scoundrels in French pay." Gessler regretted that the republic "had not exterminated these big-city sewer weeds [*Sumpfblüten*] root and branch." The pacifists, Gessler asserted, contributed to anti-Semitism because "they tore down, with cold cynicism, everything that healthy German national sentiment held sacred; because they hailed, as a sign of progress, every symptom of decadence."[16] As for the radical Right, it subjected the pacifists to the vilest terror. The pacifists Alexander Futran and the former captain Hans Paasche were murdered by nationalists; Lehmann-Russbüldt, Gerlach, Harden, and others were cruelly beaten.[17]

Even Ossietzky admitted that "leaders like Quidde, Gerlach, and Kessler achieved a great deal. At least at certain points, they broke through the dikes of German isolationism."[18] The German Peace Association, and especially the Bund Neues Vaterland or Deutsche Liga für Menschenrechte as the Bund was renamed in January 1922, made strong efforts to combat German chauvinism. As early as December 1919, they invited French pacifists to speak in Berlin. They aided unjustly accused or imprisoned leftists or brought their case to the attention of the Reichstag. They played a major role in unmasking the "patriotic" murders and illegal German rearmament. In 1926, the pacifists Kuczynski, Quidde, and Stöcker participated vigorously in the popular republican movement for the expropriation without indemnity of the rights and holdings of the German princes.[19] Following the example of the English Ponsonby, German pacifists attempted in the spring of 1927 to conduct a private plebiscite where the signatories pledged "not to take up arms, nor to support the armed forces in case of a war." Using the overwhelmingly leftist and working-class district around the city of Zwickau in Saxony for their experiment, the pacifists collected 86,000 signatures in a region inhabited by 650,000 people. Ninety-eight percent of the signatories were workers and house-wives.[20]

Fairly popular in the early 1920's, the German peace movement lost much of its support when the German government officially embraced the policy of international arbitration after Locarno. The "No More War" demonstrations and the "War on War" exhibitions had to be abandoned for lack of public interest. Hans Wehberg openly questioned in 1927 the justification of organized pacifism in the Locarno era.[21] As the moderates in the peace movement gradually dropped out, the radicals advanced into more important positions. In 1927, Quidde was replaced in the presidium of the Peace Association by a triumvi-rate in which Quidde represented the moderates, Schoenaich and Friedrich Küster, editor of *Das andere Deutschland,* the radicals.[22] An extraordinary congress of the Peace Association in the spring of 1929 brought the final triumph of the Küster faction; Quidde, Gerlach, and Kessler seceded from the association. Even Kurt Hiller failed to live up to the expectations of these radicals. He was expelled from the association in 1930 for having accused some pacifists of practicing "nationalism in reverse," and serving the interests of French imperial-ism.[23] The two previously sympathetic political parties, the SPD and the "Staatspartei" (the former Democratic Party) put the Peace Asso-ciation under interdiction, a move hastened by the association's sup-port of socialist and democratic splinter parties (SAPD [t] and "*Vereini-gung unabhängiger Demokraten*").[24] The great liberal newspapers, which until 1930 had faithfully reported on all pacifist activity, began to adjust themselves to the new temper of the nation and simply ignored the pacifists. By January 1933, the Peace Association had fewer than 5,000 members. The German peace movement had expired before Hitler came to power.

Tucholsky commented that organized pacifism with its abstract theories and philosophical loftiness never reached the "little" German. He recommended "guerilla methods": infiltration of the family and an appeal to the instinct of self-preservation. People must be told, he argued, that the only effects of war are a missing eye and a miserly pension. They must understand that one need not go to war at all. "This is a simple, a primitive, an uncomplicated, and great truism: one can just as well remain at home." [25]

---

[t] "Sozialistische Arbeiterpartei Deutschlands," the Socialist Workers' Party, a left-wing splinter group which seceded from the Social Democratic Party in October 1931. The history of the SAPD (or SAP) has been thoroughly studied by Hanno Drechsler, *Die Sozialistische Arbeiterpartei Deutschlands* (*SAPD*) (Meisenheim/Glan, 1965).

Tucholsky objected to the tendency of the German antiwar novelists, such as Erich Maria Remarque, to present war as a tragedy mitigated by the experience of human solidarity or by revolutionary zeal. War taught nothing except hatred for war: the literatis' task was to "unromanticize" war thoroughly and to show the murderer and the murdered in the soldier. As for the officer, he was a professional killer. A class-conscious aristocrat, selfish, self-indulgent, orgiastic, thievish, and profoundly reactionary, the German officer was worse than his worst social peers in civilian occupations. Corrupted by his occupation, he corrupted society. Tucholsky wrote in his postwar series of articles, *Militaria:*

> The German officer [during the war] . . . stole without hesitation, although almost always in great style. It began with some "souvenirs" (many an officer's wife still wears these souvenirs) and it ended with crammed boxcars.[26]

Or as he wrote in another place:

> In the East the *Rittmeister* [cavalry captain] posted himself before the . . . women auxiliaries [of the army] and indicated clearly that in the German army there was a far greater gap between officers and enlisted men than in the Russian army and that they should therefore have no commerce with enlisted men. "You belong to us officers!" [27]

Tucholsky's *Militaria* evoked an uproar of indignation in nationalist and even in republican circles. It was argued that most of the active officers fell in the campaign of 1914, and that thereafter the bulk of front-line officers was made up of civilians in uniform, clerks, teachers, and shopkeepers.[g] Unperturbed, Tucholsky pointed to the misbehavior of the staff officers in the wartime *Hinterland* and accused the German reserve officers of having feverishly embraced the debased values of the professional soldiers:

> The reserve officers in no way lagged behind [the professionals]. Oppressed by a strong sense of moral inferiority in respect to the "genuine" officers, they did their best to emulate their exalted prototypes, and they parodied and copied with varying ineptness the dashing lieutenant.[28]

Tucholsky cared nothing for the fact that his generalizations alienated even the officers of republican sentiment. He declared that there

---

[g] "From among the 33,000 active officers with whom the German Army had marched to war, a majority of the captains and lieutenants were killed within the first few months. But even without these losses, the old corps could not have begun to fill the need for officers. At the start of the offensive of March 1918 there were in service over 176,000 officers." Erich Eyck, *A History of the Weimar Republic* (Cambridge, Mass., 1962), I, 3.

were in the Weimar republic only a handful of republican officers and predicted rightly that even these few would be gradually eased out of active service. To court the officers in words and in deeds, as the government insisted on doing, guaranteed the continued hostility and contempt of the officer corps toward the republic:

There is no point in enlightening the officer on the anachronism and inhumanity of his mission; nor does it make sense to soften his hostility with concessions. It is not to the officers that we are talking but to our compatriots, the Germans, whom we love and whom we ask to categorically refuse obedience to those who demand of him deeds that debase the dignity of man. It debases the dignity of man to place discipline above moral insight.[29]

This last was a prophetic condemnation, to be leveled against the German nation after 1945.

In later years, when Tucholsky began to use Communist slogans, he adopted the simplistic view of the officer corps as a mere servant and defender of the capitalist class, that is, not a caste with its own interest and purpose. This approach, reflected in his *Deutschland, Deutschland über alles* (1929) blunted his antimilitarist campaign. For whether or not the Communists were correct, the *Weltbühne's* highly specialized attacks on the officers were neither useless, nor were they unpopular. More than once *Die Weltbühne* forced democratic politicians to start proceedings against the excesses of the Reichswehr, if not against the institution of the Reichswehr itself. Some of the journal's revelations involved the exploits of the short-lived "Black Reichswehr."

The Black Reichswehr had its origins in the Army High Command's preoccupation with the alleged threat of a Polish attack, and in the army's need to accommodate former members of the Free Corps who were unwilling or unable to return to civilian life.[30] The result was the formation in 1923 of the so-called "Arbeits-Kommandos," popularly known as the Black Reichswehr. The men of this secret reserve army, formed with the knowledge of President Ebert, Chancellor Cuno, and the Social Democratic Prussian Prime Minister Otto Braun, were financed, garrisoned, equipped, and trained by the army and placed under the immediate authority of the Berlin divisional commander. By September 1923, there were between 50,000 and 80,000 men in the Black Reichswehr under the organizational leadership of a Major Bruno Buchrucker and a Lieutenant Paul Schulz. The trouble came when the Free Corps element in the Black Reichswehr grew more interested in a political coup than in preparing for a defensive war

against Poland. Misunderstanding Seeckt's immediate plans, Major
Buchrucker in September 1923 ordered the mobilization of his troops
for the overthrow of the republic. When, however, he realized that
Seeckt did not desire a putsch at that time (Seeckt had just been made
temporary dictator of Germany by Ebert), Buchrucker betrayed his
own plans to the local army command. His men could no longer be
stopped, and the ensuing "Küstrin putsch" of October 1, 1923,[31] was
nipped in the bud by the regular army. The Black Reichswehr, its
secrecy betrayed by its own men, was subsequently suppressed. It was
to be replaced eventually by the "Schutzpolizei," a heavily armed
police force of almost 70,000 men. The Küstrin putsch itself was
branded a "National Bolshevist" outrage by the army command and
was soon forgotten.[h] In 1925, however, a certain Carl Mertens appeared before Siegfried Jacobsohn, identifying himself as a former,
and now disillusioned, member of the Black Reichswehr. He submitted a lengthy memorandum which Jacobsohn printed in a series of
sixteen articles, and later also published in book form.[32] The articles
contained ample evidence to show that the Black Reichswehr was
counterrevolutionary and terroristic, that its kangaroo courts (*Feme*
courts) had sentenced and executed several so-called traitors to the
Black Reichswehr, that Lieutenant Schulz at Küstrin was personally
implicated in these murders, and that there were intimate connections
between the commands of the Black and the regular Reichswehr. Soon
after the publication of these articles, the German Peace Association
submitted to the Reichstag a "white book" on the past exploits of the
Black Reichswehr.[33] In response to this campaign, the Prussian Landtag formed a special commission under Social Democratic leadership
to investigate the *Feme* murders.[34] The reports of the commission
made public in January 1926 fully corroborated Mertens' statement.
Since the Reichswehr was washing its hands of the whole affair, the
judiciary was called into action and several of the *Feme* murderers,
Lieutenant Schulz among them, were sentenced to death.[i] Now *Die
Weltbühne* again stepped into the picture. In his "Plaidoyer für

---

[h] Major Buchrucker was given ten years fortress confinement for his coup
d'etat but was released in 1927. Embittered by the army command's lack of
interest in his fate, he later developed sympathy toward "National Bolshevism"
and had friendly words for the left intellectuals. See his memoirs, *Im Schatten
Seeckts* (Berlin, 1928), and also Emil J. Gumbel, "*Verräter verfallen der Feme*,"
(Berlin, 1929), 235.
[i] According to Alfred Apfel, *Behind the Scenes of German Justice* (London,
1934), 92 f., at Schulz's numerous trials "the army experts withdrew visibly
farther and farther from Schulz," until the court had no alternative but to find
him guilty of murder. At the end, neither Schulz nor the other convicted Black
Reichswehr murderers suffered greater indignation than a few years in prison.

Schulz," written in March 1927, Berthold Jacob protested against the persecution of this young officer and indicated that persons responsible for the summary executions should be sought for in high army circles.[35] He implicated Colonel (later Field Marshal) von Bock directly in the murders and hinted that Colonel (later General and Chancellor) Schleicher and Seeckt were also responsible. As a result of the article, Jacob and the "responsible" editor of the *Weltbühne* (Ossietzky) were brought to trial. They were given sentences respectively of two and one months in prison (reduced in the appellate court to a fine and in 1928 commuted), but the *Feme* trial of the *Weltbühne* brought fresh revelations.[36] Lieutenant Schulz, who was called as a witness at the trial, did his best to protect his superiors, yet it became clear that the regular army was implicated in the murders and that the High Command had put pressure on Schulz to sacrifice himself for the prestige of the army. The "experts of the Reichswehr" who testified at the trial were repeatedly embarrassed by the defense, a humiliation for which the Reichswehr never forgave Jacob or Ossietzky.[j]

The running battle between the Reichswehr and the self-appointed investigators of army activities continued throughout the 1920's. After the Black Reichswehr affair, Friedrich Küster of *Das andere Deutschland*, Berthold Jacob, and others concentrated on secret rearmament and on the financial scandals that accompanied the army's handling of secret funds. It is more than likely that Gessler's resignation in January 1928 was triggered by a leftist press campaign against the war minister; Gessler affected ignorance of his subordinates' rather disastrous ventures into private business (*Lohmann-Skandal*).[37] Paralleling this activity was a phenomenal rise in indictments for treason. Before the war, there had been at most two or three treason trials a year; by the late 1920's they were to be counted in hundreds, with an increasing number of indictments for the hitherto unknown crime: "treason via the press."[k] [38]

It was against the judiciary, this faithful servant of military interests, that the *Weltbühne* writers ran their other campaign. In attacking the judges, these writers aimed also at the general overhaul of Weimer society: the "debarbarization" of its anachronistic mores.

---

[j] In March 1928, Jacob was sentenced to nine months' confinement in a fortress for an article written three years earlier in Küster's *Das andere Deutschland* on the Reichswehr's violation of the Versailles treaty (*Ponton Affäre*). On the Jacob-Küster trial, see Kurt R. Grossmann, "Der Landesverratsprozess gegen Pazifisten," *Die Menschenrechte*, March 31, 1928, pp. 8 ff.

[k] It must be stated in defense of Weimar, that at least until the 1930's, practically none of these treason trials landed the accused journalist in prison.

Chapter IX
FOR A HUMANE SOCIETY

THE REFORM OF JUSTICE

In Kurt Tucholsky's *Deutschland, Deutschland über alles,* published in 1929, there appeared a photograph of two young men proudly exhibiting horribly lacerated faces and bloodied aprons, surrounded by cheering friends. The photograph—of duelling law students at a traditional *Mensur* and captioned by Tucholsky, "German Judges of the Year 1940" [1]—was a reflection of the left-wing intellectuals' nightmarish view of the academic training of Germany's future masters. What the law faculties were turning out, according to this view, were self-mutilating madmen who would one day doff their blood-streaked aprons for judicial robes and sit in Bloody Assizes over progressive thought, cultural avant-gardism, and socialist aspirations.

Jabs at the German judiciary in left-wing intellectual literature were as constant as they were fierce. The German judge was presented as the quintessence of horror: brutal, power hungry, arrogant, and pompous. More unforgivably, he was a sanctimonious bookworm without charity or imagination. Solidly and stolidly ensconced on his bench, he used his overwhelming authority to regiment society and to crush the lower classes, robbing them of their dignity before robbing them of their freedom. The left-wing intellectuals viewed the members of the German judiciary as they did the military. The judges, too, transcended the authority vested in them by the ruling class to constitute a self-seeking, radically reactionary state within the state. Imagining themselves in acute danger from the republic, the judges were more ferociously antirepublican than other, less insecure groups within the establishment. With minds unopened by tutoring in the humanities, and having received the narrowest, meanest concepts of their own

122

profession, the judges stood bewildered before the ethical, philosophical, and social upheavals of their age. Exasperated by a world they did not understand, they grew more cruel with every new generation.[2] Against these people only one policy could be effective: outright and unrelenting criticism. All trials, political as well as criminal, were to be subjected to careful scrutiny and abuses brought into the open. "There is no such thing as an unpolitical criminal proceeding," wrote Tucholsky,[3] and with this dictum, he, Kurt Hiller, and other writers of the *Weltbühne* used the force of their considerable legal insight to plead the case not only of accused pacifists, Social Democrats, and Communists, but of those other victims of German class justice: common criminals.[4]

The left-wing intellectuals' image of German justice was undoubtedly overdrawn but in respect to political trials at least, it was correct in its essentials. The unethical comportment of German judges—and prosecutors—in political trials makes a separate chapter in Weimar history.[5] There is impressive statistical evidence, prepared mostly by *Weltbühne* collaborators, to prove that the judges of the republic were harsh on leftist political offenders and soft on "patriotic," nationalist, and anti-Semitic defendants. The *Weltbühne* writer Emil J. Gumbel demonstrated, and his statistics have never been challenged, that in the first four years of the republic German courts convicted 38 leftist offenders accused of 22 political murders. Ten of these defendants were executed, the rest were given an average of fifteen years in prison. In the same period, there were 354 rightist political murders but the courts convicted only 24 rightist offenders. Not one of these defendants was executed and those convicted received an average of four months in prison. Twenty-three of the confessed rightist murderers were acquitted.[6] "Political murder was not a risky undertaking," wrote Gumbel. "There were some political con men who made a good living parading as murderers, with financial support from rightist circles—until they were unmasked and done away with."[7]

Such a parody of justice could not have taken place without close cooperation from other official quarters. It was common for the police to ignore the well-known hiding place of a "patriotic" murderer or to let him escape if arrest was unavoidable. It was equally common for the prosecutor's office to delay the investigation of rightist offenses, to lose dossiers, or to suppress evidence. As to the judges, they found extenuating circumstances, or no guilt, in the face of the most blatant evidence. If sentence was meted out at all, it was invariably imposed on the little henchmen caught in the act. But it was also customary to accept the plea that the murderer had acted on higher orders. If the courts consented to name this higher authority, it was only to point an accusing finger at some republican politician. Following the 1919 massacre of Spartacist sailors in Berlin, the court gleefully cited the orders of the Social Democratic Minister Noske, without indicting the generals and officers who had given his orders (to shoot) the most liberal interpretation.[8] It was not unusual for the courts to take into consideration the political affiliation of the victim when deciding on the guilt of the murderer. In the trials that followed upon the Bavarian white terror of 1919, the murderers of pacifists, Social Democrats, or Communists were almost invariably found not guilty, while severe punishment was imposed on the counterrevolutionary soldiers who had killed a group of young Catholic workers.[9] The callousness of the judges toward the victims of nationalist terror went to ridiculous extremes; it also pointed up the courts' old-fashioned contempt of public opinion. Thus the courts consistently denied even the most miserly pension to the widows or orphans of murdered proletarians.[10]

All this is made somewhat understandable if one considers that, of the 12,000 practicing judges of the Weimar period, only 400 were members of the League of Republican Judges ("Republikanischer Richterbund," founded in 1922).[11] That none of the other judges was forced to resign, or that none voluntarily did so, was a catastrophe for German democracy.

Die Weltbühne and other radical democratic journals did their best to protest this intolerable situation. Indeed, next to the Communists and some Social Democrats, the left-wing intellectuals were the most effective in airing the scandal of political mistrials. It was as common for a defense attorney in a leftist political trial to vent his indignation in the pages of the *Weltbühne,* as it was common for the lawyer-journalists of the *Weltbühne,* Alfred Apfel, Kurt Rosenfeld, Rudolf Olden, and others, to assume the legal defense of leftist political offenders. The campaigns of *Die Weltbühne, Das Tage-Buch, Die Justiz* (the journal of the republican judges), and especially of the German League for Human Rights were neither unpopular nor always unsuccessful. They contributed significantly to the partial amelioration of the situation after the first turbulent years of the republic. As political murders declined after 1924, so did the political mistrials and, beginning that year, *Die Weltbühne* could devote its attention to general judicial reform and to the fate of common criminals.

The *Weltbühne's* indictment of nonpolitical criminal proceedings was as harsh as that of political justice and it was more often unwarranted. The humane practices of a great number of judges and their conscientious application of modern penological concepts received little acknowledgment. Nor did *Die Weltbühne* take into account the public clamor for harsh sentences on common criminals. But it is also true that there were several mistrials. There was the famous case of Josef Jakubowski, an illiterate Polish laborer who though innocent was sentenced to death for murder and executed in 1925.[12] One must agree with the *Weltbühne* that Jakubowski's foreign origin, poverty, and ignorance played a role in the hasty sentence and execution. Nor can the authorities be excused for having delayed revision procedures. The "Jakubowski revision" was the German left-wing intellectuals' Sacco and Vanzetti affair and here too they were not unsuccessful. The Jakubowski Foundation of the German League for Human Rights which included the *Weltbühne* collaborators Heinrich Mann, Hellmut von Gerlach, Arnold Zweig, Alfred Apfel, Kurt Grossmann, Helene Stöcker, Paul von Schönaich, and Veit Valentin, as well as Thomas Mann and others, was highly persevering. Finally, in 1929 the real murderers were tried and sentenced, and the dead Jakubowski was partially rehabilitated.[13] But the high functionaries responsible for the mistrial and for the delay in revision proceedings were never brought to account.

The *Weltbühne*'s criticism of criminal proceedings can be briefly summarized. It began with the contention that because of their social background and biased education, the judges could not possibly be objective toward proletarian criminals.[14] This was a convincing argument, for neither in the Imperial era nor during the republic could a judicial functionary hope to draw an income before the age of thirty-five. Then, his beginning salary amounted to a few hundred marks.[15] Consequently, judges were recruited from among the "better estates." Having been subjected to the severest discipline in his years of training, the new judge expected the same abject obedience from his underlings and from the defendants. Tucholsky was outraged by the judges' insistence that the defendant show soldierly discipline, that he be *stramm* in the dock and accept with humility the sternest pronouncements. Repeatedly Tucholsky scorned the barrack-room atmosphere prevailing in the courts, the contemptuous tone used by the judges, and their predilection for assuming the role of the prosecutor.[16] Self-respect on the part of the defendant was equated with arrogance; protestations of innocence with lack of repentance. Unusual morality or asocial behavior were taken as evidences of guilt for any crime, or at least as aggravating factors. "The judges consider acquittal a defeat not only for the prosecutor but even for themselves," wrote Tucholsky.[a] [17] They assume the guilt of the defendant "for were he not guilty he wouldn't be in the courtroom." Alfred Polgar ridiculed the judges' tendency to expect higher moral standards from a criminal than from an ordinary mortal.[18] If he falls short of this expectation he is taken for a particularly heinous criminal. The woman accused of murder is burdened with the additional crime of bestiality for having eaten something after the deed, worse even, if she happened to eat a delicacy.[19] The defendant who receives a twenty-year sentence and cries miserably is severely admonished by the judge: "You must behave correctly!" Easier said than done. How is one to behave under similar circumstances? What does the *Ehrenkodex* prescribe for such occasions? The judge first denies the status of gentleman to the defendant and then he expects from him gentlemanly behavior.[20]

One particular sore point in the eyes of the left-wing intellectuals was the seeming failure of the system of lay judges (*Schöffen*) and jurors (*Geschworene*). The introduction of laymen in certain court proceedings had been an accomplishment of the 1848 revolution; now jury trials were to be the mainstay of Weimar democracy, the popular alternative to professional jurisdiction. Unfortunately, the lay jurors proved to be as exasperating as the professional members of the court. They were either too harsh or incomprehensibly lenient in their decisions. Hans Gathmann discussed in the *Weltbühne* the famous jury trial of the butcher Trautmann: [21] Back in 1911 Trautmann had been sentenced to twelve years in prison for having killed a young girl. There was in this case not a shred of evidence, but because the victim had been masterfully dissected and because Trautmann had been guilty, among other things, of incest, the jury brought down the verdict of murder. Finally proved innocent of murder, the butcher was not rehabilitated, nor did he receive any compensation for the twelve years he had spent in prison. On the other hand, complained Ernst Emil Schweitzer in the *Weltbühne*,[22] two women who had slowly poisoned their husbands were so mildly treated by the jury that they could be given only four years each in prison.

When it came to political trials, the juries showed less inconsistency.

---

[a] Tucholsky knew that his general indictment was exaggerated. But he excused himself by saying: "Collective indictments are always unjust, but they should and ought to be unjust. The critics of society have the right to regard the lowest type in a group as representative of that group. After all, the group tolerates that type; by not expelling him, it approves of him and thus incorporates him into the group spirit." Ignaz Wrobel [Kurt Tucholsky], "Deutsche Richter," *Gesammelte Werke*, II, 773.

Invariably protective toward rightist defendants, they were vicious toward leftist offenders. They simply refuse to indict a patriotic murderer, wrote Schweitzer.[23] As a result, prosecutors interested in obtaining an indictment, any indictment, were forced to change a first-degree murder into involuntary manslaughter, and an attempted murder into an assault-and-battery charge.

A flagrant case of mistrial by a jury, one that particularly outraged the writers of *Die Weltbühne*, was that of the would-be assassins of Maximilian Harden.[24] On July 3, 1922, the 61-year-old Harden was attacked by a group of young men and nearly beaten to death. One of his assailants, a radical nationalist office clerk was immediately captured; the other, a former officer, escaped to Austria and was extradited only a year later. It became unmistakably clear at the first two trials that the assailants had been hired by a nationalist bookseller who in turn had acted as middleman for the "Organisation Consul," a notorious white-terrorist organization. The murderers' wage amounted to 766 gold marks. Despite the undisputed evidence, the jury found all sorts of extenuating circumstances at the second trial. The one assailant present was given two years and 9 months in prison, the middleman four years and 9 months.[b] Leaders of the Organisation Consul were never indicted. What seemed terrible was not so much the mild verdict of the jury but the general conduct of the trial. The defendants were treated most politely and Harden as a criminal. The attorneys for the defense—both Jews—were allowed to argue that Harden had brought upon himself the attack by his unpatriotic literature. The judge—also a Jew—and the attorneys made sarcastic references to the Jewishness of Harden. According to Tucholsky, the judge did his best to silence the witnesses for the state. "This was no bad justice—wrote Tucholsky—this was no defective justice. It was no justice whatsoever. . . . The verdict is clear. It amounts to incitement for the next [murder]."[25]

The rightist bias of most juries was only partly explained by their unrepresentative social composition. As Rudolf Olden has shown, in some rural areas, especially in East Prussia, practically all jurors were landowners or other "better people." In the cities it was rare to see a workingman among the jurors.[26] But even juries of somewhat more mixed social composition seemed to show tolerance toward "patriotic"

---

[b] Lieutenant Ankermann, who had escaped to Austria, was tried in 1924 and was sentenced to six years in prison. He benefited from an amnesty four years later. See Heinrich Hannover and Elisabeth Hannover-Drück, *Politische Justiz 1918–1933* (Frankfurt/M., 1966), 132.

offenders. As Schweitzer pointed out, juries were responsible both for the scandal of the Harden trial and for the acquittal of the Kapp putschists. Moreover, wrote Schweitzer, when in Berlin the jury sentenced to death an innocent Communist defendant, the three expert judges used their legal authority to overrule the mad verdict.[27] What then was to be done? The writers of the *Weltbühne* reluctantly suggested measures that in any genuine, democratic state would have qualified as antidemocratic. The dilemma of the left-wing intellectuals was rarely as evident as in their grapplings with legal justice. Highly suspicious of the state and of the educated public, but even more suspicious of those on the bench, they recommended state and public interference with judicial proceedings. Schweitzer dismissed the Social Democratic argument that jury justice was but the expression of the will of the people. In politically and socially divided Germany, he held, there is no such thing as the will of the people: jury trials must be suspended![28] Schweitzer also recommended that the Minister of Justice apply rigorous standards in the selection of judges to criminal courts, and that he be obliged to consult private lawyers when making such appointments. Political crimes, especially crimes committed through the press (*Pressedelikte*), mutiny and revolutionary agitation, were to be tried not by a corps of judges (*Kollegien*) but by specially selected justices (*Richter-Könige*) as it was done in England. This would provide for the individual responsibility of judges. Furthermore, Schweitzer suggested that the Minister of Justice exercise strict control over the state prosecutor's office. He cited as particularly outrageous the notorious case of the Marburg students who, in 1920, had brutally murdered fifteen suspected Spartacists and who were subsequently acquitted by a jury upon the prosecutor's recommendation.[29] The government should have the right, Schweitzer insisted, to examine and overrule miscarriages of justice. Finally, Schweitzer recommended that both lawyers and prosecutors be entitled to appeal to the Supreme Court against all miscarriages of justice. Philosophic or ethical objections to a sentence should have the same validity as legal objections.[30] Besides requesting extensive state interference, Schweitzer also asked for public, especially journalistic, control of judicial proceedings. This request was repeated by several other *Weltbühne* writers who insisted that the state prosecutor be obliged to provide the newspapers with relevant trial material. Control by "publicity," by the political parties and the trade unions, was the remedy of Manfred George.[31] The basic problem, the writers of the *Weltbühne* clearly saw, was the immunity, independence, and irremovability of the judges. In obvious reversal of the old democratic creed, they demanded an end to these privileges: "German judicial reform is simply unthinkable without the suspension by the parliament of the present irremovability of the judges," wrote Tucholsky.[32] What he and the other left-wing intellectuals sought, essentially, was the replacement of one brand of politically influenced justice by another. This was a revolutionary demand. Could it be accomplished without a revolution? And would "proletarian justice" heralded by the Communists come any closer to the ideal of humanitarian *Rechtsstaat* that these intellectuals so doggedly pursued? There was no answer to these questions.

Fortunately for the writers of the *Weltbühne* there was simply no end to the republic's juridical and penological scandals, and other battles beckoned: capital punishment (institutional murder, they called it); the archaic prison system (Tucholsky led a vigorous but unsuccessful campaign for alleviating the sexual deprivation of convicts); [33] compulsory religious training in prison; [34] the bureaucratic and social ostracism of former convicts.[35] Finally, there was the vast question of public morality, or rather the anachronistic and hypocritical public control of private morals: the legal persecution of "sexual aberration," incest, abortion, indecent exposure, pornography, and blasphemy. On all of these issues *Die Weltbühne* took a radically progressive stand.

SEXUAL ETHICS AND ARTISTIC FREEDOM

The German intellectual ferment in the first years of the twentieth century was above all a revolt against conventional morality. It was in protest against the morality of their elders that the middle class boys and girls of the "Wandervogel" movement fled to the forests, there to "live in a state of nature." The term was as ingenuous as the sentiment. What this youthful communion with nature amounted to was little more than the singing of folksongs, the celebration of the winter solstice, and the scientific discussion of sex.[36] Even those in the Wandervogel (the later Youth Movement) who went beyond that cultivated not so much the pleasures of the flesh as an exalted form of homosexuality with emphasis on the "true" friendship between men. As late as the 1920's, rebellious young Communist intellectuals engaged in free love with a dead seriousness that, according to Margarete Buber-Neumann, an early disciple, imposed harsher rules than did the worst of the philistine regulations.[37]

The tone of the campaign against conventional morality which pervaded much of the prewar German literature—particularly the dramas of Frank Wedekind, Carl Sternheim, and Walter Hasenclever —was as defiant as it was hesitant and guilt-ridden. In the final act of Hasenclever's drama, *Der Sohn* (1914), the hero triumphantly declares to his prudish father that he has just spent a night with a woman, an act to be redeemed by death—not his own, but his father's.[38]

But whereas, before the war, sexual freedom had been the prerogative of fictional heroes, or the rather ritualistic practice of some literati, it became at the war's end a concern in the everyday life of millions of Germans. If Ossietzky was correct in his contention that the sole achievement of the war and of the revolution was the emancipation of German women,[39] then a drastic change in sexual mores was an obvious concomitant.

The numerous and enormously popular books on contemporary mores (*Sittengeschichten*)[40] attest the fact that, in the Roaring Twenties, Germany offered the most to seekers of erotic freedom. It was a time when every conceivable form of sexual indulgence was given the freest expression. There was a boom in erotic literature, and in the cabarets and theaters the *nouveaux riches* were treated to a then novel display of female nudity.[41] A curious consequence of the November Revolution, and of the German predilection for forming clubs, was that homosexuals, nudists, or prostitutes could found their own organizations, complete with a board of directors and a monthly journal.[e]

But if there was a change in practice, there was none in legislation. On the contrary, because they needed Catholic support, the Social Democrats and the Democratic Party threw to the winds their enlightened moral reform program.[42] Thus the state continued as the stern guardian of private morals. While this did not seem to disturb the neoconservative intellectuals of the Stefan George type for whom sexual freedom had always been an affair of the elite, it angered the left-wing intellectuals who perceived in official puritanism a strong weapon of the bourgeoisie. For the bourgeois was allowed to punish the proletariat in public for acts he himself committed in private.

Shortly before the war, Heinrich Mann erected a monument to the repressed and repressive bourgeois in *Der Untertan* whose hero, a champion of purity, discipline, and all other German virtues, found his

----

[e] See the biting satire in the *Weltbühne* on the homosexual association "Deutscher Freundschaftsverband" (German Friendship Association): Peter Squenz, "Sexual Schlaraffia," *Die Weltbühne,* October 6, 1921, pp. 359–360. Here, the author wrote, homosexuals cultivate German pathos and idealism, i.e., they preach "pure love" as opposed to filthy carnal relations with women.

greatest satisfaction in being thrashed and humiliated by his wife in the secrecy of the bedroom.[43] Their wartime experience in officers' quarters convinced many of these intellectuals that this was no mere fiction and that sadomasochism, and the cult of the raucous and the vulgar, were indeed the dominant traits of *gutbürgerliche* or aristocratic sexuality.

Bourgeois hypocrisy created a world of intolerable contradictions. In Germany, where there were every year more than a million illegal abortions,[44] section 218 of the criminal code forbade abortion even in cases of rape or incest. The victims of this law were naturally the poor and the unwary. Section 175 threatened with prosecution any form of homosexuality, and the Law Against Trash and Smut (*Schund- und Schmutzgesetz*) adopted by the parliament in December 1926, promised severe punishment to the corrupters of youth through literature. Adultery and blasphemy, among other things, were also strictly forbidden.[45]

These laws, the left-wing intellectuals argued, were divorced from reality and invited criminal action. Starting out from the utilitarian premise that "society has only one right: to protect itself against those who threaten its order," [46] and from the Freudian premise that for the individual to flourish, he must have the right to use his body as he chooses,[47] the writers of the *Weltbühne* demanded that in sexual matters the state restrict itself to the protection of youth and of the defenseless.

Kurt Hiller, who founded the "Kartell für Reform des Sexualstrafrechts" (Cartel for the Reform of Sexual Legislation, 1927), believed that only complete sexual freedom would permit the "liberation of Eros from the Babylonian captivity of Sexus," meaning the decline of both unnatural asceticism and exaggerated preoccupation with the sexual impulse. He coupled his campaign for the "intellectualization of politics" with a call for the "intellectualization of Sexus." [48] Most of the other *Weltbühne* writers viewed the reform of moral legislation as a social rather than a philosophical problem. Compassion and charity demanded that the laws against homosexuality be abolished. In a diatribe against the part of the projected German criminal code dealing with homosexuality, Magnus Hirschfeld pointed to the ridiculous extremes of the new law which threatened with imprisonment any adult who engaged in immoral acts with minors or with his own employees. This means, Hirschfeld wrote, that a 19-year-old boy who kisses an 18-year-old can be sent to prison.[49] Such a law would only benefit the blackmailers, he warned.

Far more serious than the interdiction on homosexual practices was the law against abortion which, as the years progressed, was applied with increasing vigor. The strong stand taken on this issue by the writers of the *Weltbühne* coincided, however, with the program of the Social Democrats and was less sweeping than the postwar Independent Socialist plan. Writing in 1925, Erich Leisar imputed to the Church and the military authorities responsibility for the ever-growing number of convictions for illegal abortion.[50] He demanded that abortion be made permissible to all unmarried women within the first three months of pregnancy and also to those married women who already had two children. Charlatans were to be prosecuted, and only medical doctors allowed to perform abortion. In an earlier article, Manfred George complained about those who refused to understand the difference between conception—due to passion or drive—and birth, which was a matter of reasoned decision.[51] The state had no right to control births, especially after the abolition of universal military service, the only justification for enforcing birth after conception. Unconditionally progressive on the issue of abortion, George was more cautious when it came to the political rights of women. Confessing disappointment over the conservative voting pattern of women in Germany, he advocated in the same article the replacement of ordinary female suffrage with a separate female suffrage on questions affecting women. Thus a Chamber of Mothers was to decide on birth and war, questions related to the life of the nation.[52]

The cruelty of the anti-abortion law became conspicuous during the Depression when the government of the Catholic chancellor Brüning came down hard on poverty-stricken women who could not afford the secrecy of professional abortionists. Led by Helene Stöcker, another founder of the Cartel for the Reform of Sexual Legislation, the *Weltbühne* writers intensified their campaign against section 218.[d] In 1931, the *Weltbühne* collaborator Dr. Friedrich Wolf and his colleague, Dr. Else Kienle, were arrested for practicing abortion. Wolf was a Communist; his 1929 play *Cyankali* had most violently denounced the abortion law of the republic. Since he himself had not performed a single abortion, his arrest was undoubtedly a form of literary censorship. Dr. Kienle's hunger strike in prison and the subsequent release of the two doctors were celebrated in the *Weltbühne* as one of the few victories of that sad year.[53]

The battle between the republic and the left-wing intellectuals over

---

[d] This campaign coincided with that of Münzenberg's "Internationale Arbeiterhilfe" for the repeal of section 218.

sexual freedom had its ironical overtones. For on few other issues were both the government and the radical Left similarly attacked. Entirely innocent of the writings of Magnus Hirschfeld and the other *Weltbühne* writers, the republican government was nevertheless indicted by the entire Right for catering to these ideas. Left intellectual ethical radicalism was a heaven-sent gift to the nationalists. But as the Right would have besmirched the republic in any case, there was no reason for the left-wing intellectuals to abandon a fight in which they strongly believed.

The problem of "blasphemy" was closely connected with that of the rights of the artist. Article 118 of the Weimar Constitution guaranteed the freedom of expression "in words, writing, print, or pictures" and forbade censorship except over films and pornographic literature. Later, because of political terror from the Right, the state felt obliged to supplement this article with emergency laws for the defense of the republic. These laws were implemented more against agitators from the Left than from the Right. There were, for instance, a series of court proceedings against revolutionary proletarian writers.[54] The prosecution of the painter George Grosz, however, had less political than religious overtones. No doubt, the political caricatures of Grosz for a long time had irritated the authorities. Were this not so, matters would hardly have come to a trial in 1929 where Grosz and his publisher, Wieland Herzfelde, were condemned by a law court ("Schöffengericht") for blasphemy (*Gotteslästerung*) and sentenced to two months in prison convertible into fines amounting separately to 2000 marks.[55] The artist and his publisher were tried for the content of three drawings, one of which depicted Christ on the Cross wearing a gas mask and military boots. The inscription read: "Shut up and obey!" (*Maul halten und weiterdienen*). As it was not clear whether these words were meant to issue from the mouth of Christ, or of the onlooker, the inscription became one of the fine points debated at the trial. That the artist had not intended to insult God, religion, or the churches, was affirmed in the appellate court by the judge himself who explained that Grosz had only satirized those priests who preached war in the name of Jesus. Ruling twice, successively, that God or the churches had no reason to feel offended, Judge Siegert acquitted the defendants. It is true that the Supreme Court reversed this acquittal and referred the case to a lower court,° but Judge Siegert's rulings were nevertheless

---

° There was to be no new George Grosz trial because the artist left Germany on January 12, 1933, to settle in the United States.

considered a major triumph for artistic freedom. *Die Weltbühne,* which had helped to make this a *cause célèbre,* was again jubilant.[56] The ruling did not, however, reverse Tucholsky's earlier verdict: "We have no more justice. Il y avait des juges à Berlin." [57]

The occasional prosecution of pornography led the *Weltbühne* to discuss the exasperating problem of the sources of moral authority in a secular state. Even before the adoption by the Reichstag in 1925 of a rigorous law against pornography, some courts showed an excess of puritanical zeal by confiscating valuable literature. Thus in 1922 a criminal court ordered the seizure of a German edition of two volumes of poems by Verlaine, and the novel *Venus und Tannhäuser,* by Aubrey Beardsley. The Reichsgericht upheld the ruling of the lower court with the argument that these publications, despite their artistic merit, offended the sensibilities of a majority of Germans. Tucholsky found this ruling ridiculous on two grounds. He held that more than a minority of the population acknowledged the prerogative of the artists to use erotic subjects, and, secondly, that the Reichsgericht had no competence to inculcate morals. There are two possibilities, Tucholsky argued: either the Reichsgericht believes that it is its duty to protect existing cultural standards and thus to proclaim "what is." In this case, the majority opinion should be somehow ascertained and the minority allowed to argue its own case. For the court has no right to treat a part of the population as nonexistent. Or again the court asserts its competence to ignore public opinion and to dictate desirable standards. In this case, it erred in its ruling for it defended false, hypocritical values.[58]

The daring artist, the convicted criminal, the abortionist mother, the homosexual, and the prostitute were members of defenseless minorities. They were little people confronting a powerful state and class dictatorship. It was the duty of the *Weltbühne* to plead their case.

Part Three

A CRUSADE FOR SOCIALIST UNITY

Chapter X
UNITY ON A SOCIAL-DEMOCRATIC PLATFORM, 1918–1923

When they went down in 1933, Social Democrats and Communists could look back on fourteen years of working-class disunity, unmitigated by a single instance of genuine interparty cooperation. The Social Democrats wondered whether they could justify having collaborated with bourgeois parties that had ultimately betrayed them, and the Communists ought to have wondered whether they had been reasonable in maintaining themselves in isolation, or in voting (and occasionally working) with the Nazis. Both groups had always recognized working-class unity as a necessity; they made it their main program, and devoted infinite rhetoric—and energy—to its realization. But ideological, strategic, and personal differences, as well as the habit of appealing to members of the other party over the heads of its leaders, made even tactical alliances between the two parties almost impossible. This was the tragedy of the German Left, the impasse for which the writers of the *Weltbühne* struggled to find issue. They tirelessly canvassed the possibilities for socialist unity, reviewing in the process their own uneasy relationship to the two socialist parties and to Marxist ideology. With their views unobscured by the fetishism of the "Party," and their journal wide open to debate, they presented themselves as sincere advocates of unification.

In the first six or seven years of the republic, the journal called for the realization of socialism and for unity among the workers on the basis of the Social Democratic program, although certainly not under the auspices of the SPD *Bonzen*. When these hopes foundered, the *Weltbühne* tentatively suggested the creation of a "New Left," that is,

137

a common front of individual Communists, Social Democrats, and other leftists, independent of the SPD or KPD executives. At the same time, although they never accepted Communist ideology or the KPD leaders, most of these writers tended to look with sympathy at some manifestations of Communist militancy. They themselves were ready to cooperate with the Communists in a number of political undertakings. After 1928, when hopes for the new German Left had to be abandoned, an increasing number of *Weltbühne* writers embraced a Communist revolutionary program and tried to persuade the do-nothing leaders of the KPD, as well as the left-wing Social Democrats, to make a revolution against the growing threat of German fascism.

Socialist unity was the supreme goal of the *Weltbühne* writers. They, who knew so little of the workers, devoted a great part of their energies to ending disunity in the working-class movement. This was because they recognized that only the workers had the discipline, the courage, and the devotion to prevent the triumph of barbarism in Germany. The failure of the *Weltbühne*, insignificant compared with the massive failure of working-class leadership, does not in any way distract from the value of its efforts. The journal's running analysis of the policies of the working-class parties was, if not always profound, at least always provocative; its propositions were often utopian but just as often tempting. Who is to say today that the recommendations of the *Weltbühne* circle, had any of them been accepted and tried, would not have helped save Germany from fascism?

Essential agreement with the Social Democratic platform in the early 1920's did not mean approval of the SPD. First and foremost, it was the issue of peace and pacifism which separated the journal from this party. The Majority Socialists' role during the war, their extreme reluctance, when they headed the republic, to accept the peace terms of the Allies, their later support of passive resistance in the Ruhr, made them the object of bitter attack.

The *Weltbühne* writers were convinced, at least in the early 1920's, that only from Germany did a dangerous imperialism emanate. It was therefore rational and incumbent upon the SPD to cooperate with the Allies. The Marxist precept, that capitalism and its later stage of imperialism necessitated war, could be invalidated: violence, argued Norbert Rosenberg at the time of the Ruhr crisis, did not always enhance the prospects of capitalist competition, and some capitalist powers such as England and the United States had not really been imperialist until after World War I, and still had no highly developed war industry. If war was not inevitable, it was in the interest of socialists to ally with pacifists in mass movements against war.[1] The SPD's refusal to give such a policy whole-hearted support was irrational: "Is it really a law of nature," asked Heinrich Ströbel, "that reason should forever be excluded from the international life of peoples?"[2]

The criterion of "rationality" was frequently used in the *Weltbühne's* critiques of the socialist parties. Because of "irrationality" the journal did not side wholly with the Independent Socialists whose leaders it generally preferred to the Majority Socialists. The Independents, or at least their radical wing, espoused the program of proletarian revolution and proletarian dictatorship through a soviet regime, a doctrine which *Die Weltbühne* categorically rejected. Heinrich Ströbel's campaign against *Rätediktatur* (Soviet dictatorship) was all the more vehement, as the dominant message of the journal to the Left throughout these years was for a coalition of the SPD and the moderate wing of the USPD.

On November 21, 1918, the Spartacus League held a great public meeting. The address to the meeting by the moderate Independent Emil J. Gumbel was printed in its entirety in the subsequent issues of the *Weltbühne.* Gumbel stressed his lack of sympathy with the Majority Socialists who had betrayed the workers all through the war, and who now seemed unwilling or unable to counter the reassertion of the militarists. And yet, Gumbel asserted, the National Assembly had to be supported because proletarian dictatorship had no chance of survival. In the first place, the proletariat of the rest of Europe, that is, of the Entente countries, could not be counted on to be as revolutionary as it was in a defeated country. In the second place, any program which went too far in nationalizing the economy would antagonize the rest of the country outside of a few centers such as Berlin. A breakdown in production would follow, and the prospects of counterrevolution greatly enhanced. Only through the National Assembly, said Gumbel, could a program of reform be instituted because only the Assembly could control the old-régime bureaucrats. If the proletariat truly constitutes a majority, then socialists should have nothing to fear from a Constituent Assembly, Gumbel concluded. Anything else would merely show a lack of faith in the working class.[3]

The main themes of this address—the inevitable isolation of the working class when acting in its own interests alone, the inevitability of economic chaos were such action successful, and the superiority of the counterrevolutionary forces—were essentially those expounded time and again by the *Weltbühne* writers during the next five years. *Rätediktatur* was irrational, that is, impossible, therefore it was in the best interests of the proletariat to support parliamentary democracy.

All this did not prevent the *Weltbühne* from expressing contempt for the government Social Democrats. "The wretched state of politics in Germany is reflected in the condition of German Social Democracy," wrote Ströbel. Scheidemann and Ebert were too dull, soft, and narrow to be real leaders. They "connect an undeniable business sense and the unspeakable self-confidence of mediocrity with the greatest ability for self-adjustment" to any situation.[4] While covering the SPD leaders with invectives, the *Weltbühne* called the Spartacus League leaders Rosa Luxemburg and Karl Liebknecht "children of fire" and "tragic heroes."[5] Contradictory as this might seem, it expressed the journal's conviction that Ebert and his friends were traitors to a good cause, or at best inadequate to their task, while the Spartacist leaders were courageous and attractive champions of a false idea. Following the suppression of the Spartacists, the *Weltbühne* accused the SPD of ignoring the real need of the workers, of relying on reactionaries for their suppression, and thereby driving the workers to all the more revolutionary illusions. It was a critique of the SPD on the basis of its own program.

When in the spring of 1919 the Socialists in the Prussian government called in the army against the Communists, or when the Reich government used the army to break the strikes of the Ruhr miners, these actions were condemned in the *Weltbühne*. Although, wrote Heinrich Ströbel, the demands of the miners were economically impossible, the workers should have been won over through understanding and reason. The SPD ought to get rid of its Noskes; "a Socialist republic can never be achieved through a pact with militarism, but only through a block of the democratic Left."[6] The workers' uprising in Hamburg in the autumn of that year, against which Noske had sent the Free Corps, exasperated Ströbel. The workers had risen, he wrote, because of their wrath "against the scandalous capitalist economy which endures despite revolution and republic."

All these sections [of the population] are embittered by privation and indignant about capitalist profiteers who are getting rich at the expense of the working classes . . . ; they are disappointed in the government which recoils from any effective intervention into the rotten system. . . . What has the clique in Weimar done for us? It has allowed the war profiteers to drag away their billions abroad and intends neither to carry out a radical taxation of the rich nor a real socialization . . . We . . . want them to put an end to capitalism and its exploitation. If the class-state cannot fulfill our demands, if capitalism thereby is ruined, so much the better! We do not want to galvanize it, but to build up a new social system on the rubble of the old, collapsed system.[7]

Such militant language, not at all infrequent in the *Weltbühne* stemmed from a genuine concern with human suffering; it did not stem from any real belief in the necessity of overthrowing capitalism and was indeed belied by the journal's concrete politics. For, as Ströbel continued in the same article, it was a "fatalistic self-destructiveness which has befallen the masses of people," against which the government was desperately fighting but with the most unenlightened and helpless methods. Noske's prohibition of strikes was oil cast on fire. Because of men like Noske, the radical Left was growing in the whole country along with all the other signs of inevitable political and economic dissolution. Economic anarchy cannot be reined in with the machine guns of the officers' guard.[8] Obviously, the exhortation to rid the country of capitalism could not be squared with a concern over the dissolution of the state and economy. Ströbel's editorials in the *Weltbühne* were intended, rather, to warn the SPD that unless it used its power to reintegrate the rebellious workers into the current social order, the result would be a bloody revolution. Certainly, wrote Ströbel, still in 1919, capitalism had "outlived its time . . . socialism is the order of the day." A planned economy should take the place of an arbitrary market in which labor was so unproductively allocated. But there were two ways of attaining socialism: "organically," or through "painful convulsion";

those who want to bring the world, recently brought out of balance, back into equilibrium, and wish for a peaceful balance of social forces in place of the brute force of both Left and Right, must make all effort to participate in the execution of socialist economic principles.[9]

What Ströbel meant by these principles was the amelioration of the living conditions of the proletariat.[10] Thus, his socialism was not different from the program of reform advocated and eventually carried out by Social Democrats wherever they were in power in Europe. The *Weltbühne* was telling the SPD to be consistent with its own reformist platform.

As to the USPD, and the Communists, they were to give up their basic programs. The Spartacists, through their "uncritical parroting of the Bolshevik ABC, which has not even been adequate for the primitive economic conditions of Russia, have forfeited any right to be considered as agents for political and social transformation." The USPD had to break with these elements decisively, ally itself with the SPD, preferably under the leadership of Rudolf Hilferding and Karl Kautsky.[11] When, in October 1920, at the Halle Congress, the majority of the USPD leaders followed Zinoviev's exhortations and joined the KPD, Ströbel commented in the *Weltbühne* that ultimately Zinoviev's real "allies" in this deplorable act were the miserable conditions of the German workers and the arrogance of the wealthy.[12]

The *Weltbühne's* opposition to *Rätediktatur* was in part determined by its early evaluation of the Bolshevik revolution. The journal had a keen analyst of Soviet affairs in Elias Hurwicz, a Russian emigré, who shared with Ströbel and other writers the conviction that the Soviet regime was a dictatorial, utopian experiment in a backward country, entirely the product of Russian history and having nothing to do with Marxism.[13] He tended to sympathize with the exiled Constituent Assembly, but opposed any foreign intervention as well as Menshevik hopes for deposing the Bolsheviks.[14] Nevertheless, articles condemning "Tartar Socialism" were very frequent.[15] The Bolshevik goal of world revolution, pronounced particularly at the Second Congress of the Third International in July 1920, was regarded by Ströbel as proof that the Bolsheviks were "determined that no country should avoid that period of economic destruction resulting from the irrationality of a soviet directed economy."[16] World revolution meant sabotage of the world economy, on the shambles of which the Bolsheviks expected to take over. What would actually result, as was clear from the history of Béla Kun's Hungarian Soviet Republic, was the triumph of counterrevolution.[17] At the same congress, Trotsky had attempted to refute these arguments, publicly posed by Karl Kautsky. Trotsky's protestations— that economic stagnation was due to the blockade, intervention, and the necessity imposed on Soviet Russia to fight a civil war—were, wrote Ströbel, correct but irrelevant. Here lay "the basic mistake of Bolshevik calculation":

They proclaimed the Soviet dictatorship without realizing that this step would tear Russia up, plunge it into the bloodiest civil war and make it prey to foreign imperialism! They were satisfied with the incredible illusion that Russia's example would spark world revolution everywhere. . . . Instead of learning from their first mistake, Trotsky and Lenin have made a system out of it: the theory and strategy of world revolution, to be unleashed in all of Europe. Once again, they see nothing but their own strength, calculate only their own chess-moves, without considering the enormous counter-forces. Their world-revolutionary speculations must end in the same Russian failure.[18]

Economic chaos, inevitably resulting from a transfer of power, was the lesson to be learned from the Bolshevik experience. For, speculated Ströbel, if the working class in North Germany were successful in setting up a Soviet republic—an admitted impossibility—what then? They would face "the break-away of the Rhineland and South Germany, the most terrible shortages of coal, iron, ore, wheat; in short, the same economic catastrophe that Soviet Russia has undergone." [19] Neither a civil war nor the truncation and destruction of Germany was in the interest of general cultural development and world socialization; the building of socialism is only possible in peace. [20]

The argument that *Rätediktatur* was irrational because of the economic chaos it would incur is based on the assumption that a revolutionary proletariat was, and would indefinitely remain, only a small part of society as a whole. The ultimate argument against *Rätediktatur* during these early years was therefore determined by the *Weltbühne* writers' view of the German working class. The 1918 revolution, in Germany, as Ströbel wrote in an early criticism of Georg Ledebour's *Räteschwärmerei* (Soviet fanaticism), had not been "the result of revolutionary perception and determination," but "only due to momentary exhaustion and helplessness." [21] He and the other *Weltbühne* writers argued correctly that the 1918 revolution was a manifestation of general despair and of a vague longing for a better society and not an expression of socialist consciousness. Therefore, the *Weltbühne* reasoned, the workers would only play a limited role in bringing about socialism. The proletariat must first be educated for socialism, wrote Ströbel, and continued: "An adequate possibility for such schooling is practice in social and political life, the participation in democracy." [22] Not only Ströbel, but Hurwicz and Karl Rothammer (the latter was the journal's other editorialist in the early 1920's), maintained that the only kind of revolution historically, socially, and economically possible at that juncture was a democratic revolution in the style of 1848. The revolution in 1918 was to be carried on by a block of the democratic Left. The similarity to the ideas of the Forty-Eighters is striking in a passage by Karl Rothammer written in his attack on the KPD for its abortive March Action in 1921: [a]

---

[a] The March Action was the KPD's two-week campaign for general strike and armed insurrection. It was, at first, to take place in Saxony in retaliation for police occupation, and then to spread throughout Germany as an "offensive" against all state authority. The strike did not spread beyond Central Germany, and the whole action was marked by isolated, confused, and senseless incidents, sharply condemned by Paul Levi, former leader of the KPD who had resigned because of the putschist tactics of the Comintern agents in Germany.

The right to revolution is a natural basic right of the majority of the people. It is a moral obligation to raise the Red Flag when a feudal minority . . . sets itself up in opposition to the highest law of democracy. . . . The excesses of the Communists [show they are] nothing else but saboteurs of the right to revolution.[23]

This conviction, that a democratic and not a proletarian revolution was the order of the day, caused the *Weltbühne* to oppose any extraparliamentary moves by the working-class parties. Thus the USPD-KPD action against the new law on factory councils of January 1920, was condemned as having, predictably, merely incurred greater dictatorial measures by the government.[24] The one exception to this approach was the *Weltbühne's* celebration of the general strike which brought Kapp down in March. Obviously, the workers were allowed to act on their own only in defense of the bourgeois republic. Otherwise, as Ströbel wrote, the workers would only isolate and weaken themselves by pursuing nonsensical, unattainable goals in their struggle against capitalism:

As long as the left-wing socialists chase after the *Rätediktatur*, and carry on a senseless policy of sabotage, they will frighten into the arms of a scornfully laughing capitalist class all those social layers who basically would be the natural allies of the revolutionary proletariat. But those circles —the Christian and Democratic workers, the officials, many intellectuals, even hundreds of thousands of self-employed middle-class people—would join a radical workers' party which would fight for a democratic anti-capitalist program with convincing, effective arguments and intelligible goals . . . Why do we not want to finally try things with reason, instead of biting into our own flesh? [25]

"Reason" and "intelligible goals" stood for a policy of economic reconstruction—consisting of the nationalization of such basic industries as coal and steel—and a social welfare program.[26] When the Second and Second-and-a-Half Internationals united, in 1923, over the objections of such Independents as Ledebour, the *Weltbühne* called it an important step in the right direction. "Not only the fate of the socialist parties," wrote Eugen Lanz, "not only that of the workers, but of all mankind depends on the development of the new International." Lanz, however, noted that there would be no real International unless Communist workers were induced to work with it.[27]

The journal's conception of working-class unification in the early twenties did not include cooperation with the KPD as a party, but rather foresaw winning Communist workers over to an essentially Social Democratic platform. At first, the *Weltbühne* welcomed the Saxon "workers' government" of 1923 in which Social Democrats and

Communists were united. As Hans Bauer wrote, in spite of the fact that the Communists were inherently "not good company, particularly in Saxony, where they lack minds," coalition was a positive step because Saxony thus provided a balance to the rightist rule in Bavaria. There was no danger of a Soviet Saxony, for the "Red Hundreds" were in fact unarmed and defensive rather than aggressive. Further, Prime Minister Zeigner was an admirable and capable person: "He is an intellectual, and as an intellectual, he is a socialist." [28]

When the Reich government, with the consent of the Majority Socialists in it, ordered the army to dissolve Zeigner's government, arrest its leaders, and declare martial law, the *Weltbühne* writers were outraged. The events in Saxony prove, wrote Hermann Windschild, that there was no hope for a republic and democracy in Germany.

The action of the federal government—in which there were two Democrats and three Social Democrats—against the constitutional Saxon state government is a perfectly worthy counterpart to the treatment of Belgium in 1914. . . . He who experienced the dull, desperate, helpless anger in the faces and words of the workers in the Saxon cities last week, as well as the entry of the Reichswehr, the bloodletting in Freiberg, and the spiteful glee of the order-loving *Bürger*—is forever disabused of every illusion about the German republic. . . . Throughout the nation the workers are today decimated, leaderless, discouraged, enfeebled because of years of privation. . . . On the other side stands the Reichswehr . . . well-fed, well-clothed, and well-armed, and ready to fight against "Marxism" and democracy. . . . We want to raise our voices again and again, with all the radicalism in our hearts, and prepare for that day of the German, which must come, if German history is to make any sense at all.[29]

The suppression of the Saxon government elicited some of the *Weltbühne's* most passionate statements for democracy and for the cause of the German working class. Arno Voigt, writing in the *Weltbühne*, nevertheless imputed the blame directly to Zeigner:

Instead of basing himself on all willing republican forces, Zeigner made an alliance with the Communists. The Communists want to overthrow the republic and that is why they cannot be a government party. The Communists act according to Moscow orders, and that is why the people of Germany must stand up against their rule. It is self-negation if we allow ourselves to have somewhere in Germany a Communist minister, who wants nothing else but to destroy our constitution. . . . For that matter, we might as well have a Hitler.[30]

Zeigner's mistake, wrote Voigt, was to make an uneducated Communist a minister, thus destroying the balance which Saxony was to offer in regard to Bavaria. Zeigner's one-sided policy awakened great opposition among the non-Socialists of Saxony, and Voigt's concluding implication was that the army's arrival was unavoidable.[31]

Voigt's article was not commented upon by other *Weltbühne* writers. Yet, many of his assumptions, if not his conclusions, were similar to those of the leading political writers of the journal in the first five years of its republican existence. But the 1923 events marked a turning point in the history of the German working-class parties. Not only were the exponents of *Rätediktatur* defeated throughout Germany for a long time to come, but the Social Democrats suffered political setbacks as well. The *Weltbühne* writers were quick to sense the change resulting from the defeat. The current crusade against Marxism, wrote Morus, was showing itself ever more clearly to be a class struggle, involving not only guns being used against the workers, but the loss of many of their former gains, such as the eight-hour day.[32] And Otto Flake, commenting on "the move to the Right," wrote:

Marxism has failed, quite true . . . because Marxism has failed, they want to take away from the working classes their right to advocate their beliefs. . . . They want to turn the workers into an object instead of a factor in the state. Hunger for power is behind that.[33]

Flake's piece ended on a note often to be heard subsequently in the *Weltbühne:* subjecting themselves to a right-wing course was endemic to Germans. That was "the main defect of the German: his lack of a sense of the present, of new ideas, of an honest relationship to the ideas of progress, freedom and dignity." [34]

Blaming the German national character, or rather German historic development, was perhaps for some of the *Weltbühne* intellectuals a desperate explanation for the malaise of Weimar. As Ossietzky wrote: "The desire for a dictatorship is in our blood." [35] It may even have been a way of ending what was an obvious dichotomy in their position toward socialism and toward the working-class parties at that time. But that dichotomy remained. The *Weltbühne* espoused the politics characteristic of Social Democracy, that of working within bourgeois society for democratic processes and institutions. Whenever the SPD showed itself inadequate to this task, the *Weltbühne* writers expressed their solidarity with the immediate victims of this inadequacy, the German workers. Yet their counsels to the working class were to reject any other program but the only "reasonable" one, essentially the program of the Majority Social Democrats. This dichotomy was strikingly expressed in the *Weltbühne* at the time of the SPD Congress at Görlitz, in 1921. The commentary on the congress was divided into two parts. One, entitled "Verstandskritik" (Reasoned Criticism) by Karl Rothammer, was a report on the outcome of the congress, approving the SPD's affirmation of coalitions, which showed its elasticity, and its affirmation of political strikes, which showed it still had revolutionary will.[36] The other part was a poem by Tucholsky, entitled "Gefühlskritik" (Criticism from the Heart), expressing a less sanguine view of the SPD's revolutionary will:

Once we were sitting in prison and in chains.
We had sacrificed for the sake of the party
Money, freedom, position, and security.
Today we are blasé about ideologies,
We sneeze at the hardy old Bebel,
We smile when we see young people rebelling,
And while we are being attacked in hundreds of conventicles
By new wage laws and in editorials
We remain Realpolitiker.
Class struggle is good for the Bolshevists.
Once we poked fun at cabinet ministers—
That was long long ago [b]
Today we see things in different light.

We are thrilled by
Cigars, automobiles and polite conversation—
After all, we aren't Bolshevists;
We are philistines [*Skatbrüder*] who have read Marx.
We have never been farther away
From the road shown to us by Lassalle.[37]

---

[b] Last three words are in English.

Chapter XI
A NEW GERMAN LEFT, 1924–1927

Beginning in 1924, *Die Weltbühne* became decidedly more radical. First of all, it found that the economic stabilization initiated by the Dawes Plan on reparations payments was being carried out at the expense of the working and middle classes. Morus described the harsh conditions of the workers victimized by economic reconstruction and "rationalization" which, he said, meant longer hours and layoffs. Leo Lania, after traveling in Saxony in 1925, wrote:

This is the German hunger area. It is not located on the Volga—no crop failure, no civil war, and no Bolshevism is to blame for this ghastly misery. There is peace in the land and the reconstruction of our economy proceeds splendidly. The intelligence and sobriety of its inhabitants have saved Germany from revolution. This exalted realization may make dying easier for them.[1]

Even when the bourgeois coalition government [a] of Wilhelm Marx in 1927 passed a series of welfare laws which definitely improved the material conditions of the workers, Morus called this mere "enlightened despotism." [2]

Secondly, as has been already noted, none of the *Weltbühne* writers considered Stresemann's policy a real path to international peace.[3] England, upon whose urging and cooperation the Locarno policy was

[a] The term "bourgeois coalition" is misleading to some extent as would be any other designation. There were, between 1919 and 1930 (end of parliamentary government), essentially four types of coalition cabinets in Weimar: 1) Weimar coalition (SPD, Democrats, and Center); 2) Great republican coalition (SPD, Democrats, Center, and People's Party); 3) Bourgeois coalition (Democrats, Center, People's Party), 4) Great bourgeois coalition ([Democrats], Center, People's Party, Nationalists).

148

based, was no longer looked upon with such sympathy as in the early years of the republic. It was recognized as an imperialist power, determined to hold its own in its colonies and in China. Ramsay MacDonald's Labor government of 1924 was at first celebrated in the *Weltbühne* as the historic alternative to Leninism,[4] but subsequently Jacobsohn printed as editorials a series of letters by Joseph Friedfeld, the journal's London correspondent, which described the misery of the English workers, the radicalism of the British trade-union movement, and its hostility to MacDonald's evolutionary policy. Friedfeld called the Labor cabinet a useful tool for big business at home and British imperialist interests abroad.[5] When, early in 1925, the Allies refused to evacuate the Cologne zone of occupation, the radical pacifist Hans Schwann put the immediate blame on Stresemann's devious disarmament policy, but the larger blame on the Allies for not bringing about world disarmament.[6] Socialists and pacifists, wrote Ossietzky in 1926, had little to hope for with Germany's entry into the League of Nations.[7]

Thirdly, once the danger of *Rätediktatur* had been averted, *Die Weltbühne* no longer felt compelled to attack the far Left. With Ströbel as the leader of the left opposition in the SPD, the journal concentrated its attacks on the antirepublican, right-wing nationalist organizations. In so doing it had to criticize the SPD for its ambivalence and weakness as well as champion the cause of Communists or pro-Communists who made up the bulk of Germany's 7,000 political prisoners. Erich Zeigner now received unequivocal support after his trial in Leipzig, which was simultaneous with the Hitler-Ludendorff trial in Munich. When Zeigner was imprisoned for three years, while the Munich defendants were mildly punished, if at all, Jacob Altmeier protested in the *Weltbühne:* "In Munich, judicial murder (*Justizmord*) has been pronounced on the republic; in Leipzig, on a human being."[8] Propagating the slogan, "Travelers avoid Bavaria," *Die Weltbühne* led a relentless campaign against the reactionary Bavarian government in these years, and published, among others, the prison experiences of Ernst Toller.[9] It also brought to light the cases of arrested and detained Communists, particularly that of Arkady Maslow[b] who, although an ultra-leftist, was one of the few KPD

---

[b] Arkady Maslow, a Marxist theoretician, belonged to the left wing of German Communism. In 1921, he argued—together with Ruth Fischer and Ernst Reuter —for continued revolutionary activity regardless of the foreign political needs of Soviet Russia. In 1923, he opposed the broad united front policy proposed by party leader Heinrich Brandler, and demanded a united front from below,

leaders the journal respected.[10] As to the various trials of Soviet spies and terrorists, such as the "Cheka Trial," *Die Weltbühne* treated them as attempts to outlaw the KPD. Then and later, the journal took every occasion to defend the Communists' right to free speech. Still, the basic position of the *Weltbühne*, at least until 1925, toward the working-class parties remained unchanged: the SPD was criticized for not living up to its promises, thereby allowing the KPD to profit from its mistakes. This was immediately obvious in the *Weltbühne's* reporting of the 1924 elections. Already in February, the elections in Thuringia and Mecklenburg had resulted in great losses to the SPD in favor of the KPD and, to a lesser extent, the Nationalists. For all this, wrote the revolutionary pacifist Emil Rabold, only the Social Democrats were to blame:

Parties may be betrayed—a class does not allow itself to be betrayed for very long. . . . Both extreme wings, the Communists and the German Racialists are in the end the fruit of Social Democratic politics which . . . are unpositive, shortsighted, instinctless, and boring. The proletarians who, despite the chaos of war and postwar promises have not lost their will to life and active control over their fate, are tired of theoretical reasoning . . . tired of the old refrain about how conditions do not allow for this or that, how we just have to wait for the maturing of a better time. They live in the present, which they want to see changed and are ready to help make the change themselves.[11]

Rabold's prophecies were fulfilled in the national elections of May 1924 when the SPD lost many votes to the Communists and Nationalists. Hans Schwann now urged the Party to go into honest opposition to the new government and rejuvenate party life by giving voice to its internal opposition.[12] This dissenting voice, made up mainly by Paul Levi's followers, the Saxon Social Democrats, was always supported in the *Weltbühne*.[13]

The serious political situation in 1924 led many *Weltbühne* writers to take an even more violently polemical attitude toward both working-class parties. They accused the Communists and Social Democrats

---

that is, the winning over of the socialist workers without their leaders. In the same year, he helped to prepare—together with Fischer, Ernst Thälmann, and the delegates of the Comintern—the "Red October," the KPD's most blatant failure in staging revolutionary upheavals. A year later, he and other "ultraleftists" were condemned by both party and Comintern for having "betrayed the Fatherland of All Toilers." See Helmut Gruber, ed., *International Communism in the Era of Lenin* (Greenwich, Conn., 1967), 314 *et passim;* Ossip K. Flechtheim, *Die Kommunistische Partei Deutschlands in der Weimarer Republik* (Offenbach/ M., 1948), 125 *et passim,* and Werner T. Angress, *Stillborn Revolution* (Princeton, N.J., 1963), 102 *et passim.*

of having obstructed the emergence of *Geister*, that is, of men with imagination and foresight, not necessarily intellectuals, but individuals with moral energy and leadership capacity. Truly, the KPD did not merit much admiration at a time when its tactics, under the leadership of the left-wing Communist Ruth Fischer, consisted mainly of obstructionism in the Reichstag, with Communist deputies blowing horns and beating drums at its sessions. The *Weltbühne* disliked Fischer, "this volcano of radicalism . . . a will free of all reflection and considered thought," [14] and it kept at a distance from the German Communists although it published contributions by Radek and Trotsky, incidentally both mortal enemies of Fischer. With the *Weltbühne* gradually revising its views on Soviet Russia, the contrast between its treatment of the USSR and the German Communists became striking. More than once, what it admired in Russia it held in contempt in Germany for the simple reason that the Soviet system "fits into Europe the way a street organ fits into a chamber orchestra." [15] Hurwicz's critical articles on Soviet Russia now gave way to much more positive travelogues by other writers who presented the USSR as a land of "youth" and "the future" and argued that the proletariat constituted the ruling class there.[16] Adolf Grabowsky described the Russian Communist Party as a model structure for the emergence of pure and dedicated leaders, a sort of holy order. Although Grabowsky criticized another *Weltbühne* writer's much too optimistic report on political and intellectual freedom in Russia, he agreed that there was a measure of freedom within the limits of proletarian dictatorship and that something magnificent was happening in that country.[17] It was therefore no surprise that in 1927, when the *Weltbühne* first took notice of the Stalin-Trotsky struggle, Ossietzky hailed Stalin's triumph. Trotsky, he commented, was still harping on 1920-style revolutionary romanticism which even Lenin had given up before his death. Stalin meant sober, realistic policies.[18] All of this in no way implied an affirmation of Bolshevik doctrine and, as long as the KPD mindlessly imitated the Russian Communists, the *Weltbühne* writers rejected that party as a political alternative. Commenting on the congress of the KPD in July 1925, Morus called it an assemblage of rigid and unimpressive personalities who differed in no way from their counterparts in the SPD, and who showed the same inclination to shunt aside their best men, in this case Maslow and Arthur Rosenberg.[19] In an open letter to the KPD, Alfons Steiniger accused the Party of having broken with the intellectual tradition of Luxemburg and Liebknecht and wondered whether this had not been due to Moscow's suppression of KPD intellectuals.[20]

The rejoinder to Steiniger was written by Friedrich Schwag, one of the pro-Communist Marxists who argued with the *Weltbühne* intellectuals. Steiniger, wrote Schwag, was one of those uneasy intellectuals, that interstitial group between bourgeoisie and proletariat, who, had they not "merely confronted Noske with hand-wringing, but had declared themselves in solidarity with the revolutionary working class," could have assured "that Rosa [Luxemburg] and Karl [Liebknecht] would be alive today and fewer workers and leaders in Republican prisons." The rowdy protest actions in the Reichstag were demonstrations for the release of the 7,000 imprisoned. The KPD rejected parliamentarism as "an infamous deception of the masses" and its tactics did not diminish the image of the Party in the eyes of the workers; it was irrelevant if they annoyed the petty bourgeois and the intellectuals.[21]

It was from Kurt Hiller that the KPD received an oblique compliment in the *Weltbühne*. Between fascism and Bolshevism, Hiller wrote, only the ends were different; because the ends of Bolshevism were good, he preferred it to fascism.[22] Hiller's main target was the SPD which he criticized for its lack of *Geister*, but because he attributed this lack to the very foundations of Marxist philosophy, he incurred the hostility of both Marxist parties.

Socialism, according to Hiller, was necessary because it promised the best selection of leadership through economic equality. But traditional socialism was too "conservative"; it ignored the cultural and artistic aspects of human liberation for preoccupation with economic goals. Dialectical materialism might explain the ethos of the masses, but what about the role of the individual in history? If social revolution is inevitable, Hiller argued, then there is no ethical postulate for action on the part of the individual.[23]

Hiller was immediately accused of gross misrepresentation of the Marxist philosophy of history. In his angry retort, Hermann Wendel, a noted theoretician in the SPD,[e] left Hiller free to dispute that man acts exclusively from economic considerations but he conceded Hiller no other ground.[24] Individualistic interpretations of history, Wendel held,

---

[e] Wendel was typical of those committed SPD politicians who wrote in the *Weltbühne*. Relatively young (he was born in 1884) and highly cultivated—he became, among others, honorary doctor of the University of Belgrade—he often opposed SPD policy, without breaking party discipline. Once the youngest member of the SPD in the Reichstag, in the 1920's he gradually withdrew from active politics; he turned down an offer of the government to become German Minister in Belgrade, and engaged in writing. Wendel died near Paris in 1936. See Franz Osteroth, ed., *Biographisches Lexikon des Sozialismus* (Hannover, 1960), I, 331 f.

saw it as wild chaos, a series of accidents dependent on this or that man; in reality the awakening of the masses to culture and art was due exclusively to the day-to-day work of trade unionists and party functionaries for whom Hiller had so much scorn. But Hiller's basic misconception, the SPD leader wrote, was that Marxism thought social revolution inevitable:

. . . when Marxism speaks of the "naturally necessary" movement to socialism, it does not consider a nonhuman fatalism as the impelling force, but rather the desire of the people themselves; within the concept of economic necessity lies the will to action, from which all historical events originate.[25]

Hiller's arguments, of course, had contained strong elements of his *Logokratie;* he passionately believed that his notions of elitism transcended the old-fashioned concepts of Marxism. Actually, his conviction as to the necessity of consciously intervening into the process of history put Hiller into a closer bond with the Communists than with the Social Democrats. As he himself wrote in his first diatribe against the Marxists, his criticisms applied only partly or not at all to the Communists, and ultimately this intellectual bond made him a far more frequently radical critic of the SPD than the KPD.

Nevertheless, Hiller ended up in political support of Social Democracy. When the bourgeois coalition government was dissolved in October 1924, and new elections were to be held, Hiller wrote that everything depended on a leftist victory at the polls although, he insisted, the KPD's intransigence made a Left Block impossible. Therefore, he concluded, all leftists should vote to make a block of republican parties more left; such a government would then be able to drop the Stresemanns.[26]

The outcome of the December 1924 elections partly confirmed Hiller's predictions. A huge popular vote was returned to the SPD, and all republican parties gained in strength. The Communist seats were reduced by almost a quarter. Yet the Luther government which emerged was more right-wing than the last, for instead of the Democrats, it included the Nationalists, and the SPD went into opposition.

When President Ebert died in February 1925, Hiller proposed a single presidential candidate for the republican and socialist parties—Joseph Wirth—as a tactical move to defeat the candidate of the reactionary parties.[27] In fact, after an indecisive first round, the republican and Social Democratic parties ran the moderate Center politician Wilhelm Marx against Hindenburg in the second round of the election, and were defeated. The election of Hindenburg came as a terrible shock to most writers of the *Weltbühne*. They expected the overthrow of the republic, a German war of revenge, and the end to all hopes for democracy in Germany. "And what now?" asked Tucholsky. "Now a bitter, terrible and bloody lesson. One that has been deserved a thousand times over." [28]

Oddly enough, criticism of the KPD's performance was only occasional and indirect although it was clear that had the Communists refrained from running Thälmann, at least in the second round, Wilhelm Marx could have defeated Hindenburg.[d] Tucholsky saw the cause of the catastrophe in the moderation of the Marx campaign and the awe of the Hindenburg legend which both republican parties and Social Democrats shared.[29] Leo Lania absolved the Communists and came down hard on the SPD: the Communists had maintained their electoral following, he held, whereas the SPD could not convince hundreds of thousands of its members in Saxony, Thuringia, and Franconia, who had abstained, to vote for the candidate the SPD was finally forced to support.[30]

The Hindenburg election seems to have marked a turning point in the attitude of the *Weltbühne* writers toward the working-class parties. Bitterness toward the SPD grew perceptibly, while a shift in the leadership of the KPD was hailed as a positive step. Alfons Steiniger saw the removal of Fischer, Maslow, and Rosenberg, and the adoption of a course opposite to that of those "ultra-left Mensheviks" as the possible beginning of the German revolution.[31] Ossietzky believed that Moscow had urged the new course so as to make possible an immediate *rapprochement* with the SPD, but he cautioned the Communists lest they allow themselves to be swallowed up by the SPD as had been the case with the USPD and the Levi group.[e]

The whole idea of unification would lose its meaning if nothing else should result but a fatter Social Democracy. The purpose can only be the new, great Workers Party: not Social Democracy, not the Communist Party, but the Party born out of the struggles of this year, ready for the struggles of 1930.[32]

What made cooperation between Social Democrats and Communists seem possible in those years was the attempt of the British Trade Unions, in 1926, to rally the Social Democratic Trade Union International to a program of radical mass resistance to war and imperialism,

---

[d] The final election results were as follows: Hindenburg (candidate of the Right) 14,655,766 votes; Marx (candidate of the republicans and of the SPD) 13,751,615 votes; Thälmann (KPD) 1,931,151 votes.

[e] Paul Levi, a former Communist leader, joined the SPD in 1922 where he attempted unsuccessfully to form an autonomous left-wing group.

and to an alliance with the Communist, particularly Russian, trade unions. This move, ultimately unsuccessful in the Trade Union International, was wholly supported by the Comintern and by the German radical pacifists in the *Weltbühne*. In addition, despite disclosures of military cooperation between German militarists and the Soviet Union, the *Weltbühne* continued to exhibit, more often than not, a mildly sympathetic view to the international position of the USSR. The national liberation movements in mostly English dominated areas had become more powerful, and although writers like Friedfeld and Ossietzky disapproved of Soviet agitation in these areas, particularly China, these nationalist movements were recognized as a reality. During the war scare of 1927, when Great Britain broke relations with Russia, the responsibility for it was laid to Britain, and the treason trials and rearmament in the USSR were seen as defensive acts.[33]

The *Weltbühne* writers, therefore, pressed vigorously for cooperation between Social Democrats and Communists throughout 1925–1927, and expressed increasing annoyance over the SPD's intransigence.

The job now, wrote Hiller, was to form a Left front against entrenched, reactionary capitalism. "To join Socialists and Communists . . . into a Red unity may be like squaring the circle, but it is our task." The question as to how this should be done was to occupy the *Weltbühne* writers during the next two years.

Alfons Steiniger's proposal that the nonparty leftists should form a "Council of Republicans"[34] caused Hiller to reject the idea of republicanism. "Should the prolongers of shameful capitalist economics [*kapitalistische Schandwirtschaft*] be allowed in such a council, simply because they are 'republicans'?" he asked Steiniger. It must be a socialist unification with a definite program:

The bridge must finally be built between Communists who understand the situation today and Social Democrats who do not merely think about today and their livelihoods but also about the socialist goal. This bridge should not be made out of the cardboard of democratic principle, but out of the concrete of the following aims:

1. Proletarian policies for wages, hours, taxes, housing, and customs duties.

2. A ruthless anti-nationalist policy. No mere preaching against the war of revenge . . . rather, going beyond the resolutions of a castrated pacifism by planned preparation for active hindrance to war, by rejection of army service and sabotage.

3. A policy of freedom and social welfare in regard to elementary schools, criminal law, execution of sentences.

4. Purging the administration and the courts of corruption and counterrevolution.[35]

Hiller closed with the remark that it did not matter what system would get established, once power was taken. The important thing was to take power. This addendum would have left the interested reader more confused than clear, for if Hiller's four points were the program of a revolutionary movement for state power, then point two was obviously superfluous, whereas other points, such as the expropriation of capital, were conspicuously absent. Hiller could only have meant this as a program upon which to gain a majority in the Reichstag, or perhaps as a program for joint extraparliamentary actions, in which case "taking power" and "establishing a system" could hardly be a part of the united front he was proposing.

Alfons Steiniger envisaged the Left grouping to be made up of Social Democrats, Communists, workers, members of parliament, intellectuals, radical youth—and Joseph Wirth. All that was needed, he wrote, were

thirty activists full of strength and courage and will, of purpose and self-sacrifice; thirty determined, kind, believing people who will be ready to hammer out a unique statement of fanatical truth, to bring it to the darkest province, to go as speakers into the villages and cities—plus three hundred men ashamed of their unjustified happiness, of capitalist contentment, who will give their money to blaze the paths for truth. . . . all of you who want paradise . . . where will we meet? That is the last thing to concern us. Perhaps in Munich—it ought to be night, perhaps in the house of one of our murdered comrades.[36]

Steiniger's language was more appropriate for an early nineteenth-century secret society; it seems doubtful that it could have had any attraction for the most important elements in a block of "Red unity," namely the Socialists and Communists.

Max Peters, another *Weltbühne* writer, argued that the wretched state of the SPD, so clearly shown at the party's Heidelberg Congress in September 1925, and the basically similar state of the KPD, necessitated the building of "a new Independent Social Democratic Party, either in the form of a German Left beside or above the existing parties, or by the destruction of the colossus of those parties between whom real freedom is about to suffocate." [37] For even if the recent change in the KPD line indicated the possibility that this party would become politically constructive, Peters had no great hopes because the whole change had been carried out in a bureaucratic manner, good men had been suppressed, and narrow-minded functionaries had triumphed.

Immediate opposition to the idea of a new party came from Friedrich Schwag. If it was not born in a social and economic process,

Schwag held, if it did not have a program sharply defined in relation to that of other parties, and if its foundation was simply motivated by annoyance, the new party was doomed. After all, the Moscow directives were positive, even if the German Communists seemed to be substituting proletarian pretentiousness for that of the intellectuals. Schwag urged instead work in the trade unions, which were intrinsically supraparty institutions.[38]

Kurt Hiller agreed with Schwag that nothing could be more harmful to the united front of the proletariat than slipping a third party between its two most powerful organizations. But Schwag was wrong in requiring a social or economic justification for the German Left; the building of a great Left Block would only come about with clear purposes and work. The trade unions were a vehicle for such work only in a limited way, for not even the influence of the British Trade Unions would make the Trade Union International carry through a program of determined antiwar activity. Nor would this change if the Communists were to gain predominance in the international trade-union movement. The Communists' refusal to advocate mass resistance to the draft could easily lead them to separate themselves from the union of the German Left, a move which Hiller said would be not only theoretically wrong, but politically stupid: the next war would definitely pit Germany against the Soviet Union.[39]

It was not likely that Hiller's demands for common effort would attract two political parties whose basic programs called either for compromise with the national interests of a bourgeois state, or for subversion of the army rather than abstention from the draft. Hiller, and others sympathetic to his ideas, obviously saw the new "German Left" (*Deutsche Linke*) as an independent pressure group, coaxing the Parties into common action. But it was never clear how this was to be done. Max Peters had replaced his suggestion for a third party with one for the establishment of "political salons," on the order of the prerevolutionary clubs in France. For although

we are still convinced that political power can only be won through the victory of the revolutionary class struggle, we are also convinced that all power is without sense if at the moment of victory there is no real spiritually revolutionary society. . . . We must create an intelligent, mobile society, conscious of its purpose. The Red Block will thereby finally be attained.[40]

Peters foresaw a wide political function to these salons, for the deputies of the leftist parties, like all *Geistige*, would be attracted to them.

Then it will be a matter of tact as to how to guide this talent toward an exclusive dedication to the ideas of the German Left. The *Deutsche Linke* will become the conscience of the parties, an unparliamentary, undemocratized leadership.[41]

The culmination of the discussion was a conference held for the organization of the *Deutsche Linke* in the fall of 1926 in which many of these writers, members of the Peace Cartel, Leonard Nelson's "Internationaler Sozialistischer Kampf-Bund" or ISK (International Socialist Militant League),[f] and other independent socialists participated. The two great parties apparently sent no official representatives and the outcome was not spectacular.[42] The failure of the conference may have been symbolic of the dilemma of the left-wing intellectuals in the *Weltbühne*. Their utopianism, as, for instance, expressed by Hiller, made them more action-oriented, hence more radical, than the mass socialist parties. At the same time, it limited their effect and influence in and on these two parties. Their conception of a united Red front, despite the detailed programs advanced by Hiller, amounted to a call for individuals to reunify under the aegis of a vague and disparate *Deutsche Linke*, and therefore a call for both Social Democrats and Communists to give up their basic programs and party structures. A campaign for a united front of the working-class parties, rather than a call for unification, would have outlined a specific course of action, programmatically possible for each of the parties. Of the entire *Weltbühne* circle, only Georg Ledebour advanced such an idea. He called for joint action by both parties, as well as his splinter USPD, in the form of demonstrations and strikes for the Chinese revolution, against the imperialist ventures of any power, against all moves toward the war, against the fascist leagues, and for the eight-hour day. The more action on these issues, the greater would be the threat of a general strike if war were to break out.[43] Of all the propositions made in the *Weltbühne* on the unity of the working class, Ledebour's seems the most sensible. For if it was true that the leaders of the two mass

---

[f] Founded by the radical pacifist and idealist philosopher Leonard Nelson in 1917 as the "Internationaler Jugend-Bund" (International Youth League), the IJB was first a part of the German Communist youth organization. The Nelson League—as it was called—was however expelled in 1922 for its elitist program. It then became part of the Social Democratic youth organization only to be expelled for left-wing opposition in 1925. Thereupon it became an independent socialist organization, the ISK. Nelson's highly voluntaristic leftism and antidemocratic ideas had many sympathizers among the *Weltbühne* writers. For an excellent study of the Nelson League, see Werner Link, *Die Geschichte des Internationalen Jugend-Bundes (IJB) und des Internationalen Sozialistischen Kampf-Bundes (ISK)* (Meisenheim/Glan, 1964).

parties were misleading the masses, then it was logical to expect that they would disregard these concrete appeals for joint action and in so doing expose themselves as sectarians and traitors before their own followers.

What most *Weltbühne* writers could not accept in theory, they subscribed to in practice by supporting every attempt toward an interparty united front. When Communists, democrats, and pacifists at the University of Berlin began a campaign in 1926 against the large right-wing student organizations, the journal celebrated their collective effort and condemned the Social Democratic student groups for refusing to cooperate with the Communists.[44] Similarly, it supported the attempt of some Reichsbanner leaders to cooperate more closely with the Communist "Roter Frontkämpfer Bund" (Red Frontfighters' League), not only in defensive action against the Right Radicals, but in propagating such issues as the expropriation without indemnity of the rights and holdings in Germany of the former ruling houses.[45] It was this latter campaign for the "Expropriation of the Princes" (*Fürstenenteignung*) which brought most of the left-wing intellectuals into a temporary united front with the working-class parties.

The Weimar Constitution, which guaranteed the rights of private property, allowed the *Länder* to exercise the right of eminent domain when accompanied by payment of proper damages. The German states, however, were generally unable to assume the enormous financial burdens of the property settlements with their former rulers. Then, in November 1925, the KPD demanded in the Reichstag the outright expropriation of the princely fortunes.[46] When this was rejected, they resorted to the constitutional device of "popular demand" (*Volksbegehren*) to force the cabinet to present the proposal in the Reichstag. This required written support from at least one-tenth of the qualified voters. No sooner did the Communists announce their intentions than a Reich Action Committee was formed, on instructions by Willi Münzenberg, to collect the needed signatures.[47] Headed by the economist and *Weltbühne* collaborator Robert R. Kuczynski, the Committee included a number of Communists, but also Tucholsky, Helene Stöcker, Albert Einstein, George Grosz, Jacobsohn, Hiller, Persius, and others. The KPD, the SPD, the Peace Association, and the German League for Human Rights endorsed the committee. Ultimately, 12.5 million signatures were collected, three times the constitutionally required number but, again, the Reichstag turned down the proposal for expropriation. Now, a popular vote or referendum would be required to turn this proposal into law, a matter of first attracting 20 million

voters, more than half of the qualified electors, to the polls, and then
of securing a majority of "yes" votes. Although the SPD joined in the
campaign for a referendum—reluctantly to say the least, because most
leaders disapproved of the idea of expropriation [48]—the chances of its
success were minimal. There followed several months of extreme
agitation: the KPD resorted to its most violent invectives, while the
Right and the churches railed against an "atheistic attack on God,
order, and private property." [49] President Hindenburg came out openly
—and unconstitutionally—in favor of the princes. [50] The referendum,
held on June 20, 1926, brought 15.5 million voters to the polls; 14.6
million voted in favor of the measure. This was an impressive figure,
considering that the total number of Social Democratic and Communist votes at the previous Reichstag elections barely exceeded ten
million. Clearly, a great number of nonsocialists crossed party lines to
deny the princes their enormous fortunes.

The left-wing intellectuals had gone into this "magnificent action,"
as Emil Rabold called it in the *Weltbühne*,[51] with an overflow of
enthusiasm. In the words of Ossietzky:

> The people must rise against the Reichstag . . . against this so-called
> parliamentarism which has shown itself incapable of popular legislation.
> . . . This rotten parliament will not . . . therefore the people must salvage
> the idea of democracy.[52]

Even after the failure of the referendum, Ossietzky suggested no more
than a "soaping of heads" in the KPD for the raucousness of some
party campaigners and other tactical errors; he called for new, revital-
ized democratic actions.[53] While he praised the "efforts of these magnificent youths, whether of the Red Frontfighters' League, the Reichsbanner, or the Socialist Youth Leagues," [54] he denounced the SPD for
its inaction during the campaign and for its later participation in the
parliamentary committee which was to devise a compromise settlement with the princes (*Fürstenabfindung*). The SPD should have
used the 14.6 million votes to press for a less ignoble settlement [g] or to
bring down the government, he argued.[55]

The "popular demand" against the princes was one of Weimar's
most interesting leftist experiments. It is hard to escape the feeling
that a slight modification in the term "without indemnity" would have
brought this movement to triumph. But then this would have required

---

[g] The issue of settlement was ultimately referred to the *Länder* whose governments either consented to buy off the princes or allowed them to keep their
lands, which made the deposed rulers the greatest landowners in the Weimar
Republic. Albert Schwarz, *Die Weimarer Republik* (Konstanz, 1958), 126.

that the KPD be sincerely interested in passing the princely fortunes into the hands of the bourgeois-operated German states, and in creating a united front of equal parties. In fact, it appeared to be interested mainly in embarrassing the Social Democrats. The SPD showed itself no less opportunistic by cautiously supporting a measure it disliked, in order to save face before its followers. As to the left-wing intellectuals, they gave their full cooperation to the venture but by accepting to work for the Reich Committee, a product of the Communist propaganda machinery, they unwittingly served the private interests of the KPD. Sincerity again remained the doubtful privilege of the intellectuals.

This was not the only time that the *Weltbühne* circle subscribed to a Communist move. Back in 1921, Maximilian Harden, Leonhard Frank, George Grosz, Alfons Goldschmidt, Arthur Holitscher, Albert Einstein, and a number of others, functioned as charter members of the "Internationale Arbeiterhilfe" (IAH or International Workers' Aid), organized by the Comintern functionary Münzenberg.[56] The IAH provided aid to starving children in Russia and to striking workers elsewhere, thus combining humanitarian activities with proletarian causes. Not only in the IAH, in all other branches of Münzenberg's "propaganda empire"—in his publishing firms, newspapers, theaters, cabarets, exhibitions, and movies—such left-wing intellectuals as Tucholsky and Ossietzky, the sculptor Ernst Barlach, Käthe Kollwitz, Ernst Toller, Kurt Hiller, Erich Mühsam, Leo Lania, Heinz Pol, and Kurt Kersten constituted the main work force.[h] No doubt, many of them would also have collaborated with a similar, nominally independent Social Democratic propaganda organization, but there was no such undertaking. In 1926, Tucholsky wrote to a socialist friend:

I shall always remain a stranger [to the proletariat]; there is something that separates us. I hold the average German intellectual—including myself—unfit to lead the German proletariat. But, then, why don't you call on us more often? (*Aber warum benutzt ihr uns nicht mehr?*). Why is it so terribly hard, even with the best of will, to put our labor at the disposal of both parties? Suspicion and pride militate against us. We wear our white collar like a brandmark.[57]

Their collaboration with Münzenberg gave the *Weltbühne* writers the satisfaction of addressing a working-class audience; it also pro-

---

[h] Although Münzenberg broke with the Comintern in the late 1930's, in the Weimar period he was still a dogmatic Communist, irreproachably faithful to Moscow's orders. It is true, however, that he allowed his non-Communist collaborators a good deal of thematic freedom as long as it did not involve criticism of the KPD, the USSR, or International Communism.

vided them with the means—or so they thought—of gaining the ears of the KPD leaders. They regarded Münzenberg as the most "reasonable" of the Communist functionaries; through him the KPD was to be persuaded to initiate a united front of all leftists. Repeatedly, some writers of the *Weltbühne* campaigned to reach an understanding with Münzenberg, not the generous employer, but the Communist leader. There was no such understanding. These writers hoped to use Münzenberg as a Trojan horse to penetrate the walls of the Communist Party. They were used instead by Münzenberg, the Trojan horse of Communism. Münzenberg converted the Weimar left-wing intellectuals, together with such non-Germans as Romain Rolland or Martin Andersen-Nexö, into the first fellow travelers in the history of international Communism. A fellow traveler is thought to be either opportunistic or gullible. There is some evidence to show that a handful of German left-wing intellectuals answered to the first characterization; all answered to the second.

Babette Gross, Münzenberg's lifelong companion, relates in her biography of Münzenberg that in 1924 she herself had seen Münzenberg transfer a substantial sum in dollars from the Soviet Embassy in Berlin to Karl Vetter's and Ossietzky's ill-fated Republican Party. But, Gross continues, only Vetter was likely to solicit or accept such largesse while Ossietzky, "this determined enemy of the Communists," probably knew nothing of this transaction.[58] If such cases of bribery were extremely rare and the left-wing intellectuals generally incorruptible, they certainly showed a good deal of that gullibility which came to characterize all fellow travelers in Communist front organizations and which stayed with them even after their disillusionment with the God that failed.

In 1931, reports Babette Gross, Münzenberg launched a highly successful campaign among the left-wing intellectuals on behalf of an alleged "secretary of a pan-pacifistic trade union" who, together with his wife, had fallen into the hands of the Chiang Kai-shek clique in Shanghai. No sooner did Münzenberg print in *Inprekorr*, the journal of the Comintern, the news of this double arrest when scores of protest telegrams were rushed off to China by, among others, Ossietzky, Lion Feuchtwanger, Alfred Kerr, Hugo Gropius, Mies van der Rohe, and the publisher Ernst Rowohlt. This campaign of protest was soon joined by Paul Klee, Theodore Dreiser, and many others. Several months later, when Münzenberg finally identified the two victims of Chiang Kai-shek as the Swiss couple Ruegg, intellectuals in many countries formed a "Central Committee to Save the Rueggs" and rushed off new telegrams to China. As a result, the prisoners, although under sentence of death, were released some time later. These protesters did not know, but Münzenberg did, that the real name of the prisoners was not Ruegg but Luft, and that the husband was not a Swiss pacifist but a Ukrainian Communist who had gone to China as a Soviet intelligence agent.[1] The real Ruegg was a Swiss Communist whose passport had been borrowed by the Comintern.[59]

After all this had been said, it is still difficult not to sympathize with these early fellow travelers or to disapprove of their actions. For even if they failed to recognize the cynicism of the Comintern, they alone stood up for real or alleged victims of man's inhumanity to man. In a way, they represented the conscience of humanity. Nor can they be considered equally misguided in their support of every conceivable cause which was likely to bring the men of the Left together in common political action. Only in Münzenberg's International Workers' Aid could such divergent personalities as Albert Einstein, the Social Democratic leader Paul Löbe, and Communist politicians work together and occasionally engage in an exchange of opinions.

In 1927, when the *Weltbühne* made renewed efforts to promote interparty encounters, such dialogues seemed more urgent than ever. Although the SPD was in opposition to the rightist government of Wilhelm Marx, it appeared no less unprincipled and compromising than it had been as a direct or indirect government party.[60] The Social Democrats had moved from being weak and unreliable opponents of the Reichswehr to the champions of "parliamentary control" over the army;[61] the KPD could think of nothing better to do than drive out

---

[1] If Münzenberg knew of this subterfuge, Babette Gross most likely knew also; she herself was a militant Communist and director of several of Münzenberg's political enterprises. In view of her past activities, there is some incongruity in the bemused moral indignation with which she spices her account of Münzenberg's politics. It is indeed a pity that no one has as yet written a biography of Babette Gross, daughter of a Protestant petty bourgeois in Potsdam. In 1933, Babette followed Münzenberg to Paris where she continued to work on Communist publications. Five years later, upon the expulsion of Münzenberg from the German Communist Party, she herself broke with the Party and with the Comintern. In 1941 she went to Mexico, returning to West Germany in 1947, where she now lives. Her sister Margarete, who was the wife of the German Communist leader Heinz Neumann, fled to the Soviet Union after Hitler came to power. Subsequently, she spent three years in the concentration camps of Stalin and in 1940 was handed over to the Gestapo, together with other German anti-Nazi refugees. She then spent five years in the Ravensbrück concentration camp. Since then Margarete, too, has been living in the German Federal Republic. Her autobiographical works shed light on the lives of both sisters. Margarete Buber-Neumann, *Von Potsdam nach Moskau* (Stuttgart, 1957) and *Under Two Dictators* (London, 1949).

one of its best members, Arthur Rosenberg. "Be he a moderate or an ultra, the intellectual always ends up by being cast aside. Only the servants of the holy party machinery seem indispensable: the functionaries, the guardians of the cash register, the managers of the file cabinet." [62] The theoretical debates on socialism and pacifism continued in the *Weltbühne* throughout 1927, but the journal's professed hope for working-class unity was as far from reality as ever.

Chapter XII
REVOLUTION AGAINST FASCISM, 1928–1932

In the late period of the Weimar Republic, the *Weltbühne's* leading political commentators moved far to the left of their previous position. They were not converted to Bolshevism but the KPD became what the SPD had been for their counterparts in the early *Weltbühne:* that party with which they basically identified and which they vigorously criticized for not living up to its program. In the early 1920's, these writers had formed a Left opposition to the SPD because it was not doing its job of protecting bourgeois democracy; now they criticized the Communists from the left for not leading a truly revolutionary struggle against fascism, and for refusing to initiate a united-front policy with the SPD. This was, with some points of difference, the position of Léon Trotsky. To be sure, Ossietzky, Hiller, Fritz Sternberg, Heinz Pol, Morus, Hanns-Erich Kaminski, and the other political commentators of that period, still conceived of their revolutionary role as *überparteilich,* above the parties; they reproached the two working-class parties for calcification and rigid adherence to mechanical Marxist materialism. But they also held that "republicanism" had lost all reality and that bourgeois democracy was disintegrating in a great social and economic crisis. They therefore called on the only democratic force left in Germany, the workers, to defeat fascism. This, however, was inconceivable without the working class taking power. Thus, these writers eventually gave some form of support to the Communist Party, the traditional advocate of this program, until it became increasingly evident that the KPD was incapable, or unwilling, to fulfill its revolutionary promises. At that point, many of them found themselves in close agreement with Trotsky and his supporters.

165

Paradoxically, *Die Weltbühne* had always chosen to become more radical when the republic and the democratic parties seemed to stabilize their position. During the uprisings of 1919, or in the political and economic chaos of 1922–1923, the journal rallied to the republic. In 1924–1925, however, when the mark was again stable and Germany readmitted into the concert of European powers, *Die Weltbühne* repudiated bourgeois democracy and called on the SPD to remain in opposition. And in 1928, when Social Democracy scored its greatest electoral victory since the elections of January 1919, and a Social Democrat, Hermann Müller, again became chancellor, the journal repudiated the SPD, and embraced the cause of proletarian revolution. These shifts to the left were not arbitrary; they were supported by insistent arguments on the fundamental shortcomings of what the moderate republicans believed were favorable developments.

The first months of 1928 did indeed hold out good promise for the republicans. For three years the economy had been stable; private industry was expanding; the states and the municipalities were engaged in grandiose construction projects; industrial wages were high, and unemployment reached a new low early in that year. Encouraged by this state of affairs, the bourgeois republican leaders decided to withdraw from their uneasy governmental alliance with the Nationalist Party and to bring the Social Democrats into the cabinet. The champion of this move was the foreign minister, Gustav Stresemann, who saw Nationalist participation in the government as a threat to his Locarno policy of obtaining concessions from the Allies through conciliation.[1] In February the Great Bourgeois Coalition cabinet of Wilhelm Marx was dissolved, and in the following Reichstag elections held in May 1928, the SPD increased the number of its seats from 131 to 152. At the same time, the Nationalists suffered heavy losses and the National Socialists were reduced from fourteen to twelve deputies. The new chancellor, the Social Democrat Hermann Müller, presided over a Great Republican Coalition of Social Democrats, Democrats, Centrists, and members of Stresemann's People's Party.

Yet all was not well with the republic. Prosperity remained tenuous, achieved as it had been through short-term foreign loans which were easily revocable and often poorly invested. A few months after the elections—that is, well before the Great Depression—the country began to experience economic difficulties. By the winter of 1928–1929, the number of unemployed reached two million. More importantly, the right-wing enemies of the republic remained undefeated and stepped up their militancy. Frightened by the victory of the Social

Democrats and the prospect of further workers' agitation, a number of important industrialists began to put pressure on Stresemann's People's Party, their parliamentary interest group, to withdraw from the Great Coalition. The hostility to the republic of the Junkers and the officers remained unchanged, and in September 1928, President Hindenburg's own Stahlhelm, that powerful reactionary veterans' association, hurled its "Message of Hate" in the face of the republic: "We hate the present state with all our soul; we hate its form and its essence, its future and its present."[2] In the same year began, and thereafter continued unabated, the shift to the right of the bourgeois republican parties. The first step in this direction was taken by the Center whose congress in December 1928 repudiated the politics of its left-wing faction, led by Joseph Wirth and the trade unionist Adam Stegerwald, by electing the conservative and antirepublican Monsignor Ludwig Kaas as its chairman.[3]

All through that year *Die Weltbühne* demonstrated that it did not share in Social Democratic and republican perspectives. Hiller, who before the December 1924 elections had advocated "biting into the sour apple of the SPD," urged before the May 1928 elections that its readers "bite into the Communist apple—it is sour but juicy!"[4] After the elections, Ossietzky commented that the SPD would not fulfill its promises and that its electoral success was more harmful than good for it would mislead the workers into thinking that they now had power.[5]

Ossietzky's predictions were fulfilled in August 1928 when the Müller government announced that it would proceed with the construction of an armored cruiser, the famous "Panzerkreuzer A," whose budget had been approved by the previous legislature. Before the May elections, the SPD had flaunted its resolve that if successful, it would "feed children instead of building armored cruisers." Now the SPD ministers in the cabinet surrendered to the pressure of their coalition partners, particularly to that of the new minister of defense, General Groener. An immediate outcry of indignation in the Social Democratic camp forced the party leadership to demand in the Reichstag the postponement of the armored-cruiser program. The Social Democratic cabinet members bowed to party discipline and, in November 1928, the Reichstag was treated to the ridiculous spectacle of the Reich chancellor and the SPD ministers voting against a resolution they themselves had adopted in a Cabinet meeting.[6] Meanwhile, the Communists Pieck and Münzenberg had announced in the Reichstag a "popular demand" for the enaction of a "Law Forbidding the Construction of Armored Cruisers and Other Warships." Although Ossietzky showed little enthusiasm for this undertaking which he correctly judged hopeless [7] (the Communists collected only 1.2 million signatures to support their petition) he called the Social Democratic performance a "national scandal" and accused the SPD ministers of having surrendered to Groener's "pronunciamento against the democratic republic." [8] Lothar Persius conducted a campaign in the *Weltbühne* against the armored cruiser, and even the moderate Quidde demanded in a pacifist journal that the German Peace Association support the Communist action.[9] When on May 1 of the following year, the Social Democratic police of Berlin clashed with Communist demonstrators, and there were at least twenty-five killed, *Die Weltbühne* sided entirely with the Communists. Today it is clear that the May Day demonstration, held despite official interdiction, was meant to embarrass the SPD, and that the Communist leaders misled their followers in asserting that the interdiction had been recalled at the last minute.[a] But there can be no doubt either about the brutality of the police acting under the orders of the Social Democratic police president Karl Zörgiebel. Ossietzky began an immediate campaign in the *Weltbühne* against Zörgiebel, accusing him of provocation and of wanting to exterminate the Communists in Berlin.[10] Ossietzky, Alfred Döblin, Stefan Grossmann, Alfons Goldschmidt, Alfred Apfel, and Heinrich Mann participated in the labors of a "Commission for the Public Investigation of the May Events," set up, not surprisingly, by Willi Münzenberg. The commission held several public hearings,[11] mostly under the chairmanship of Ossietzky: it listened to a long harangue by the chief witness, Wilhelm Pieck, and ended up with a clear indictment of the Berlin police and its president.[b] Ossietzky was at the beginning of his long campaign against Zörgiebel when he presented in the *Weltbühne* a balance of Müller's first year in office. Although it would be unrealistic to expect, he wrote, that the SPD would undertake such socialist reforms as the nationalization of coal and steel and the redistribution of latifundia in East Germany, the

---

[a] Harvey L. Dyck shows in his *Weimar Germany and Soviet Russia, 1926–1933* (New York, 1966), 153, that the clash between the Berlin police and the Communist demonstrators on May Day had been anticipated in the Soviet press, and that illegal demonstrations had been encouraged by Moscow as part of the Communists' campaign of increased hostility toward the SPD. For similar revelations, see Friedrich Stampfer, *Die ersten 14 Jahre der deutschen Republik* (Offenbach/M. 1947), 536 f.

[b] The German League for Human Rights, led by Kurt R. Grossmann, set up a rival committee of investigation and came up with a more balanced judgment. See Kurt R. Grossmann, *Ossietzky* (Munich, 1963), 225 ff., and "Die Ergebnisse der Maiuntersuchung," *Die Menschenrechte*, October 1, 1929, pp. 1–8.

party in power had also proved itself incapable of fulfilling any of the most urgent demands for peace and democracy. It had compromised on German rearmament and on social welfare; its only accomplishments were the dissolution of the Red Frontfighters' League, and a de facto anti-Communist law. Yet the SPD's attempt to drive the Communists underground could only hurt Social Democracy, Ossietzky warned. Its watchdog protection of the bourgeois state would not be rewarded by the bourgeoisie when the latter no longer needed the Social Democrats. Further, Ossietzky sounded a note which was to become the main theme of all *Weltbühne* articles on the socialist parties: the SPD's campaign for the suppression of the KPD was deepening the split in the working class, from which only the Right would benefit.[12] In the fall of 1929, Hiller announced a petition for the re-legalization of the Red Frontfighters' League. This move was supported by a number of *Weltbühne* writers, although it is noteworthy that Heinrich Mann, who had participated in the May Day commission, withheld his signature as did, not surprisingly, Thomas Mann.[13]

Throughout 1929, Hiller was again active organizing his campaign for a supraparty "Left Front." It was the duty of the independent leftists, the "intellectual centers" outside of the parties, Hiller argued, to form a propaganda group to urge such a unity. As a novel measure, Hiller suggested that such Communist-affiliated but ostensibly autonomous organizations as the International Workers' Aid, the Red Aid ("Rote Hilfe"), and the League Against Imperialism join with independent socialists and revolutionary pacifists in such a propaganda group.[14] When, however, the Rote Hilfe was purged by the KPD of all "anti-Party Communists," that is of dissident Communists who had been cooperating with left Social Democrats on issues of common interest, Hiller attacked the KPD stormily for its narrow-mindedness.[15] This elicited a response from Wilhelm Pieck in the *Weltbühne* which showed that no KPD-led organization could deviate from the KPD line.[16]

The Communist line at that time was that of "class against class," adopted by the Sixth Congress of the Communist International in the summer of 1928. This memorable Congress initiated the Communist trend toward branding the Social Democrats as "Social Fascists" and the worst enemies of the proletariat. It called on the national communist parties not to collaborate under any conditions with Social Democracy or with trade unions belonging to the Second International. The congress also announced a policy of "united front from below," which meant that the socialist workers were to be won over to Communism. The theory behind this policy was that the final sharpening of the contradictions of capitalism was imminent and so was the final revolutionary struggle. The Social Democrats who defended the bourgeois state were delaying the process of capitalist disintegration and thus had to be annihilated if history was to take its proper course. The practical reason for the new tactics was Stalin's decision to introduce forced collectivization and industrialization in Soviet Russia, a process which required unconditional obedience to Moscow on the part of all Communists.[17] The "ultraleftist" policy of the Comintern, faithfully executed by the KPD, put the left-wing intellectuals in a difficult position. On the one hand, they were still encouraged to work for Münzenberg, the only Communist permitted by the Comintern to set up a miniature popular-front operation in Germany; [c] on the other hand, they were subjected to increasingly bitter criticism in the official Communist press and by individual party members. It is significant, however, that no one in the KPD called the left-wing intellectuals fascists, which made them the only "nonfascist" group in Germany outside of the Communist Party. In an exchange of arguments between Tucholsky and the Communist writer Hans Conrad, the latter claimed in the *Weltbühne* that "the German tragedy was due in great part to the lamentable inefficiency of the so-called *linke Intellektuellen*." [18] It is high time, wrote Conrad, that the intellectuals exercise a little self-criticism and become "simple soldiers of the revolution" by entering the KPD. Even harsher criticism was heaped upon the *Weltbühne* writers in the *Linkskurve*, the new journal of the Communist literati. Edited by the "League of German Proletarian-Revolutionary Writers," this journal belittled the left-wing intellectuals for refusing to "go all out" and fight "the war against war." [d] The tension between the *Weltbühne* and the *Linkskurve* increased after 1930, when the Communist journal outdid its own party in ignoring the "National Fas-

---

[c] Heinz Pol, a close collaborator of Münzenberg was expressly told by the latter not to join the KPD. See Helmut Gruber, "Willi Münzenberg's German Communist Propaganda Empire, 1921–1933," *The Journal of Modern History,* September 1966, p. 290.

[d] Founded on August 1, 1929, by the poet Johannes R. Becher, the Hungarian journalist Andor Gábor, the proletarian writer Kurt Kläber, the satirist Erich Weinert, and the former army captain and aristocrat Ludwig Renn, *Die Linkskurve* advocated socialist realism and relentlessly tracked down bourgeois objectivism, formalism, and idealism in the writings of Communist and pro-Communist writers. The journal folded, because of financial difficulties, in December 1932. For an excellent analysis, see Werner T. Angress, "Pegasus and Insurrection: *Die Linkskurve* and Its Heritage," *Central European History,* March 1968, pp. 35–55.

cists," in other words the National Socialists, and used all its venom against the "Social Fascists." Nor could *Die Weltbühne* forgive the other journal for making the former National Socialist officer, Lieutenant Scheringer, one of its editors in 1931. When Scheringer announced in the *Linkskurve* the he would now combine his fight for a "national revolution" with the fight against "international capitalism," Ossietzky bemoaned what he called a "thorough confusion of leftist and rightist slogans in the KPD." [19]

While the writers of the *Weltbühne* bristled under the impact of the new Comintern policy, and rejected some of its unpleasant manifestations, they attacked the KPD's basic program only because they found it inappropriate for the revolutionary struggle. Reporting on the Sixth Congress of the Comintern, Heinz Pol, one of the youngest and most astute political analysts of the *Weltbühne*, wondered whether the Communists knew what they were talking about when they proclaimed the ultimate crisis of capitalism and the immediacy of revolution. Pol agreed with the Comintern's analysis of capitalist disintegration and with its contention that the Social Democrats, by supporting vanishing and increasingly antidemocratic bourgeois parties, were helping fascism to win. But, Pol wrote, this analysis was contradicted by Bukharin's and Thälmann's [*] proposed tactic, namely that the KPD should fight both Social Democrats and left-wing socialists while building the party into a multimillion-member organization. Since the majority of the workers were Social Democrats, the KPD had a long way to go, especially since "winning over" the workers meant in effect that they had to enter the Communist Party.[f] As the congress also called for the extirpation of all those elements in the Communist Party friendly to the "Social Fascists," the final struggle would be even further off in time.[20] Thus Heinz Pol saw clearly that the KPD's program was ultraleftist rhetoric rather than any real revolutionary strategy. Following the 1929 congress of the German Communist Party, Pol again criticized the tactics of the Communists and accused Thälmann of deliberately using abstract Marxist phraseology—"sharp-

---

[*] Ernst Thälmann (Hamburg, 1886—KZ Buchenwald, 1944) was the chairman of the KPD from 1925 until his arrest by the Gestapo in 1933. Originally a teamster, he was—and still is—idolized by party propaganda as the "Führer of the German Proletariat." In fact, he was conceited, coarse, and unimaginative. His loyalty to Moscow, however, could never be called into question.

[f] In 1928, the KPD had at most 150,000 dues-paying members while the SPD had 867,000. See Siegfried Bahne, "Die Kommunistische Partei Deutschlands," in Erich Matthias and Rudolf Morsey, eds., *Das Ende der Parteien 1933* (Düsseldorf, 1960), 660. Also Hunt, 100.

ening of the conflict"—to hide the fact that the party was stagnating. It had not succeeded in turning its millions of voters into party members, and instead of confronting this stark fact with honesty, it merely repeated the old formula that those who opposed the KPD were automatically counterrevolutionary. Thälmann had the cheek to call Communist clashes with the police "pre-victories" along the road to the final struggle, yet these fights against the better armed police were self-defeating and merely alienated the sympathetic Social Democratic workers who could not condone such futility.[21] Then and later, Pol and other *Weltbühne* commentators pleaded with the KPD to initiate a new united-front policy, not from "below," but in a way which would accept the differing ideological persuasions of the non-Communist workers.

The journal's fundamental sympathy for the domestic goals of the KPD did not mean agreement with the foreign policy of the German Communists, or rather, with that of Soviet Russia. *Die Weltbühne* still rejected any attempt at Soviet-German cooperation, and disapproved of the savage Communist campaign against the Young Plan on reparation payments. When, in the summer of 1929, the Nationalists and the Nazis proposed a plebiscite in favor of a "Law Against the Enslavement of the German People," in other words, a law forbidding the ratification of the Young Plan, and the Communists gave indirect support to the Right by fighting their own war against the *Sklavengesetz*,[22] Morus argued in the *Weltbühne* that the Young Plan represented a "lesser evil" and that the price to be paid for the final Allied evacuation of the Rhineland was not unduly heavy.[23] Ossietzky agreed with the Communists that, ultimately, the workers would bear the costs of the reparation payments, but still he called the signature of the Young Plan a great political victory for Germany and recommended that the treaty be ratified. If the costs were high, he wrote, this was due to the façade of prosperity that Germany had been presenting to the world in the preceding years. Now it was too late to dress in Käthe Kollwitz fashion and appeal to the good will of the American bankers![24] Besides, Ossietzky argued, neither France nor England would benefit from the German payments, for these countries were in heavy debt to the United States. He suggested as an ideal solution "an alliance of all European debtor states against America,"[25] a plan he was certain would fail since the German manufacturers were tied to the United States for credit, and preferred economic enslavement by America to a common European front. The agitation of the Nationalists against the Young Plan was but a clever camouflage, Ossietzky concluded. These, and subsequent arguments in the

Weltbühne on reparation payments, proved that most of these writers considered the capitalist offensive against the workers a specific German problem and that they did not share in the Marxist analysis of a world-wide conflict between proletarians and exploiters. The aggressive behavior of the German bourgeoisie was, for them, a "Germanic deviation" as was, incidentally, the fanaticism, intolerance, and stupidity of the German Communist leaders. In international affairs, most of these writers remained pacifists and democrats who looked to one or more of the Western powers for salvation.

Weimar Germany's last Great Coalition cabinet broke up in March 1930 over a dispute between the SPD and the People's Party on how to eliminate a heavy deficit in the unemployment fund. Pressed by the trade unions and a left-wing rebellion in the party, the SPD asked for new taxes on business, while the People's Party, under similar pressure by its industrialist supporters, advocated a cut in unemployment benefits. Behind it all loomed the growing threat of depression, the socialists' fear for the future of the country's welfare system, and the manufacturers' desire to lower wages as a means of sustaining them in competition in the world market. In the controversy over free enterprise versus welfare state, writes K. D. Bracher,[26] parliamentary democracy itself came under fire, as an increasing number of industrialists felt that only an authoritarian state could save them and free enterprise from ruin. Still, the fall of the Müller government could have been averted had not Hindenburg and the crucial Center party been eager to see the end of the Great Coalition. Hindenburg, General Schleicher, and the two leaders of the Center—Kaas and Brüning—tolerated the crisis, if they did not actually promote it, because they saw in it a long awaited opportunity for authoritarian government.[27] With the SPD in opposition, the formation of a majority government was impossible. Heinrich Brüning, whom Hindenburg appointed as chancellor, was forced to rely (and relished doing so) on the doubtful constitutional privilege of the President to authorize emergency legislation. In March 1930, Weimar Germany's parliamentary government was replaced by a "state standing above parties" (*Staat über den Parteien*), to use Werner Conze's apt definition.[28] Three years later, the latter ceded to a "state without parties" (*Staat ohne Parteien*).

In July 1930, the combined votes of Social Democrats, Communists, Nazis (NSDAP), and most of the Nationalists, upset Brüning's first two emergency decrees aimed at the restoration of the budget. The President thereupon dissolved the Reichstag and called for new elections on September 14, 1930. In these elections the National Socialists emerged with 107 seats. All other parties, with the exception of the KPD and the Center, lost heavily, and the People's Party, as well as the Democrats (now *Staatspartei*) were fatally weakened. Since Brüning's moderate Conservative-Catholic camp would not, and could not, form a coalition with either the radical Right or the SPD, the future of the minority government depended on the Social Democrats' willingness to "tolerate" Brüning.[29]

The success of the NSDAP and the decline of the bourgeois republican parties presented the socialist camp with a new set of problems. Starting out from the premise that the present crisis of capitalism was temporary—it represented a "trough" (*Wellental*) in capitalist production—the Social Democratic leaders argued that it was too early for the workers to seize power. Consequently, they should tolerate the Brüning cabinet as a "lesser evil" (*kleineres Übel*) while exerting every effort to combat the National Socialist danger. Conscious of their role as the last defenders of democracy and the republic, the SPD leaders authorized the creation in December 1931 of a new militant mass organization: the "Iron Front for Resistance Against Fascism" composed of the Socialist Youth, the Reichsbanner, and all sympathetic republicans. Led by such enthusiastic young men as Carlo Mierendorff, Theodor Haubach, Julius Leber, and Kurt Schumacher, as well as the Reichsbanner leader Höltermann, the new organization achieved wonders in mass mobilization, in launching popular slogans, and even in arming the Social Democratic workers.[30] But the SPD leadership did not point to positive goals beyond the defeat of fascism; it did not hold out to the workers the promise of power, nor the abolition of capitalism,—the cause of the depression—and finally, it did not dare call for an armed fight against fascism. Trained in the tradition of legality, anxious about the lives of the workers and the tremendous financial assets of the trade unions, these leaders insisted to the end on democratic procedure. Thus Social Democracy succumbed to Hitler without final resistance.[g]

As for the Communists, they were convinced that, with Brüning, German capitalism had reached its penultimate stage of "fascist transformation." The proper timing for a revolution would be the ultimate stage: Hitler's appointment by the capitalists. Hitler as chancellor

---

[g] Whether or not the Iron Front was capable of effective resistance in July 1932, when the Prussian republican government was illegally dissolved by Chancellor Papen, or again in February–March 1933, is today an academic question. Erich Matthias maintains in his authoritative "Die Sozialdemokratische Partei Deutschlands," Matthias and Morsey, 142 ff., that strong elements in the Iron Front were ready to fight in both instances and that they would at least have put up a good showing.

would automatically bring about the collapse of the bourgeois order. This interpretation was responsible for the virtual immobilization of the German Communists between 1930 and 1933; they accomplished nothing of significance, which was what Stalin had wanted the German Communists to do in the first place.[h] As Kurt Hiller wrote in 1931, on the one side are the Social Democrats holding up a wall which they wish to wreck later; on the other side advance the cohorts of the KPD sounding trumpets, horns, bassoons, and bullhorns. Unfortunately, the walls of capitalism are not those of Jericho.[31]

The policies of both the SPD and the KPD were strongly opposed by a substantial leftist minority in the Social Democratic Party. Max Seydewitz, Kurt Rosenfeld, Heinrich Ströbel, and other left-wing socialists gathered around the journal, *Der Klassenkampf*, rejected the SPD's policy of "lesser evil" and demanded that in the event of an attack by the Right on the democratic foundations of the republic, the proletariat seize power and establish a temporary dictatorship. They also called for a tactical united front of Social Democrats and Communists. The left-wing Socialists were repudiated by the SPD leadership, while the KPD called them the worst of the "Social Fascists." When they seceded—or were expelled—from the SPD, they bereft themselves of influence. Their Socialist Workers' Party or SAPD, founded in October 1931,[i] received almost no popular support during the subsequent elections.[32]

Léon Trotsky had relatively few avowed political supporters in Weimar Germany, and some of these, for instance Paul Frölich, went along with the SAP in 1931, but Trotsky's views on the German crisis were so refreshing, and they were so strongly represented in the *Weltbühne*, that a brief presentation is in order.[33] Indeed, it is enough to know what Trotsky had to say at that time, to understand how some *Weltbühne* collaborators, especially Fritz Sternberg,[34] evaluated the situation.

The economic crisis, Trotsky argued, rendered it impossible for the

---

[h] So at least argue such critics of Stalin as Franz Borkenau, *The Communist International* (London, 1938), 337 ff., and Buber-Neumann, *Von Potsdam nach Moskau*, 284 ff. Trotsky, of course, held similar views.

[i] Most writers of the *Weltbühne* identified themselves closely with the left-wing socialists and the SAPD, even if they harbored grave doubts about the future of the splinter party. On the other hand, Fritz Sternberg criticized the SAPD's hesitancy and wrote that if the KPD had a rational and truly revolutionary policy in the trade unions, it could attract the SAPD members into its ranks immediately. (K. L. Gerstorff [Sternberg], "SPD Gespalten!," *Die Weltbühne*, October 6, 1931, pp. 504–508.) Similarly, Trotsky discounted the SAPD as a mere propaganda group to be won over by the KPD like all Social Democrats. ("Et maintenant," *Écrits*, III, pp. 146 f., and 166 ff.)

great industrial and business class to maintain its rule through parliamentary democracy. Those hardest hit by the depression, the working class and the middle class, were no longer content to follow their parliamentary parties. The Social Democrats were now more than ever manifesting their inability to fight for the living standards of the workers; the middle class was deserting the moderate bourgeois parties for National Socialism. Nazism, wrote Trotsky, was a movement of "counterrevolutionary despair," springing from the depths of the petty bourgeoisie *acharnée*. Ruined by continual crises, threatened by both monopoly capitalism and the organized proletariat, these small shopkeepers, artisans, and officials hated big business as much as they hated the working class. They envied both for their ability to defend themselves through their political and economic organizations, something that the middle class was unable to do. The plebian movement of these middle strata, Nazism, was a conglomeration of irrational and neurotic fears: Jewish finance, big business, corrupt political parties, Bolshevism. Having no independent or realistic politics, these strata would follow either the bourgeoisie or the proletariat. Nazism could never fulfill any of its demagogic promises for the alleviation of the lot of the middle class and would eventually make a deal with industrial and financial interests in order to solve the latter's problem of maintaining power. This solution was nothing less than the wholesale destruction not only of the revolutionary proletariat, but the entire labor movement. The fascist solution was dangerous for the capitalists, however, because it involved open confrontation with the revolutionary proletariat in a civil war. All antagonisms in this protracted struggle, Trotsky argued, made for a very volatile situation, in which the working-class parties must seize the initiative, or else fascism would triumph. For only by demonstrating its thorough determination to take power could the proletariat win these impoverished and desperate masses to its cause.

But this is exactly what the German working-class parties were not doing, Trotsky continued. Through their passivity, they were forcing the petty bourgeois into the ranks of the Nazis, and already some workers were following in their footsteps. The Social Democrats, by supporting anyone short of Hitler, were defending a status quo no longer tolerable to their own rank and file, and were buttressing the comparatively moderate bourgeois parties which the middle class was deserting precisely for their moderation. As for the KPD, it would make itself even more responsible for the coming colossal defeat if it did not take the necessary determined action. By lumping the SPD,

Brüning, and the Nazis all in the same "fascist" category, by telling the masses that Brüning was no different from Hitler, and that the SPD leaders Wels and Severing were no different from Brüning, the Communists were not only deceiving their followers but were also disarming them before the onslaught of real fascism. Thälmann was a fool to pride himself on the fact that in September 1930 the KPD had increased its votes by over a million—he ought rather to worry about the five million new Nazi votes. If the fascists, Trotsky wrote, were able to mobilize such a vast following at the beginning of the crisis, how much more support would they receive with its intensification![35] Although parliamentary democracy and fascism were both forms of capitalist rule, there was a distinction, even if Brüning ruled by decree. In parliamentary democracy, the bourgeoisie governed by compromise with the working-class organizations, and therefore had to tolerate them as autonomous agents with which to bargain. Working-class organizations were "islands of proletarian democracy within bourgeois democracy," from where sallies could be made against capitalist rule. Even Brüning had to do some bargaining, and would and could not destroy these islands because the forces he represented were too weak to do so. The most pressing task for the KPD was openly and honestly to insist on a united front with the SPD in order to defend these proletarian islands, just as the Bolsheviks and Mensheviks had defended the Kerensky government from the counterrevolutionary army of Kornilov. In this united front each party was to organize its separate armed combat units in the factories and trade unions, but they were to strike together against fascist attacks on working-class organizations, or on the government. Further, the KPD was to demand that the Social Democratic organizations disaffiliate with the bourgeois republican organizations in the Iron Front. On their part, the Communists were to give up their sectarian "red" trade unions ("Revolutionäre Gewerkschafts-Opposition" or RGO).[j] Trotsky also recommended that the KPD end its submission to Soviet

---

[j] The meaning of the term RGO was not always clear and it was often interpreted as "Rote Gewerkschafts-Organisation" or something similar to that. Finally, however, the term "Revolutionäre Gewerkschafts-Opposition" prevailed, reflecting the determination of the KPD to treat the Red trade unions not as a separate organization but, rather, as a revolutionary movement within the Social Democratic trade unions. In the winter of 1930–1931, the RGO and affiliated "red groups" (*rote Verbände*), boasted approximately 136,000 members. At the same time, the Social Democratic Free Trade Unions (ADGB) had a membership of about 4.8 million. See Bahne in Matthias and Morsey, 664, and Hunt, 168.

bureaucracy and restore internal democracy; failing this, it would not make the right moves at the right time. Finally, Trotsky urged the KPD to make propaganda within the united front and elsewhere for Soviet power.[36]

But what was the KPD actually doing? Not only did it show every sign of sectarianism, Trotsky observed, but it also exhibited crass opportunism by trying to outdo the Nazis with its chauvinistic slogans. This was just as self-defeating as the smug assertion of the KPD leaders that an eventual Nazi takeover would immediately be overthrown by the working class. In waiting for that day with such complacency, Trotsky declared, the KPD was actually declaring the battle already lost. By then, the fascists would have absorbed so much of the state apparatus and bureaucracy, that the latter would be ready to do what they were meant to do, namely, to "ride like a great tank" over the skulls and spines of the workers, and launch a period of unprecedented barbarism. Anyone who minimized this threat, or the necessity to rally immediately, was a criminal.

Excerpts from Trotsky's evaluation of the German crisis first appeared in the *Weltbühne* in Ossietzky's laudatory review of Trotsky's pamphlet *Soll der Fascismus wirklich siegen?* [37] In March 1932, *Die Weltbühne* printed Trotsky's attack on Soviet bureaucracy occasioned by the Eleventh Plenum of the Executive Committee (ECCI) of the Comintern which had proclaimed an even more vitriolic hostility to all sorts of socialists.[38] In the fall of that year another article by Trotsky appeared in the journal.[39] Ossietzky, Erich Mühsam, Hiller, Heinz Pol, and above all Fritz Sternberg, echoed most of Trotsky's brilliant analysis frequently and vehemently. They appealed for a recognition of the fascist threat,[40] condemned the suicidal "armed uprisings" staged by the Communists as well as their chauvinistic slogans, and exhorted the Communists to initiate fraternal SPD and KPD combat units in the factories and trade unions.[41] Even Ossietzky, usually so averse to military action and violence, regretted that youth groups of both parties had not moved to attack the Nazi and Nationalist rioters who had prevented the presentation of the film "All Quiet on the Western Front" in December 1930 in Berlin. "Fascism can be beaten only in the streets," he wrote. "Against the National Socialist mob there is only one logic, that of the heavier club: *À un corsaire—corsaire et demi!*" [42]

Despite a similarity of views, the *Weltbühne* writers often differed from Trotsky's theses. They were, for one, generally less critical of Communist policy than was Trotsky, particularly because of their

Siegfried Jacobsohn, 1925
Photo: Kurt Tucholsky Archiv

Kurt Tucholsky, 1923
Photo: Kurt Tucholsky Archiv

Revolutionary soldiers and sailors in the courtyard of the Imperial Palace in Berlin, November 1918.

United Press International Photo

II. Jahrg.   Berlin, 8. Februar 1906.   Nr. 6

Die
Schaubühne

Herausgeber:

Siegfried Jacobsohn

Inhalt:

Preis 20 Pf., vierteljährlich 2,50 M.

Erscheint jeden Donnerstag

Oesterheld & Co., Verlag, Berlin W. 15, Lietzenburgerstraße 60.

The title page of the *Schaubühne*

Die Weltbühne

Der Schaubühne XXV. Jahr

Wochenschrift für Politik · Kunst · Wirtschaft

Begründet von Siegfried Jacobsohn

Unter Mitarbeit von Kurt Tucholsky
· geleitet von Carl v. Ossietzky

Erscheint jeden Dienstag

XXV. Jahrgang   10. September 1929   Nummer 37

Versandort Potsdam

Verlag der Weltbühne

Charlottenburg · Kantstrasse 152

The cover of the *Weltbühne*

Die neue Weltbühne

Wochenschrift für Politik·Kunst·Wirtschaft

Der Weltbühne XXXII. Jahrgang
Begründet von Siegfried Jacobsohn

Erscheint jeden Donnerstag

XXXII. Jahrgang   26. November 1936   Nummer 48

Prag   Zürich   Paris

The cover of the *Neue Weltbühne*

The Independent Socialist leader Georg Ledebour leaving the Chancellor's office in Berlin, 1919

United Press International Photo

The pacifist leader Ludwig Quidde, 1919
United Press International Photo

President and Mrs. Ebert leaving the polling place in Berlin, 1920
United Press International Photo

Berlin housewife using inflated marks to light fire for breakfast
United Press International Photo

"This parchment face with a pointed nose, this Pater Filucius with the Iron Cross First Class on his rosary."—Ossietzky on Chancellor Brüning, 1930.

From the cover of Wilhelm Busch, PATER FILUCIUS

Ernst Toller in his New York exile, 1938
Photo: New York Public Library

Kurt Tucholsky, 1920
*Photo: Kurt Tuchol-
sky Archiv*

Kurt and Mary Tucholsky, 1927
Photo: Kurt Tucholsky Archiv

Ossietzky in 1919
Photo: Kurt Tucholsky Archiv

Ossietzky entering prison in Berlin-Tegel, in May 1932, flanked on his left by his lawyer,
Kurt Rosenfeld
Photo: Wide World

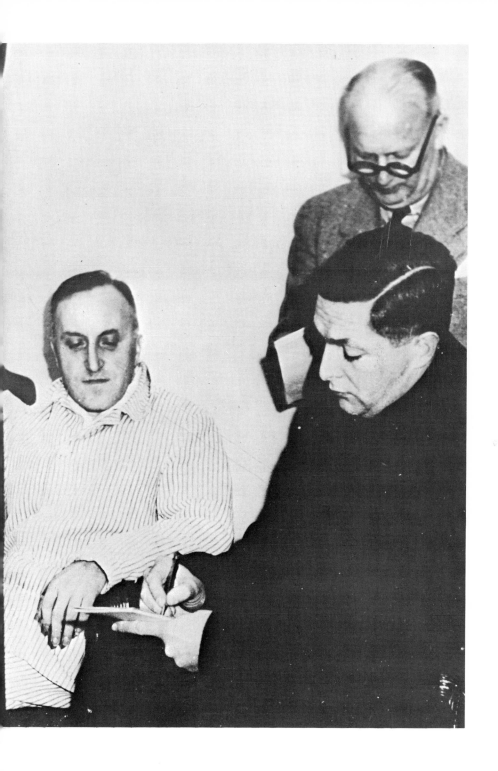

Ossietzky interviewed by newspapermen after receiving the Nobel Price for Peace in 1936.

Photo: Wide World

Nummer 562: Carl von Ossietzky

Weil er rechtzeitig auf die Kriegsvorbereitungen der deutschen Generalaclique hinwies und vor einer Entwicklung warnte, die der Nürnberger Prozeß in ihren verbrecherischen Folgen zeigt, wurde Ossietzky, ein mutiger Mann aus dem demokratischen Bürgertum Deutschlands, im KZ Oranienburg zu Tode gemartert.

Prisoner No. 562: Ossietzky in the Oranienburg concentration camp.
Photo reproduced from Neue Illustrierte Zeitung

annoyance with the SPD. In the summer of 1931, the so-called "National Opposition," that is the Nazis, Hugenberg's Nationalists, and the Stahlhelm, launched a "popular demand" for the dissolution of the Prussian parliament which, in turn, would have brought about the fall of the SPD-led coalition government in Prussia. The KPD first condemned this move as a "fascist swindle," then suddenly reversed itself and joined in what it now called the "Red Referendum." This plebiscite, held in August 1931, brought only 9.8 million votes in favor of the measure, not enough to make it binding, but the hitherto inconceivable idea of a "united front" combining the far Left with the far Right had nevertheless become a reality.[43] Trotsky in his "Contre le national-socialisme" described the "Red referendum" as the most heinous example of the KPD's ultraleftist tactics. The Communists had participated in the plebiscite merely to oppose the SPD; no lessons were posed for either the Social Democratic or Communist workers, and the latter were not differentiated in any way from the Nazis.[44] Ossietzky, on the other hand, did not blame the KPD at all; rather, he attacked the SPD for its refusal to come to an agreement with the Communists. All that the KPD had asked, according to Ossietzky, in proposing its abstention from the fascist referendum, was that its civil rights be restored in Prussia. But the SPD had refused this offer.[45]

Again, as opposed to Trotsky, the *Weltbühne* showed tolerance and understanding toward Soviet Russia and Stalin. All *Weltbühne* writers, including Fritz Sternberg, refused to accept Trotsky's contention that the self-destructive program of the KPD was due to the Soviet Party apparatus. *Die Weltbühne* tended to view Thälmann as the real culprit, and to exonerate Stalin of any blame for Comintern policy. Paradoxically, the KPD was spoken of during this time as being a parrot of Moscow, and the author of its own vicious and foolish propaganda. Back in 1928, Ossietzky sided with Stalin against Trotsky, calling the latter's "pure" Leninism unrealistic and dangerous to world peace.[46] In the following year, Heinz Pol denied that Stalin, "the only man finally able to bring socialism to Russia," could be responsible for Thälmann's stupidity.[47] In his 1931 review of Trotsky's pamphlet, Ossietzky admonished Trotsky for his attacks on Stalin and the Soviet Party.[48] Even Fritz Sternberg who condemned the KPD's trade-union policies most vehemently, held that these policies were contrary to Moscow's advice.[49] Trotsky, of course, argued that the reason for the ultraleftist and ultimately counterrevolutionary tactic of the KPD lay in the Soviet bureaucracy's need to stifle opposition to its erroneous policy. The bureaucracy's rule had been rendered precarious by defeats abroad, and by a crisis situation at home brought about by the bureaucracy's autarchic and brutal industrialization policy. Cooperation with Social Democracy abroad would have strengthened the left-oppositionary elements in Soviet Russia which looked to the victory of the European working class as a solution for Soviet Russia's economic and social problems.[50]

The *Weltbühne's* defense of Stalin was all the more remarkable as the journal welcomed Trotsky's contributions and strongly denounced Stalin for having driven Trotsky into exile.[51] More than once, *Die Weltbühne* accused Stalin of mad imperial ambitions, and voiced increasing anxiety over the forced industrialization and collectivization program. And it sharply condemned the first Moscow show trials, for instance, that of the "Forty-Eight Specialists."[52] In the words of Arnold Zweig, it was a biological error to treat human beings as ants or bees, and it was criminal to sacrifice masses of citizens for the sake of a doubtful program.[53]

The contradictory views on Stalinism can be explained only by the utter contempt in which the *Weltbühne* writers held the German Communists. If the Russian Communists were bad, they were not as bad as the German Communists, who in turn could not be as bad as the other great German parties. Further, the *Weltbühne* writers had much less confidence in the revolutionary potential of the European working class than did Trotsky, which caused them to look with some sympathy at Stalin's "national Communism" and his program of "socialism in one country."

Finally, although they repeatedly interpreted the rise of National Socialism with a clairvoyance similar to Trotsky's, many *Weltbühne* writers, above all Ossietzky, faltered in their detachment. In fact, only Sternberg, Mühsam, Toller, Hiller, and Pol were really consistent in recognizing both the supreme danger posed by National Socialism and the genuine antagonism between the Nazis and other groups in the bourgeois camp.

For one, the Nazis were often described in the *Weltbühne* as puppets of the Nationalist leader Alfred Hugenberg and the industrialists. This was the line of the KPD, and incidentally also the firm conviction of Hugenberg. Early in 1930, Ossietzky called Hitler the "Golem" of Hugenberg, and added:

Hugenberg will never let his Golem become too independent; when Hitler will no longer fit his plans, he will cut off his resources and the National Socialist movement will disappear as mysteriously as it mushroomed during the past two years.[54]

Writing on the night of the Reichstag elections in September 1930, but before the results were announced, Ossietzky derided the Social Democrats for having campaigned against "the little Goebbels who does not exist at all, instead of concentrating on the real candidate for dictatorship, Herr Brüning."[55] Even after the Nazi electoral victory, and well into January 1933, scores of commentators announced in the *Weltbühne* the forthcoming disappearance of the National Socialist movement or its replacement by the industrialists with a more reliable and better lead mass party.[56]

There was an unfortunate tendency to present the Nazis as a bunch of psychopaths who could not possibly garner lasting popular support and would soon be repudiated by the masses. Goebbels, for instance, generally figured as "Goebbeles" in the *Weltbühne*, and was endowed with the characteristics of a Jewish peddler. The Nazi leaders were "scatter-brains and lunatics" and Hitler a "cowardly, effeminate *Pyjamaexistenz*, a petty bourgeois rebel inclined to obesity."[57]

Their acceptance of Communist terminology caused a great deal of semantic confusion among writers untrained in Marxist ideology. Tucholsky wrote in March 1932, that is, at a time when Brüning was still chancellor:

Satire has its upper limits: Buddha is beyond its reach. But there are lower limits also: in Germany, for instance, the ruling fascist powers. Not worth it. One cannot shoot that low.[58]

Not only did Tucholsky repeat verbatim the current KPD slogan in regard to Brüning's government: "the ruling fascist powers" (*die herrschenden faschistischen Mächte*), but he unwittingly denied his life purpose which was to fight with all the brilliant talent at his disposal against the clericalists, militarists, and monarchists, all of whom Brüning united in his person. In fact, Tucholsky hardly ever "shot" at the real fascists, the National Socialist Party.

Finally, *Die Weltbühne* repeatedly voiced the sentiment that the Nazis could never sustain their assumption of power and therefore it might be best to let them come to power. This was again the line of the KPD, as well as of a growing number of republicans and non-Nazi rightists. Let them take over, argued "Quietus" in the *Weltbühne* after the elections in September 1930: power would not only burden Dr. Frick[k] and Company with the responsibility for such oppressive measures as increased taxation but would also destroy their popularity by

---

[k] Wilhelm Frick, executed at Nuremberg in 1946, was the parliamentary leader of the NSDAP in the Weimar era.

making bosses (*Bonzen*) and bureaucrats out of the Nazi leaders.[59] "If given power, the Nazis will soon ruin themselves by mismanagement (*sie werden bald abwirtschaften*)," argued H-E. Kaminski at the same time. If Germany wants to have a strong man, let her have one.[60] And Ossietzky wrote in 1931:

Like a horrible enchanted forest, the fascist era lies ahead of us. It is crowded with frightening creatures and secret traps. Never mind. We must pass through it.[61]

Ernst Toller protested the collective masochism inherent in the let-them-take-over theory:

They are forgetting that the National Socialist Party is characterized by its will to acquire and sustain power. The NSDAP will luxuriate in a power legally acquired, but once at the top, it will never surrender this power at the behest of democracy.[62]

Toller urged the Communist and Social Democratic trade unions to form a united front against National Socialism, and warned:

Unless we act now, we will have to face the age of European fascism where all social, political, and spiritual freedoms will disappear: an age which will culminate in a horrible and bloody war, and in chaos.[63]

There were many reasons for the repeated departure of Ossietzky and other *Weltbühne* writers from their basically perceptive views on National Socialism. For one, many of these writers still trusted the "educated people" and felt that the latter would not tolerate or follow the National Socialist madness in the long run. Their hatred and contempt for Brüning was certainly another factor. Ossietzky, who in these years wrote twice as many political editorials in the *Weltbühne* as any of the other writers, spent an inordinate amount of time excoriating Brüning. He was outraged to learn that Brüning's selection for office was based in large part on this machine-gun officer's wartime heroism: "With him the *Frontgeneration* came into power. The nation sets out on a new road in a thunder of steel [*Stahlgewittern*], but who in England or France cares whether Baldwin or Tardieu knew how to shoot."[64] The anticlerical in him seethed against the priestlike asceticism of Brüning, his esteem for eloquence and dynamic leadership against the cautious reserve and cultivated aloofness of the chancellor. He disliked the very looks of Brüning. "This parchment face with a pointed nose, this Pater Filucius with the Iron Cross First Class on his rosary, when will he disappear at last?"[65]

In the spring of 1932, President Hindenburg's seven-year term in office expired. Anxious to secure continued support for his austerity program and also to prevent the election of Hitler, Brüning persuaded the 85-year-old field marshal to run again for office. To Hindenburg's utter embarrassment, he was opposed on the Right not only by Hitler but by the candidate of the Nationalists, the Stahlhelm leader Duesterberg. The moderate conservatives, bourgeois republicans, and Social Democrats supported Hindenburg, while the Communists nominated Thälmann. As the first round of elections on March 13 brought no decision, a runoff election was held on April 10 with Hindenburg, Hitler, and Thälmann the only candidates. In the second balloting, most of the Nationalists voted for Hitler,[66] and Hindenburg's final victory was due entirely to the loyalty of the republicans, essentially the Social Democratic voters. The 3.7 million ballots cast for Thälmann (as opposed to Hindenburg's 19.3 million votes and Hitler's 13.4 million) only helped to demonstrate the Communists' weakness.

In January 1932, Trotsky had written that even the Trotskyists should vote for Thälmann, and that the KPD should under no conditions support the candidate of any other party.[67] The choice of the *Weltbühne* writers had not been all that simple, but after some hesitation they also ended up in support of the Communist candidate. There was, at first, some talk in the journal about a unitary candidate for the two working-class parties; Hiller devoted a good deal of energy trying to find the person acceptable to all socialists. Having dismissed, successively, Georg Ledebour, whom at 82 he found too old; Willi Eichler, leader of the International Socialist Militant League (ISK) as too little known; Albert Einstein, Ernst Toller, and Alfons Goldschmidt because they were Jewish, Hiller urged the Social Democrats and Communists to agree on the candidacy of Heinrich Mann. He recalled for the benefit of the German Left the case of Czechoslovakia where Masaryk, a professor of philosophy, was president, and added that Heinrich Mann would be acceptable both to Moscow and Paris. He knew that his proposition would meet with "irony and laughter," [1] but then Hindenburg as a candidate of socialism was, for him, no less an ironical proposition.[68] Hiller eventually came out in favor of Thälmann. Ossietzky was undecided for several weeks before the election. In a private letter to a *Weltbühne* reader early in February 1932, he recommended abstention as the only honest course of

---

[1] Because of his electoral propositions, Hiller was indeed called a "camp follower of the united front," "a dangerous madman," and a "child" by Bruno Frei in Münzenberg's *Berlin am Morgen*. See Hiller, *Koepfe und Troepfe*, 37.

action.[69] In his editorial, he predicted that millions would stay away from the polls.[70] By March 1, he came to a decision. Dismissing the Social Democratic argument that a vote for Hindenburg was a vote against fascism, he announced in the journal that he would vote for the candidate of the KPD.

Let me make it clear that by voting for Thälmann, I am not voting confidence in the Communist Party. . . . But to be a leftist means to direct all one's efforts in the direction of the battle position of the Left. Thälmann is the only leftist [in this campaign]; all the others represent varying shades of reaction. This makes the choice easier.[71]

He knew well, Ossietzky continued, that the first round of elections would bring no decision. Every vote cast for Thälmann would therefore underscore the need for a unitary socialist candidate in the second ballot. A week later, he repeated his argument in favor of Thälmann:

Our republican friends lift a wagging finger at us asking: "What if the votes cast for Thälmann lead to the election of Hitler?" To this we answer with another question: "And what if Hindenburg is elected?" [72]

Yet when the first ballot was over, Ossietzky praised the Social Democratic voters:

Without the heavy infantry of Social Democracy, without the engineers of the trade unions, the "Hindenburg battle" would have been lost from the very start. This Imperial field marshal, who once openly proclaimed his belief in the stab-in-the-back legend, was saved by the votes of the "November criminals." This time again, as in every single political battle since 1918, the real hero of the struggle was the unknown soldier of Social Democracy. With a last desperate effort he once more saved the remnants of democracy. . . . Unknown soldier of Social Democracy, you most patient of all fighters! When you die, none of the finely caparisoned Treviranuses [m] will lift his top hat at your memorial . . . if you ever get one! [73]

Following the elections, Chancellor Brüning ordered the dissolution of the SA, the SS, and other fighting organizations of the NSDAP. But the joy of the republicans lasted only a few weeks. In the Landtag (state parliament) elections of April 24, the National Socialists again made great advances, especially in Prussia, scoring twice as many votes there as did the Social Democrats. This was the end of Prussia as a "fortress of democracy" in a reactionary Reich, even if, for the time being, the coalition cabinet of the Social Democratic Otto Braun

---

[m] Gottfried Treviranus, member of the Brüning cabinet, was the leader of the "People's Conservative Association," an attempted moderate conservative answer to the Nationalist and National Socialist challenge.

remained in office as a caretaker government. Commenting on the Prussian elections, Sternberg argued that now was the time for the Communists to initiate a united front with Social Democracy: the weakened SPD could not possibly turn down an overture from the KPD.[74] Hiller published excerpts from Lenin's *Left-Wing Communism —an Infantile Disorder* to remind the KPD how far it had strayed from the correct Communist program.[75] Ossietzky implored the Social Democrats to abandon their toleration of the Reich government and start negotiations for a united front with the Communists:

I ask you Social Democrats and Communists, do you think you will have a chance to begin talks tomorrow? Do you think that they will let you negotiate tomorrow? I certainly do not ignore the magnitude of the antagonisms that have arisen between you. I know them better than anyone else, for in the past I have received blows from both of you.[76]

Ossietzky proposed that nonparty intellectuals act as go-betweens for the two parties: "In these days, the future of all German Social Democrats and Communists will be decided. . . . There is somewhere a round table—waiting." [77]

Part Four

LOSING THE BATTLE

Chapter XIII
THE *WELTBÜHNE* TRIAL

When Ossietzky was preparing his dispirited appraisal of the 1932 Prussian elections for the press, he was already under prison sentence; on May 10, the editor in chief of the *Weltbühne* began his confinement. The provocation for what became the "Ossietzky affair" was an article written by Walter Kreiser, an expert on German aviation; it appeared in the *Weltbühne* on March 12, 1929, under the title "Windiges aus der deutschen Luftfahrt" (approximately: "Hot Air in German Aeronautics").[1] Kreiser, who wrote under the pen name Heinz Jäger, was an aircraft designer and president of a German airmen's association;[2] his intimacy with government aviation policy was undeniable.

In his article, Kreiser dealt initially with various abuses in Germany's aviation industry and with useless government subsidies to failing aviation plants. He then went on to declare that the marine research institute, "Severa," ostensibly associated with the civilian Lufthansa, was in reality a heavily financed undertaking of the German Admiralty. When parliamentary critics requested the liquidation of this secret naval air plant, Kreiser related, its name but not its function was changed. "Similar tricks" were played, Kreiser asserted, by Minister of Defense Groener in connection with a certain "Abteilung M," a civilian plant testing military aircraft from an airport near Berlin. When a year earlier (Februay 3, 1928), the Social Democatic deputy Richard Krüger requested clarification regarding the function of "Abteilung M" from the representative of the government in the budget commission of the Reichstag, he received no reply. Subsequent to that incident, the plant changed its name and its location (elsewhere on the airport) but its function remained the same. "Severa" and "Abteilung M" operated between thirty and forty (military) aircraft each, the writer reported. Worse still: "Not all the airplanes are always in Germany. . . ." [3] In the manuscript prepared for the press, Kreiser had named Soviet Russia as the alternate resting place of the aircraft but Ossietzky deleted this particular.[a] The three dots replacing Ossietzky's deletion presented no mystery to anyone aware of the military rapport between Soviet Russia and Germany, that is, to almost any newspaper reader. Kreiser's printed revelations were also quite unsensational. Most of his facts were already in print in the protocols of the 312th session of the budget commission of the Reichstag held on February 3, 1928. These circumstances did not affect the Reichswehr's request for an indictment of the author of the article and of the *Weltbühne's* "responsible" editor.

Kreiser and Ossietzky were interrogated by a magistrate of the Reichsgericht (Supreme Court) in Leipzig in August 1929 [b] and, after an incomprehensibly long delay, were indicted on March 30, 1931, for "espionage and treason." [4] They were accused, specifically, of having divulged information on "Abteilung M," with "the preconceived purpose of thereby drawing the attention of foreign governments to facts which should have been kept secret in the interest of national defense." [c]

---

[a] Alfred Pohlmann, "Wer war Carl von Ossietzky? Weitere Dokumente zu einem heute wieder vieldiskutierten Fall," *Die Zeit* (Hamburg), November 23, 1962, p. 9. Pohlmann wrote his article at the time of the famous *Der Spiegel* controversy in Western Germany which pitted the minister of defense, Franz Joseph Strauss, against this much too inquisitive Hamburg journal.

[b] According to the German legal code, crimes involving treason had to go before the Reichsgericht, against whose judgment no appeal was possible.

[c] Quoted in André Pironneau, "Les révélations du procès Kreiser-Ossietzky," *L'écho de Paris*, February 21, 1932. As both the investigation and the trial of Kreiser and Ossietzky were conducted in secret, with silence imposed on the defendants and their counsels, details of the procedures could not be divulged in Germany at that time. Early in 1932, however, Walter Kreiser fled to Paris where he published his story in the French nationalist newspaper, *L'écho de Paris*. Kreiser put at the disposal of the newspaper several important documents: the bill of indictment of March 30, 1931, prepared by Reich Prosecutor-General Werner; the correspondence between Werner and von Bülow, secretary of state at the Foreign Ministry, and a stenographic transcript of the verbal opinion of the judges taken during the trial by Dr. Apfel. Kreiser gave no indication how he had acquired these documents, but their detailed presentation in the newspaper seems to confirm their authenticity. As the official records of the trial, kept in the "Deutsches Zentralarchiv" in Potsdam are closed to the public, the revelations of *L'écho de Paris* must be accepted for what they are worth. It should be noted, however, that the German Ministry of Defense denied the accuracy of the documents in a short statement distributed by the Wolff news

Ossietzky and Kreiser appeared before the "red robes"—as the judges in Leipzig were called—of the Fourth Senate (*IV. Strafsenat*) of the Reichsgericht on November 17, 1931. The presiding judge was the same Reichsgericht Councellor Baumgarten who, in the fall of 1930, had presided over the so-called Reichswehr trial of Lieutenant Scheringer and his two companions.[d] Baumgarten's polite patience toward an arrogant Hitler in the witness stand drew an acrimonious commentary at the time of that trial from Ossietzky.[5]

Ossietzky and Kreiser were defended by Max Alsberg, Alfred Apfel, Rudolf Olden, and Kurt Rosenfeld, all well-known collaborators of the *Weltbühne.* The defense counsels argued that Kreiser's data had been cited in the report of the Reichstag's budget commission, that articles 198–203 of the Versailles treaty, which after all was a German law, had denied Germany the right to maintain an air arm, and that the defendants were exercising the prerogative of citizens to remind the authorities of their responsibilities. The judges, in turn, questioned neither the authenticity of Kreiser's data, nor the illegality of German rearmament. According to the account of the trial in *L'écho de Paris,* the expert witnesses of the Ministry of Defense (Major Himer) and of the Ministry of Transport (Dr. Wegert) confirmed the accuracy of Kreiser's statements; the French newspaper also reported that the Ministry of Foreign Affairs submitted a letter to the state prosecutor affirming that the facts cited in the article were indeed contrary to the terms of the Versailles treaty.[6] But, the prosecutor explained, this was exactly what damned the defendants. The silence of the Ministry of Defense when questioned by deputy Krüger in 1928 should have been sufficient warning to the defendants that the problem was not to be publicly aired. The judges agreed with the prosecutor: "The informa-

---

agency on February 27, 1932. The very secrecy of the trial shows that Kreiser could not have been far off the mark. For the account which appeared in the Paris newspaper, see André Pironneau, "Les révélations du procès Kreiser-Ossietzky," *L'écho de Paris,* February 21, 22, 23, 25, 1932, and Walter Kreiser, "La politique militaire de l'Allemagne," *ibid.,* April 9, 10, 14, 16, 1932. All articles were printed on the first page and were given equal space with the report on the formation of France's new Tardieu cabinet.

[d] It was at this trial (at which three young officers of the Reichswehr were sentenced to various terms in prison for National Socialist agitation) that Hitler made his well-kept promise to acquire power by legal means only and, once in power, to exterminate the "November criminals." It is noteworthy that the officers were tried and sentenced at the insistence of General Groener. See Freiherr Kurt von Reibnitz, "Das Reichsgerichtsurteil gegen die Ulmer Offiziere vom 4.10.1930," *Die Justiz,* January 1931, pp. 187 ff.; Otto-Ernst Schüddekopf, ed., *Das Heer und die Republik* (Hannover, 1955), 265 ff., and Ossietzky, "Der Prozess der Offiziere," *Die Weltbühne,* October 1, 1930, p. 501.

tion was in no sense known to foreign governments before its publication. . . . The 'Heeresleitung,' despite the Versailles treaty and the Aeronautic Agreement of Paris, considered itself obliged, from the point of view of an imperious necessity above the laws to carry out this reorganization in the interest of national defense." [7]

Both Kreiser and Ossietzky were sentenced on November 23, 1931, by the Reichsgericht, to eighteen months in prison for "betrayal of military secrets." As instruments of the alleged betrayal, all copies of the *Weltbühne*, issue no. 11 of the year 1929, as well as the printing plates, were ordered destroyed. [8]

The harsh sentence was undoubtedly due to the growing irritation of the Reichswehr Command with the antimilitarist campaign of the *Weltbühne*. Groener was probably a sincere republican but he could see no redeeming grace in pacifism either. Speaking on the defense budget in the Reichstag on March 19, 1931, he discussed, among other things, the coming disarmament negotiations in Geneva, and announced the introduction of an emergency law against the pacifists, these "defamers of the state" (*Staatsverleumder*). He denied the antimilitarists their idealism when he claimed that they were "motivated either by fanatical hatred for all things military or by base greed." [9] While the emergency law against the pacifists was never adopted, it was Ossietzky's misfortune to become a victim of the reinvigorated administrative campaign against antimilitarists.

When the defense counsels of Kreiser and Ossietzky sought commutation or remittance of the sentences imposed on November 23, 1931, the request was turned down by Hindenburg. [10] So was a later collective appeal—for a commutation of the prison sentence to fortress confinement—by the German Section of the P.E.N. Club and the German League for Human Rights. A great number of protests followed, both at home and abroad.

The first protest meeting of the German League for Human Rights, held at the end of November 1931 was attended by 3,000 people. [11] The appeal for the commutation of the sentence bore 33,000 signatures. [12] The foreign press, such as the *Neue Zürcher Zeitung*, the *Manchester Guardian*, *The Times*, *Le Monde*, and *The New York Evening Post* came out strongly in favor of the defendants. [13] In Germany, Theodor Wolff railed in the *Berliner Tageblatt* against a willful act which, beyond violating elementary human rights and the freedom of the press, could lead to serious international repercussions. [14] In France, Henri Barbusse and Romain Rolland led a protest movement; unfortunately, any movement directed by these two human-rights defenders

en pérmanence was barely noticed. Somewhat more significant was
the protest raised in England both in the pages of *The Times* and in
the House of Commons by Sir Austen Chamberlain, former conservative foreign secretary.[15] At home, Rudolf Breitscheid—incidentally one
of Ossietzky's favorite journalistic targets—and twenty-nine other Social Democratic deputies in the Reichstag asked the government
whether it was fully prepared to explain the circumstances of the trial,
and requested that the government prevent the execution of the sentence.[16] There were, further, protests by prominent individuals such as
the historian Veit Valentin, the sociologist Alfred Weber, the theolo-
gian Paul Tillich, and the writers Lion Feuchtwanger, Heinrich and
Thomas Mann, Arnold Zweig, and Alfred Döblin: "It is both frightening and humiliating to live in a country," wrote Thomas Mann in an
open letter to Dr. Apfel, "where the judiciary must be used to enforce
silence over irregularities in public life: one would think that the
muzzling   of   public   criticism   was   the   privilege   of   fascist
dictatorships." [17]

On the other side, at least one Social Democratic newspaper found
the moment opportune to indict the "despicable *Literatenklüngel* (literary clique) of the *Weltbühne* who deserve no sympathy." [18] The
press of the extreme Right was jubilant over the fall of Ossietzky, the
"hireling of the Jews," * while the conservative Right's interpretation
of the affair was reflected in the *Deutsche Allgemeine Zeitung* which
emphasized Ossietzky's pacifist past, and Kreiser's connections with
the "infamous pacifist" journal *Die Menschheit*.[19]

In the campaign for Ossietzky, as in all their campaigns against a
partisan judiciary, the leftist journals appealed to everyone with a
sense of responsibility and justice. But because political lines were too
sharply drawn in the Weimar era, no force of any consequence from
either the conservative camp or from the Center came to Ossietzky's

---

* The National Socialist *Illustrierter Beobachter* celebrated Ossietzky's imprisonment with a poem that was as prophetic as it was vulgar:

> "Wer verfasst nun die Artikel,
> die für Panjudäa werben—?
> Wai, der Untat Aktfaszikel
> muss in Feuerbrand verderben.
>
> . . . .
>
> Einmal noch weht vor dem Fasten
> lind um dich das Knoblauchdüftchen
> wenn du raus kommst aus dem Kasten,
> säuselt wohl ein andres Lüftchen."

Pidder Lüngs, "Marsch der Literaten," *Illustrierter Beobachter,* May 1932.

aid. Only once it would seem was momentary unity achieved among people of disparate political beliefs. That was in the strange case of Lieutenant Scheringer. Scheringer, who had been the chief defendant in the Reichswehr trial of 1930, and had been sentenced to one and a half years in a fortress, broke with Hitler shortly after the trial. He then entered the Communist Party. The Reich prosecutor who remained indifferent to the stream of National Socialist manifestoes which Scheringer was issuing from his cell, suddenly became interested when Scheringer's missives hawked the Communist line. Early in 1932, Scheringer was indicted for "preparation for high treason," and was transferred to a regular prison. A "Scheringer-Komitee" was formed in Berlin to protest the action. The committee obtained the signatures of such divergent personalities as Georg Ledebour, Ernst Toller, Kurt Hiller, Veit Valentin, Otto Strasser (leader of the dissident National Socialist "Schwarze Front"), and the Black Reichswehr leader, Major Buchrucker.[20] If there was any bond common to all the signatories of the protest note, it was that there were among them neither Communists, Social Democrats, nor Nazi party members, and that they belonged either to political splinter groups or to no party.

Ossietzky, who shortly after his trial had been deserted by a fugitive Kreiser, was determined to turn the circumstances of his conviction into a major political issue. Now that persecution had hit the editor of a popular non-Communist journal, he saw renewed hope for the creation of a wide antifascist front: "However attractive and flattering to Kreiser and to myself are all these expressions of sympathy, the issue should not rest there. Let us turn this movement of protest into a political campaign against the powerful forces of counterrevolution. . . . The time for individual action is over."[21] Resorting to the practice of open political debate—so skillfully manipulated in France and England but little understood in Germany—he challenged General Groener to a polemical exchange in the *Weltbühne*. In November 1931, Groener again commented on the Ossietzky affair in an article written for the *Deutsche Allgemeine Zeitung*: "Can the state tolerate propaganda activity which attempts systematically to obstruct our progress toward [international] understanding, toward the development of international confidence, toward a forceful representation on our part of Germany's vital interests?" The laws now in force do not sufficiently protect the state against these "organized informers." Why, just recently it took almost three years to mete out well-deserved punishment to two slanderers.[22]

Ossietzky's reply was immediate. In one of his most eloquent editorials,[23] he challenged Groener's every statement. The minister's very choice of a public forum, Ossietzky began, was an indication of the dilemma of "conservative republican" Germany: here was a confessed republican who found no better vehicle for his ministerial pronouncements than the antirepublican *Deutsche Allgemeine Zeitung*. Referring flippantly to Groener's dual position as minister of interior and minister of defense, he cautioned the minister of interior against the machinations of the minister of defense. Particularly dangerous, he wrote, is the military mania for dividing the population of Germany into two camps: those with an exalted view of the soldier's life (*Wehrfreudige*), and the "shirkers" disinclined to bear arms. A victim of this mania, Groener saw in the pacifists the chief enemies of the state: "How poorly informed you are, Herr Minister! If you knew more about the German Peace Association, you would understand that pacifism and political influence are two diametrically opposed concepts!" Groener should stalk the enemies of the state in their true lair —on the Right—not in the sad little band of pacifists. He should show some consideration for the few "who consider it an honor to fight with their pen in an age when all problems are settled with knife and bludgeon."[24] Ossietzky ended his open letter to Groener with a friendly call to the minister to reconsider his position, and offered the pages of the *Weltbühne* for the minister's reply. But there was no reply.

Ossietzky's prison date was set for May 10, 1932. On the same day there appeared in the *Weltbühne* his "Account" (*Rechenschaft*), a twenty-odd-page résumé of the treason affair and his only *apologia pro vita sua*.[25] As he explained to his readers, his decision to undergo imprisonment was entirely his own: the authorities had left him with ample time to leave the country; friends had exhorted him to leave; his passport was not withdrawn until the day before his scheduled imprisonment.[†] Why then did he stay in Germany? "It is not of loyalty [to the state] that I am going to prison but because by so doing I can become the more embarrassing [to the government]. I do not bow before the red-velveted authority of the Reichsgericht but I am remaining here: an inmate of a Prussian prison, a living symbol of protest."[26] Several other considerations had prompted this decision, Ossietzky explained. He felt bound by loyalty to the many thousand proletarian victims of the Fourth Senate of the Reichsgericht who had

---

[†] As Ossietzky told a friend later, General Schleicher himself had let him know that his passport would be left with him and that he was free to pass the border whenever and wherever he chose. See Grossmann, *Ossietzky*, 288.

not been given the unique and sensational publicity enjoyed by Kreiser and himself. He was bound by loyalty to the *Weltbühne* whose very existence was based on the courage of its editors to stand up to censure. In any case, he saw little point in fleeing: "I belong to no political party; where could I go? No International would receive me in its arms, no one would assign me to a new post." [27]

Nor would he sell his pen and his pacifist convictions to foreign militarists who knew of only one militarism: that of Germany. He foresaw the dilemma of subsequent German refugees. "The dissenter who crosses the borders of his country would soon sound hollow when he began to address his countrymen across the frontiers." He knew that the political activities of an exile inevitably have an adverse effect on the position of comrades at home. The case of Walter Kreiser taught him his first (but not final) lesson. This brave young man, wrote Ossietzky, who had behaved so admirably at the trial, by his sudden flight and his irresponsible behavior abroad had completely paralyzed the campaign for justice and democratic action. Kreiser's decision to offer his pen to *L'écho de Paris* might well have been motivated by antimilitarist idealism, yet he could have done no greater disservice to the cause of pacifism; writing for this nationalist and reactionary newspaper, Kreiser was in reality in the service of Schneider-Creusot and the French armaments industry, sponsors of the newspaper. *L'écho de Paris* was a bitter enemy of Franco-German reconciliation; every anti-German attack in its pages served to strengthen French militarism. What, after all, was the point in unmasking German rearmament, Ossietzky asked; in 1932, the secret militarization of Germany was as well known as it was of little interest to other nations. It had been overshadowed as a major concern by the ascendancy of German fascism and the international repercussions which that would inevitably provoke. Only Kreiser and his Swabian *Landsmann,* General Groener, persevered in the delusion that secret rearmament itself was a major international issue. *Die Weltbühne* was not waging a campaign against clandestine rearmament, but against the insidious usurpation of political power by the German generals. The idolization of the uniform was the monster which was devouring the republic and which was leading to fascism in Germany. During the trial, he wrote, the indifference of the judges suddenly vanished when mention was made of his pacifist past. It little mattered that his association with organized pacifism had been a passing episode in his life, that he had subsequently fallen out with almost all pacifist leaders, that he himself had condemned the tactics of organized pacifism:

there loomed before the judges only the long-standing feud between himself and military authority. "These pathetic judges of Leipzig," he went on, "were but puckered provincial patriots, baffled by a world they could no longer comprehend; they were frightened by an era where great industrial combines were collapsing, where young people went swimming in the nude, where the globe was spinning to the tunes of a jazz orchestra, where the worth of old family estates was steadily dwindling." [28] No wonder that the judges and all the *Spiessers* were desperately looking for a solid post in this tottering world. It was in the Reichswehr that they found this ultimate source of authority and power, and they bowed deep before the boots of the officer. The pedestal of the army should have been shattered by the republic. The genuine revulsion of returning soldiers to the specter of war should have been understood; these men could have been pressed into salutary service. Now, Germany was living under a *Generalswirtschaft:* under the myopic, bungling regime of military juntas. Everyone had capitulated to the generals: the Marxists who shrug their shoulders and chatter of militarism as an inevitable phenomenon of class society; the orthodox Stalinists who hasten to assert that proletarian countries, too, have their national armies; the democrats who wring their hands in exasperation and do nothing. Militarism has swallowed both its friends and opponents. Even Brüning, "the only chancellor to have a program since 1918," [29] who had labored hard for the establishment of an authoritarian democracy upheld by the Cross and by the Sword, who had sought a "strict militaristic state imbued with Catholic ethics" he too, was betrayed by the army.[ᵉ] This chancellor who had labored to mold the army into a *rocher de bronze,* begat a host of intriguers who incited the President to spurn his faithful chancellor. Today, domestic and foreign policy are synonymous with military policy, and "the citizen is no longer asked how he feels toward the republic but whether or not he is zealous about bearing arms." [30]

With his "Little Testament" *à la* Villon, Ossietzky concluded his "Account." He left the *Weltbühne* to the care of his old friend, Hellmut von Gerlach; to his other friends, he left warm admonitions. To the chief intriguer, General Schleicher, he bequeathed "a pair of

---

[ᵉ] By the time Ossietzky's article was published, the dismissal of Brüning and Groener by the President was known to be impending. Groener was forced to resign on May 13 and Chancellor Brüning on May 30. These acts of legendary ingratitude on the part of Hindenburg were prompted chiefly by the army command's disapproval of the government's anti-Nazi measures. See Karl D. Bracher, *Die Auflösung der Weimarer Republic* (Villingen, Schwarzwald, 1960), 490 ff.

attractive tortoise shell spectacles with blue glasses sent to me by one of my female admirers to facilitate my flight; *item,* the false beard, proffered by a faithful reader in Prague. He [Schleicher] might make good use of them." [31] (Two years later, Schleicher was murdered by the Nazis.) To his fellow countrymen, Ossietzky submitted the plea that they not "exterminate each other so that *Die Weltbühne* would not suffer for lack of topics in the future." And he added: "I believe that life will not be dull in Germany during the next eighteen months."

Ossietzky's entry into prison led to a leftist demonstration fittingly held before the prison gates. He was accompanied to the Tegel penitentiary by a few hundred admirers, their cars displaying the black red and gold flag of the republic. After a short oration by a friend, and his own brief farewell, Ossietzky, the chain smoker, threw away his last cigarette and disappeared behind the prison gates. [32]

Chapter XIV
"WALKING A TIGHTROPE"

Although about 8,500 political offenders were incarcerated in Germany in 1932, a non-Communist *Politischer* was still such a rarity in a regular prison that Ossietzky was treated with great courtesy. The warden at Tegel allowed him books and paper and, subsequently, under the pseudonym Thomas Murner,[a] there appeared in the *Weltbühne* a series of articles on Germany's "conservative revolution." Prison isolation was an opportune time for Ossietzky to come to grips with the political message of Germany's right-wing intellectuals.

At a time when poverty and fear drove the educated classes rapidly to the right, the "conservative revolutionaries" alone presented an intelligent ideological alternative to Marxism, democracy, and pacifism. And their ideology gave a respectability to the uncommonly coarse and boorish German rightist movement, for these journalists, novelists, and poets—young men for the most part—garnished their political polemics with a wealth of sociological, psychological, philosophical, and "geopolitical" interpretations. Carried on a wave of popular enthusiasm, they failed to understand that the new Germany would have no need for their intellectual honesty and that their usefulness to the Right would terminate as soon as the Right was securely in power. National Socialist anti-intellectualism soon superseded all conservative revolutionary thought.

Fierce individualists as they were, it is difficult to group these right-wing intellectuals under a common denominator. But ever since

---

[a] Thomas Murner (1475–1537), a Franciscan polemicist, satirized the Lutherans in his writings, but also abuses in the Catholic Church.

the Austrian poet Hugo von Hofmannsthal, himself a vague sympathizer, coined the term "conservative revolution" in a 1927 address to the students of the University of Munich,[1] it has been adopted to describe a movement whose participants variously referred to themselves as "neoconservatives," "young conservatives," "German socialists," "conservative socialists," "national revolutionaries," and "national bolshevists." And when, in 1941, the former National Socialist Hermann Rauschning entitled his historical study, *The Conservative Revolution*,[2] he established a precedent for a number of books with similar titles.[3] It became customary to group together such antithetical personalities as Oswald Spengler, the much admired doomsayer of Western civilization; Ernst Jünger, the poet of war and naked power; the rebellious National Socialists Otto Strasser and Count Ernst Reventlow; the indomitable National Bolshevist Ernst Niekisch; the respectable conservative Edgar J. Jung, whom the Nazis murdered in 1934 and, finally, Hans Zehrer, Ferdinand Fried, and Giselher Wirsing, the young enthusiasts of the *Tat* circle. Armin Mohler, their foremost chronicler, distinguishes about one hundred political trends—and the appropriate number of clubs, leagues, and parties—within the conservative revolution, ranging from "German Leninism" to "pagan imperialism," and from "people's socialism" to "new realism."[4] Mohler goes so far as to lump together the conservative "Herrenklub" in Berlin with the Free Corps, the Youth Movement, the homosexually tainted "Männerbünde," and the North German revolutionary peasant movement, the "Landvolkbewegung." It is true that they all had many things in common: they hated liberalism, parliament, pacifism, rational thought, bourgeois morality, Marxism, and capitalism. What differentiated them from the fascists was their contempt for mass propaganda methods. Like the pre-Marxian socialists, the conservative revolutionaries relied on persuasion, except for the Free Corps which used revolvers, and the revolutionary peasants who threw bombs. Generally, they were satisfied to gloat over the troubles of the November republic and to confidently predict the coming of the great *Kladderadatsch*, the apocalyptic collapse of Western civilization. On the positive side, there was a vague longing for "a new faith, for a community of believers, a world with fixed standards and no doubts, a new national religion." Exceptionally, there was also a detailed program for an authoritarian state. The essentially negative philosophy of the conservative revolutionaries is summed up by Fritz Stern:

The term conservative revolution . . . denotes the ideological attack on modernity, on the complex of ideas and institutions that characterize our

liberal, secular and industrial civilization. . . . The conservative revolutionaries denounced every aspect of the capitalistic society and its putative
materialism. They railed against the spiritual emptiness of life in an urban,
commercial civilization, and lamented the decline of intellect and virtue in
a mass society. They attacked the press as corrupt, the political parties as
agents of national dissension, and the new rulers as ineffectual mediocrities.
The bleaker the picture of the present, the more attractive seemed the
past, and they indulged in nostalgic recollections of the uncorrupted life of
earlier rural communities, when men were peasants and kings true rulers.[5]

Increasingly popular in the Weimar era, the conservative revolutionaries achieved their greatest fame during the Depression when
they voiced the wishes of the troubled middle class in predicting the
end of capitalism, the coming of a corporative parliament, an agrarian
brotherhood of men, and a true leader. Some, like Ferdinand Fried,
announced the end of the technological revolution (the putative
source of the sufferings of shopkeepers and artisans) and asserted that
new mechanical inventions were neither likely nor needed.[6] How
these miraculous developments would come to pass was never made
quite clear; it was enough for the middle class, especially for the
young generation in this class, to stay out of the struggle between
capital and labor.[7] When these two monsters had devoured each other,
then the farmers, artisans, shopkeepers, civil servants, employees,
professionals—the only Germans with spiritual values—could again
assert themselves and bring about an orderly and socially harmonious
nation.

Understandably, there was no love lost between the *Weltbühne*
writers, self-appointed champions of the working class, and the conservative intellectuals, who fought for the middle strata. Yet a lively
dialogue developed from the mutual fascination of the two groups. In
Germany, where the level of political debate was abysmally low,
left-wing intellectuals and conservative revolutionaries enjoyed the
articulateness of their opponents, the occasional sharp repartees. Fritz
Sternberg praised Ferdinand Fried for his excellent statistical analyses
of the pauperization of the German middle class, and expressed hope
that the *Tat* circle would give up its unrealistic and romantic propositions that were but "indirect support given to monopoly capital," and
choose instead the revolutionary workers' movement.[8] On his part, the
conservative revolutionary Wilhelm Stapel, whom a *Weltbühne* writer
once called "Ossietzky's favorite opponent [*Lieblingsgegner*],"[9] wrote
in his unpublished postwar apology that he had enjoyed being "the
only sharp-witted opponent of a Karl Kraus, a Maximilian Harden, a
Kurt Tucholsky, a Siegfried Jacobsohn, and a Stefan Grossmann."[10]

When the Left disintegrated, after 1932, the conservative revolutionaries found themselves without a target and they, in turn, gradually disappeared. In connection with Hans Zehrer's article, "Das Ende der Links-Intelligenz," Tucholsky wrote: "They miss us now; if one has no enemy, one must look for one: 'Come, play with me.' I wouldn't think of it. . . . What's over is over."[11]

Ossietzky's prison articles, which epitomize left-wing intellectual criticism of the conservative revolution, reveal a patience and a will to understand that he was never able to muster toward the traditional conservatives. "We are often told," he wrote in his article on the Wandervogel enthusiast Hans Blüher[b] "that there is a ready jester behind Charles Maurras, the saber-rattling Bayard of the 'Action Française.'"[c] The same must be true of Hans Blüher for how else could he, a man of talent and creative ideas, write so much anti-Semitic nonsense?"[12] Does Blüher really believe that every Jew is a delegated servant of the great Jewish Prince in Exile? Does he really tremble at the thought of an innocent German maiden subjected to the whim of a Jewish doctor? "An unbearable thought—Blüher had written—the Jew at the gates of the Germanic race!" Blüher denies that there is such a thing as an honest Jew, yet he lashes out at political anti-Semitism and at Hitler.

Ossietzky insisted that Blüher was but a "deeply troubled and suffering intellectual"; for Blüher's friend, Wilhelm Stapel, he could find no redeeming feature. He called Stapel a "high-school teacher run wild," a false prophet whose "intellectual and literary" anti-Semitism served only to hide a deep-seated hatred.[13] Stapel was intelligent enough to deny the existence of a Jewish race—of any race—but he was also vicious enough to insist on contrasts between the Jewish and German *Volkstum*. He rejected violence as a solution of the Jewish problem and discoursed on the economic advantages of Jewish presence in Germany, but he also declared that the Jewish *Volk* must be

---

[b] Hans Blüher (b. 1888) is best known for his three-volume *Wandervogel: Geschichte einer Jugendbewegung* (1912), and his *Die Rolle der Erotik in der männlichen Gesellschaft* (1917), where he paid tribute to the history-making power of male associations (*Männerbünde*) and advocated their right to place themselves above common morality.

[c] In a 1925 article, Tucholsky praised Charles Maurras and the *Action Française* as fanatical truth seekers who had the courage to say "no" to the entire liberal-democratic establishment. Here, finally, was the challenge to awaken "the 'progressive' opportunists, the me-too socialists, the liberal culture monopolists" from their exasperating complacency. Ignaz Wrobel, "Herr Maurras vor Gericht," *WB*, September 22, 1925, pp. 436–440. Also in *Gesammelte Werke*, II, 217–223.

kept separate from the Germans, and denied the former any access to intellectual professions. Stapel asserts, Ossietzky continued, that "tactful Jews and tactful Germans can get along with each other," but then goes on to say that tact is something that a Jew can never acquire.

None of the scorn he heaped on Stapel is palpable in Ossietzky's attitude toward the "Black" National Socialist Otto Strasser. He called Strasser "a soft-spoken intellectual whose main weapon is persuasion"; and compared Strasser to Ulrich von Hutten, one of his [Ossietzky's] historical heroes.[14] Strasser was a true individualist who, by "his peculiar disposition was the quintessence of a liberal." His socialism is genuine, wrote Ossietzky, but so is his intellectual confusion. It was the same confusion that plagued the writings of the other conservative revolutionaries: Ernst Jünger, Ferdinand Fried, and Hans Zehrer. Their socialist theories were spun with a romantic longing for feudalism, autarchy and a return to an agrarian society. Do these people really believe, asked Ossietzky, that the inhabitants of a metropolis can be rehabilitated into genuine rustics? "Is it economically and ethically really more valuable to pick potatoes than to exert oneself over a complicated blueprint?"[15] Ossietzky saw correctly in the idea of a "sacred soil" the middle class's growing anxiety over its future; the conservative revolution, he argued, was the revolt of the *Bürger* against an industrial civilization. Besides, Ossietzky continued, there was nothing new in these theories. They were derived from the teachings of a Viennese professor, Othmar Spann, who himself had taken most of his incoherent ideas from Adam Müller, the nineteenth-century economist of romanticism. For these people everything is "organic," Ossietzky commented, but what in the world is organic about a return to the medieval guilds and estates? Where is progress in their desire to put the women back into the kitchen? They imagine, Ossietzky continued, that an independent butcher is somehow a better human being than an industrial worker. The conservative revolutionaries know nothing about workers. Ernst Jünger's *Arbeiter* resembles more an entombed pharaoh then the worker he strives to depict.[16] Jünger pretends to hate bourgeois society, but what he hates is not its ugliness and hypocrisy but its historic achievements, the conquest of feudalism and absolutism, and the adoption of basic human rights. And Hans Zehrer or Ferdinand Fried? As long as these two young men were sitting peacefully at Ullstein's in the Kochstrasse, they had no prophetic inclinations; the Depression turned them into apocalyptic philosophers.[17] They proclaimed the end of the bourgeois age and the coming of "total chaos." But their predictions were only a palliative for the bourgeois, something pleasantly frightening to think about on a quiet Sunday. All that Zehrer and Fried did, Ossietzky wrote, was to "outhitler Hitler" (*sie haben Hitler überhitlert*), and to translate into sophisticated language the coarse nonsense of National Socialism.

Ossietzky understood well the changes that had taken place in the "*Tat* circle" since 1930. The former doomsayers became by 1932 the prophets of *auctoritas*, of a presidential dictatorship under Hindenburg and Schleicher. What a fallacy, Ossietzky exclaimed, to believe that the capitalists, militarists, and agrarian feudalists who now are in power in Germany would voluntarily destroy their society for the sake of some corporative-socialist utopia! [18] He interpreted the *Tat* circle's support of Schleicher as a last outburst of its energy. The conservative revolution, he concluded, was on its deathbed.

There has been occasional speculation on the spiritual affinity between conservative revolutionaries and such left-wing intellectuals as Tucholsky and Ossietzky in Weimar. This is a tempting proposition that ought not be carried too far. The rightists were mainly sons of officers, of civil servants, and of Protestant clergymen; the leftists were likely to be sons of businessmen, of artists, and of educators. In the second group the Jews formed a majority, in the first there were almost none. On the ideological level these groups differed in their conception of human nature, in their judgment of the perfectibility of man, on the relative merits of tradition and of human rights, on the meaning of liberty, on the possibility of a systematic solution of men's problems, on the usefulness of initiative and of collective wisdom, and, in practical terms, on the political and economic course of Weimar Germany. One side preached peace, humanism, and democracy; the other excoriated these as useless sentimentalities and glorified war as an act of purification. Opposing the idea of "Germanic freedom" (a synonym for submission) to the "superficial" freedom of Western man, the conservative revolutionaries denied the greatest spiritual achievements of modern society. "Can one abjure reason," asked Fritz Stern in concluding his work on the three prophets of the conservative revolution— Paul de Lagarde, Julius Langbehn, and Moeller van den Bruck— "[Can one] glorify force, prophesy the age of the imperial dictator, can one condemn all existing institutions, without preparing the triumph of irresponsibility? The Germanic critics did all that, thereby demonstrating the terrible dangers of cultural despair." [19]

Certainly, there were some similarities: both left-wing intellectuals and conservative revolutionaries were the products of the same cultural and political crises. Before 1914, they voiced the same contempt for the materialism and phony medievalism of the Wilhelmian age. In August 1914, and again in November 1918, they experienced similar exaltations and soon the same despair. Later they expressed similar contempt toward the plodding republic. Again, the conservative revolutionaries cloaked their basically regressive ideas in terms borrowed from Marxist ideology and radical leftist postulations. They achieved their popularity by preaching chauvinism and reaction in the words of the prophet of a more humane society. They could sometimes be mistaken for leftists.

Ossietzky's prison reflections were interrupted by two more collisions with the law. During his Tegel confinement, he was twice tried for libel as "responsible editor" of the *Weltbühne*.[d] The first instance involved the minister of finance, who had been offended by some remarks in the *Weltbühne;* the affair was settled by Ossietzky's apology. The second case, involving the minister of defense, led to repeated judicial proceedings and ended with a minor triumph for the *Weltbühne.* Earlier, in August 1931, the journal had published a 1915 pastoral exhortation by Pope Benedict XV. Here, the pope had termed the World War "a horrible butchery" and a "dishonoring massacre." To this document, Tucholsky had appended his commentary which contained the following passage: "For four years there existed several square miles of land where murder was an obligation, while only half an hour away, murder was strictly forbidden. Did I say murder? Naturally, I did. Soldiers are murderers!" [20] Minister Groener took offense, and in the name of the Reichswehr sued for libel. The trial was held on July 1, 1932, in Berlin-Charlottenburg. Tucholsky, who had been living in Sweden since 1929, refused to return to Germany for the trial; he wrote in letters to his wife that his return would not have helped matters.[21] This may have been true but once again Ossietzky stood alone.

At the trial, the state prosecutor demanded the maximum punishment of six months; Ossietzky's lawyers, Alfred Apfel and Rudolf Olden, who argued for acquittal, submitted forceful reminders of famous statesmen who had likewise called soldiery butchery. The court acquitted the defendant.[22] The state prosecutor pressed for a re-trial, and Ossietzky was tried a second time in November 1932.

---

[d] Following Ossietzky's imprisonment, Walther Karsch signed as "responsible editor" of the *Weltbühne.* For understandable reasons Karsch continued to sign even after Ossietzky's release from prison in December 1932.

Again, he was acquitted, for as the judge argued, the Reichswehr could not take offense in its quality as a separate estate (*Stand*): the accusation applied to soldiering of all times.[23]

Despite the confinement of its editor in chief, *Die Weltbühne* appeared regularly. But now the left-wing intellectuals had truly become isolated. They were gradually eased out of the theater, the big daily papers, and the previously progressive Berlin radio stations; their efforts to reach the Communists had been fruitless; the splinter parties on the Left disappeared from the scene as did the peace movement. In a pemanent column entitled, "Weekly Review of Retrogression and of Progress" (later to be captioned "Casualty List"),° *Die Weltbühne* registered the gradual deterioration of the political situation. For Tucholsky the hope for a humane society faded into a future he knew he would not live to see:

And when all this will be over; when all this will have fizzled out—the madness of the rabble, the thrill of marching, of shouting and waving flags with the masses—when this present malady which calls for the idolization of man's basest instincts, will come to an end . . . when the last freedom-loving emigré will be dead—; then, one day, it will again be very modern to be a liberal.ᶠ

In January 1932, Tucholsky wrote in the *Weltbühne:*

> Anthems and flags on every spot.
> What about Europe? Europe may rot!
> Everything else can go to hell
> As long as the Nation is doing well!
> People? Who cares if they survive—
> Britain! Italy! Poland must thrive!
> The State devours us. A specter, a myth.
> The State, that's a thing to be reckoned with.
> The thing grows skyward into the blue—
> there even the Church can learn something new.
> Come all and buy! Yet there are no buyers.
> Up flare the tribal funeral pyres.
> Glow, tribal fires of immolation:
> the goal of existence is the taxation.

° "Wochenschau des Rückschritts—Wochenschau des Fortschritts." By the end of 1932, the column under "Fortschritt" was often deliberately left empty.

ᶠ Ignaz Wrobel, "Blick in die ferne Zukunft," *Die Weltbühne*, October 28, 1930, p. 665. Also in *Gesammelte Werke*, III, 580. This quotation was cited here not only to show Tucholsky's growing discouragement, but also his inconsistent use of political terms. He who had so often denounced liberalism in the name of revolutionary socialism, here again identified himself as a liberal. But then, he was a socialist only because of the failure of German liberalism.

Let Heaven be our estate's receiver:
this age has medieval fever.

The State becomes a sacrament—
may God protect this Continent! [23a]

A few months later Tucholsky fell silent. At the time of Ossietzky's imprisonment, Tucholsky had promised in the name of the *Weltbühne* to provide its readers "with goods of unchanged quality." [24] Instead, he wrote nothing. He used his illness, a nasal complication, as an excuse for his silence.[25]

The remaining political editorialists of the *Weltbühne*—Sternberg, Kaminski, and Gerlach—continued to scan the political horizon for the first signs of a leftist resurgence. They found that the chancellorship of Franz von Papen (appointed by Hindenburg on May 31, 1932), offered definite possibilities for a *ralliement* of the German Left. First of all, there could be no question about the unpopularity of this arch-conservative regime; here at least *Die Weltbühne* found itself at one with the overwhelming majority of the nation. Secondly, there was hope in the chaotic political situation and the endless feuds rocking the rightist camp. Thirdly, Social Democracy had finally abandoned its policy of toleration and was now in unconditional opposition to the government. *Die Weltbühne* sought to impress on the Social Democrats and other republicans the need to continue in this opposition. There was, the journal agreed, nothing to expect from a government which clearly depended for its survival on the good will of the Reichswehr. Since May 13, 1932—when Groener was dismissed by the President—there has been a military dictatorship in Germany, wrote Kaminski.[26] "Some people wonder whether it is better to be shot by a military dictatorship or to be hanged by a fascist regime. As far as I am concerned, it makes no difference." [27] Writing before the Reichstag elections of July 31, 1932, Fritz Sternberg found the time for a united front more propitious than ever. The Nazis, he argued, had reached the zenith of their popularity and were now on the decline. Having become part of the rotten parliamentary game, they were losing their mass appeal. What was more, certain capitalist circles were no longer willing to resort to the Nazis, at least not for the time being. Now that there was no chance of the SPD being taken into the government, not even as a loyal opposition, the united front had become a real possibility. The terrible economic situation, combined with the SA raids on working-class organizations, were causing local workers' groups to cooperate in defiance of their party leadership. The "united front from

below" was about to be born: SPD, KPD, and Reichsbanner units
were defending each other against the attacks of the SA. But this
could come to full fruition only, Sternberg continued, if the two parties
finally form an alliance and coordinate their defense measures in a
"Cartel of Anti-Fascist Organizations." The cartel was to go into the
Reichstag elections with a unified list of candidates.[28]

The elections did not confirm Sternberg's expectations. There
were no unified lists of socialist candidates, and the Nazis increased
the number of their mandates from 107 to 230. Still, Sternberg remained undaunted. He admitted that the NSDAP had been endorsed
by the unemployed and the young voters, but he argued that although
the two socialist parties had lost 500,000 votes during the April Prussian elections, this time the cadres of the working class remained
intact. The losses of Social Democracy were equaled by the success of
the KPD, and in the cities the Nazis had registered no further gains.[g]
He attributed the decline of the SPD to Papen's putsch on July 20
against the Prussian government of Otto Braun. In the past, the Social
Democratic workers had tolerated Brüning to save Braun. Now there
was no democratic Prussia and hence no reason for the workers to vote
the Social Democratic ticket.[29]

In the following months, the writers of the *Weltbühne* turned with
guarded optimism to developments within the National Socialist
Party. Clearly, this party had succeeded in attracting a certain number
of workers, or at least the unemployed workers; no less clearly this
would lead to class antagonisms in the NSDAP.[h] Fritz Sternberg
predicted that no matter what Hitler would undertake in the near
future, the young proletarian and *Lumpenproletarier* element in the

---

[g] In the Reichstag elections of July 31, 1932, the SPD lost 600,000 votes and
ten mandates as compared with the elections of September 1930; the KPD
gained 700,000 votes and twelve mandates. (Total number of votes: SPD:
7,959,700; KPD: 5,282,600.) Sternberg failed to emphasize that there had been
almost two million more votes cast in 1932 than in 1930 and that the percentage
of KPD-SPD votes declined from a total of 37.6 in 1930, to 35.9 in 1932. See
Milatz in Matthias and Morsey, 776 ff.; also Bracher, 601 ff.

[h] In 1929, Heinz Pol, incidentally the first one in the *Weltbühne* to warn
against the Nazis, detected the signs of a growing class struggle in the NSDAP.
He distinguished among three groups within the party: the "true fascists" under
Hitler and Gregor Strasser who were in the pay of the industrialists; the petty
bourgeois and rustic (*bäuerisch*) element under Goebbels, and the "young nationalists" under the writer Ernst Jünger(!). This last group, and perhaps even
that under Goebbels, were aware of the significance of class struggle and were
therefore liable to split from Hitler's movement. Heinz Pol, "Die Nationalsozialisten," *WB*, July 16, 1929, pp. 77–81. For a similar appraisal see Ossietzky,
"Nach der Sintflut," *ibid.*, April 14, 1931, pp. 519–522.

SA would rebel against him. For if Hitler entered the Papen government, the proletarian Nazis would turn against him for making common cause with the reactionaries; and if he remained outside the government, they would rebel against him for failing to bring his followers to promised power. In addition, wrote Sternberg, the revolutionary conservatives within the NSDAP, led by Count Reventlow, would soon repudiate Hitler.[30]

Kaminski saw not only a crisis in the Nazi movement but a European-wide retreat from fascism. He elaborated, rather jubilantly, on the leftist turn of events in Mussolini's Italy, Yugoslavia, Rumania, and Bulgaria. Even in Hungary—he wrote—there was now, for the first time in many years, something resembling an opposition to the fascist regime of Admiral Horthy. "The reactionaries are everywhere on the retreat. In Spain, France, and Sweden they have already been defeated." [31]

These writers were, of course, correct in detecting a crisis in the NSDAP in the fall of 1932. Caught between his boast to his followers that he could assume power whenever he wanted, and his promise to the conservatives that he would not make a coup d'état, Hitler found himself in an embarrassing situation. Moreover, there was truly a rebellious "socialist" element in his party which momentarily forced Hitler to remain in opposition to the Papen government.[32] But the partial proletarization of the NSDAP, and other internal problems, did not lead to a fatal split. In two consecutive, and most eloquent, articles Kurt Hiller attacked the prophets of the "split theory." [33] If the Marxists were right, he wrote, the Depression should have benefited the KPD at least as much as it benefited the Nazis. Yet what happened instead? Between 1928 and 1932, the Communists increased their votes by 70 percent, the NSDAP by 1700 percent. Obviously, it was not only in search of social justice that so many workers went over to Hitler. Nor should they be considered as misguided and therefore redeemable socialists. These proletarians had left the socialist parties because Marxism had not satisfied their emotional needs. The past few years had shown, Hiller continued, that "the wider the proletarian sector of society, the smaller the political power of the proletariat." [34] This was because the Marxists failed to understand the little man's need which was not for harsh dogmas, but for a mystique, a tempting idea. The Marxists would have their followers deny God and the nation, surrender their traditions, their prejudices, and their entire cultural heritage; the Nazis asked for no such sacrifices but dazzled their followers with an array of colorful promises. They allowed the little man to guard his *Spiesser* tradition while striving for social justice, a combination he had vainly sought in the past. The Marxists' aim was to "galvanize the little man's proletarian condition," but what the little man wanted was to achieve bourgeois respectability and forget his proletarian origins. The decadence of the conservative, liberal, and bourgeois democratic parties and their transformation into small economic pressure groups, and the magnificent survival of the Catholic Center prove, Hiller continued, that only a party with an "idea," however narrow, with a spiritual banner flying over all economic considerations, could appeal to the German masses.

Confident that he could wear down his opposition by a series of elections, Papen prevailed upon Hindenburg to authorize the dissolution of the Reichstag almost as soon as it met after the August elections, and to set a date for new elections on November 6, 1932. On that day the Nazis registered serious losses (down to 196 mandates from the previous 230), but Papen failed much more abysmally when he proved incapable of gaining the support of more than 10 percent of the voters.[35] Since none of the party combinations achieved a majority, Papen himself realized the necessity for new tactics if he wished to continue in office. As an ultimate measure, he suggested to the President the establishment of a dictatorial "new state," requiring the suppression of all political parties, trade unions, and professional organizations. Since such repression risked both Communist and National Socialist revolutions, the chancellor turned to the Reichswehr for support. This was not forthcoming. It was denied to Papen on the same grounds that had six months earlier caused the ousting of Groener from Brüning's cabinet: any plan which would have required the dissolution of the SA and other paramilitary organizations, and interfered with the nation's military preparedness, was anathema to the Army Command. It was also objectionable because it would have alienated large segments of the population.[36] On November 17, Papen resigned, and two weeks later President Hindenburg gave the chancellorship to the political leader of the army, General Schleicher.

Surprisingly enough, Schleicher, an intriguer who was generally disliked, began his career as chancellor under favorable auspices. The National Socialists, whose severe losses at the November elections appeared to dissipate their energies, decided to tolerate the chancellor lest an eventual dissolution of the Reichstag with its attendant elections further weaken their position.[37] With the exception of the Social Democrats and the Communists, the other political parties likewise decided to support the chancellor. As both the economy and Germany's international position showed signs of improvement, Schleicher felt free to engage in his grandiose project. This was to harness the NSDAP, or to split it along class lines, and to establish a popular dictatorship with the support of the army, the trade unions, and the socialists in the NSDAP. With the help of this "popular front," he hoped to introduce some urgent social and economic reforms.[38] Whether or not these plans owed their origin to the circle around the *Tat*, as Zehrer liked to claim, it is certain that *Die Tat* had long been heralding a "revolution from above"[39] and "the necessity of unifying nationalism and socialism, whether right or left, into a new *Volksgemeinschaft.*"[40] *Die Tat* had for some time looked benignly on the "socialist" National Socialist leader, Gregor Strasser, and on the trade unions.[41] Following Schleicher's assumption of power, *Die Tat* and *Die Tägliche Rundschau* (the daily newspaper of the *Tat* circle) acted as Schleicher's spokesmen for the chancellor's reform program.[1] For the first time in their history, a small group of the "homeless" Right took an active part in politics and supported a government.

Schleicher's program left the writers of the *Weltbühne* indifferent. "Republicans stay out," warned Kaminski, in a reversal of Hans Zehrer's old antirepublican slogan. Let the Right ruin itself by mismanagement just as the republicans had ruined themselves a few years earlier. The Left should exploit the weaknesses of the Right and exacerbate the crisis by preventing the toleration of Schleicher by the National Socialists, Kaminski concluded.[42] Or as he had put it in an earlier article: not only the Left, the reactionaries also face a dilemma. It is therefore essential for the Left to abstain from state affairs completely and keep the masses alert and on the move against Hindenburg, Hugenberg, and Hitler.[43]

The prediction that the Social Democratic trade unions would reject Schleicher's proposals proved correct,[44] but it was perhaps not quite logical on the part of the left-wing intellectuals to gloat over the failure of the chancellor's undertaking. Schleicher was the first conservative chancellor attempting to rely on support from other than the President and the Reichswehr. He did not ask the trade unions to tolerate a reactionary government but to help form a new state. The

---

[1] The *Tat* circle acquired the *Tägliche Rundschau* on September 1, 1932. Kurt Sontheimer maintains in his "Der Tatkreis," *Vierteljahrshefte für Zeitgeschichte,* July 1959, p. 249, that Zehrer received substantial subsidies from Schleicher in launching the journal. This was denied by Zehrer in an interview given to this writer (Hamburg, May 1961).

dictatorship that he proposed, with its combination of rightist and leftist political forces, would perhaps have allowed the Left to regain the political initiative. The resolution that "in no case must Schleicher be given a chance," voiced by almost the entire Left, invited a holocaust. After all, Hitler was the only alternative to Schleicher. But the Left, now including the Social Democrats, saw no difference between "Bonaparte" Schleicher and the Führer.

In at least one respect, *Die Weltbühne* profited from the mild dictatorship of Schleicher. Early in December 1932, the KPD and the NSDAP presented in the Reichstag a joint motion for a general political amnesty. The motion received the support of the SPD and was passed on December 9 by a great majority in the Reichstag.[45] On the insistence of the SPD it carried a proviso extending the amnesty to persons guilty of having betrayed military secrets but who were guiltless of selfish motivation.[46] The proviso was a favor granted by the Social Democrats to Ossietzky.[47] On December 22, Ossietzky was released. "Well, now he can insult us again," a Social Democratic deputy commented in the Reichstag upon Ossietzky's release.[48]

"The session continues," Ossietzky announced in the *Weltbühne* following his return to his editorial office in Kantstrasse, but his writings would soon show that he had lost much of his fire. His health had suffered in prison, and his friend, Walter Mehring, noticed that his hands were now trembling.[49] Lacking solid information, his commentaries became rambling and colorless during the eight weeks of his new-found freedom. The political situation in January 1933 was more than ever unfathomable; there was, behind a calm façade, a rush of mysterious activity. "At the close of 1932, an eventful yet frustrating year," writes Bracher, "the political scene was still under the sign of a *power vacuum* [Bracher's italics] determined by the partly forced, partly spontaneous elimination of democratic mechanisms, the solidification of the political fronts and the feverish busyness of middlemen and intriguers in the President's palace."[50] The most significant of these maneuverings which, in the words of Bracher, "marked the birth of the Third Reich,"[51] took place on January 4, when Hitler met with Papen in Cologne. The meeting paved the way to the joint National Socialist and Nationalist government of January 30 and the chancellorship of Hitler. The secrecy of the meeting was penetrated almost immediately, yet so great had been the number of furtive negotiations that *Die Weltbühne* did not recognize its importance. "Papen meets with Hitler; Schleicher negotiates with [Gregor] Strasser and even with [Captain] Röhm," wrote Ossietzky.[52] "We register these occurrences on the Right and in government circles with the interest of an observer from the outside, without espousing the cause of any one of these heroic knights of the Grail." He addressed the republicans: "Must we remind certain people over and over again that these are but family quarrels?" Here democracy, socialism, and the republic, there authority and militarism, he asserted; the conflict between the people and the ruling class should absolutely not be obscured by temporary concessions to some "lesser enemy." [j]

Although it refused to "solve the puzzle" of the Right, *Die Weltbühne* was absorbed by the crisis that rocked the NSDAP shortly before its coming to power. In December 1932, *Reichsorganisationsleiter* Gregor Strasser broke openly with Hitler and, worse still for the party, the NSDAP's financial bankruptcy could no longer be veiled. Berlin was treated to the curious spectacle of SA men soliciting party contributions from pedestrians. In mid-January, an anonymous writer in the *Weltbühne* proclaimed the end of the Nazi adventure: "The NSDAP is still alive—yet it is already dead—or at least wounded to death. . . . Adolphus Imperator, Rex, Lord of his Hosts—our readers should be spared his obituary: Adolphus was a man of missed opportunities." [53] Ossietzky was more concerned with the moral consequences of National Socialism than with the political significance of its ostensible demise. "Years of brutality, swagger, and stupidity will not disappear without leaving their mark," he wrote on January 3.[54] National Socialism had fulfilled the secret yearnings of the German *Bürger:* he could rid himself of the intellectual attire, the spiritual pretensions, and the academic façade of wealthier decades. Never in his history had the *Bürger* been more honest than during the years of Nazi ascendance: "The economic collapse had unmasked the inner coarseness, gross anti-intellectualism, harsh lust of power of the *bürgerliche* cast. . . . The great *völkisch* Leader with the looks and manners of a gypsy bandleader might have had his season and might vanish with it, but the ugly and evil instincts that he had evoked will not disappear as simply.[55]

On January 28, President Hindenburg caused Schleicher to resign; two days later, he appointed Hitler chancellor. For history this event closed an epoch and opened another; for his contemporaries, Hitler's appointment was another stage in the rise of authoritarianism. Accord-

---

[j] Not all left-wing intellectuals were as uncompromising toward Schleicher as Ossietzky. Leopold Schwarzschild, for instance, in *Das Tage-Buch* was sympathetic toward Schleicher as he had been toward Chancellor Brüning. See *Das Tage-Buch,* December 10, 1932, p. 1931.

ing to a study made at the University of Erlangen of fifteen "leading intellectual journals" of the period, the rightist journals were generally elated over Hitler's appointment, while the democratic and socialist journals "maintained their composure, if not their indifference." For those on the Left, Hugenberg's appointment as "economic dictator" was the event of greater importance.[56] Ossietzky wasted no words on Schleicher's dismissal: "another flop," he commented.[k] Still unaware of Hitler's appointment, he demanded the resignation of Hindenburg, the "true cause of all these crises." He asked for an immediate return to constitutionality lest the extraparliamentary practices from above lead to extraparliamentary defense measures from below: "For there exists an emergency right [*Notrecht*] of the people against the adventuresome practices of authority."

When they learned that Hitler had become chancellor, the writers of the *Weltbühne* were not alarmed. One reason for Schleicher's fall had been his refusal to cover up for Hindenburg's friends, the East-Elbian landowners who profited enormously from the *Osthilfe*, a financial program originally designated to help peasant settlers.[57] In an open letter to the new chancellor, Gerlach demanded that Hitler make clear his position on the scandal of the *Osthilfe*. This, he argued, would be both "honorable and useful [to Hitler]," especially in view of the coming Reichstag elections.[58] Ossietzky thought that the new regime had good chances of survival. Provided that it managed to ease the depression and not tamper with welfare legislation, the system could last a generation. In his last editorial, on February 14, he urged social and economic reforms and announced that the working class had given Chancellor Hitler a "decent headstart." "Germany is waiting —but not for more intrigues, not for new machinations . . . the people ask the government to work seriously. Its mandate is inexorable: *Hic Rhodus, hic salta!*" [59]

In the last weeks of its existence, *Die Weltbühne* showed a curious dichotomy in its revolutionary socialism and a revival of its bourgeois republican faith. In a sudden burst of optimism some writers expressed confidence that the Reich Constitutional Court would again, as in October 1932, reverse the President's decree and restore the

---

[k] Carl von Ossietzky, "Kamarilla," *Die Weltbühne*, January 31, 1933, pp. 153–155. On the issue of Schleicher's dismissal *Das Tage-Buch* once again was of different opinion. Its editorial expressed regret over the fall of the General, "who had to go because he was much too socialistic and not sufficiently *junkerlich*." Leopold Schwarzschild, "Kanzler Hitler," *Das Tage-Buch*, February 4, 1933, p. 165. Also in Leopold Schwarzschild, *Die letzten Jahre vor Hitler* (Hamburg, 1966), 233.

democratic government of Otto Braun in Prussia. They speculated with interest on the coming Reichstag elections; they foresaw a cabinet crisis as a result of the election, the entry of the Center in the cabinet, and a possible return to political normalcy. Other commentators expected the proletariat to rise in self-defense against Hitler.[1] The working class is ready to wage battle, wrote Kaminski on February 7. A united front of all trade unions, even the Christian, democratic, and Nationalist unions, is in the making. Class against class is the order of the day. The battle lost in the political arena can be won in the plants and factories.[60]

Eventually it became impossible to ignore the physical dangers that threatened the left-wing intellectuals. "Journalists today gaze with envy at the practitioners of such unrisky professions as tightrope walking," Kaminski wrote on February 21.[61] Now, finally, Walter Mehring prevailed upon Ossietzky to abstain from political commentaries.[62] His contributions to the *Weltbühne* again dealt with the conservative tradition and the conservative revolutionaries.[63] When his last article was printed, Ossietzky was already in the hands of the SA. He, Erich Mühsam, and Heinz Pol were arrested on February 27, the night of the Reichstag fire. Others, like Kurt Hiller, Axel Eggebrecht, and Paul von Schoenaich, followed shortly thereafter. Still *Die Weltbühne* continued publication: its last issue in Germany appeared on March 7. In it Kurt Hiller proclaimed his indomitable belief in a world of peace, socialism, and intellectual freedom.[64] The same night, the SA raided the officers of the *Weltbühne* and confiscated the property of the journal. Walther Karsch, the *Weltbühne's* 27-year-old editor, escaped only because the SA could not believe that a youth was in charge of such a monstrous publication.[65]

---

[1] It was at the press conference of the Reich Chancellery that Heinz Pol learned of the appointment of Hitler on January 30, 1933. He expected not to be able to return home because of the general strike of the workers. The failure of the strike to materialize caused his pessimistic prediction—and this set him apart from most of his contemporaries—that Hitler would last two years. Interview with Heinz Pol, New York City, May 14, 1962.

Epilogue
PRISON AND EXILE

In premonition of things to come, Siegfried Jacobsohn's widow, the owner of the journal, had established a Vienna edition of the *Weltbühne* in September 1932. *Die Wiener Weltbühne* was not a replica of the German edition in that only half of its articles came from Berlin, the other half followed Austrian developments. Its editor Willi Schlamm[a] was a disciple of Karl Kraus and a journalist in the best Vienna tradition: witty, eurdite, pugnacious, and melancholy. Schlamm was also a follower of Trotsky, and he opened his journal to the exiled Soviet leader.

Unlike most card-carrying Communists and Social Democrats, Schlamm did not interpret Hitler's rise to power as the beginning of National Socialism's inevitable collapse. He ridiculed the Communist slogan: "Hitler governs—Communism is on the march" (*Rote Fahne*),[1] and he attributed Hitler's "complete and lasting" victory to the bankruptcy of the entire German Left.[2] This was a daring pronouncement at a time when none of the great antifascist parties was, as yet, engaged in self-examination. The Communists were particularly satisfied with themselves: on April 1, 1933, when the KPD was already thoroughly

---

[a] Willi (today William) Schlamm was born in 1904 in Galicia, the son of a merchant. He studied political science at the University of Vienna and worked as a journalist. In 1938, he emigrated to the United States where he must have undergone a fundamental political change for he became assistant to the editor in chief of *Time, Life,* and *Fortune* (1941–1951). Between 1951 and 1957 he edited the *National Review* and other magazines. Since 1959 he has contributed to *Stern* in Germany, and to other European magazines. Among his works, see *Diktatur der Lüge* (1937); *Germany and the East-West Crisis* (1959); *Die Grenzen des Wunders* (1959), and *Who Is a Jew?* (1964).

216

smashed, with its leaders in prison or in exile, and many of its members in the SA, the Executive Committee of the Communist International adopted a resolution lauding the policy of Thälmann and the Central Committee of the Party "up to, and, including the day of Hitler's seizure of power."[3] Schlamm's colleague, Paul Krey, listed in the journal some of the well-worn slogans that "ought finally to be discarded":

The German worker will never let it happen. . . .
But these people don't even have a program. . . .
Well, then Russia will march against him.
That much is certain: in four weeks he will ruin himself by mismanagement. . . .
Berlin is Red.
In that very instant the proletarian United Front will come into being!
Most of them are only fellow-travelers. . . .
Then there will be bloodshed!
The Iron Front stands ready for every eventuality.
The trade unions will have something to say about that!
Hitler doesn't even want power![4]

The journal's views on the National Socialist *Machtübernahme* were at first determined by Trotsky who elaborated in a series of articles his thesis that Hitler would not ruin himself by his inability to fulfill his economic and social program. Hitler's program had been but a means to power, Trotsky argued; now that the National Socialists were in power, they would mobilize all of Germany's human and natural resources for imperialist expansion. The historical mission of fascist dictatorship was imperialism—that is, preparation for war. Fascism could neither be reformed nor forced internally to surrender power. Only the international proletariat mobilized in a united front against fascism could overthrow Hitler.[5] Trotsky called "the unparalleled defeat of the German proletariat the most important event in modern history since the assumption of power by the Russian proletariat,"[6] and he again identified the KPD's policy of united front from below as the greatest impediment to the antifascist struggle. The KPD, wrote Trotsky, should have profited from the genuine antagonism between Social Democratic reformism and fascism to weaken fascism, and "while so doing, demonstrate to the workers the inadequacy of the Social Democratic leadership—and thereby weaken reformism."[7]

In April 1933 Schlamm renamed his now lonely publication, *Die Neue Weltbühne,* and moved his headquarters to Prague, a safe distance from the reactionary regime of Chancellor Dollfuss. But neither he nor Trotsky would be heard from much longer through the journal.

In March 1934, Jacobsohn's widow [b] dismissed Schlamm whom she had found too Trotskyist for her taste and made the left-wing socialist Hermann Budzislawski editor of the journal.[8] Shen then sold *Die Neue Weltbühne* to a group of German businessmen and journalists in Prague. In 1936, Budzislawski obtained ownership of the financially unsuccessful journal.[9] Budzislawski, now a professor of international journalism at the University of Leipzig, had had almost no connection with the *Weltbühne* except for a few brief contributions on economic problems at the end of 1932. Kurt Hiller exaggerates somewhat when he recounts in his *Weltbühne* reminiscences that once Budzislawski took over, the journal hawked the Stalinist line.[10] Its many non-Communist contributors, Hiller included, assured continued diversity to the *Neue Weltbühne*. Yet it is true that after 1934 there would be no more criticism of the KPD, the USSR, or international Communism. Trotsky's name disappeared from the list of contributors;[11] the show trials in Moscow were hardly even mentioned except to praise the wisdom of the judges, and the SPD was attacked with unprecedented brutality and venom. The journal's pessimism under Schlamm now gave way to confident evaluations of the revolutionary situation in Germany. "Who will overthrow Hitler?" the new editor asked in July 1934: "Most probably the German bourgeoisie itself. Not of its free will, but under the pressure of the masses." [12] In 1934, *Die Neue Weltbühne* revived the tradition of interparty discussion on the German Left, a quantitatively most successful undertaking. Unfortunately for the quality of the debate, all participants were convinced that they were talking "into" Germany, and that their proposals would be adopted by a vigorous socialist underground movement. As the Popular Front had not yet come into being, the debate was restricted to the radical socialist camp, that is, to the Communist Party, individual left-wing Social Democrats, the Socialist Workers' Party (SAPD), the International Socialist Militant League (ISK), and the group called New Beginning ("Neu Beginnen") [13]. The spokesman of left-wing Social Democracy, Siegfried Aufhäuser,[e] insisted that the Communist and Social Democratic cells in Germany coordinate their programs and create "common executive committees

---

[b] Edith Jacobsohn moved from Vienna to Zurich in the spring of 1934. She died in London at the end of the next year. See *Die Neue Weltbühne*, January 23, 1936, p. 110.

[e] Aufhäuser was a member of SOPADE, the exiled executive of the SPD, but he consistently represented independent views.

from both camps."[14] The spokesman of the Communists, "Walter," that is, Walter Ulbricht, demanded that the Social Democrats break away from their Prague leaders and collaborate with the KPD "in the spirit of Marx, Engels, Lenin, and Stalin." Cooperation between the two parties was out of the question: the Social Democrats, if they wanted to fight the bourgeoisie, "had to become members of the Communist Party."[15]

The policy of a united front from below was first challenged by some French Communists in February 1934 when they joined with the French Socialists in a strike against the fascist leagues. Soon thereafter Stalin decided that the main threat to the Soviet Union came no longer from France or Great Britain, but from Hitler's Germany. He then inaugurated a policy of "collective security" on the international scene and, at the Seventh World Congress of the Comintern in August 1935, ordered all Communist parties to create a wide front of antifascists.[16] Budzislawski made the shift to the united front from above and from there to the Popular Front without any difficulty; as a result, the best of the emigré intellectuals, and all left-wing politicians, joined in signing the many Popular Front manifestoes published in the journal.[d] *Die Neue Weltbühne* voiced the sentiments of the majority of exile intellectuals when it castigated the right SPD leadership for not joining with the Communists in the common struggle.[17] There was energetic debate on the practical application of the Popular Front idea, and a general atmosphere of expectation. Yet, *Die Neue Weltbühne,* for all of its positive commitments and the excellent collaborators it was still able to attract, was losing its luster. As a prestige publication of the German exiles, it occupied second place behind Leopold Schwarzschild's *Das Neue Tage-Buch* with its profound analyses of German economics and politics.

In June 1938, the journal moved to Sèvres, near Paris. There, on August 31, 1939, the last issue of the *Neue Weltbühne* was published. The writing of the editorial must have pained Budzislawski. Entitled

---

[d] The *Volksfront-Aufruf* of January 1937 (*NWB*, January 14, 1937, pp. 64–68) contained the names of—among others—the Social Democrats Rudolf Breitscheid and Alexander Schiffrin; the Communists Franz Dahlem, Walter Ulbricht, Wilhelm Pieck, Bruno Frei (Karl Franz), and Willi Münzenberg; the SAPD leaders Willy Brandt, Max Seydewitz, and Kurt Rosenfeld, and the free intellectuals Georg Bernhard, Lion Feuchtwanger, Emil J. Gumbel, Kurt Kersten, Otto Lehmann-Russbüldt, Heinrich and Klaus Mann, Ernst Toller, and Arnold Zweig. See also *NWB*, January 30, 1936, entirely devoted to discussions on the Popular Front.

the "Moscow Agreement," it deplored Stalin's "mistake" in keeping the toiling masses ignorant of the true purpose of the Ribbentrop-Molotov treaty.[18]

With National Socialism's triumph, Germany lost its best intellectuals. When, in 1936, a debate erupted between a National Socialist sympathizer on the staff of the *Neue Zürcher Zeitung* and Leopold Schwarzschild over the merits of literature in the Third Reich,[19] Schwarzschild pointed out with pride that sixty-seven of the best known German writers, poets, and journalists were in exile.[20] Of the twelve "loyal" German writers mentioned by his opponents, some wrote nothing, while others hardly deserved the epithet "well known." As Schwarzschild commented with pleasure, one of the better known German writers, Friedrich G. Jünger, chose that moment to go into exile.

Most *Weltbühne* writers managed to get abroad after 1933, but escape was not always easy. Hiller, who was arrested on March 23, 1933, knew the worst prisons of the Gestapo and a concentration camp before he was released in 1934. He then fled to Prague where he printed his experiences in the *Neue Weltbühne* in a long series of fascinating articles.[21] Emigré life itself took its toll among the intellectuals. Poverty, discouragement, their relative anonymity, and the callousness of the French and other authorities, drove Kurt Tucholsky, Walter Hasenclever, Ernst Toller, Klaus Mann, Stefan Zweig, Max Alsberg, and several more to suicide.[22] Berthold Jacob was kidnapped from Portugal by the Nazis during World War II and died in captivity. And there were those who never made it abroad. Erich Mühsam was tortured to death shortly after his capture in 1933. Ossietzky, following his arrest on February 27, 1933, was taken to the citadel of Spandau. From there he was sent to the prison of Sonnenburg, and, finally, in 1934 to the *Moorlager* of Papenburg-Esterwegen, a concentration camp. Bullied by the SS guards who called him a Polish swine, he presented a pitiful spectacle to the rare foreign visitors admitted to the camp. In November 1936, when the arduous and often frustrating campaign for the Nobel Peace Prize was triumphantly concluded,* he was no longer in the camp. Suffering from tuberculosis, he had been transferred in May 1936 to a closely guarded section of the Virchow hospital in Berlin. Prevented from accepting the Nobel Prize in per-

---

* A violent journalistic attack by the Norwegian writer Knut Hamsun on the "traitor Ossietzky" (November 22, 1935) seems to have done more good than harm to the cause of the campaigners. See Grossmann, *Ossietzky*, 402 ff.

son, Ossietzky was formally released in the same year, and transferred to a private hospital in Berlin.[23] He died on May 4, 1938.

On June 1, 1946, *Die Weltbühne* reappeared in Berlin under the joint editorship of Ossietzky's widow, Maud von Ossietzky, and Hans Leonard. Printed under Russian license, it was identical with the original *Weltbühne* in format and color. In its early editions, the journal paid homage to the dead and printed reminiscences by the survivors. Today, it is again devoted to politics, the theatre, literature, film, and social problems. Published primarily for the export trade, it resists criticism of conditions in the German Democratic Republic; in fact, its enemies are all abroad—in Bonn and the United States. At home the new *Weltbühne* has only friends. This, admittedly, distinguishes it from its predecessor.

CONCLUSION

The writers of the *Weltbühne* thrived on the journal's political radicalism. It invigorated their literature and inspired their hopes for the
future at a time when men of liberal and democratic convictions were
already despairing. But as politicians these writers were utterly unsuccessful. Decried by the Right as enemies of humanity, they were also
rejected by the great republican and left-wing political parties. Unlike
the French *philosophes* or the prerevolutionary Russian writers, they
did not even influence the political activists of the following generation. The members of the German resistance movement against Hitler
were no followers of the left-wing intellectuals; on the contrary, they
were mainly former ideological enemies who drew their moral arguments from conservative revolutionary or Catholic philosophies. And
of the two Germanies of today, neither bears the slightest resemblance
to the aspirations of the left-wing intellectuals.

The prime reason for this failure lay in the anti-intellectualism of
German politics. The same writers who were allowed to glorify party
and ideology in verse, in novels, or on the stage, were contemptuously
brushed aside by the *Bonzen* when they attempted to meddle in the
serious business of party politics. Undoubtedly the left-wing intellectuals had been at their most effective when they were still cultural
rebels, before World War I, poking fun at academic arts and at the
supreme paladin of established art, the emperor. Those who experimented with surrealism, cubism, expressionism, or the *Bauhaus*, did
more than their share in tearing down the fabric of old society. The
difficulty began when these literati turned to politics with all the
impatience, venom, and fierce independence of artists. The politicians

222

could never forgive the intellectuals for the fresh air they breathed into party politics.

It was World War I, and the parallel crisis of the middle class, which turned the left-wing intellectuals into militants. By the end of the war they were all prophets of peace, justice, and universal fraternity. There was a good deal of naïveté in their wartime propositions, but then they were novices at the political trade and surely no more foolish than all those other Germans who viewed the extermination of German youth at the front as the guarantee of national survival.

As befits political novices, these writers developed inordinate hopes during the war and, in 1918–1919, they were terribly disappointed. It was a healthy disappointment, however, for it was followed by increasing lucidity in politics. The *Weltbühne*'s collective analysis of developments in the Weimar Republic remains superior to that of most other contemporary journals.

In November 1918, these writers showed, the collapse of the monarchy presented those who in the past had opposed the monarchy with a unique opportunity. Because the upholders of the old order were thoroughly frightened, while the republican bourgeoisie remained weak, the working-class movement alone was in a position to take power in Germany. Unfortunately for Germany, those who chose to close the gap kept open by the forces of the old order were the Majority Socialists, a group bereft of pride, of the will to rule, and of ideological consistency. It was no less unfortunate that the radical socialists had not only missed the initial opportunity to seize power peacefully, but then attempted to wrest power from the Majority Socialists with insufficient means. In the crucial two months between November 1918 and January 1919, the Majority Socialists strengthened their position in the country and secured the support of the Army High Command. When the radical socialists revolted in January, they were easily defeated. The writers of the *Weltbühne* generally approved of the defeat of the far Left by the Majority Socialists but they did not condone the excessive brutality of the government troops, nor the unwillingness of the government to extend a friendly hand to the defeated radicals. Ebert and Scheidemann should have used the victory over the left-wing opposition to rally the working class by turning against their right-wing enemies. For this fatal omission the Social Democrats themselves had to pay the heaviest price. The working class remained forever split, while the majority of the bourgeoisie felt neither gratitude nor did it truly accept the republic. Indeed, the upper class never forgot, nor forgave, their humiliation in 1918–1919, a humiliation exacerbated by the parallel setback they suffered on the international scene. For all these miseries they held the Majority Socialists equally responsible with the radical socialists. The republic which had emerged from the events of 1918–1919 reflected both the momentary triumph of Social Democracy and the continued hostility of a great part of the German bourgeoisie. The tolerant and democratic constitution was sabotaged by an increasingly intolerant and reactionary bourgeoisie which despised its own state and allowed it to survive only as long as there was no alternative. During the Depression, when the second great crisis of Germany ensued and the ruling class again experienced the fear of bankruptcy and of social upheaval, it unhesitatingly cast aside the republic. Unsupported by the majority of its social and economic elite, the republic disappeared from the scene.

In the first years of the Weimar Republic, when the writers of the *Weltbühne* still believed in the republic, they preached a reformist policy to be initiated by the government. These reforms were not a matter of the promulgation of new laws—the best of laws became worthless in the hands of an uncooperative civil service; they were to consist of the creation of a new elite. Only by dismissing the old-regime bureaucrats, army officers, judges, and educators, and by creating a new national leadership could democracy and socialism be secured in Weimar Germany. The left-wing intellectuals saw themselves as part of this new elite for which they felt qualified by their erudition, their cosmopolitan views, their unsullied past and, above all, their firm socialist beliefs. They were convinced that intellectuals made the best socialists and that there was no place in the new German elite for nonsocialists. "He is an intellectual, and as an intellectual he is a socialist," a *Weltbühne* writer said in 1923 in reference to the prime minister of Saxony. This was a forced equation but an understandable one in view of the terrible weakness of the nonsocialist republicans and the lack of imagination among the socialist politicians.

Later, when these writers deserted the republican cause and turned an expectant eye toward revolutionary socialism, they made the same demand on the Communist Party that they had previously made on the bourgeois republic. They insisted that the KPD leadership give way to radical intellectuals by dismissing its dull-witted functionaries, a demand that was to be voiced again in the 1950's by radical intellectuals in Poland and Hungary, and in 1968 in Czechoslovakia. When it became successively clear that the KPD leadership was hardly less narrow-minded, rigid, and conservative than the Social Democratic and republican politicians, the major writers of the *Weltbühne* gradually moved to the left of the Communist Party. By then, however, the national emergency had become so pressing that the idea of substantial reform within state or party was abandoned in favor of a desperate call for the antifascist unity of all socialists.

All through the Weimar years, *Die Weltbühne* showed consistent sympathy toward one political group only, the left-wing opposition within Social Democracy. These writers approved of the demand of Paul Levi and the Saxon Social Democrats that the SPD go into unconditional opposition to the bourgeois parties and that it make overtures to the Communists. The latter was not necessarily an untenable proposition, for there were periods in the history of the KPD when the Communists were genuinely seeking cooperation with other socialists, and there were, at least until 1929, always some leading Communists who fought against the isolationist tendencies of their own party. It was surely not by unconditional hostility to the KPD that Social Democracy was to win the cooperation of the Communist workers. Unfortunately for the *Weltbühne* circle, and most probably for Germany, the left-wing opposition in the SPD remained an outcast in the socialist movement and exercised no influence on contemporary or future German socialism.

It has become customary in Western liberal circles to reproach the left-wing intellectuals for having refused to embrace the gradualist policy of Weimar Social Democracy. Because of this refusal, asserts Kurt Sontheimer, the republic was "squeezed in hopelessly between a literary Left and a nationalist Right," and "the republic had no breathing space between the eccentricities and absolutes of the Left and Right." [1] The radical *Literaten* caused great harm to the republic, writes Golo Mann, for "while they mercilessly exposed all its weaknesses, they were nevertheless regarded [by the Right] as a valid expression of the republican spirit." [2] They did not belong to the republic at all, he argues, only to a republican era which allowed them to shout at the top of their voices. Yet, writes Golo Mann in another place, this weak and struggling republic "would have deserved help, rather than hilarious comment." [3] The left-wing intellectuals deserted the Weimar Republic, comments the American historian Gordon A. Craig: "This defection was a grave one, and one that was not made good." [4]

What is implied here is that the Right, acting alone, could not have engineered the republic's destruction. This contention is scarcely supported by history. For one thing, the "literary Left" lacked the power to destroy. Nor was the Communist Party alone a match for the forces of the Right. Admittedly, the disagreeable noise that the Communists were making did not help matters, but there is little likelihood that their polite silence would have been salutary. The masses who voted the Communist ticket did so precisely because the KPD aggressively opposed the republic; had this party decided to behave "correctly," these voters would probably have turned to the other antirepublican mass movement, the National Socialist Party. Even with the KPD mounting a constant propaganda barrage against republicanism, thousands of Communist rank and file went over to the NSDAP in search of a truly efficient antirepublican leadership. On the other hand, one is at least permitted to wonder what would have been the consequences of the SPD's joining the Communists in their unconditional opposition to the bourgeoisie. This tactical alliance might have prevented the working class from going down in 1933 without offering resistance to the Nazis. In any case, it was a tactical error for the SPD to seek support in the political center after 1930 when that center was rapidly disintegrating. It ought to be recognized, finally, that the Nazis and the Communists did not destroy the Weimar Republic: it had been destroyed by the German bourgeoisie and the bourgeois political parties, the Center, the People's Party, and the Nationalists who, after 1929, consistently favored an authoritarian solution. Because they clearly perceived the fallacy of the SPD's course, the writers of the *Weltbühne* could not submit to that party's discipline. Their contempt for the "party of Noske and of petty trade union functionaries" played only a minor role in this decision.

Why then did they fail to become "simple soldiers" of the proletarian revolution? Even today, their biographers in the German Democratic Republic bemoan the fact that these "magnificent antifascists," who saw clearly the internal contradictions of *bürgerliche* society, could not bring themselves to take the final step and join the Communist Party. Only then, do the East German historians argue, would the *bürgerliche Linke* have found fruitful ground for its ideas. Instead of addressing a bourgeoisie deaf to their calls, they could have used their literary force to appeal to the workers and win over the Social Democratic voters to the only revolutionary organization of the proletariat.[5] The Communist argument falters on two grounds. To begin with, the German Communists were impotent revolutionaries and ineffectual antifascists: they manifestedly would neither overthrow the bourgeois state nor act as a responsible parliamentary party within that state.

One had to be very shortsighted—and there were such myopic individuals in the *Weltbühne* circle—to believe that the KPD could be reformed from within and transformed from a tool of Moscow into an independent political force. Secondly, the vast majority of the *Weltbühne* writers did not desire the triumph of Communism; they were drawn to the KPD primarily as a vehicle of antifascist militancy. The fact that only a handful of those who survived chose to settle in the German Democratic Republic testifies to a reluctance to accept the ultimate consequences of the Communist program. Their willingness to fight the forces of reaction, however, on the side of the Communist Party was undermined by the sectarianism of the Communist leaders.

There was indeed no place for a left-wing intellectual in Weimar Germany. Still, the writers of the *Weltbühne* helped contribute to their own ineffectiveness. They were never able to conciliate their longing for revolution with their pacifist convictions. Nor did they ever concede that their refusal to shed blood reduced them to the role of reformers. And there were other inconsistencies which weakened their position. They asked for an egalitarian society often without bothering to ask for the socialization of private property; they clamored for a government by the intellectual elite but they never ceased to idolize the worker; they admired Soviet Russia but they consented to the quarantining of Soviet Bolshevism by the great powers; they decried the German Communist Party for parroting the policy of Moscow at the same time that they declared the German Communists inherently incapable of independent thought or action.

Clearly, the writers of the *Weltbühne,* too, were products of their time and society. As urban, bourgeois intellectuals they suffered from the limitations of a class which had no tradition of public service. They had no contact with those who ruled and they were also far removed from the workers and the peasants. As Germans they often engaged in the favorite German pastime of blaming the national character for misfortunes that had only little to do with the boundaries of their country. Finally, those among them who were Jews tortured themselves for being Jewish and often doubted their title to existence. Indeed, the Jewish writers of the *Weltbühne,* more than their Christian colleagues, shared in the contradictions of Weimar society. They profited from the peculiar fascination that the average middle-class German—unfree, frightened, and desperately respectable—bore toward the free, irreverent, and outwardly self-assured Jewish intellectuals. They created their literary pieces for this German, titillated him with satire, wit, eroticism, and permitted themselves applause at the same time that they suffered enormously from the contempt which went hand in hand with the fascination.

Fallible, conceited, often hedonistic, the writers of the *Weltbühne* were never destructive. On the contrary, they aimed at redemption. They dreamed of a socialist society with democratic instrumental forms; this was and still is everywhere an intellectual utopia. But these writers acted on behalf of their utopia; they were participants, not bystanders in the political arena.

APPENDIXES

Appendix I

BIOGRAPHIES OF THE *WELTBÜHNE* CIRCLE

Note to the Reader

The writers listed in this biographical series were selected for the frequency and importance of their contributions to the *Weltbühne*. Several writers mentioned in the text do not figure in the biographies either because they were infrequent collaborators of the journal or because not enough is known of their lives. Others, who were not mentioned in the text, are included in the biographical series to establish a balance between the journal's political and literary contributors. Ultimately, this selection must be regarded as arbitrary.

There are many valuable source books on the politicians and writers of the Weimar period. The most useful for this series were:

Wilfried Adling *et al.*, eds., *Lexikon sozialistischer deutscher Literatur von den Anfängen bis 1945* (Halle, 1963); Günter Albrecht *et al.*, eds., *Deutsches Schriftstellerlexikon* (Weimar, 1963); Paul Fechter, ed., *Geschichte der deutschen Literatur*. Vol. II. (Gütersloh, 1960); Siegmund Kaznelson, ed., *Juden im deutschen Kulturbereich* (Berlin, 1962); Hermann Kunisch, ed., *Handbuch der deutschen Gegenwartsliteratur* (Munich, 1965); *Neue Deutsche Biographie* (Berlin, 1955 ff.). This will hereafter be referred to as *NDB;* Franz Osterroth, ed., *Biographisches Lexikon des Sozialismus* (Hannover, 1960), and *The Universal Jewish Encyclopedia* (New York, 1940). This will hereafter be referred to as *UJE*.

ALSBERG, MAX (Bonn, 1877—Samaden, Switzerland, 1933), one of Weimar Germany's foremost legal experts and a counsel for the defense in numerous sensational political and criminal trials, was the son of a Jewish merchant in Bonn. He defended, among others, the conservative politician Helfferich in the latter's "Erzberger treason trial" (1920) which led to the resignation of Finance Minister Erzberger. Alsberg also figured in most of the *Weltbühne* and pacifist trials. In 1931 he was appointed lecturer at the University of Berlin. Two years later he fled to Switzerland where he committed suicide. Of his numerous legal studies, *Der Beweisantrag im Strafprozess* (1930) is considered the most significant, and *Der Prozess des Sokrates im Lichte moderner Jurisprudenz und Psychologie* (1926) the most challenging. His drama, *Voruntersuchung* (1930) about guilt and legality was filmed in 1931. See *NDB*, I, 205, and Kaznelson, 230 *et passim.*

APFEL, ALFRED (Düren, Rhineland, 1882—Marseille, 1940), was the son of a well-known physician of liberal political views. He became a junior barrister (*Referendar*) in 1903. While on active duty in the army, he completed officer's school but, being Jewish, was not commissioned. He nevertheless volunteered in 1914 and earned the Iron Cross First Class on the Western front. Discharged in 1916 because of illness, he became legal adviser to a business syndicate and, after 1918, a successful criminal lawyer and political lawyer. He defended, among others, Max Hölz, the founder of the revolutionary "Soviet Republic of Central Germany" (1922); George Grosz, accused of blasphemy; Friedrich Wolf, charged with propagating illegal abortions; and Ossietzky and Jacob at all of their trials. Apfel headed several Zionist youth organizations. In 1933 he fled to France. See his *Behind the Scenes of German Justice* (1935) and *Jüdisches Lexikon*, I, 383.

BAB, JULIUS (Berlin, 1880—New York City, 1955), well-known theater critic, director, speech expert, and literary historian, was a major contributor to the *Schaubühne* and the *Weltbühne.* The son of a Jewish salesman, Bab studied at the universities of Zurich and Berlin. Before the war he belonged to the Freie Volksbühne movement in Berlin and through that organization discovered his interest in politics. (See his *Das Erwachen zur Politik*, 1920.) He was a member of the German Democratic Party. After 1933 he went abroad and in 1940 settled in New York as theater and film critic at the *New York Herold und Staatszeitung.* He was the author of at least thirty volumes on literature and theater, for example, *Kritik der Bühne* (1908); *Bernard Shaw* (1910); *Der Mensch auf der Bühne,* 3 vols. (1909–11); *Chronik des deutschen Dramas,* 5 vols. (1911); *Gustav Landauer* (1923); *Arbeiterdichtung* (1924); *Das Theater im Lichte der Soziologie* (1930); *Kränze dem Mimen* (1954), on great actors. See Kaznelson, 217 *et passim.*

BALÁZS, BÉLA (Szeged, Hungary, 1884—Budapest, 1949), whose original name was Herbert Bauer, was one of the greatest critics of cinematic art. Balázs was of Jewish descent. After obtaining a doctorate in philosophy at the University of Budapest in 1909, he became a teacher. Soon, he joined the "Nyugat" (West) circle in Budapest, a group of democratic intellectuals who aimed at political and social reform through the propagation of Western, especially French, cultural values. At first a realist and a naturalist, Balázs soon changed to symbolism and a preoccupation with the inner self ("Aesthetics of Death," 1907; "The Wanderer Sings," poems, 1910). In 1914 he volunteered for front-line service to gain fresh artistic experience, becoming a revolutionary socialist in the process. He was among the first to join Béla Kun's Hungarian Communist Party and, under the Soviet Republic, he was put in charge of the theaters. When the Hungarian Soviet Republic was overthrown in August 1919, he fled to Vienna and subsequently settled in Berlin. There he established his literary reputation through his neo-objectivist novels and socialist film aesthetics (*Sieben Märchen,* 1921; *Der sichtbare Mensch,* on cinema, 1924; *Unmögliche Menschen,* an attempt to deal with the ideals of his youth, 1922–1930, and *Menschen auf der Barrikade,* 1929). His pieces in the *Weltbühne* concentrated on film as an art form and a political weapon. In 1931 he migrated to the U.S.S.R. where he wrote filmscripts, essays, and short stories, and was appointed professor at the Moscow Film Academy. Returning to Budapest in 1946, he published his autobiographical novel, *Álmodó Ifjúság* (Dreaming Youth). His most lasting contributions are probably the librettos he wrote for the operas of his friends Béla Bartók and Zoltán Kodály, such as *Bluebeard's Castle, The Wooden Prince,* and *Czinka Panna.* In these, he combined folk-tale elements and ballads with a modern psychological approach. See Adling, 78 ff., and letter by Erich Lukacs in *Aufbau* (New York), May 12, 1950.

BALTHASAR: see SCHACHT, ROLAND

BAUER, HERBERT: see BALÁZS, BÉLA

BIE, OSKAR (Breslau, 1864—Berlin, 1938), musicologist and art historian, was a contributor to the *Schaubühne* and the *Weltbühne.* Bie was the son of a Jewish manufacturer. He converted to Christianity. In 1890 he became "Privatdozent" at the Technological Academy in Berlin, and after 1921 he taught at the Berlin Academy of Music. He was the successor of Otto Brahm as head of the Freie Bühne, and was for many years the editor of the famous *Neue Rundschau.* Of his numerous works on opera, dance, ancient art, modern music (Richard Strauss) see, especially, *Rätsel der Musik* (1922) which was translated into several languages. On Bie, see *NDB*, II, 219 f.; Kaznelson, 65 *et passim*, and *UJE*, II, 349.

BÖTTICHER, HANS: see RINGELNATZ, JOACHIM

BREUER, ROBERT (Rereki, Poland, 1878—Martinique, West Indies, 1943), whose real name was Lucian Friedländer, was the son of a Jewish grain merchant and of a Christian mother. He joined the SPD in his youth, worked at the *Vorwärts*, and lectured to workers on fine and practical arts. He was one of the founders (1909) of the "Schutzverband deutscher Schriftsteller," the professional organization of German writers. During the war he was chief editorialist of the *Schaubühne* under the name of Germanicus. In 1918 he became deputy press chief of the Reich Chancellery. Later, he edited *Die Glocke*, the journal of the controversial Social Democratic millionnaire, Dr. Helphand-Parvus. In 1933 he fled to Paris where he worked for the *Pariser Tageblatt*. Interned in 1939, he managed to reach the Antilles where he died literally of hunger. See Arno Scholz, ed., *Robert Breuer: Ein Meister der Feder* (Berlin, 1934), and Osterroth, I, 48.

BROD, MAX (Prague, b. 1884), J. D. from the University of Prague, novelist, essayist, dramatist, and literary critic, whose greatest service to literature was putting Franz Kafka into print, was also instrumental in promoting Franz Werfel's fame. At first an expressionist writer and a cultural pessimist, he later became an advocate of social and ethical reforms. He was most successful in blending Jewish, Czech, and German cultural elements in his historical novels (for example, *Tycho Brahe's Redemption*, 1916. In English: 1928). His *Der Meister* (1952) represented Jesus as a social redeemer. Brod wrote several novels and essays on Jewish nationality, relations between Jews and Christians, and the importance of the Jewish outlook on life (*Sozialismus im Zionismus*, 1920; *Heidentum, Christentum, Judentum*, 1921, etc.). In the *Weltbühne* he wrote mainly in defense of his pacifist Zionism. During World War I he engaged in pacifist propaganda in Switzerland; in the early 1920's he headed the press department of the Czechoslovak Council of Ministers. He then was theater and music critic at the *Prager Tagblatt* and in 1939 went to Tel Aviv. See his memoirs: *Streitbares Leben* (1961). On Brod, see *UJE*, II, 537 f., and Kunisch, 135 f.

DÖBLIN, ALFRED (Stettin, 1878—Emmendingen, Schwarzwald 1957), grew up in Berlin as one of five children of a poor Jewish tailor. He became a physician, and between 1911 and 1933 practiced neurology among the Berlin proletarians. In 1910 he was one of the founders of the expressionist magazine *Der Sturm*. In the Weimar period he achieved fame with his great novels: *Die drei Sprünge des Wang-Lun* (1915); *Wallenstein* (1920); the utopian *Berge, Meere und Giganten* (1924), and especially *Alexanderplatz* (1929), a portrait of the Berlin underworld and the conversion to goodness of Biberkopf, a former convict. Döblin was a member of the Prussian Academy of Arts; politically, he stood close to the Social Democrats. Some of his pieces in the *Weltbühne* discussed the relationship between the intellectuals and the masses. He renounced Judaism in 1917 and converted to Catholicism in 1941. Having barely escaped the Nazis in 1933, he had to flee from France in 1940. He then lived in San Francisco but was one of the first exiles to return to Germany after World War II. For further details on one of Weimar Germany's greatest novelists see, among others, *NDB*, IV, 12 f.; Kunisch, 162 ff., and Fechter, 271 ff. *et passim*.

DOMBROWSKI, ERICH (Danzig, b. 1882), who wrote in the *Weltbühne* under the pseudonym Johannes Fischart, was the son of a Lutheran customs officer. He studied economics and business and became a journalist in 1907. He was deputy editor in chief of the *Berliner Tageblatt* from 1916 to 1926, and editor in chief of the *Frankfurter Anzeiger* from 1926 to 1936. He was one of the *Weltbühne*'s best political contacts. A member of the German Democratic Party, Dombrowski contributed a series of astute political portraits to the *Weltbühne* that were critical of the far-Left leaders. These biographies appeared in book form as Johannes Fischart, *Das alte und das neue System*, 4 vols. (1919–1924). Forbidden to practice journalism in 1936, he lived quietly until after World War II when he became one of the founders and the editor in chief of the *Frankfurter Allgemeine Zeitung*.

EGGEBRECHT, AXEL (Leipzig, b. 1899), was the son of a Christian physician; his mother was a *von*. An officer's candidate in 1917–1918, he was critically wounded at the front. He then studied at a university, practiced a variety of professions, and in 1925 became a free publicist. He joined Münzenberg's Red Aid in 1928. In the *Weltbühne* he wrote mainly on cinematic art but also enthusiastic accounts of Soviet Russia. A left-wing socialist, he was arrested in 1933 and spent two years in a concentration camp. Thereafter he worked in film studios as a script writer. Between 1945 and 1949 he was an executive with the Northwest German radio station and since that time has been an unattached writer in Hamburg. He is the author, among other books, of *Weltliteratur* (1948) and *Volk ans Gewehr: Chronik eines Berliner Hauses, 1930–1934* (1959).

ELOESSER, ARTHUR (Berlin, 1870—Berlin, 1938), the son of a Jewish textile merchant, was born and raised in the heart of Berlin, the Alexanderplatz area. The family could boast of noted intellectuals such as Ludwig Lewisohn. After acquiring a doctorate in history, he became increasingly involved with the world of the theater. He began writing theater criticism for the *Vossische Zeitung* in 1899 and went on to become, next to Julius Bab and Alfred Kerr, one of Germany's most important literary critics. Although he dabbled in directing at the Lessing Theater, his main contribution was as historian and critic of drama and literature, and in developing the critical essay as an art form. His works include *Das bürgerliche Drama: Seine Geschichte im 18. und 19. Jahrhundert* (1898); *Thomas Mann: Sein Leben und sein Werk* (1925); *Die deutsche Literatur vom Barock bis zur Gegenwart* (1930–1931). Eloesser remained in Germany after the Nazis came to power. Eventually deprived of the right to work, he died in 1938. See *NDB*, IV, 461 f.; *UJE*, IV, 89, and Kaznelson, 1 ff.

EMERENZER, ANTON: see SCHNOG, KARL

FASSLAND, FRANK (Birnbaum a/W., 1880—?), who also wrote under the name of Felix Pinner, was the son of a Jewish merchant. He studied law; in the Weimar period he was editor in chief of the *Handelszeitung*, a special supplement to the *Berliner Tageblatt*. His contributions to the *Weltbühne*, written in a socialist vein, dealt mainly with financiers and with economics. See Felix Pinner, *Deutsche Wirtschaftsführer* (1926) and *Die grossen Weltkrisen im Lichte des Strukturwandels der kapitalistischen Wirtschaft* (1938).

FEUCHTWANGER, LION (Munich, 1884—Pacific Palisades, Calif., 1958), the internationally known novelist, was born into a family of orthodox Jews. His father was a prosperous manufacturer whose nine children all became noted professionals. From 1903 to 1907 Feuchtwanger studied German philology, philosophy, and anthropology in Munich, completing a doctorate in 1907. In the same year he began writing drama reviews for the *Schaubühne* and soon became editor of the magazine *Der Spiegel.* Interned in Tunisia after the outbreak of World War I, he escaped and returned to Munich where he wrote some antiwar pieces. After the war, he directed for the stage, collaborating with Bertolt Brecht on *The Life of Edward II* in 1923. In 1925 he settled permanently in Berlin and began to devote himself more seriously to writing novels and short stories. Among his best known works are *Jud Süss* (1925), *Erfolg* (1930), the trilogy *Josephus* (1932–35), and *Goya* (1951). Feuchtwanger's dominant concerns were with the problem of the Jew in a non-Jewish world and with the psychological analysis of historic individuals. His political interest was never too apparent in his writings, and indeed developed only gradually. In 1918, he had objected to the transformation of the *Schaubühne* into the *Weltbühne* because he felt that politics and culture were incompatible. With the rise of fascism, however, he became increasingly sympathetic to Communism. His 1930 antifascist novel *Erfolg* was followed by numerous international propaganda efforts against Nazism. By 1937, his sympathy for the Communist movement was so strong that he publicly criticized André Gide for his partly negative commentary on the U.S.S.R. Feuchtwanger spent his first years of exile in France, was interned during and after the German invasion, and in 1941 made his way to the United States, where he remained until his death. His acclaim has been widespread both in his adopted land and in East Germany, which awarded him the National Prize for Literature in 1953. He also received an honorary degree from Humboldt University in East Berlin in 1954. On Feuchtwanger, see his autobiographical novel *Die Geschwister Oppenheim* (1933); Hiller, *Koepfe und Troepfe,* 203 ff.; *NDB,* V, 109 f.; *UJE,* IV, 284 f.; Fechter, 248 ff., and Kaznelson, 50.

FISCHART, JOHANNES: see DOMBROWSKI, ERICH

FLAKE, OTTO (Metz, Lorraine, 1880—Baden-Baden, 1963), a wartime "activist" and a fighter for the *Vergeistigung* of political life, was also "the most important German essayist next to Heinrich Mann" (Tucholsky). Like René Schickele, a true son of Alsace-Lorraine, he was proud to have grown up in a mixed German-French cultural atmosphere. He studied at the University of Strasbourg and became a follower of Nietzsche. During the war he worked in the political section of the German army at Brussels, but in 1918 he went to Switzerland to engage in pacifist propaganda. After the war, he was editor of the *Leipziger Tageblatt.* A member of the Democratic Party,

Flake moved in the Weimar years from a pacifist-socialist to an increasingly conservative position. His *Weltbühne* articles show his growing interest in elitist ideas and in a conservative revolution. In 1927 he was expelled from Italy for his active sympathy with the cause of the South-Tyrolean Germans. In 1933 he remained in Germany but was relegated to obscurity because of his Jewish wife and his fierce individualism. Flake was a fascinating storyteller and an accomplished literary portraitist of female personalities. His autobiography, *Es wird Abend* (1960) is of great interest to the student of Weimar literature. See also the autobiographical *Eine Kindheit* (1928); *Nein und Ja,* novel (1920); *Das Ende der Revolution* (1920); *Unsere Zeit,* essays (1928); *Spiel und Nachspiel,* novel (1962). On Flake, see Kunisch, 184 ff., and Fechter, 74 ff.

FRANK, LEONHARD (Würzburg, 1882—Munich, 1961), was the son of a Catholic carpenter. He was an apprentice bicycle mechanic, factory worker, chauffeur, house painter, and hospital employee. In 1904, he tried painting and joined the starving but happy company of the artistic coffee-house society in Munich-Schwabing. In 1910, he moved to Berlin and became one of the first expressionist writers with *Die Räuberbande* (1914; Fontane Prize, 1918), a semi-autobiographical presentation of youthful revolt against petty-bourgeois parents and society. During the war, he went to Switzerland where he edited, with Schickele, the pacifist *Die weissen Blätter,* and achieved fame with the sentimental antiwar novel, *Der Mensch ist gut* (1917). After the war, he joined the Independent Socialists. When this party was dissolved in 1922, he remained an unattached left-wing socialist although he collaborated closely with Münzenberg in the Red Aid and elsewhere. In the Weimar period, he received numerous literary accolades (Kleist Prize, 1920; membership in the Prussian Academy of Writers, 1927) for his expressionist stories and novels (*Karl und Anna,* 1927, on the popular theme of the returning soldier; *Im letzten Wagen,* 1925, where he found lasting human value only in the symbolic figure of the worker, etc.). In 1933, he fled to Switzerland, from there to London, later to Paris, and then, after some concentration-camp experiences in France in 1940, to Portugal. In the same year, he went to the United States where he settled in Hollywood swelling the ranks of those German refugee writers whom the film industry paid but neglected. In 1950, he returned to live in Munich but received more recognition in the East than in the West. He visited Russia (1955), received the Tolstoy Medal of the U.S.S.R. (1960), obtained the National Prize of the German Democratic Republic (1955), and was made an honorary doctor of the East-Berlin Humboldt University, for which reason the Bavarian Christian Democrats blocked a move in 1962 to name a street after him in his native Würzburg. See his autobiographical *Heart on the Left* (1954); *Gesammelte Werke,* 6 vols. (1957); Fechter, 255 ff., and Kurt Kersten, "Leonhard Frank," *Aufbau,* August 25 and September 7, 1961.

FRANZ, KARL: see FREI, BRUNO

FREI, BRUNO (Bratislava, b. 1897), whose real name is Benedikt Freistadt, and who also wrote under the name of Karl Franz, was one of the few left-wing socialists in the *Weltbühne* who consistently favored the Communist Party. Born to a Jewish family of modest circumstances, he managed to take up studies and obtained a doctorate in philosophy at the University of Vienna in 1922. The experience of the war led him into the left wing of the Austrian Socialist Party. Between 1922 and 1925, he was the Berlin correspondent of *Abend,* a socialist newspaper in Vienna and, between 1925 and 1929, he was the editor of that newspaper. He also contributed regularly to the *Weltbühne.* He wrote enthusiastic reports on Soviet Russia and engaged in controversies with the other *Weltbühne* writers about the place of the intellectual in the workers' movement. Between 1929 and 1933, he was editor in chief of *Berlin am Morgen,* a Münzenberg publication. He was especially active in exile politics where he entered the KPD (1934) and edited *Der Gegenangriff* (Prague and Paris) and the *Nouvelles d'Allemagne,* the news bulletin of the German Popular Front in Paris. Arrested by the French in 1939, he escaped to Mexico in 1941. He returned to Austria in 1947, and became the editor in chief of the Communist *Abend.* Since 1959 he has been editing *Das Tagebuch* in Vienna. Of his works, all of documentary character, see *Das Elend Wiens* (1921); *Die roten Matrosen von Cattaro* (1927); *Im Lande der roten Macht* (1929); *Wie Hitler zur Macht kam* (1933); *Mit eigenen Augen* (1955), about his experiences in Austria, Italy, Mexico, the U.S.S.R., etc.; *Frühling in Vietnam* (1959), and *Carl v. Ossietzky* (1966). On Frei, see Adling, 165 ff.

FREISTADT, BENEDIKT: see FREI, BRUNO

FRIEDELL, EGON (Vienna, 1878—Vienna, 1938), whose real name was Friedmann, was the son of a prosperous Jewish silk manufacturer.

At 27, Friedell converted to Lutheranism and developed an ambivalent, even hostile attitude toward Judaism. After obtaining a doctorate in German philology in 1904, he turned to the theater. Between 1908 and 1910 he directed the Vienna cabaret "Fledermaus" and wrote, together with Alfred Polgar, several short, satirical plays. He also wrote philosophical and literary essays during this time, such as *Ecce Poeta*, 1912; *Von Dante bis D'Annunzio*, 1915; *Das Jesusproblem*, 1921, and several plays, of which the 1920 *Judastragödie* is the best known. Under the aegis and encouragement of Max Reinhardt, Friedell also began acting, and pursued this profession in both Vienna and Berlin until 1927 when he returned to serious literary and cultural studies. One result was the much translated three-volume *Kulturgeschichte der Neuzeit* (1927–1931), in which modern times are depicted as heralding the end of rationality and the beginning of an ethos "beyond logic." His brilliant and provocative analyses were no less evident in his subsequent cultural histories of ancient civilizations, written in the late thirties but published posthumously after World War II. Friedell took his life in Vienna just after the "Anschluss" by throwing himself out of the window when the Nazis entered his apartment. For more on Friedell, see Peter Haage, "Ein unbekannter Friedell," *Der Monat*, March 1965, p. 82.; *NDB*, V, 446.; *UJE*, IV, 447.; Fechter, 127 ff., and Alfred Polgar, "Erinnerungen an Egon Friedell," *Aufbau*, April 24, 1953.

FRIEDLÄNDER, LUCIAN: see BREUER, ROBERT

FRIEDMANN, EGON: see FRIEDELL, EGON

GEORG(E), MANFRED (Berlin, 1893—New York City, 1965), the son of a Berlin businessman, was descended from a family of prominent Jews. He volunteered for military service in 1914. Seriously wounded, he was discharged a year later and returned to his studies. He began working as a journalist in 1916 while obtaining his doctorate in law, and collaborated with such German expressionists as Walter Hasenclever and Kurt Pinthus. Between 1916 and 1933 he worked for both the House of Ullstein and Mosse, edited Berlin newspapers, and contributed to the leading periodicals of the day, particularly the *Weltbühne*. As correspondent of the *Vossische Zeitung* in 1920, he covered the Upper Silesian events and was in Breslau at the time of the Kapp putsch; he narrowly escaped a firing squad set up by right-wing forces. Besides his numerous essays on law, politics, Zionism (of which he was a supporter), he also wrote radio dramas, plays, short stories, novels, and a musical comedy. In 1924 he founded, with Karl Vetter, Berthold Jacob, and Carl von Ossietzky, the Republican Party of Germany. In 1933 he fled to Prague where he founded and edited the *Jüdische Revue* and edited the *Prager Montagszeitung*. He was also correspondent for the *Nationalzeitung* in Basel and a reporter, in Spain, for many European newspapers during the Civil War. After his arrival in New York City in 1938, he created the *Aufbau*, the prestige publication of the Jewish and democratic emigrés. See his *Der Rebell*, short stories (1921); *Rathenau* (1924); *Theodor Herzl* (1932), and *The Case of Ivan Krueger* (1933). On George, see *Current Biography*, October 1965, pp. 13–16, and *UJE*, IV, 535.

GERLACH, HELLMUT VON (Mönchmotschelnitz, Silesia, 1866—Paris, 1935), was the scion of a Junker family. As a young man, he resigned his civil service career to join Adolf Stöcker's "Christian Social Movement" toward which he was driven by his violent anti-Semitism and his preoccupation with social questions and land reform. When he fell out with the domineering Stöcker, he approached Friedrich Naumann and Göhre and was, with them, one of the founders of the "Nationalsoziale Partei" in 1897. In 1903 he was elected to the Reichstag. After the dissolution of the Nationalsoziale Partei, he entered the "Freisinnige Vereinigung" (League of Free Thinkers); he was defeated at the Reichstag elections in 1907 and, in 1908, participated in the establishment of the Demokratische Vereinigung. His anti-Semitism and his interest in state socialism had by that time completely evaporated. During the war he was one of the most outspoken advocates of peace; he put his weekly journal, *Die Welt am Montag*, at the service of every conceivable humanitarian, democratic, and pacifist cause. In 1918–1919 he was, for a short time, a member of the Prussian revolutionary government but he turned against the Weimar coalition when it hesitated in accepting the Versailles treaty. He became a leader in the postwar pacifist movement and in the Reichsbanner, as well as a permanent contributor to the *Weltbühne*. For his efforts, he was almost killed by nationalists at a meeting in 1920. Gerlach was a member of the German Democratic Party from which he seceded when the Staatspartei (the successor to the Democratic Party) accepted the support of an anti-Semitic youth league in 1930. He then helped found a radical democratic splinter party. When Ossietzky went to prison in May 1932, Gerlach acted as editor of the *Weltbühne*. In February 1933, he fled abroad to escape arrest by the

SA; he died in his Paris exile. Gerlach was a reformist pacifist: he supported what he considered Germany's justified claims but he was uncompromising toward illegal rearmament and chauvinism. An exceptionally short man, Gerlach, with his red beard and his great eloquence, was one of the best known of the left-wing intellectuals. See the autobiographical *Erinnerungen eines Junkers* (Berlin, n.d.), and *Von Rechts nach Links* (1937). Also *NDB*, VI, 301 f.

GERMANICUS: see BREUER, ROBERT

GERSTORFF, K. L.: see STERNBERG, FRITZ

GLAESER, ERNST (Butzbach, Hesse, 1902—Mainz, 1963), had the most checkered political career of all *Weltbühne* writers. Born the son of a minor judge of Lutheran background, he studied at several German universities, then became a free writer and stage director in a Frankfurt theater. Between 1928 and 1930, he was the literary director of the Southwest German Radio Station. He made his fame with the still popular neo-objectivist novel, *Jahrgang 1902* (1928), the autobiographical story of youthful awakening—erotic and political—under the impact of war and the parallel deterioration of bourgeois values. Perhaps nowhere was the happy mood of 1914 and the subsequent general disillusionment better illustrated than in this humorously melancholy account of a little German town. At that time Glaeser was a left-wing socialist and a member of the group of proletarian revolutionary writers. His *Der Staat ohne Arbeitslose* (1931) presented a flattering image of Soviet Russia. In 1933, his works were burned by the Nazis on Opera Square in Berlin. Glaeser fled to Switzerland but returned to Germany six years later. During World War II he was editor in chief of a German army newspaper. After the war, he presented a dismal picture of the corruption and war-mongering of West German society in his *Glanz und Elend der Deutschen* (1960), but he also wrote a series of laudatory essays on West German politicians.

GOLDSCHMIDT, ALFONS (Gelsenkirchen, 1879—Mexico City, 1940), was a collateral descendant of Heine. He was a finance editor at Mosse's *Berliner Tageblatt* and at Ullstein's *B.Z. am Mittag*. For his *Weltbühne* pieces he drew chiefly on his economic expertise, and he also contributed some enthusiastic accounts of Soviet Russia. Although a revolutionary pacifist and former member of the Council of Intellectual Workers, he stood close to Communism and worked for Münzenberg's International Workers' Aid. He also taught economics at the University of Leipzig. After 1933, he became a member of the "Antifascist Literature Committee" (1937) and contributed to the *Neue Weltbühne* as well as to the *Wort* (Moscow). Of his works, see *Moskau 1920: Tagebuchblätter; Die Wirtschaftsorganisation Sowjet-Russlands; Wie ich Moskau wiederfand,* and the violently anti-Weimar *Deutschland heute,* all published between 1920 and 1928 by Rowohlt in Berlin. On Goldschmidt, see Hiller, *Koepfe und Troepfe,* 273 ff., and *UJE,* V, 29.

GUMBEL, EMIL J. (Munich, 1891—New York City, 1966), professor of mathematical statistics and mathematical engineering, received his habilitation at the University of Heidelberg in 1923. By then he was already well known and much hated for his pacifist politics and his shattering documentary revelations on "patriotic" murders and reactionary justice. His appointment, in 1930, as associate professor (*ausserordentlicher Professor*) of mathematics, statistics, and "social politics" at the University of Heidelberg led to an extensive rightist student campaign, supported by most members of the Heidelberg faculty, for his immediate resignation. Two years later, Gumbel went to Paris and, in 1934, became "Maître de Recherches" at the University of Lyons. Between 1940 and 1966 he taught at, among other institutions, Columbia University in New York City. Gumbel was also interested in philosophy and translated Bertrand Russell into German. Among his political works, see *Vier Jahre Lüge* (1919); *Zwei Jahre Mord* (1920); *Vier Jahre politischer Mord* (1922); *Das Stahlbad des Krieges* (1924); *Vom Russland der Gegenwart* (1927); "*Verräter verfallen der Feme*" (1929); *Lasst Köpfe rollen* (1932); *Freie Wissenschaft* (1938), and *Vom Fememord zur Reichskanzlei* (1962). On Gumbel, see *Aufbau,* September 14, 1966.

HASENCLEVER, WALTER (Aachen, 1890—Aix-en-Provence, 1940), one of the most noted playwrights of the Weimar era, was born to an old Rhenish family, among whom there were Jews as well as Protestants. His father, a reputed physician, was apparently excessively authoritarian. The young man broke with his father and set out to study in Oxford, Lausanne, and Leipzig. He began writing poetry and plays at Oxford, but the real turning point in his life came in 1910 at Leipzig where he became part of a circle of expressionist writers through friendship with Karl Pinthus and Franz Werfel. He produced some of his most important work between 1910 and 1917, despite having volunteered in the war and having been wounded. His output included a volume of poems, *Der Jüngling* (1913); the expressionist drama *Der Sohn* (1913), on the conflict of generations; and the drama *Antigone* (1917), dominated by radical pacifism and political activism. This last play earned him the Kleist Prize in 1917. Disappointed by the outcome of the events of 1918–1919, Hasenclever turned to literary mysticism under the influence of the occultism of Swedenborg, and later experimented with literary realism. He also wrote comedies, collaborating with Kurt Tucholsky on occasion. Forced to flee in 1933, he spent most of the subsequent years in France where he was interned in 1940. He took his life at the internment camp near Aix-en-Provence in March 1940 at the approach of the German army. See Kunisch, 244 ff., *UJE*, V, 236.; Fechter, 175 ff., and *Gedichte, Dramen, Prosa* (1963).

HEGEMANN, WERNER (Mannheim, 1881—New York City, 1936), son of a manufacturer, was a foremost architect and city planner, but he also held degrees in political science from Columbia University, Harvard, and other universities. In the Weimar period he edited the *Städtebau*, an architectural monthly, and wrote several historical studies. Although not Jewish, he went to Geneva in 1933 and from there to the United States where he lectured on architecture and city planning at several universities. Besides his many professional works, see *Fridericus oder das Königsopfer* (1926); *Napoleon oder der Kniefall vor dem Heros* (1927); *Das Steinerne Berlin* (1930) and *Entlarvte Geschichte* (1934).

HENSCHKE, ALFRED: see KLABUND

HERMANN, LAZAR: see LANIA, LEO

HILLER, KURT (Berlin, b. 1885), is according to his own account a "rebel with veneration for certain traditions." He has candidly admitted that his judgments have been dominated by the "crassest subjectivity." On his father's side he was a descendant of famous rabbis, on his mother's side of socialists. His father was a merchant. Having obtained his degree in law at the University of Heidelberg, Hiller became, before World War I, one of Germany's coffee-house *Literaten* and helped to found several expressionist magazines. In 1920 he joined the German Peace Association and, in 1926, he founded the revolutionary pacifist movement. Four years later, he was excluded from the Peace

Association for his violent attacks on Fr. W. Foerster and other alleged "agents" of French and Russian imperialism. Feverishly active, Hiller edited his own *Ziel Jahrbücher;* contributed to the *Weltbühne* and other independent leftist periodicals; lectured to students and philosophers; praised the philosopher Leonard Nelson and the latter's Internationaler Sozialistischer Kampf-Bund (ISK), and fought for sexual freedom at the head of his Kartell für Reform des Sexualstrafrechts (1927). His own publications were: *Geist werde Herr* (1920); *Verwirklichung des Geistes im Staate* (1925) with a full exposition of his views on humanism, rationalism, logokratic activism, and free socialism; *Das Ziel: Die rote Einheit* (1931), which demanded socialist unity to combat fascism; *Der Sprung ins Helle* (1932); and *Selbskritik links!* (1932). Arrested by the Nazis in the spring of 1933, Hiller was released from the Oranienburg concentration camp in April 1934. In the same month, he fled to Prague where he wrote articles for the exiled *Weltbühne.* While in Prague, Hiller published, in partnership with Otto Strasser, ex-National Socialist and conservative revolutionary, a manifesto (1938) calling for an elitist society and the world rule of intellectuals. In 1938, he went to London and founded the "League of Independent German Writers" (1939–1946). After World War II, Hiller returned to Germany, and in 1956 in Hamburg founded the "New Socialist League." Living more in the present than in the past, and active as a polemicist, Hiller at eighty-three seems loath to write his autobiography. His *Koepfe und Troepfe,* however, sheds light on his past. See also, Kaznelson, 65 *et passim.*

HIRSCHFELD, MAGNUS (Kolberg, 1868—France, 1935), was the son of a Jewish physician. He studied philosophy and medicine, and became one of Berlin's best-known neurologists. His Institute for Sexology and his *Zeitschrift für Sexualwissenschaft* were the subject of constant controversies. In the *Weltbühne* he wrote mainly on psychoanalysis and against the homosexuality and abortion paragraphs of the criminal code. He belonged to the left wing of the SPD: in 1921, an attempt was made on his life by an anti-Semite. His exotic Berlin apartment *cum* Institute housed, among others, the Communist leaders Heinz Neumann and Willi Münzenberg (see Buber-Neumann, *Von Potsdam . . . ,* 132 *et passim*). Apart from his numerous writings on sexology and psychiatry, see *Racism* (1938). On Hirschfeld, see *UJE,* V, 382.

HOLITSCHER, ARTHUR (Budapest, 1869—Geneva, 1941), was the son of a wealthy Jewish businessman. He broke away in early youth from his religiously orthodox and politically Hungarian nationalist family to return to the fold of German (Western) culture which his parents had abandoned. He quit his original profession of bank clerk in Fiume and Vienna and began to travel widely, writing his first novel, *Leidende Menschen* (1893), while abroad in the various capitals of Europe. He settled in Munich a few years before the outbreak of World War I and wrote for the satirical magazine, *Simplizissimus.* His many travelogues (*Amerika heute und morgen,* 1912; *Reise durch das jüdische Palästina,* 1922; *Das unruhige Asien,* 1926) reflect his strong identification with revolutionary socialist movements. His accounts of Soviet Russia (*Drei Monate in Sowjet-Russland,* 1921; *Das Theater des revolutionären Russland,* 1924) were almost unreservedly enthusiastic. Politically, he stood close to the Communist Party, but he also had sympathies with the socialist wing of the Zionist movement and was involved with "Heduth Avoda," a labor group in Palestine. Holitscher left Germany in 1938 for Switzerland where he remained until his death. See the autobiographical *Lebensgeschichte eines Rebellen* (1926) and *Mein Leben in dieser Zeit* (1928). Also, Adling, 229 ff.

HORVATH, ÖDÖN VON (Fiume, 1901—Paris, 1938) was the son of a Hungarian Jew and petty noble who was a diplomat in the Dual Monarchy. At the end of World War I, the family moved to Munich, where Horvath studied philosophy and German philology. After his studies, he became a free-lance writer, residing variously in Berlin, Salzburg, and Vienna. Besides contributing to the journals of the day, he wrote plays and novels in which the main themes were the fate of little men buffeted by forces they could not control, and their struggle for decency and dignity. (See *Die Bergbahn,* 1929, the story of striking railroad workers.) His stories were sometimes compassionate and humorous, sometimes bitingly satirical; the latter was particularly true of his vignettes from the lives of the lower-middle class, such as the play, *Geschichten aus dem Wienerwald* (1931) or *Italienische Nacht* (1930). From 1934 on he lived in Vienna until the Nazi take-over in 1938 when he fled to France. He was killed by a falling tree-branch in Paris that same year. Aside from his autobiographical novel, *Ein Kind unserer Zeit* (1939), see Kunisch, 298 f.

HUTH, ERNST: *see* SCHNOG, KARL

JACOB, BERTHOLD (Berlin, 1889—Berlin, 1944), whose full name was Berthold Jacob Salomon, was the son of a merchant of graphic arts in Berlin. His brother was a novelist. After the war, he became a staff-member of the *Berliner Volks-Zeitung* and in 1924 helped found the "Republican Party of Germany." He was also a regular contributor to Harden's *Zukunft,* Gerlach's *Die Welt am Montag,* and *Die Weltbühne.* In March 1928 he was sentenced to nine months' confinement in a fortress for an article written three years earlier in Küster's *Das andere Deutschland* on the Reichswehr's violation of the Versailles treaty. Jacob left Germany for Strasbourg in 1932, and was among the first Germans to be deprived of citizenship by the Nazis. In March 1935 he was kidnapped by German agents from Basel on Swiss territory and questioned by Heydrich himself on his amazing familiarity with the German military organization. The Swiss government protested, and Jacob was released to the Swiss police a few months later. (See Eduard Zellweger, "Die Affäre Jacob: Politische Entführung und ein Schweizer Beispiel," *Die Zeit* [Hamburg], July 5, 1963, p. 4.) In 1936, he published in Paris *Das neue deutsche Heer und seine Führer* (Paris: Éditions du Carrefour—Willi Münzenberg's exile publishing house—1936) which again proved his precise knowledge of the German military establishment. Jacob was again kidnapped, this time from Portugal, in 1941. He died, a prisoner of the Gestapo, in the Jewish Hospital in Berlin. See Lehnau, "Berthold Jacob und Rudolf Olden," *WB*, October 15, 1946, pp. 232–237, and Hermann Lewy, "Nochmals: Berthold Jacob," *ibid.,* March 1, 1947, pp. 222–223.

KÄSTNER, ERICH (Dresden, b. 1899), one of Germany's most famous writers and popular feuilleton humorists, was born to a poor Christian saddler. His mother was a seamstress. In 1917 he was drafted in the army and served on the Western front. He completed his doctorate in philology in 1925 when already a writer. Two years later he was fired from the *Neue Leipziger Zeitung* for publishing an erotic poem. He then settled in Berlin and contributed drama, literary reviews, reportages, and feuilleton items to the leading periodicals and newspapers of that city. He was one of the *Weltbühne's* most popular contributors, and provided the luxury of publishing apolitical poems and essays in that journal. His first volume of poetry, *Herz und Taille,* appeared in 1928. A witty, aphoristic style, and a compassionate optimism for mankind pervaded his work as in *Fabian* (1931) and *Drei Männer im Schnee* (1935). His children's books (*Emil und die Detektive,* 1928) remain as popular today as do his witty and socially critical verses known as *Gebrauchslyrik.* Although his works were burned on Opera Square in Berlin in May 1933, Kästner chose to stay in Hitler's Germany. He wrote several film scenarios (*Münchhausen,* 1942), but most of what he wrote could only be published abroad. After the war he edited the *Neue Zeitung* and directed the *Kleine Freiheit,* a literary cabaret theater in Munich. He was elected president of the German PEN Club in 1951, and vice-president of the International PEN Club in 1965. He was awarded the Georg Büchner Prize in 1957. See his autobiographical *When I Was a Little Boy* (1959). Also, Kunisch, 323 ff., and Fechter, 359.

KARSCH, WALTHER (Dresden, b. 1906), the youngest member of the *Weltbühne* circle, was one of Ossietzky's editorial assistants and, in February–March 1933, the editor of the journal. The son of a Christian businessman, Karsch became a journalist in 1928, contributing among others to the pacifist *Die Friedenswarte* and *Die neue Generation.* In the *Weltbühne* his contributions were mainly on the theater. He was then a socialist. Karsch remained in Germany in 1933 and became a businessman. Since 1945 he has been the editor in chief of the West Berlin *Der Tagesspiegel,* a moderate conservative newspaper. See his *Was war—was blieb?,* a collection of critiques on the Berlin theater in 1945–1946.

KERSTEN, KURT (Welheiden, Kassel, 1891—New York City, 1962), the son of a peasant, held a doctoral degree from the University of Berlin. His wife was Jewish. During World War I, he was an officer and won the Iron Cross First Class. Kersten was a successful journalist, translator, and writer of historical biographies; in the Weimar period he contributed, among others, to the *Prager Tagblatt* and to Münzenberg's *Arbeiter Illustrierte Zeitung.* In the *Weltbühne* he wrote mainly on Soviet Russia. He was a left-wing socialist, if not a Communist, and he was one of Münzenberg's main collaborators. In 1933 he fled abroad, living mostly in Paris. He contributed, among others, to the *Pariser Tageblatt, Das Neue Tage-Buch,* and the Moscow *Das Wort.* Between 1940 and 1945, he lived on Martinique island and, after 1946, in New York where he contributed to the *Aufbau.* See his *N. Lenin* (1920); *Fridericus Rex und die Krise des Absolutismus* (1922); *Moskau-Leningrad: Eine Winterfahrt* (1924); *Der Moskauer Prozess gegen die Sozialrevolutionäre* (1926); *Bakunins Beichte* (1927); *Peter der Grosse* (1935), etc.

KESTEN, HERMANN (Nuremberg, b. 1900), refers to himself as a *Café-Dichter,* the title of an autobiographical book written in 1958.

Yet the implication that an author can find inspiration in one place, the coffee house, is contradicted by Kesten's own life. The son of a prosperous Jewish merchant, he traveled widely in Europe and Asia after completing his university education. He had already known many cultural milieus before he became an editor, in 1927, at the Kiepenheuer publishing company in Berlin. His first novel, *Joseph sucht die Freiheit* (1928), concerning the impossibility of total freedom, earned him the Kleist Prize. This novel, as well as his short stories and essays, show the influence of German neo-objectivism. Kesten also became noted for his travelogues. After 1933, he lived in Paris and Amsterdam, heading the Amsterdam publishing house, Albert de Lange. In exile he wrote his "Spanish" novels: *Ferdinand und Isabella*, 1936; *König Phillip II*, 1938; *Die Kinder von Guernica*, 1939. When war broke out he moved to the United States, but returned to Europe at war's end. Today, he lives and writes in Rome. See Kunisch, 344 f.

KIAULEHN, WALTER (Berlin, b. 1900), a well-known figure in contemporary German journalism and the theater, came from a Berlin working-class family. He was at first trained as an electrician. Having served in World War I, he took up university studies and in 1924 became a journalist and an actor. He wrote theater critiques and related articles for Mosse's *Berliner Tageblatt* from 1924 to 1930, and for Ullstein's *B.Z. am Mittag* from 1930 to 1933. He was also editor in chief of the *Münchner Merkur*. Kiaulehn continued to live and work in Germany after the Nazi take-over. Although his satirical collection of essays, *Lehnaus Trostfibel* (1933), was banned by the Nazis, subsequent humorous collections, such as *Lesebuch für Lächler* (1938; reprinted in 1958), were published. He also worked for the German film industry as a newsreel commentator. During World War II he was again drafted and was captured by the Red Army. In 1958 he published an excellent illustrated documentary history, *Berlin: Schicksal einer Weltstadt*, and has continued to live and work in Munich. See also his *Die eisernen Engel* (1935; reprinted in 1953) on the culture of the machine age.

KISCH, EGON ERWIN (Prague, 1885—Prague, 1948), one of the world's best reporters, often called a "private eye for Communism," was born of a German-Jewish upper-middle class family. He began his journalistic career in 1906 at the Prague newspaper *Bohemia;* he belonged to the Prague coffee-house society and was a close friend of

Rilke, Kafka, Brod, Werfel, and Paul Kornfeld. He became famous through his journalistic exposure, in 1913, of the sensational Redl affair: the life and death of an Austro-Hungarian colonel and chief of army counterintelligence who had been blackmailed by the Russians into spying for them. (Alfred Redl, a homosexual, committed suicide at the orders of his superiors.) In 1913, Kisch went to Berlin for the first time where he tried both acting and directing. He became a radical socialist during the war while a corporal in the Austro-Hungarian army and, after the proclamation of the Austrian republic, participated in the Communist general strike movement in Vienna and headed a Red Guard unit. He stormed, among others, the editorial offices of the *Neue Freie Presse* where his brother, Paul, was a staff member. As legend has it, his brother warned him on that occasion that he would "tell it all to mother." Arrested by the Social Democratic authorities in Vienna, he was imprisoned for three months and then expelled to Germany. From then on, he worked for scores of leftist papers as a peripatetic reporter (*Der rasende Reporter*), traveling widely and pouring out innumerable articles on imperialism, the sufferings of the colonial peoples, bourgeois callousness and corruption, religious superstition, and so on. For the *Weltbühne* he wrote some of his most militant travelogues, and also political commentaries and short stories. A member of the KPD, Kisch helped found the "Bund proletarisch-revolutionärer Schriftsteller Deutschlands" (League of German Proletarian-Revolutionary Writers) in 1928, and was a staff member of the *Linkskurve*. Despite a tone of Marxist militancy, some of his reportages on Soviet Russia were suppressed there because they were much too accurate (*Zaren, Popen, Bolschewisten*, 1927). His most shattering revelations concerned the misery of the Asiatic peoples (*Asien gründlich verändert*, 1932; *China geheim*, 1933). In 1933, he was arrested by the Nazis but was soon released because of Czechoslovak protest. He then went to Paris and worked for the Münzenberg enterprises, reporting, among other assignments, on the Civil War in Spain. In 1940 he fled to Mexico where he worked for the Communist *Freies Deutschland* until 1946; he then returned to Prague. Rühle recounts in his *Literatur und Revolution* (p. 231) that by that time Kisch was a disillusioned Marxist, having shown even as early as the 1930's an ambivalent attitude toward the eventual triumph of Communism. [His close friend and colleague, Otto Katz (André Simon)—incidentally also a collaborator of the *Weltbühne* in the 1920's—became one of the highest-ranking members of the Czechoslovak Communist Party and was executed in Prague in the early 1950's as a Zionist agent.] See, among others, *Schreib das auf, Kisch: Soldat im Prager Korps,* war diaries (1920); *Der Fall des Generalstabschefs Redl* (1924); *Marktplatz der Sensationen* (1953); *Gesammelte Werke in Einzelausgaben* (1960 ff.), and Emil Utitz, *Egon Erwin Kisch* (1956). These last three works were published by Aufbau-Verlag in East Berlin.

KLABUND, whose real name was Alfred Henschke (Crossen/O., 1890—Davos, 1928), lived the short and intense life typical of romantic poets. The son of a pharmacist in a small Prussian town, his adult life was plagued by recurring attacks of tuberculosis. His profound poetic talent was discovered early through his contributions to the magazine *Pan* in 1913. In that year the first volume of his poetry (*Morgenrot*) was published. A mixture of neo-romanticism (Rilke was an early model) and expressionism permeates his "soldiers' songs" and other war poems written between 1914 and 1918. The war experience turned his neo-romantic nationalism into confirmed pacifism, but although he wrote political satire and chansons for the cabaret and for newspapers, he was not primarily a political poet. He was widely noted for his lyrical rendering of translations from Chinese poetry, and for the linguistic beauty of his novels and short stories which often centered on historical figures. Before his premature death in the Swiss sanatorium town of Davos, Klabund had also written some plays. One of these was "The Chalk Circle" (1924), an adaptation of an ancient Chinese tale which was also later adapted by Bertolt Brecht. In a well-known and moving funeral address, the great German poet Gottfried Benn, voiced the loss to literature occasioned by Klabund's death. See Kunisch, 345 f.

KOBLENTZ, KARL: see SCHNOG, KARL

KOESTLER, ARTHUR (Budapest, b. 1905), was the son of an unsuccessful Budapest inventor-businessman. He studied at the University of Vienna where he joined a Zionist student fraternity which fought weekly engagements with members of "Aryan" fraternities. He then went to Palestine to become first a laborer in a kibbutz and then a lemonade vendor in Tel Aviv. Later he worked as the Middle-East correspondent of the House of Ullstein and moved in 1928 to Berlin where he was the science editor of the *Vossische Zeitung* and foreign editor of the *B.Z. am Mittag*. He participated, among other ventures, in the "Graf Zeppelin" expedition to the North Pole. At the end of 1931 he became a secret member of the German Communist Party and an agent of its intelligence apparatus; when he was fired from Ullstein's seven months later, he went to Soviet Russia. After 1933 he worked for the Münzenberg enterprises in Paris and was sent to Spain to write on the Civil War. Arrested by the Nationalists and almost executed, he became disillusioned with Communism while waiting—according to his own account—to be shot by the fascists. Later, he was interned in France. In 1940 he settled in England where he became a British soldier. For more details on "this typical case history of a Central European member of the educated middle classes, born in the first years of our century" (Koestler), see the autobiographical *Arrow in the Blue* (1952–1954), which describes his childhood and youth up to his joining the KPD in 1931, and *The Invisible Writing* (1955), a sequel to *Arrow in the Blue*.

KOLB, ANNETTE (Badenweiler, 1875—Badenweiler, 1967), was a novelist equally versed in German and French. Her father was a Christian landscape architect to the Bavarian Court, her mother a French pianist. Her early short stories and her novel, *Das Exemplar* (1913), won for her the attention of Rilke and Thomas Mann. For the recurring theme in her novels of the frantic frivolity and malaise of affluent life (*Daphné Herbst*, 1928, and *Die Schaukel*, 1934), she drew upon her childhood experiences in the aristocratic circles in *fin de siècle* Munich. An even stronger theme in her work was pacifism and Franco-German conciliation as, for instance, in *Sieben Studien, l'âme aux deux patries*, written in 1906, *Wege und Umwege* (1914), *Briefe einer Deutsch-Französin* (1917), and *Versuch über Briand* (1929). She was among the first to leave Germany in 1933, living in Paris until 1940 and then in New York. After the war she returned to Badenweiler where she continued to write mostly on music and musicians. She received the Fontane Prize in 1915, the Gerhart Hauptmann Prize in 1928 and 1931, and the Frankfurt Goethe Prize in 1955. See Fechter, 80 ff., and *Aufbau*, December 8, 1967.

KUCZYNSKI, ROBERT RENÉ (Berlin, 1876—Berlin, 1947), son of a Berlin Jewish banker, was a student of Lujo Brentano and became a labor economist. Between 1906 and 1921 he headed the Office of Statistics in Berlin. A left-wing socialist and a pacifist, he was chairman, in 1926, of the Reich Committee on the Expropriation Without Indemnity of the Rights and Holdings of the German Princes. Between 1933 and 1945, he taught at the London School of Economics.

Of his numerous works on immigration policy, demography, agriculture, wage policy, labor conditions, see *American Loans to Germany* (1927); *Postwar Labor Conditions in Germany* (1925), *Lebensraum und Bevölkerungsproblem* (1939). His son Jürgen is the foremost economic historian of the German Democratic Republic. See Kaznelson, 697.

LANIA, LEO (Kharkov, Russia, 1896—Munich, 1961), born Lazar Hermann, was the son of a professor of medicine at Kharkov University who, although Jewish, was decorated by the tsar in 1905 for his medical services to the Dowager Empress. In the same year, the family moved to Vienna where Lania later studied at the university. He became a pacifist and a socialist when he served as an officer in the Austro-Hungarian army during the war. After World War I, he first worked at the *Wiener Arbeiterzeitung*, and then settled in Berlin where he became a dramatist. In 1922 he helped Piscator create the proletarian theater. Later he also worked with Reinhardt, wrote political editorials, and published several documentary collections, plays, essays, novels, and film scenarios, such as that for the *Dreigroschenoper*. He insinuated himself into Nazi circles and published one of the earliest interviews with Hitler. In the *Weltbühne* he wrote mainly on socialist unity and against the Reichswehr. As a left-wing socialist, he collaborated both with Paul Levi and Willi Münzenberg. In 1933 he fled to Paris where he was interned at the outbreak of World War II. He then fled to England, via Portugal, and in 1941 came to the United States. After the war, he returned to live in West Germany. Of his numerous works, see particularly *Die Totengräber Deutschlands* (1923) and *Das Urteil im Hitlerprozess* (1924); *Gruben, Gräber, Dividenden* (1924); *Gott, König und Vaterland,* drama (1928); *Wanderer ins Nichts,* novel (1935); the autobiographical *Today We Are Brothers* (1952) and *Welt im Umbruch* (1953); also *Willy Brandt,* a biography (1960). His novel, *Der Aussenminister* (1960), based on the last days of Jan Masaryk, describes a confrontation between Masaryk and Otto Katz, the former *Weltbühne* writer and Communist, who became a leader in the Czechoslovak regime after 1948. On Lania, see Kurt Kersten in *Aufbau,* August 3, 1956, and November 17, 1961.

LANZER, ROBERT: see LEONHARD, RUDOLF

LEDEBOUR, GEORG (Hannover, 1850—Berne, 1947), the oldest member of the *Weltbühne* circle, was the descendant of North-German peasants, and the son of a civil servant. Orphaned at ten, he was trained to be a businessman by his guardian but chose journalism as soon as he was legally free to do so. He served in the Franco-Prussian war of 1870–1871 as a medical orderly. At first a liberal, he joined Social Democracy in the 1890's and was elected in 1900 to the Reichstag where he represented the district Berlin-Pankow until 1924. An early advocate of revolutionary socialism, he became one of the founders of the Independent Socialist Party. In November 1918 he was elected into the Executive of the Berlin Workers and Soldiers Council where he advocated mass demonstrations and a general strike—not violence—as the proper revolutionary method, thus siding with Rosa Luxemburg against the radical Spartacists and revolutionary shop stewards. In January 1919, he barely escaped death at the hands of the counterrevolutionary soldiers. Sent to prison for four months, he was acquitted at his trial. (See *Der Ledebour-Prozess,* and *Ledebour vor den Geschworenen: Seine Verteidigungsrede,* both published by the *Freiheit,* in 1919 in Berlin). Although a strong advocate of Soviet dictatorship, he turned against Zinoviev at the Halle Congress of the USPD (1920) and fought against the acceptance of Lenin's 21 Propositions as well as against the entry of the USPD into the Third International. In 1922, he refused to follow his moderate colleagues into the SPD and founded—together with the son of Karl Liebknecht —a new USPD. Their splinter party never acquired a mandate. When his Reichstag mandate expired in 1924, Ledebour turned to political journalism, advocating a united action front of all socialist parties. In 1931, he joined the SAPD; two years later he fled to Switzerland. In 1945 he protested sharply against the expulsion of Germans from Polish-occupied territories. Hiller and many other left-wing intellectuals esteemed Ledebour as the greatest German socialist, but at least one *Weltbühne* writer, Johannes Fischart, that is, Erich Dombrowski, regarded him as a cheap comedian and a fool (*Das alte und das neue System,* 1919, pp. 64 ff.). On Ledebour, see Osterroth, I, 183 f., and Minna Ledebour (his wife) *et al.,* eds., *Georg Ledebour* (Zurich, 1957).

LEHMANN-RUSSBÜLDT, OTTO (Berlin, 1873—West Berlin, 1964), the son of a customs official, was one of the *Weltbühne's* most dedicated pacifists. A bookseller by profession, he became interested in social philosophy (monism) and social criticism while still a young man. (See *Metaphysik der Geschlechtsliebe* and *Weckruf an Deutschlands junge Geister,* both written in 1901). He was one of the found-

ers, in 1914, of the Bund Neues Vaterland which later became the
Deutsche Liga für Menschenrechte. His main work was *Der Kampf
der deutschen Liga für Menschenrechte,* written in 1927. He was
typical of many leftist intellectuals in that he combined adherence to
left-wing Social Democracy with assiduous work in several of Willi
Münzenberg's Communist-front organizations, and a conviction that
lasting peace would be achieved even among capitalist societies. Although a moderate among the German pacifists, he was a strong
antimilitarist and coauthor of the exposé *Weissbuch über die
Schwarze Reichswehr* (1925), a fierce attack on the military establishment. Further polemical works, many of which reflected his moderate
views, were: *Die blutige Internationale der Rüstungsindustrie* (1929);
Die Reichswehr (1930); *Wer rettet Europa? Die Aufgabe der kleinen
Staaten* (1936). *Aggression: The Origin of Germany's War Machine*
(1942) was written in London, where Lehmann-Russbüldt spent his
exile after 1933. At the close of World War II, he edited for a short
while a publication for German emigrés, *Rundbriefe des Flüchtlings*
(1947), and then returned to Germany in 1951. He lived in West
Berlin where he continued to write about European reconciliation in
such books as *Europa den Europäern* (1948), and *Wie gewinnen wir
den Frieden?* (1956). He received a high decoration (*Grosse Bundes-
verdienstkreuz*) from the Federal Republic of Germany in 1953. A
year later he felt compelled to resign from the German League for
Human Rights when it turned to propaganda among the inhabitants
of East Germany. See "Konflikte in der deutschen Liga für Menschenrechte," *Aufbau,* August 13, 1954.

LEONHARD, RUDOLF, whose real name was Levysohn (Lissa,
Posen, 1889—East Berlin, 1953), was the son of a wealthy Jewish
lawyer. He obtained a doctorate in law at the University of Berlin. In
1914 he volunteered for front service. The war turned him into a
radical pacifist and revolutionary, a conversion indicated in his 1916
play, *Die Vorhölle.* In 1918 he became a follower of Karl Liebknecht
and the Spartacists even though he had joined the Council of Intellectual Workers and, later, Kurt Hiller's revolutionary pacifist movement.
He then lived in Berlin as a writer and reader for the publishing house
Die Schmiede. At first an expressionist, he came to advocate a human-
istic socialism in his poems, essays, and dramas. In 1927 he went to
Paris where several of his works were published in French translation.
After 1933 he became one of the founders of the "Schutzverband
Deutscher Schriftsteller im Exil" (Association of German writers in

Exile) and was a Communist advocate of the Popular Front. Interned by the French in 1939, he escaped to join the French underground movement during the German occupation. Some of his illegally published writings aimed at the German soldiers (see Robert Lanzer, *Deutschland muss leben,* poems, 1944). In 1947, he attended the first German Writers' Congress in Berlin and three years later settled in the Eastern sector of the city. By then, however, he was almost blind. His best-known expressionist writing is the *Angelische Strophen,* poems (1913). See also his revolutionary *Spartakus-Sonette* (1921); *Das nackte Leben,* poems (1925); *Segel am Horizont,* drama (1925); *Gedichte* (1936), a collection of poems that was smuggled into Germany; *Der Tod des Don Quijote* (1938), poems on the Spanish civil war; *Geiseln* (1945), a drama about the French resistance, and *Unsere Republik: Aufsätze und Gedichte* (1951) written in praise of the German Democratic Republic. On Leonhard, see Adling, 321 ff.

LEVYSOHN, RUDOLF: see LEONHARD, RUDOLF

LEWINSOHN, RICHARD (Graudenz, West Prussia, 1894—Brazil?), who wrote under the name Morus, was the best economics reporter of the *Weltbühne.* Born of a fairly prosperous Jewish family, he became a medical doctor but interest in the problems of urbanization and in demography led him to acquire a doctorate in economics and to join the Social Democratic Party. He gave up his medical practice after World War I to become economics specialist and foreign correspondent for the *Vossische Zeitung.* In 1921 he also joined the *Weltbühne* where he became one of Jacobsohn's favorite writers. He published works on political theory (*Sozialismus und Bevölkerungspolitik,* 1922); tersely written and well researched analytical articles on socioeconomic problems, and several biographies on the "lords of the economy." (*Das Leben Sir Basil Zaharoffs,* 1925; *Wie sie gross und reich wurden: Lebensbilder erfolgreicher Männer,* 1927). Some of his other works are *Jüdische Weltfinanz?* (1925); *Histoire de l'Inflation* (1926), and *Das Geld in der Politik* (1930). He wrote *The Profits of War through the Ages* (1936) in exile which eventually led him to Brazil. Nothing has been heard of him in recent years.

LINKS, JACOB: see POL, HEINZ

MANN, HEINRICH (Lübeck, 1871—Santa Monica, California, 1950) is one of the great names in twentieth-century German literature. His background, that of north German merchant-patricians, is well-known from the novels and short stories of his younger brother, Thomas. As a young man he was trained for the publishing business with the Fischer-Verlag, but soon began traveling and writing on his own. In the decade before World War I he settled in Munich where he became a leading literary figure, moving through the literary influences of naturalism, neo-romanticism, expressionism and, after the war, neo-objectivism. His most frequent and successful genre was the novel, in which at first two themes predominated: the dichotomy between artist and *Bürger*, and the moral and social decline of the Wilhelmian bourgeoisie. Among his early novels were *Professor Unrat* (1905), which was later made into the classic film *The Blue Angel; Die kleine Stadt* (1909), and *Der Untertan* (published in 1918 but written between 1912 and 1914). After the war, when he settled in Berlin, his novels concentrated on dissecting bourgeois society and became increasingly political, reflecting what was to be his life-long connection, despite ideological differences, with the Communist Party. His personality, much more patrician than that of his brother, made this connection sometimes seem incongruous. As Hermann Kesten noted in *Lauter Literaten* (1963), Heinrich Mann was an "anti-bourgeois satirist with almost upper-class (*hochbürgerlich*) manners." In 1930 he was elected to the Prussian Academy of Arts. His sympathies for the KPD and his marriage to a Jewish woman (Mimi Kahn) made it impossible for him to remain in Germany in 1933. In exile in France, he continued to write for the *Weltbühne* as well as to head numerous Popular Front undertakings, but he slowly returned to literary themes which had occupied him earlier. The two volume *Henri Quatre* (1935–1938) is a break from his political novels of the interwar period. His commitment to Communism remained, however, until his sudden death in 1950: he was about to return to East Germany where he had been named president of the Academy of Arts. In 1961 he was reburied in East Berlin. See Kunisch, 408 ff.; Fechter, 47 ff.; *Deutsches Dichter Lexikon*, 388; his own *Geist und Tat*, essays (1931), and the autobiographical *Ein Zeitalter wird besichtigt* (1944).

MARCUSE, LUDWIG (Berlin, b. 1894), is a noted biographer and cultural critic. Born of a prosperous Jewish family, he studied philosophy, wrote a dissertation on Nietzsche, and would have become, in another day and age, an academician. World War I made him discover his interest in journalism and politics. Fresh out of the university at the close of the war, he wrote theater critiques, feuilleton articles, and political commentaries for the *Frankfurter Anzeiger*, the *Berliner Tageblatt*, the *Vossische Zeitung* and, of course, the *Weltbühne*. He also wrote learned essays on philosophy and drama and gradually found his best form in biographies; his choice of figures were those whom he considered representative of a revolutionary historical change. (*Georg Büchner*, 1922; *Strindberg*, 1924; *Ludwig Börne*, 1929; *Gerhart Hauptmann*, 1929; *Heinrich Heine*, 1932; *Ignatius von Loyola*, 1934, and others). In 1933 he fled to the United States via France. He taught philosophy at the University of Southern California in Los Angeles from 1947 until his recent retirement and return to Germany. He reentered the German literary scene shortly after World War II, and most of his recent works, such as his well-known biography of Sigmund Freud (1958), appeared both in English and German. See Kunisch, 422 f., and his own *Mein zwanzigstes Jahrhundert*.

MEHRING, WALTER (Berlin, b. 1896) was born to a Jewish family of artists. His father, Sigmar, was a writer and editor of the Berlin magazine, *Ulk*. His mother was an opera singer. He finished high school before World War I but refused to go on to university studies, plunging instead into the expressionist movement. He wrote poetry for *Sturm* and for Harden's *Zukunft*, and was one of the originators of the Berlin circle of Dadaists. After the war he began writing cabaret shows and political chansons for which he became famous, starting out in this career in Max Reinhardt's cabaret in 1919. He also worked with George Grosz and Erwin Piscator. Many of his savage and brilliant lyrics are contained in *Ketzerbrevier* (1921) and *Arche Noah SOS* (1931) as well as in other volumes published in those years. His play, *Der Kaufmann von Berlin*, produced by Piscator in 1929, created a scandal partly because of its alleged anti-Semitism. Characterized by iconoclasm, irreverence, and above all wit, his poems—the *Gebrauchslyrik* type of verse—combined the rhythms of jazz and other foreign song forms with the German language, particularly Berlinese. Politically, Mehring was a revolutionary pacifist with anarchist tendencies. He lived in Paris from 1924 to 1928, and again after 1933. Interned in a Vichy detention camp in 1940, he escaped to the United States after a series of wild adventures; he remained there until some time after World War II. In 1952 he wrote a satirical, sociopolitical account of twentieth-century German history, by way of a description of the fate of his father's library, called *Die verlorene Bibliothek: Autobiographie einer Kultur.* He now lives in Switzerland. See *UJE,* VII, 996, and Kunisch, 424 f.

MENENIUS: see SCHACHT, ROLAND

MORUS: see LEWINSOHN, RICHARD

MÜHSAM, ERICH (Berlin, 1878—Concentration Camp Oranienburg, 1934) is distinguished among the *Weltbühne* writers because he was utterly and unambiguously a revolutionary. The purpose of his entire life was, as he put it, "Struggle, Revolution, Equality, Freedom." He never hesitated to act for this purpose and devoted his art to it. Son of a Jewish pharmacist in Berlin, he spent his youth in Lübeck where his secondary schooling ended with his expulsion for socialist agitation. He spent the next few years traveling around Germany as a pharmacist's apprentice, and received most of his subsequent education in coffee houses and through reading. By 1901 he was launched as a free-lance writer in Berlin, collaborating with the Hart brothers on the periodical, *Neue Gemeinschaft.* Through his Bohemian Berlin circle, he met the philosopher Gustav Landauer and the dramatist Frank Wedekind who were to have a decisive literary and political influence on him. In 1909 he moved to Munich where, a year later, he was arrested but not convicted for socialist agitation. In Munich he wrote theater criticism, cabaret plays and songs, essays and verse for *Simplizissimus* and *Fackel.* He also edited his own literary periodical *Kain,* described as a "magazine for humanity." By this time he was on the far Left of the socialist movement, a revolutionary pacifist who, when the war broke out, declined even to carry out alternate labor service. For this he was confined to the Traunstein fortress in Bavaria. The strike wave of January 1918 found him agitating among factory workers for a socialist revolution to end the war. In the winter of 1918–1919 he opposed the revolutionary prime minister of Bavaria, Kurt Eisner, from the left and, in April 1919, he helped set up the short-lived Bavarian Soviet Republic. As one of the most hated revolutionaries, he was sentenced by a Bavarian tribunal to fifteen years' imprisonment in a fortress. While incarcerated, he wrote a series of revolutionary songs which became highly popular among both Social Democrats and Communists. Many of these songs were published in the book, *Revolution: Kampf-, Marsch-, und Spottlieder* (1925). In the same period he wrote novels and nonfictional accounts of his own revolutionary experience and on revolution in general, such as *Brennende Erde* (1920) and, in 1921, the play *Judas*. Amnestied in 1925, he returned to full-time propagandizing for the revolutionary cause. Although he was associated with Münzenberg's Red Aid, his basic creed remained anarchism, and he was often critical of the KPD. He edited the monthly *Fanal* and wrote didactic and agitational novels, short stories, and poems for workers, according to the tenets of *Proletkult*. Other noted works are *Von Eisner bis Leviné* (1929), his account of the Bavarian Soviet Republic; *Unpolitische Erinnerungen* (1931); *Die Befreiung der Gesellschaft vom Staat: Was ist der kommunistische Anarchismus?* (1932). When the Nazis took power, Mühsam was immediately arrested and sent to the Oranienburg concentration camp. There this bearded and hirsute apostle of unchained humanity became the obvious target of the SS guards. He died at the hands of his captors on July 11, 1934. For more information on Mühsam, see his "Selbstbiographie" in *Auswahl: Gedichte, Drama, Prosa* (1961); *UJE* VIII, 32; Kunisch, 437 f., and Adling, 367 ff.

NATONEK, HANS (Prague, 1892—Tucson, Arizona, 1963) was born into a family of noted Jewish scholars. Destined for his father's profession in the insurance business, he chose to leave Prague for study in Vienna and Berlin. Later he was to write that his greatest regret in life was having been too fearful of taking a job as publicity agent with a traveling circus. His need for variety and excitement was, however, at least partly requited when he became a free-lance writer. From 1920 on he was feuilletonist for the *Neue Leipziger Zeitung* and contributed to the leading journals of the time. By 1931, when he received the Goethe Prize, his literary output was prolific: he wrote short stories, drama, novels, and literary and cultural criticism. As a moderate liberal, his works were only mildly polemical. Among his most popular novels were *Der Mann, der nie genug hat* (1927), and *Geld regiert die Welt* (1930). After 1933, he returned to Prague, then went on to Paris in 1938. Before his arrival in the United States in 1940, he wrote for the *Neue Zürcher Zeitung* and the Paris *Weltbühne*. Apart from some published poems, Natonek had little success in the United States and was obliged at times to take up manual labor. He married and settled in Arizona where he died after a long illness. See his autobiography, *In Search of Myself* (1943), and Manfred George, "Hans Natonek," *Aufbau*, November 8, 1963.

OLDEN, RUDOLF (Stettin, 1885—At sea, 1940), was the son of a Berlin actor and playwright. He served in an aristocratic Dragoon

Regiment and was a *Leutnant der Reserve*. After the war he left his civil-service career to become a reporter for Theodor Wolff's *Berliner Tageblatt*. When already a well-known journalist, he acquired a doctorate in law and passed his bar examination. He made a name for himself as a lawyer with his successful defense of a proletarian woman accused of child murder, and with his defense of Ossietzky and other opponents of the Reichswehr. Olden was a pacifist and a leading member of the German League for Human Rights. Politically he was a moderate with sincere admiration for Gustav Stresemann. In the *Weltbühne* he first wrote a series of "Austrian Portraits" (1925) and then articles on the judiciary. Although a Christian, he fled to Czechoslovakia in 1933 and settled, in the following year, in England. He and his wife were on their way to the United States when their ship, the "City of Benares," was sunk by a German submarine. Olden was described as an aristocratic personality, a "noble snob in the spirit of Baudelaire," and a "true *homo eroticus*." He was the author of a number of astute biographies (*Stresemann*, 1929; *Hindenburg*, 1933, published in 1948; *Hitler*, 1936), and *The History of Liberty in Germany* (1946). On Olden, see Lehnau, "Berthold Jacob und Rudolf Olden," *Die Weltbühne*, October 15, 1946, pp. 232–237.

PERSIUS, LOTHAR (Kyritz, East-Prignitz, 1864—Ascona, Switzerland, 1944), naval captain and dedicated pacifist, came from an old Protestant family; his ancestors were Prussian officers and civil servants. His father, a civil servant in Breslau, was a conservative member of the Prussian Upper House. Persius' biographer, Johannes Fischart [Erich Dombrowski] remarks that the father had testified to his cultural liberalism by allowing the presentation of Gerhart Hauptmann's "Weavers" in Breslau. (*Das alte und das neue System*, I, 250.) Persius studied nautical engineering, witnessed the Spanish-American war in the Philippines and, in the early 1900's, was commander of an armored cruiser in the Far East. While there, he published pseudonymous articles in the *Ostasiatische Lloyd* criticizing German colonial policy in China. When his identity became known, he was recalled to Germany. He resigned his commission in 1908 and wrote newspaper articles on Tirpitz' naval program which he found inadequate. Instead of battleships, he proposed the construction of submarines, which he saw as purely defensive weapons. Beginning 1912 he was a staff member of the *Berliner Tageblatt*, but also wrote for other liberal papers. He held World War I for lost before it had begun and became an ardent pacifist. In the *Weltbühne* he wrote several series of articles on the Imperial Navy, on World War I and, in 1928, against the "armored cruiser" program. See his *Die Tirpitzlegende* (1918), and *Warum die Flotte versagte* (1924), both of which originally appeared in the *Weltbühne*.

PINNER, FELIX: see FASSLAND, FRANK

PINTHUS, KURT (Erfurt, b. 1886) is one of the most important German expressionists. He was cofounder of the Kurt Wolff Verlag, famous for its support to expressionist writers, and author of the analytical anthology of expressionism, *Menschheitsdämmerung* (1920). Born of a Jewish family in Erfurt, he studied German philology and literature in Leipzig where he completed his doctorate in 1911. As chief reader for Rowohlt as well as for Wolff, he brought many future expressionist writers together, such as Franz Werfel and Walter Hasenclever. He was also a friend and collaborator of Oskar Kokoschka and Max Reinhardt. After World War I, he became a leading theater critic and feuilleton contributor to *Das Tage-Buch, 8 Uhr-Abendblatt*, and the *Weltbühne*. He did not immediately leave Germany after Hitler came to power but lectured at the "Jüdisches Lehrhaus" in Berlin. He came to the United States in 1937 where he wrote for *The New York Times* and the *Aufbau* and, in 1947, began to lecture on theater at Columbia University. There he also worked on the *Columbia Dictionary of Modern European Literature* (1947). He retired in 1961 and now lives in New York. See Kunisch, 673 ff., and *UJE*, VIII, 539.

POHL, GERHART (Trachenberg, Silesia, b. 1902), one of the *Weltbühne's* most polemical cultural critics, was born to a Silesian Catholic family. His father owned a saw-mill. Pohl joined the Youth Movement and earned a doctorate in German philology. As a young man he settled in Berlin, swelling the ranks of the many Silesian writers who constituted a separate group in Berlin literary circles. He came under the influence of the expressionists Klabund and Kasimir Edschmid and published his first novel, *Fragols Kreuzweg*, in 1921. Between 1923 and 1930 he edited the youthful and iconoclastic literary review, *Die neue Bücherschau*. In the *Weltbühne* he wrote far left essays on politics, many of which later appeared in book form (*Deutscher Justizmord: Der Fall Fechenbach*, 1924; *Vormarsch ins XX. Jahrhundert*, 1931). He also wrote literary essays on Lessing, Büchner, Zola, Mehring, as well as short stories (*Partie verspielt*, 1929, etc.). After the triumph of Hitler, Pohl retired to his Silesian homeland to live in "inner emigration." He continued to write, however, and his novels and short stories made him famous. *Der Ruf* (1934); *Die Brüder Wagemann* (1936); *Der verrückte Ferdinand* (1939) reflect his fascination with Silesia, as well as with his own tragic "generation of 1902," previously described by Ernst Glaeser (*Jahrgang 1902*). At war's end, Pohl found himself in Silesia under Polish occupation. In 1946 he conducted the transfer of the remains of his friend and fellow Silesian, Gerhart Hauptmann, from Polish Silesia to Berlin. Four years later, he himself moved to West Germany. He resides today in Munich and has continued to write about the fate of Silesia. See Fechter, 117 ff., and Kunisch, 462.

POL, HEINZ (Berlin, b. 1904), who often used the pseudonym Jakob Links in the *Weltbühne,* was the son of a Berlin Jewish manufacturer of progressive liberal convictions. Pol studied at an exclusive *Gymnasium* in Berlin and later at Berlin University where he was expelled for his satirical articles on members of the faculty; these had appeared in the *Vossische Zeitung*. He also turned against his father under the influence of expressionist literature and for a while toyed with the idea of killing him. In 1923 he joined the *Vossische Zeitung* as assistant editor but also became a regular contributor to the *Weltbühne* and the *Literarische Welt.* He published his first political novel, *Entweder-Oder* in 1927: its socialist hero, a refined intellectual moulded in the image of Paul Levi, is murdered by Communist workers. Four years later, he published *Die Patrioten,* another political novel, and in the same year he left the *Vossische Zeitung* because of censorship of his articles. Between 1931 and 1933, he was editor of the *Neue Montagszeitung* and assistant editor of the *Welt am Abend,* both published by Willi Münzenberg. Although sympathetic to Communism, he criticized the KPD in his pseudonymous *Weltbühne* articles from a Trotskyist point of view. Pol was arrested by the Nazis on the night of the Reichstag fire but was released from Spandau prison eight days later when he artfully convinced his captors that he was the wrong man. He then fled to Prague where he stayed until 1936 as part-owner and regular collaborator of the *Neue Weltbühne* and editor of the anti-Nazi satirical weekly, *Der Simpl.* Between 1936 and 1940, he lived in Paris as editor of the antifascist news and feature agency, Mitropress. Interned by the French in 1939, he left France in May 1940 on the last French passenger ship bound for New York. There he published the *Suicide of Democracy* (1942), a study on the fall of France; the first biography of De Gaulle, and *The Hidden Enemy* (1943), a study on the origins of National Socialism. He also contributed to the left-wing *Nation* and *Protestant*, as well as to *The New York Times* and other New York newspapers. Between 1946 and 1948, he was U.S. correspondent for the Paris weekly, *L'Action*, and since 1949 he has been the New York correspondent of the *Frankfurter Rundschau, Basler National-Zeitung*, and several other West German and Swiss papers. He is also the author of numerous volumes of poetry and essays published in Germany.

POLGAR, ALFRED (Vienna, 1873—Zurich, 1955), was the son of a Jewish composer and music teacher in Vienna. He set aside his studies in music to become one of the most celebrated feuilleton writers of the *Weltbühne*. He began by writing theater critiques for the *Montagblatt* in Vienna, and contributed to the *Schaubühne* as early as 1905. Twenty years later, he moved to Berlin and wrote regularly for the *Weltbühne*, the *Tage-Buch*, and a number of other Berlin journals. His celebrated style—Jacobsohn always referred to him as "Marquis Prosa"—was characterized by aphorisms, crystallized ideas, and lapidary sentences. He wrote thousands of music and theater critiques many of which appeared in the four volume *Ja und Nein* (1926–1927); *Stücke und Spiele* (1929); *Ich bin Zeuge* (1928), and *Schwarz und Weiss* (1929). He also translated the Czech author Hašek and the Hungarian Ferenc Molnár. He escaped to Austria in 1933, five years later to France, and then to Spain. He landed in Hollywood in 1940 where he was paid but politely ignored. He succeeded, however, in publishing a collection of essays in German (*Geschichte ohne Moral*, 1942). He died unexpectedly while on a European trip. See Kunisch, 463 f., and Kaznelson, 62 *et passim*.

QUENDT, EUGEN: see SCHACHT, ROLAND

QUIDDE, LUDWIG (Bremen, 1858—Geneva, 1941), was the son of a Lutheran wholesale merchant in Bremen. His ancestors were mainly civil servants with democratic, *grossdeutsch* political leanings. His wife was Jewish. Quidde was a historian and founder of the *Deutsche Zeitschrift für Geschichtswissenschaft* (1886). In 1894, in an ostensibly innocent essay entitled, *Caligula: Eine Studie über römischen Cäsarenwahnsinn*, he delivered a biting and sensational attack on William II. Two years later, Quidde drew a prison sentence for lese majesty allegedly committed while addressing a Social Democratic audience.

He had joined the peace movement at its very start; in 1894, he became president of the Bavarian branch of the Peace Association and, in 1914, president of the German Peace Association. In 1907 he was elected to the Bavarian Landtag on a progressive liberal ticket. He spent most of the war years in Switzerland and was, in 1919, elected to the Weimar National Assembly on a German Democratic Party ticket. Quidde came into conflict with the Party leadership over the question of the Reichswehr and failed to be elected to the Reichstag. As president of the German Peace Association and of the Friedenskartell, he came under attack from the left for supporting international arbitration and a peaceful revision of the Versailles treaty, as well as for being anti-Soviet. In 1927, he received the Nobel Prize for Peace. Having seen his movement disintegrate in the early 1930's, he left Germany after Hitler came to power. See Utz-Friedebert Taube, *Ludwig Quidde* (Kallmünz, Opf., 1963).

RINGELNATZ, JOACHIM (Wurzen, near Leipzig, 1883—Berlin, 1934), whose assumed name fits his extraordinary life better than his real one (Hans Bötticher), was one of Weimar Germany's best-known lyricists. His father was a lieutenant in the reserve, an artist of applied arts, and a writer of children's books. By the time he was thirty, Ringelnatz himself was a jack of all trades: he had been an actor, sailor, cabaret entertainer, painter, and an announcer in a reptile act as well as having had approximately thirty other occupations. To these he added poetry with his first volume of verse, *Kleine Wesen,* appearing in 1910. Best described as *Gebrauchslyrik*—aphoristic and slightly absurd verse about the common yet universal concerns of life—Ringelnatz' poetry reflected the language of those places he knew best: harbor bars (he was a heavy drinker), ships, backyards of lower-class neighborhoods, and amusement parks. Yet the language was musical, and the poems, said to be akin to the poetry of Christian Morgenstern, unexpectedly beautiful. Many of Ringelnatz' lyrics became popular chansons, especially those contained in *Seemann Kuddel Daddeldu* (1920), a volume commemorating the four war years he had spent in the Imperial Navy. Ringelnatz was one of the *Weltbühne's* most prolific poetic contributors. His works were suppressed in 1933 and were not collected and republished until 1951, when they appeared under the title . . . *und auf einmal steht es neben dir,* a line taken from one of his poems. On Ringelnatz, see his autobiographical *Als Mariner im Krieg* (1929), and *Mein Leben bis zum Kriege* (1931). See also Fechter, 259 ff., and Kunisch, 488 f.

RODA RODA, ALEXANDER (Zdenci Puszta, Slavonia, 1872—New York City, 1945) was actually Sándor Friedrich Rosenfeld, son of a Jewish estate manager for a Hungarian landlord in that part of Southern Hungary's black belt region which is now Yugoslavia. His father had also been an active officer in the Austro-Hungarian army, a career at first chosen for or by Alexander as well. Entering the army in 1892 as a "one-year volunteer," he was discharged ten years later with the rank of first lieutenant in the artillery; eventually, he was deprived of his rank (in 1907) when he published his criticism of the Austro-Hungarian generals. By that time he had taken up residence in Berlin and in Munich, and had become a free-lance writer. His plays were banned from the stages in Austria-Hungary. He spent the next few years before World War I as a correspondent for Vienna newspapers in Belgrade and Balkan cities and also wrote for the Munich *Simplizissimus*. His Balkan experiences were gathered in a volume of tales, *Rosenland* (1918). During the war he served as reporter in the Austro-Hungarian Army Command Headquarters. In the following years, he produced a great number of plays, novels, reviews, travel stories, as well as stories about Vienna written in Viennese Jewish jargon. He was also a frequent contributor to the *Weltbühne*. In 1933 he fled to his Austrian homeland from which, in turn, he had to flee in 1938. He made his way to the United States in 1940 and spent the last five years of his life in New York. See *Das grosse Roda Roda Buch* (1950).

ROSENFELD, KURT (Marienwerder, West Prussia, 1877—United States, 1943), son of a Jewish manufacturer, became a lawyer in 1905. He joined the SPD, and in 1909 was elected to the Municipal Council in Berlin. During the war he was a soldier. In 1917 he was elected to the executive committee of the Independent Socialist Party, and in November 1918 he was delegated to the Prussian Ministry of Justice. In the following year he was elected to the Prussian Constituent Assembly on a USPD ticket, and in 1920 to the Reichstag where he served until 1932. In 1922 he rejoined the SPD but remained in opposition to the party's coalition policy; in October 1931 he was among the founders of the SAPD. Rosenfeld was one of the lawyer-collaborators of the *Weltbühne;* he defended Ossietzky at all of his trials. He was also a leading member of the German League for Human Rights. After his immigration to the United States, he edited the *German-American,* a trade-union newspaper. See Osterroth, 255.

ROSENFELD, SÁNDOR FRIEDRICH: see RODA RODA, ALEX-
ANDER

SALOMON, BERTHOLD JACOB: see JACOB, BERTHOLD

SCHACHT, ROLAND (Reichenberg, Bohemia, 1888—Berlin, 1961)
wrote for the *Weltbühne* under a variety of pseudonyms such as
Eugen Quendt, Menenius, and Balthasar. His father was an actor at
the Royal Theater in Reichenberg. His mother was a member of the
aristocracy. Having studied at the universities of Paris, Munich, Berlin, and Göttingen, Schacht settled in Berlin where he became a
grammar-school teacher. When the republic was declared, he entered
the foreign service but soon gave up this career in favor of free-lance
writing. His contributions to the leading periodicals of the time were
mostly on literature, literary history, aesthetics, and art history. He
edited the periodical *Jahresberichte für neuere deutche Literaturge-
schichte.* Himself a painter, he wrote about artists, publishing a biography of Matisse in 1923 and of Archipenko in 1924. He also wrote
successfully for the theater, his most noted works being *Christine von
Schweden* and *Die Schauspielerin.* He remained in Germany after
1933, wrote comedies and film scenarios, but turned increasingly to
translating, paticularly after the war.

SCHICKELE, RENÉ (Oberehnheim, Alsace, 1883—Vence, Provence,
1940) was a noted German expressionist and pacifist. Born to a Christian German-Alsatian wine grower and local police official, and to a
French mother, he always considered himself a *Grenzvogel* or "fron-
tier bird" and devoted himself to conciliation between French and
Germans. His writings, which often dealt with Alsace, reflected a
combination of French rationalism and German romanticism. At fifteen, he published his poems in the *Strassburger Zeitung* and in the
Heimat in Berlin. Five years later, in 1903, he founded the magazine
Der Stürmer, devoted to modern poetry in Alsace; his partner in this
venture was his fellow Alsatian and later colleague on the *Weltbühne,*
Otto Flake. While studying natural sciences and philology at Strasbourg, Munich, and Paris, he brought out his first volume of poetry,
entitled *Sommernächte* (1902). From 1904 to 1909, he edited the
internationally known literary review, *Das neue Magazin für Literatur,* during which time he also wrote his first novel, *Der Fremde*
(1909), a story about a young Alsatian in Bohemian Paris. From 1909
to 1913 he was foreign correspondent for the magazine, *Nord und Süd,*

and for the newspaper, *Neue Strassburger Zeitung.* He then became coeditor of the pacifist journal, *Die weissen Blätter.* When the war broke out Schickele declared himself a conscientious objector and wrote his first pacifist play, *Hans im Schnakenloch* (1916). Because of his pacifist activity, he was forced to move to Switzerland where he lived until after the war. He returned to Germany at the time of the revolution, which he described in *Der 9. November* (1919). Thereafter, he lived near Munich until 1933. He continued writing for the *Weltbühne* and other journals, and also published his famous Alsatian trilogy, called *Erbe am Rhein* (1927–1931). These novels described the destructive effect on the Alsatians of the revanchism of both France and Germany. Schickele died in exile. His collected works were edited by Hermann Kesten in 1961. For his role in the formative years of German expressionism, see Kurt Pinthus, *Menschheitsdämmerung.* See also Kunisch, 519 f., and Fechter, 73 f.

SCHNOG, KARL (Cologne, 1897—East Berlin, 1964), one of the *Weltbühne's* far left contributors, was the son of an artisan and a descendant of famous Jewish scholars. He himself was entirely self-taught. He became a political radical in World War I, and in November 1918 he helped set up a Workers' and Soldiers' Council in Hagenau. At first an actor, he also tried directing in various Berlin theaters and political cabarets. In addition, he wrote feuilleton pieces, reviews, and satirical verse for the *Weltbühne* and similar journals under such assumed names as Ernst Huth, Anton Emerenzer, and Carl Coblentz. Much of his satirical verse was published in the volume *Gerumpel* and *So sehen sie aus! Sehen sie so aus?* (1928). After 1927, he worked for various radio stations as the author of successful plays. He also wrote for the left-wing Social Democratic satirical magazine, *Lache Links.* In 1933 he went to Switzerland and from there to Luxemburg where he was captured by the German army in 1940. The next five years he spent in several German concentration camps (see his *Unbekanntes KZ,* 1945). In 1945 he returned to Luxemburg; a year later, he became editor in chief of the Berlin satirical newspaper *Ulenspiegel* and, in 1948, editor in chief of the East-Berlin Radio Station. He was awarded the East German Heine Prize in 1957. See, among others, *Zeitgedichte-Zeitgeschichte* (1949), and Adling, 448 f.

SCHOENAICH, PAUL FREIHERR VON (Reinfeld, Holstein, 1886—Reinfeld, Holstein, 1954), scion of East-Elbian aristocracy turned pacifist militant, was at first a naval officer. From 1887 to 1907 he served in the Second Guard Dragoons Regiment and then in the War Ministry. Between 1913 and 1919 he was regimental commander at the front and rose to the rank of major general. In 1920 he resigned from the army and became a full-time propagandist for a series of German and international peace organizations, such as the German Peace Cartel and the German League for Human Rights. The ideas and experiences which led him to change his philosophy and way of life are described in *Mein Damaskus: Erlebnisse und Bekenntnisse* (1926). Having joined the German Democratic Party in 1918, he repeatedly attempted to win a Reichstag seat but was always defeated. He was not among those left-wing pacifists willing to modify their opposition to the bearing of arms for the sake of anti-capitalist, anti-imperialist revolution. His rejection of any form of military service included the socialist idea of a citizen's militia. Besides writing numerous pacifist works, such as *Abrüstung der Köpfe* (1922) and *Vom Chaos zum Aufbau* (1923), he also aroused the wrath of his former military colleagues by traveling to and reporting favorably on the Soviet Union in his book *Lebende Bilder aus Sowjet-Russland* (1925). His articles in the *Weltbühne* were often leading political editorials. He was immediately arrested by the Nazis in 1933 but went on a hunger strike in prison and was released after a few months. Living in retirement on his family estate, Schoenaich became increasingly embittered after World War II by political developments in West Germany and by the slim chances of East-West reconciliation. On Schoenaich, see his own *Mein Finale* (1947) and Kurt R. Grossmann's tribute in *Aufbau,* January 15, 1954.

STERNBERG, FRITZ (Breslau, 1895—Munich, 1963), who wrote in the *Weltbühne* under the names K. L. Gerstorff and Thomas Tarn, was one of the journal's foremost economic and political analysts. Born to a Jewish middle-class family, he embarked on an academic career shortly after World War I, and as a Ph.D. in economics taught at the University of Frankfurt. His scholarly works, *Der Imperialismus* (1926) and *Der Niedergang des deutschen Kapitalismus* (1932) reflected his left-wing socialist orientation and inclinations to Trotskyism, as did the many editorials he wrote for the *Weltbühne* in the early 1930's. A political activist since his youth, he first belonged to the SPD, then to the USPD, again to the SPD, and finally became a major theoretician for the SAPD. The bulk of his work appeared after 1933, when he went to live in Austria, then Switzerland and, finally, in 1939, in the United States. In this country, he taught at New York University, returning to West Germany after the close of the war. During this period he wrote economic and political analyses of German developments (*Deutschland wohin?*, 1937); on the war effort (*Die deutsche Kriegsstärke*, 1939, and *Fivefold Aid to Britain*, 1941), and anticipations of the Cold War (*The Coming Crisis*, 1947; and *How to Stop the Russians Without War*, 1948, the latter translated into fifteen languages.) One of his most widely read books among socialists is *Capitalism and Socialism on Trial* (1951). For his differences with Trotsky, see "Erinnerungen an Trotsky," *Gewerkschaftliche Monatshefte*, 14 (1964), 711–722. For a tribute to Sternberg, see Kurt R. Grossmann in *Aufbau*, November 8, 1963.

STÖCKER, HELENE (Elberfeld, 1869—New York City, 1943), militant feminist and pacifist, studied at the universities of Berlin and Glasgow and was the first woman in Germany to earn a doctorate in philosophy. In 1905, she founded the "Bund für Mutterschutz und Sexualreform" (League for the Protection of Mothers and for Sexual Reform). In the same year she founded *Die neue Generation*, a feminist periodical which she edited until 1932. She was among the first in 1914 to join the Bund Neues Vaterland and after the suppression of this antiwar organization in 1916, carried on pacifist propaganda at the head of her own "Frauenausschuss für einen dauernden Frieden" (Women's Committee for a Lasting Peace). This too was suppressed, however, in the same year. After the war, she cofounded numerous international pacifist and feminist organizations; she became a leading member of the German Peace Cartel and was most active in the International League for Sexual Reform where she pleaded, among other things, for the protection of unwed mothers and illegitimate children, and against the laws forbidding abortion. The elimination from German birth certificates of the term "illegitimate" was almost entirely her doing. Politically, she stood to the left of Social Democracy. She considered herself one of Kurt Hiller's "revolutionary pacifists" and she belonged to the left-wing opposition within the German Peace Cartel, favoring the Soviet peace projects. She worked with Münzenberg in the League Against Imperialism and other organizations, and in the *Weltbühne* she expressed admiration for the Soviet educational system and social legislation. In 1933 she fled to Switzerland, later to England and Sweden, and finally, in 1941, to the United States. Of her numerous works, see *Die Frauen und die Liebe* (1906); *Liebe*, novel (1922); *Erotik und Altruismus* (1924); *Verkünder und Verwirklicher* (1928). On Stöcker, see Fischart, *Das alte und das neue*

System, II, 255 ff. and Hiller, *Koepfe und Troepfe*, 259 ff. where Hiller insists that Stöcker was not a suffragette in the conventional sense but rather an advocate of equality between the sexes based on the recognition of the different social roles of the male and female.

STÖSSINGER, FELIX (Prague, 1890—Zurich, 1954), wrote for the *Weltbühne* both on music and on Social Democratic tactics. His political point of view represented an interesting mixture of revisionist Social Democratic theory and radical practice. He wrote mainly for the periodical, *Sozialistische Monatshefte*, in which he advocated a Franco-German *Kontinentalpolitik* directed against Great Britain. He was also the editor of a 1920 series called, *Die Revolution: Jahresbericht;* the owner of his own Felix Stössinger publishing firm (which published the Independent Socialist *Die Freiheit*), and the author of radio programs on music. As a Jew and well-known activist in the SPD, Stössinger was forced to emigrate in 1933 to his home city of Prague; he then went for a short while to Nice, and subsequently to Zurich where he remained for the rest of his life. He resumed writing at the end of World War II, but his works were no longer political. Besides contributing to the *Neue Schweizer Rundschau*, he translated Upton Sinclair, Hillair Belloc, and John Hershey, and edited a volume of Heine's poems, all in the early 1950's. For more on Stössinger, see Kurt Kersten's tribute in *Aufbau*, September 10, 1954.

STRÖBEL, HEINRICH (Bad Nauheim, 1869—Berlin, 1945), was one of the *Weltbühne*'s chief editorialists and a leading left-wing Social Democrat. Of Christian middle-class background, he studied literature, history, and economics at several German universities and, in 1892, began writing for various Social Democratic newspapers in Kassel and Kiel. After 1900, he was a staff member of the party's main organ, *Vorwärts*. He resigned in 1916 to join the antiwar Independent Socialists. Beginning in 1908, he had also been a member of the Prussian Landtag. In November 1918 he entered the Prussian revolutionary government but resigned a month later when the USPD withdrew from the coalition with the SPD. During the next three years, he wrote weekly editorials for the *Weltbühne* and published several political tracts, such as *Wider die Pfaffenherrschaft* (1919) and *Die Bilanz der Revolution* (1919), as well as his major work, *Die deutsche Revolution* (1922; translated into English as *The German Revolution*). Along with the USPD moderates, Ströbel rejoined the SPD in 1922 and thereafter devoted himself to leading the left-wing opposition within the party. In 1924 he was elected to the Reichstag by the workers of the Saxon industrial town of Chemnitz, and retained his seat there until 1932. His contributions to the *Weltbühne* were few in this period, but he remained in close association. He also wrote for the *Welt am Montag* and was editor of the left-wing Social Democratic journal, *Der Klassenkampf*. He continued to write theoretical works, such as *Die Sozialisierung: Ihre Wege und Voraussetzungen,* and *Sozialismus und Weltgemeinschaft*. In 1931, together with Rosenfeld and Seydewitz, he led the left wing out of the SPD to form the Socialist Workers Party (SAPD). Ströbel remained in Germany after 1933, but his life during the Nazi regime is not traceable. See Osterroth, 305.

TARN, THOMAS: see STERNBERG, FRITZ

TOLLER, ERNST (Samotschin, Posen, 1893—New York, 1939), was the son of a shopkeeper. He volunteered for the army in 1914 and was still a soldier when he wrote his antiwar play, *Die Wandlung* (1917). Imprisoned for a short time for his participation in the antiwar strikes in Bavaria in January 1918, he was the youngest of the five Jewish *Literaten* (Kurt Eisner, Gustav Landauer, Erich Mühsam, Eugen Leviné) who made history in Munich during the revolutionary events of 1918–1919. Sentenced to five years by a Bavarian court after the suppression of the revolution, he earned popularity while in captivity by his melancholy *Schwalbenbuch* and his socialist dramas: *Masse Mensch, Die Maschinentürmer,* and *Hinkemann*. An expressionist writer at first, he turned to neo-objectivism around 1925 (*Feuer aus den Kesseln*). He had been a member of the USPD, but after the dissolution of that party he remained uncommitted. He was often chided by the Communists for his bourgeois idealism. After he fled Germany in 1933, he felt that his creative energy was spent. He committed suicide in 1939 in New York by hanging. Toller was a genuine humanitarian who longed to become a *Volksdichter,* a poet of the masses, but his audience was limited to the sophisticated. Most of Toller's works have been translated into English: see, for instance, *Man and the Masses* (1924); *I Was a German: An Autobiography* (1934); *Look Through the Bars: Letters from Prison, Poems, and a New Version of the "Swallow Book"* (1937). There are in German two collections of his writings: *Ausgewählte Schriften* (1959), and *Prosa, Briefe, Dramen, Gedichte* (1962), with an excellent introduction by Kurt Hiller. See also, Kaznelson, 55 *et passim*.

VALENTIN, VEIT (Frankfurt/M, 1885—Washington, D.C., 1947) an eminent historian, came to the *Weltbühne* through his affiliation with the German Democratic Party. He was born to a highly cultured family of French background; among his ancestors were poets and scholars. His father was a teacher, art critic, and expert on Goethe, and his mother a musician. He was educated at Heidelberg, Berlin, and Munich and began to teach history at the University of Freiburg when he was twenty-five. During World War I he was a soldier, and between 1915 and 1916 was attached to the Foreign Ministry. After the war, he taught at the Technological Academy in Berlin where he was also director of the *Reichsarchiv* from 1920 to 1933. During this time, he wrote some historical essays with democratic political over-tones, such as *Die erste deutsche Nationalversammlung* (1919) and *Schwarz-weiss-rot und schwarz-rot-gold* (1925). Among his many studies in German history, the best known are those on the revolution of 1848, on Bismarck, and on Frederick II. In 1933 he went to England and in 1940 to the United States where he taught at the University of Pennsylvania and at Harvard. It was at that time that he wrote his comprehensive history of Germany, *The German People* (1946).

VICTOR, WALTHER (b. Oeynhausen, Westphalia, 1895), was the editor of several left-wing Social Democratic newspapers in the Weimar period and an assiduous contributor to the *Weltbühne*. Of Jewish middle-class background, he obtained a doctorate in literary history and experimented with apolitical avant-garde literature before joining the Social Democratic *Hamburger Echo* in 1919. Between 1923 and 1931, he was editor of the left-wing Social Democratic *Sächsisches Volksblatt* in Zwickau where he took a militantly critical position toward the politics of his party. Although he refused to follow his Saxon left-wing Social Democratic friends in 1931 in founding the SAPD, he quit Social Democratic journalism in that year and, for the next two years, worked for the left-wing intellectual *8 Uhr-Abendblatt* in Berlin. In the Weimar period he published several political and social essays, such as *Abseits vom Tempo* (1921), and *Atemzüge der Besinnung* (1928), as well as a biographical sketch of Heinrich Heine, entitled *Mathilde* (1931). When Hitler came to power, Victor re-mained in Germany to carry on illegal anti-Nazi activity. He fled abroad in 1935 and thereafter lived, successively, in Switzerland, Lux-emburg, France and, beginning 1940, in the United States. In 1947 he returned to East Germany where he is now an author and a playwright. His autobiographical *Kehre wieder über die Berge* (1945) sheds light on his political development but the chapter entitled "The Three Great Men of the Weltbühne" (Jacobsohn, Tucholsky, Ossietzky) is unfortunately, unreliable. See Adling, 506 f.

WEHBERG, HANS (Düsseldorf, 1885—Geneva, 1962), a noted pacifist and international jurist, was born to a Düsseldorf physician. He studied law at Jena, Göttingen, and Bonn, and embraced the pacifist cause while yet a student. After obtaining his doctorate, he became co-editor of the pacifist *Zeitschrift für Völkerrecht*. During World War I he engaged in active antiwar propaganda, proudly shouldering the accusation of treason. (See his *Als Pazifist im Weltkriege*, 1919.) From 1917 to 1919 he was a staff member of the Kiel Institute on World Economy and thereafter became a leader in the pacifist movement. He was president of the German Association for the League of Nations; member of the Executive Committee of the German Peace Cartel, and editor of the important pacifist journal, *Die Friedenswarte*. From 1921 to 1925 he worked for the Reichstag Committee investigating Germany's attitude toward the peace conference. Among his many works on the prospects of world peace and international organization, see *Der Völkerbund: Vorschlag der deutschen Regierung* (1920) and *Die Völkerbundbewegung* (1924). From 1928 until his retirement in 1959, Wehberg was professor of international law at the Institut Universitaire des Hautes Études Internationales in Geneva. In 1955 he was decorated for his services to peace by the government of his homeland.

ZWEIG, ARNOLD (Gross-Glogau, Silesia, b. 1887), the most famous writer of the German Democratic Republic, was not a Communist during his *Weltbühne* years but a pacifist and a Zionist. His father had been a saddler who, after marrying rich, became a food merchant and was ruined when Jews were forbidden to supply the Prussian army. The father was once again eking out a living from saddling when Zweig started attending a *Gymnasium* at Kattowitz. During his last years there he began to write, and had his first short story published in 1909. He also attended several German universities. His writing at that time was still quite romantic, and his 1912 novel, *Novellen um Claudia*, is unlike the social realism which was to become his genre. His next work, the 1914 drama, *Ritualmord in Ungarn* precursed the central theme of his later writing, that of the identity of the Jew in European society. He received the Kleist Prize for this play in 1915, the year he volunteered for military service. His experience in World

War I, in which he served near Verdun and in the East, turned him into a pacifist, a process which he described in the 1935 novel, *Erziehung vor Verdun*. After the war, he made fame with his Sergeant Grischa stories. *Das Spiel um den Sergeanten Grischa* (1921) and *Der Streit um den Sergeanten Grischa* (1927) tell a true wartime incident about a Russian prisoner of war whose fate is decided in a struggle between the progressive and reactionary forces of German society. When the Nazis came to power, Zweig emigrated to Czechoslovakia, Switzerland, and France, where he worked for various German emigré newspapers and magazines. During the Popular Front period, his connection with the Communist movement grew. He reached Palestine in 1940 and remained there for the duration of the war, co-editing the journal *Orient* and heading the "Liga Victory," an organization waging propaganda for the U.S.S.R. and the Red Army. Zweig returned to East Berlin in 1948 and has remained in the German Democratic Republic ever since; he represented East Germany at the World Peace Conference in 1949. He has continued to write prolifically, although with diminishing artistic inspiration, and has received many awards (Lenin Prize, 1958). He was president of the East German Academy of Arts and deputy in the People's Parliament. A reworking of some of his earlier novels became the *Zeitgeschichte* epic, *Der grosse Krieg der weissen Männer* (1958). See his *Ausgewählte Werke* (1957 ff.; as of today in thirteen volumes). Also, Kunisch, 642 f.; Fechter, 265 f., and Adling, 565 ff.

Appendix II

SOME FRIENDS AND ENEMIES OF THE *WELTBÜHNE*

BERNHARD, GEORG (Berlin, 1875—New York City, 1944), was the son of a merchant. At first a stockbroker, he began his journalistic career at the *Welt am Montag* in 1896; two years later, he became financial editor (*Handelsredakteur*) of Ullstein's *Berliner Zeitung.* He also wrote for Harden's *Zukunft* but quit all his posts in 1903 when the Social Democratic Party forbade its members to work for the bourgeois press. When he eventually left the SPD he found his way back (1908) to Ullstein's where he became co-editor of the *Vossische Zeitung.* At first an annexationist, he came out in 1917 for a peace of understanding. As editor in chief of the *"Voss"* after 1920, he advocated Franco-German reconciliation, and a *Kontinentalpolitik* directed against England (the Right called his paper *Gazette de Foch*). In 1928 he was elected to the Reichstag on a Democratic Party ticket; he also taught at the Business Academy in Berlin. His resignation from the *Voss* in 1930 was provoked, according to his own account, by a rightist turn at Ullstein's. (See Bernhard's letter to Ossietzky: "Verlegertragödie," *WB*, July 15, 1930, pp. 82–86.) In 1933 he fled to Paris where he edited the *Pariser Tageblatt,* later to be renamed *Pariser Tageszeitung.* He resigned his post four years later in the midst of an émigré scandal. (He had accused Léon Poliakov, the publisher of the newspaper, of having attempted to make a business deal with the German embassy in Paris. A "Jewish Court of Honor" found Bernhard guilty of libel. See *Das Neue Tage-Buch,* July 4 and 25, 1936.) In 1941 he fled to the United States where he worked at the Institute of Jewish Affairs in New York. Bernhard was an excellent journalist and a

276

foremost financial expert, but he was rather disliked in radical circles and in the *Weltbühne*. Of his own works, see *Die deutsche Tragödie* (1933). On Bernhard, see Schay, 267 ff.; Peter de Mendelssohn, *Zeitungsstadt Berlin* (Berlin, 1959), 76 *et passim*, and *NDB*, II, 117 f.

BREITSCHEID, RUDOLF (Cologne, 1874—Buchenwald, 1944), was the son of a bookstore salesman. He began his political career as a liberal. In 1903 he joined the progressive Freisinnige Vereinigung. Five years later he founded with Gerlach and Theodor Barth the Demokratische Vereinigung. Defeated at the Reichstag elections of 1912, Breitscheid joined the SPD and, in 1915, identified himself with those socialists within the party who two years later were to found the USPD. Between November 1918 and January 1919 he was Prussian minister of interior in the coalition cabinet of Social Democrats and Independent Socialists. Having rejoined the SPD in 1922, he became one of its parliamentary leaders. He supported Stresemann's Locarno policy and was known as an advocate of Franco-German reconciliation. In March 1933 Breitscheid went to Switzerland and from there to Paris. He was extradited to the Germans by the Vichy government and died in an air attack on the Buchenwald concentration camp. A celebrated orator, Breitscheid was, around 1920, the great hope of the *Weltbühne* writers. See *Osterroth* I, 46 ff., and *NDB*, II, 579 f.

DEUTSCHE LIGA FÜR MENSCHENRECHTE: see GERMAN LEAGUE FOR HUMAN RIGHTS
DIEDERICHS, EUGEN: see *TAT, DIE*
FACKEL, DIE: see KRAUS, KARL

FRIED, FERDINAND (b. Hamburg, 1898), whose real name was Friedrich Zimmermann, was the son of a merchant. He worked for the *Vossische Zeitung* and went over, with Zehrer, to the *Tat* during the Depression. He became a main contributor to the *Tat* and to the *Tägliche Rundschau*. Fried's *Das Ende des Kapitalismus* (1931) created a sensation. In 1934, Fried boasted—probably without justification—that he had been in close contact with the NSDAP since 1930. In the same year, he was made an *Obersturmführer* in the SS and assigned to the "Race and Settlement" office of the *Reichsführer SS* Himmler. Between 1940 and 1944, Fried was a professor at Prague University. After 1954, he was a leading collaborator of Zehrer in the *Welt* in Hamburg. See Fried's *Die Wende der Weltwirtschaft* (1937) and *Der Umsturz der Gesellschaft* (1950). On Fried, see K. L. Gerstorff

[Fritz Sternberg], "Ferdinand Fried und 'Die Tat,' " *WB*, May 26, 1931, pp. 751–756; Alexander Gabriel "Kryptomarxismus," *Die Gesellschaft* (Berlin), May, 1932, pp. 415–428, and Poliakov and Wulf, 368 ff.

GERMAN LEAGUE FOR HUMAN RIGHTS (Deutsche Liga für Menschenrechte), originally Bund Neues Vaterland, dedicated itself to "pacifism and to the struggle against fascism and injustice." The League was headed by Kurt R. Grossmann (b. Berlin, 1897) himself an occasional contributor to the *Weltbühne.* Grossmann, who descended from a family of Berlin merchants, served in World War I, and after his return from capitivity by the British, became a journalist and an activist in the antiwar movement. Threatened by arrest, he fled to Prague in February 1933 and was among the first Germans to be deprived of citizenship by the National Socialist regime. In New York City since 1939, Grossmann is active as a journalist and an adviser on Jewish affairs. Of his many works, see *Die unbesungenen Helden* (1957), on Christian Germans who helped save Jewish lives in the Nazi era, and *Ossietzky* (1963). In the Weimar period, the League enlisted the support of some of Germany's greatest lights, among them Albert Einstein. Obviously unsuccessful as a political force, the League was an efficient protector of the victims of both political and criminal justice and succeeded in reversing many an illegal conviction. On the activities of the League, see Lehmann-Russbüldt, *Der Kampf der Deutschen Liga für Menschenrechte,* as well as *Die Menschenrechte,* the League's monthly periodical.

GROSSMANN, KURT R: see GERMAN LEAGUE FOR HUMAN RIGHTS
GROSSMANN, STEFAN: see TAGE-BUCH, DAS

HARDEN, MAXIMILIAN (Berlin, 1861—Switzerland, 1927), was the most formidable polemical journalist of the Wilhelmian era. A fierce individualist, he escapes every attempt at classification. His original name was Witkowski, and he converted to Christianity at sixteen. He was first an actor, then, from 1892 to 1922, he edited—and mostly wrote—*Die Zukunft,* a political, cultural, and theatrical weekly, of which 119 volumes appeared. Harden became an intimate friend of Bismarck and a mortal foe of Bismarck's successors, but he himself departed from Bismarck's path with his advocacy of a German *Weltpolitik* and a preventive war against France (1913). His hero at that time was Admiral Tirpitz; his whipping boy William II. In 1914 he was a determined annexationist, but two years later he foresaw Germany's defeat and began to agitate for an early peace. By the end of the war he was a republican, a pacifist, and a socialist. He asked for unconditional acceptance of the Versailles treaty—a "work of art" as he called it—and for unilateral German disarmament. He reproached the Majority Socialists for lack of sophistication, brutality, and cowardice. He hated the bourgeois aspects of the republic and he toyed with elitist ideas. This helps to explain why he despised the liberal Jewish press and why he found kind words for the reactionary multimillionaire Hugo Stinnes, the White terrorist Captain Ehrhardt, General Ludendorff, and the Communist revolutionary Max Hölz. By 1921, he was a staunch friend of Soviet Russia. A year later he was severely beaten by some young "patriots," and he never quite recovered from this attack. Harden was very erudite and an excellent, if somewhat pompous, stylist; the writers of the *Weltbühne* held him almost unanimously in great esteem. See *Die Zukunft*, 1892–1922; *Köpfe*, four vols. (1910–13; 1924), *Krieg und Friede* (1918). On Harden, see Harry F. Young, *Maximilian Harden* (The Hague, 1959); Hans Delbrück, *Kautsky und Harden* (Berlin, 1920), very critical; Wilhelm Herzog, *Menschen, denen ich begegnete* (Bern, 1959), 70 ff., appreciative of Harden's talent and courage; Helmuth Rogge, "Aus Maximilian Hardens politischer Publizistik, 1912–1922," *Publizistik*, September–October, 1961, pp. 301–337, and *NDB*, VII, 647 ff.

HERZOG, WILHELM (Berlin, 1884—Munich, 1960) earned his first literary laurels with a biography of Heinrich von Kleist (1911). A year earlier he had founded with Paul Cassirer the avant-garde magazine *Pan;* in 1913 he became the editor of the progressive-liberal *März*, and in 1914 he founded the *Forum*. The latter was suppressed from 1915 to 1918 for pacifist propaganda. After the war, Herzog became editor in chief of the socialist *Hamburger Volkszeitung*. In exile, beginning 1933, he was interned by the Vichy authorities but escaped to Trinidad. Between 1945 and 1947 he lived in the United States and thereafter in Switzerland. To the Western reader he is best known for his *From Dreyfus to Pétain* (1947). See his autobiographical *Menschen, denen ich begegnete*.

HILFERDING, RUDOLF (Vienna, 1877—La Santé prison in Paris, 1941), was a physician but he seldom practiced his profession. A socialist from his youth, he became famous as the author of *Das Finanzkapital* (1910), often called the "fourth volume of *Das Kapital*."

As a member of the German Reichstag, he opposed the SPD's voting for war credits in August 1914. Three years later, he became one of the founders of the USPD, and edited *Die Freiheit*, the party newspaper. He rejoined the SPD in 1922 as a member of its executive committee. He was twice minister of finance, and a member of the Reichstag from 1924 to 1933. He also edited *Die Gesellchaft*, the SPD's prestige monthly to which some *Weltbühne* writers contributed. Having fled abroad in 1933, Hilferding was handed over to the Germans by the Vichy authorities in 1941. A few days later, he was tortured to death by the Gestapo. See Alexander Stein, *Rudolf Hilferding und die deutsche Arbeiterbewegung* (Hannover, 1946), and Osterroth, I, 131 ff.

KRAUS, KARL (Jičin, Bohemia, 1874—Vienna, 1936), poet, dramatist, linguist, cultural and social critic was, after Heine, the greatest satirist in German literature. The son of a Jewish paper manufacturer, he converted to Catholicism to spite his parents. He studied law and philosophy in Vienna. At first an actor, he soon became a journalist and free-lance writer. In 1899 he founded *Die Fackel*, a journal which he published, edited, and wrote from 1911 to the day of his death, filling 20,000 pages in the process. Before the war his greatest enemy was the Vienna liberal (Jewish) press which he accused of linguistic sloppiness, moral decadence, and corruption. Then and later he predicted, and confidently expected, the end of the bourgeois-capitalistic world order without, however, suggesting anything more precise in its stead than the replacement of *Ungeist* by *Geist*. During the war he wrote *Die letzten Tage der Menschheit* (1918–1919), an engrossing monster drama made up of documents and of diatribes against the imperialistic war, stock-market speculators, generals, and yellow journalism. In the 1920's he wrote, among others, the satirical drama *Literatur oder Man wird doch sehen* (1921), directed against Franz Werfel and expressionist literature, and *Die Unüberwindlichen* (1928), a condemnation of the bloody suppression of the 1927 workers' revolt in Vienna. Kraus also made a name for himself with his public lectures where he read from his own works and from those he liked: Goethe, Hauptmann, Wedekind, Brecht, and Nestroy. Basically an elitist and a conservative, in the 1930's Kraus supported the Austrian dictator Dollfuss. The writers of the *Weltbühne* held him in the greatest esteem, but he was the mortal enemy of Jacobsohn. Although Kraus is very popular in German-speaking countries, he is almost unknown abroad—his writings are considered untranslatable, but a representative selection of his principal work, *Die letzten Tage der Menschheit*, by Max Knight and Joseph Fabry is being prepared for publication. See, among other writings, *Sprüche und Widersprüche* (1909); *Pro Domo et Mundo* (1911); *Die Sprache* (1937),—these three mainly on language; *Worte in Versen*, 9 vols. (1916–1930), one of the many collections of his poetry; *Untergang der Welt durch schwarze Magie* (1922), and *Literatur und Lüge* (1929), both containing essays and satire; *Dokumente und Selbstzeugnisse* (1945), and *Gesammelte Werke* (12 vols.; Munich, 1952 ff.). On Kraus, see among others, Werner Kraft, *Karl Kraus* (Salzburg, 1956); Hans Kohn, *Karl Kraus, Arthur Schnitzler, Otto Weininger* (Tübingen, 1962), and Kunisch, 363 ff.

LEVI, PAUL (Hechingen, 1883—Berlin, 1930), was the son of a manufacturer; he first made a name for himself as a Social Democratic lawyer in his defense of Rosa Luxemburg in February 1914 when the latter was tried for inciting soldiers to disobedience. Levi contributed to the *Spartakusbriefe* in 1916 and, at the end of the war, became a member of the central committee in the Spartacus League. In January 1919, after the murder of Liebknecht and Luxemburg, he became leader of the Spartacus League and, subsequently, of the United Communist Party. Opposed to what he termed the "Bakuninist" and "putschist" tactics of the party majority (see *Unser Weg wider den Putschismus*, 1921), he broke with the KPD in 1921. Following a brief experiment with his own splinter "Kommunistische Arbeits-gesellschaft," he rejoined the SPD in 1922. Reelected to the Reichstag in 1924, he was recognized as the intellectual leader of the SPD's left wing although he always remained a loner. Levi edited the important *Sozialistische Politik und Wirtschaft*, a journal which in 1928 merged with the *Klassenkampf* of Ströbel, Seydewitz, and Rosenfeld. His greatest professional triumph came in April 1929, when, as a defense lawyer, he achieved the acquittal of the journalist Josef Bornstein, "responsible" editor of the *Tage-Buch*. Bornstein was accused of having defamed the character of public prosecutor Jorns by repeating the old charge that Jorns had abetted the murderers of Liebknecht and Luxemburg in his capacity as military judge advocate. At the trial, Levi proved Bornstein's innocence by establishing Jorns's guilt. (See *Der Jorns-Prozess: Rede des Verteidigers Dr. Paul Levi*, 1929.) Less than a year later, Levi fell to his death from a window while in a state of delirious fever. According to the obituary of the Communist *Rote Fahne*, the death of this "arch-opportunist" had deprived the "left-wing Social Fascists" of their only orator and writer. The writers of the *Weltbühne*, Ossietzky in particular, admired Levi and freely recognized their indebtedness to him for many of their political views. Thus, they voiced Levi's demand for a united front of all socialists without regard to ideological differences, and insisted with Levi that the SPD maintain itself in strict opposition to all bourgeois ministries. They were particularly attracted by Levi's antimilitarism, his willingness to defend nonsocialists (Bullerjahn), his brilliance as a writer and debater, and his refined tastes and inclinations. See Ossietzky, "Als Gast Herr Dr. Paul Levi," *WB*, June 4, 1929, pp. 841 ff., and "Paul Levi," *ibid.*, February 18, 1930, pp. 280–282. Levi is also the hero of Heinz Pol's political novel, *Entweder-Oder*. See, further, Osterroth, I, 191 f, and Helmut Gruber, "Paul Levi and the Comintern," *Survey* (London), October 1964, pp. 70–85. Documents on and by Levi are reproduced in Gruber, *International Communism*, 161 ff. *et passim*.

MÜNZENBERG, WILLI (Erfurt, 1889—Forest of Caugnet, France, 1940), was the son of an innkeeper who was a drunkard and a brute; his mother was sickly. Orphaned at thirteen, he became a barber's apprentice, then a worker in a shoe factory and, beginning in 1910, a pharmacist's aide in Zurich. By then he was an old hand at revolutionary socialist activity and a sharp critic of the SPD. A genuine self-made man, Münzenberg read voraciously, at first Kropotkin and Bakunin (for a while he belonged to an anarchist group in Zurich), then Ibsen and Strindberg, and, finally, Marx, Engels, and Mehring. As coordinator of various international youth organizations, he advocated in 1914 a general strike against the war. During the war he remained in Switzerland where he became an intimate of Lenin, the organizer of the Socialist (later Communist) Youth International, and the editor of the *Jugend-Internationale*. The Swiss authorities, after imprisoning Münzenberg for about a year, deported him in November 1918 to Germany where he joined the Spartacus League and participated in its uprisings. Again he went to prison for a few months, emerging as an even stronger advocate of putschist policy (as opposed to Paul Levi's parliamentary tactics). This did not prevent him from associating with bourgeois elements when, in 1921, he organized the International Workers' Aid (IAH) at Lenin's behest. From then on, he was at home in the Central Committee of the KPD, in the Moscow Comintern, in the Reichstag, and in non-Communist literary circles. He won over almost every left-wing intellectual for one or more of his enterprises. The propaganda empire that he created with Comintern money, and which proved to be financially profitable, consisted of ideological, political, and illustrated dailies and journals; a film company (*Mezhrabpom*) which had studios in Moscow and produced, among others, "Storm over Asia"; theaters; cabarets; cinemas; a publishing company (Neuer Deutscher Verlag), managed by his wife, Babette Gross, and other undertakings. As director of these organizations, Münzenberg was tolerant and understanding; as a party member, he unwaveringly towed the Comintern line. Thus in 1932 he furiously denounced Trotsky for suggesting a KPD-SPD action front against the Nazis. This might have been the price he had to pay for relative independence but it disappointed those who had thought Münzenberg "reasonable," and who wanted to use him just as they were used by him. (See, for instance, Hans Wesemann, "Interview mit Willi Münzenberg," *WB*, September 23, 1930, pp. 474–477, and Kurt Hiller, "Undurchführbar," *ibid.*, March 3, 1931, pp. 303–306.) In 1932, Münzenberg organized the League Against War and Fascism which won the cooperation of some of the world's most famous literati. In the following year, he went to Paris where he set up a new propaganda network. His Éditions du Carrefour published among others, the famous and often distorted "Brown Books" on the Reichstag fire and on Nazi atrocities. He organized a mock countertrial to discredit the Leipzig Reichstag-fire trial and persuaded some of the world's greatest legal authorities to indict—wrongly so it seems—the Nazi leaders for having set fire on the Reichstag. The Comintern's Popular Front policy, inaugurated in 1935, permitted Münzenberg an enormous expansion of his activities but it also sealed his fate. For the first time he worked not for Communist ascendancy in his supra-party organizations, but for genuine cooperation with the SPD and a common front of all antifascists. This was a mistake that neither Ulbricht nor Pieck would overlook: in 1936 he was recalled to Moscow and almost purged. His friends in the Party helped to get him back to Paris but he was no longer trusted; in the following year he himself broke with the Comintern. Termed a "vermin," a "parasite," and a "Trotskyite viper," he set up an independent antifascist propaganda network and, after August 1939, openly criticized the U.S.S.R. When the Germans invaded France, Münzenberg fled from Paris and was found dead, sitting with a rope around his neck in the Isère valley. The identity of his murderer[s] remains unknown. This "grey eminence" of Communist propaganda was not only one of modern history's greatest impresarios but a political theoretician and writer of talent. He did more to win sympathy for the U.S.S.R. and Communism than all the German Communists combined and, in the years of exile, provided the emigrés with a sense of community and purpose. See Babette Gross, *Willi Münzenberg* (Stuttgart, 1967); Koestler, *The Invisible Writing*, 205 ff.; Ruth Fischer, *Stalin and German Communism* (Cambridge, Mass., 1938), 610 ff.; Buber-Neumann, 97 *et passim*; Kurt Kersten, "Das Ende Willi Münzenbergs: Ein Opfer Stalins und Ulbrichts," *Deutsche Rundschau*, April 1957, pp. 484–499; Jorgen Schleimann, "The Organisation Man: The Life and Work of Willi Münzenberg," *Survey* (London), April 1965, pp. 64–91; Helmut Gruber, "Willi Münzenberg's German Communist Propaganda Empire, 1921–1933," *The Journal of Modern History*, September 1966, pp. 278–297, and, by the same author, "Willi Münzenberg: Propagandist for and against the Comintern," *International Review of Social History*, X, 2 (1965), 188–210. The latter is definitive on the period after 1933.

REVENTLOW, ERNST GRAF ZU (Husum, 1869—Munich, 1943), a captain in the Imperial navy, resigned his commission at the age of thirty to devote himself to writing. Before the war he was a Pan-German; beginning in 1920, he edited the conservative revolutionary journal, *Reichswart*, and in 1923 was co-founder of the radical rightist "Deutschvölkische Freiheitspartei." In the same year, he created a sensation by contributing to the Communist *Rote Fahne*. In 1924 he was elected to the Reichstag on the ticket of the "Nationalsozialistische Freiheitspartei;" three years later, he joined the NSDAP. After 1933 he headed the "Deutsche Glaubensbewegung." Despite his association with Hitler, Reventlow stood closer to National Bolshevism and to the circles of the "homeless Right" than to the Nazi movement. His influence on Nazi party politics was insignificant. Of his numerous writings, see especially *Völkisch-kommunistische Einigung* (1924) and *Deutscher Sozialismus: Civitas Dei Germanica* (1933). See also Armin Mohler, *Die konservative Revolution* (Stuttgart, 1950), 60 *et passim* and Schüddekopf, *Linke Leute von Rechts* (Stuttgart, 1960), 114 *et passim*.

SCHWARZSCHILD, LEOPOLD: see *TAGE-BUCH, DAS*

STAPEL, WILHELM (Calbe, Altmark, 1882—Hamburg, 1954), a political writer and Lutheran religious philosopher, was one of the founders of the "Fichte-Gesellschaft" and the director of the Hanseatische Verlagsanstalt, a social-conservative publishing house in Hamburg, financed by the powerful "Deutschnationaler Handlungsgehilfen Verband," the trade union of shop attendants. From 1918 to

1933, Stapel edited the *Deutsches Volkstum,* a monthly journal. He was a prolific author, equally versed in theology, ethics, and in anti-Semitic "Germanic" mystification. See, for instance, *Antisemitismus und Antigermanismus* (1927), *Literatenwäsche* (1930), *Der christliche Staatsmann* (1932), and *Die Kirche Christi und der Staat Hitlers* (1933). On Stapel, see Heinrich Kessler, *Wilhelm Stapel als politischer Publizist* (Nuremberg, 1967).

TAGE-BUCH, DAS, a weekly magazine, was founded in 1920 in Berlin by the Austrian journalist Stefan Grossmann (Vienna, 1875—Vienna, 1935) who was joined, two years later, by the economic analyst Leopold Schwarzschild (Frankfurt/M., 1891—Italy, 1950). When Grossmann retired from journalism in 1930, Schwarzschild became the journal's sole editor. Of the latter, Golo Mann writes: "His political sagacity stands almost without parallel in the history of German journalism. He rarely used satire and then only as a means to an end. He moderated his fury because he hoped to reach the ears of the men in power. All in all, he wanted to help. Deep down he was a conservative, as were most Jewish Germans, and he belonged to the Left only . . . because the Right allowed him . . . no other alternative." *Das Tage-Buch* was consistently democratic, but never radical, although it printed contributions from the far Left. Both its circulation (10,000 to 20,000) and the excellence of its collaborators matched that of the *Weltbühne;* it was also often better informed than its competitor. In 1933, Schwarzschild fled to Paris where he edited *Das Neue Tage-Buch* which won the collaboration of Churchill, Chancellor Dollfuss, G. B. Shaw, Ilya Ehrenburg, Leon Trotsky, Bertrand Russell, Aldous Huxley, Julien Benda, François Mauriac, and, of course, the best of the German exile-intellectuals with the exception of the orthodox Communists. In his last years, which he spent in the United States, Schwarzschild became a conservative. His *The Red Prussian: The Life and Legend of Karl Marx* (1947), shows little of his earlier judiciousness and wisdom. His other works are, *Das Ende der Illusionen* (1934), and *World in Trance: From Versailles to Pearl Harbor* (1942). *Die letzten Jahre vor Hitler* (1966) contains a selection of Schwarzschild's *Tage-Buch* articles. Valerie Schwarzschild, ed., *Die Lunte am Pulverfass* (Hamburg, 1965) contains a selection of Schwarzschild's articles written in exile. See also Wolfgang Weyrauch, ed., *Ausnahmezustand* (Munich, 1966), and Hans-Albert Walter, "Schwarzschild and Das Neue Tage-Buch," in Walter Laqueur and George L. Mosse, eds., *The Left-Wing Intellectuals Between the Wars, 1919–1939* (New York, 1966), 103–116. On Stefan Grossmann, see his autobiographical *Ich war begeistert: Eine Lebensgeschichte* (Berlin, 1931), which unfortunately does not go beyond the beginning of Grossmann's journalistic career in Berlin.

TAT, DIE, one of Weimar Germany's most prestigious cultural magazines, was founded in 1909 by Eugen Diederichs (1867–1931), a publisher, essayist, and political philosopher. Convinced that religion and religious-ethical education must be made the foundations of German society, Diederichs opposed Wilhelmian Germany and capitalism. In 1913, he helped to organize the congress of the Free German Youth on the Hoher Meissner Mountain. Although a follower of Fichte and Lagarde, and an advocate of a national and socialist revival built on religious-*völkisch* grounds, Diederichs occasionally opened the pages of his journal to radical leftists (Ernst Toller). In 1927, Diederichs made the young poet Adam Kuckhoff (executed in 1944 at Plötzensee) the journal's editor in chief. In 1928, the latter's place was taken by Hans Zehrer who turned *Die Tat* into Germany's leading conservative revolutionary journal. The small circle of friends around Zehrer, the "Tatkreis," presented a coherent revolutionary program for an authoritarian state. On Eugen Diederichs, see, among others, *Leben und Werk,* Lulu von Strauss und Torney-Diederichs (his wife), ed. (Jena, 1936), and Klaus Dietze, *Eugen Diederichs als Zeitschriftenverleger* (Würzburg, 1940). On *Die Tat* and the Tatkreis, see, among others, Kurt Sontheimer, "Der Tatkreis," *Vierteljahrshefte für Zeitgeschichte,* July, 1959, pp. 229–260; H. P. Brunzel, "Die 'Tat,' 1918–1933" (unpublished Ph.D. dissertation, University of Bonn, 1952), and Klemperer, 74 *et passim.*

ULLSTEIN, Germany's and Europe's foremost newspaper concern, was founded in 1877 by Leopold Ullstein (1826–1899), the son of a Jewish paper wholesaler. Within a few decades, the firm acquired scores of Berlin newspapers and founded new ones. The House of Ullstein revolutionized German journalism by employing hundreds of foreign correspondents, setting up its own wire service, and giving straight news understandable to everyone. Besides publishing dozens of dailies and weeklies aimed at the lower classes, it also published the most respectable German paper, the *Vossische Zeitung* (acquired in 1913). Under the active direction of the five Ullstein brothers, sons of the founder, the firm attained its greatest fame in the 1920's when its *Berliner Illustrirte Zeitung* alone attained a circulation of 1.8 million. Regarded as a bastion of solid republicanism, by the early 1930's Ullstein's was nevertheless thoroughly infiltrated by National Socialists. In 1934, the owners sold their enterprise to a Nazi publishing firm and went abroad. After World War II the House of Ullstein in Berlin never matched the fame of its predecessor; it was recently absorbed by the new giant, Axel Springer. See Mendelssohn, *Zeitungsstadt Berlin*, almost entirely devoted to the Ullsteins; Hermann Ullstein, *The Rise and Fall of the House of Ullstein* (London, 1944); Max Krell, *Das alles gab es einmal* (Frankfurt/M., 1961), by the former head of Ullstein's book publication department, and Heinz Ullstein, *Spielplatz meines Lebens* (Munich, 1961), by a rebellious younger member of the family.

WOLFF, THEODOR (Berlin, 1868—concentration camp Oranienburg, 1943), became at nineteen a contributor to Mosse's *Berliner Tageblatt* of which he was the Paris correspondent from 1894 to 1906, and its editor in chief from 1906 to 1933. Before the war he was also active in the Freie Bühne movement. In 1914, he wrote editorials accusing the German government of responsibility in the outbreak of the war. As one of the founders of the Bund Neues Vaterland, he led a journalistic campaign for a negotiated peace and a parliamentary government. In November 1918 he helped found the German Democratic Party which he left seven years later because of that party's support of the clerical Law on Pornography. Wolff was one of the three or four best known journalists in Weimar and a consistent democrat. In 1933 he fled to Switzerland and then to Nice. He was extradited to the Germans by the Vichy authorities and put in the Oranienburg concentration camp where he died. Of his numerous works, see especially, *Pariser Tagebuch*, essays written for the *Berliner Tageblatt* (1908; new ed. 1927); *Vollendete Tatsachen* (1918), political editorials written between 1914 and 1917; *Der Krieg des Pontius Pilatus* (1934), in English: *The Eve of 1914* (1936); *Der Marsch durch zwei Jahrzente* (1936), also published as *Durch zwei Dekaden* (1936), and in English as *Through Two Decades* (1936), and *Die Lächelnde Sphinx* (1937). On Wolff, see Hiller, *Koepfe und Troepfe,* 358 ff.; Mendelssohn, 117 *et passim; UJE,* X, 557 f., and Schay, 261 ff.

YOUTH MOVEMENT, THE, began in 1896 with the formation of small groups of students, the Wandervögel, organized for hiking through the countryside in symbolic protest against the grimness of city life and the banalities of bourgeois society. It found support for its ideals in the elitist doctrine of the poet Stefan George, who saw the irrational (poetic) essence of man as the regenerative force within politics and society. Very popular among educated youth before

World War I, the Youth Movement wasted its energy in romantic (pseudo-medieval) escapism. The war, seen as a supreme purification, decimated the ranks of the movement. After the war the Youth Movement became political, dividing into a large nationalist (often violently anti-Semitic), and much smaller republican and Communist camps. Both the National Socialist "Hitler Jugend" (HJ) and, after World War II the East German "Freie Deutsche Jugend" (FDJ) consciously harked back to the tradition of the Youth Movement but without its essence: withdrawal from adult society. For two valuable accounts of the Youth Movement, see Walter Z. Laqueur, *Young Germany* (New York, 1962) and Mario Domandi, "The German Youth Movement" (unpublished Ph.D. dissertation, New York: Columbia University, 1960).

ZEHRER, HANS (Berlin, 1899—Hamburg, 1966), son of a civil servant, was of Protestant background. He was a member of the Youth Movement and in 1916 volunteered for the war. After 1918, he studied alternately medicine, history, national economics, and theology. In 1920, he participated in the Kapp putsch where he was wounded. Despite his nationalist background, he worked as foreign political commentator between 1923 and 1929 for the *Vossische Zeitung*. When it was discovered that he had been secretly editing *Die Tat* he was forced to resign his post at the *Vossische Zeitung* and was made the *Tat's* official editor in chief. Following the death of Diederichs in 1931, Zehrer also became the *Tat's* publisher. In 1932, he acquired the *Tägliche Rundschau*, a conservative daily, which he put at the service of General Schleicher and the latter's authoritarian program. The triumph of National Socialism disappointed Zehrer. He withdrew from public life and spent the Hitler years as a businessman. Between 1947 and 1953, Zehrer edited the *Sonntagsblatt* in Hamburg. After 1953, he was editor in chief of the liberal daily *Die Welt*, also a Hamburg paper. Besides his numerous editorials in the *Tat* and the *Tägliche Rundschau*, see *Der Mensch in dieser Welt* (1948) and *Stille vor dem Sturm* (1949). On Zehrer, see Walter Struve, "Hans Zehrer as a Neoconservative Elite Theorist," *The American Historical Review*, July 1965, pp. 1035–1057.

ZIMMERMANN, FRIEDRICH: see FRIED, FERDINAND

ZUKUNFT, DIE: see HARDEN, MAXIMILIAN

NOTES

Notes for the Introduction (pp. 1-9)

[1] Jürgen Rühle, *Literatur und Revolution* (Cologne, 1960), 173.

[2] Carl von Ossietzky, "Kulturbolschewismus," *Die Weltbühne*, April 21, 1931, pp. 559-563. Also in Carl v. Ossietzky, *Schriften* (Berlin [East], 1966), I, 343-349. *Die Weltbühne* will hereafter be referred to as *WB*.

[3] Ossietzky, *Schriften*, I, 344.

[4] *Ibid.*

[5] Kurt Tucholsky, "Fünfundzwanzig Jahre," *WB*, September 9, 1930, p. 382. Also in Kurt Tucholsky, *Gesammelte Werke* (Hamburg, 1960-1961), III, 521.

[6] Leonhard Frank, *Links wo das Herz ist* (Munich, 1952), 258 ff. The English translation is from L. Frank, *Heart on the Left* (London, 1954), 191 f.

[7] Kurt Hiller, *Der Sprung ins Helle* (Leipzig, 1932), 201.

[8] Kurt Hiller, "Aufstieg, Glanz und Verfall der Weltbühne," *Konkret* (Hamburg), April, 1962, p. 19.

[9] Hermann Behr, *Die goldenen zwanziger Jahre* (Hamburg, 1964), 30.

[10] For a detailed description of the book-burning ceremony in Berlin and a list of the authors personally cited, see *Neuköllner Tageblatt*, May 12, 1933, quoted in Léon Poliakov and Josef Wulf, eds., *Das Dritte Reich und seine Denker* (Berlin, 1959), 119 ff.

[11] Arnold Zweig, *Bilanz der deutschen Judenheit, 1933* (Amsterdam, 1934), 274.

Notes for Chapter I (pp. 13-29)

[1] Cited by Alfred Kantorowicz, *Deutsches Tagebuch* (Munich, 1959), I, 22.

[2] See Hellmut von Gerlach, *Von Rechts nach Links* (Zurich, 1937).

[3] See Lothar Persius, "Erinnerungen eines Seeoffiziers," *WB*, April 7, 1925, pp. 501-504, *et passim*.

[4] Hughes, 49.

[5] See Utz-Friedebert Taube, *Ludwig Quidde* (Kallmünz, Opf., 1963), 4 *et passim*.

[6] Heinrich Mann, *Der Untertan* (Leipzig, 1918). In English: *The Patrioteer* (New York, 1921).

[7] Hughes, 338.

[8] Ernst Glaeser, *Jahgang 1902* (Berlin, 1931), 185.

[9] See especially, Arthur Koestler, *The Invisible Writing* (Boston, 1955).

[10] Heinz Ullstein, *Spielplatz meines Lebens* (Munich, 1961), 58 f.

[11] Kurt Hiller, *Koepfe und Troepfe* (Hamburg, 1950), 345.

[12] See Rühle, 184.

[13] Ernst Toller, *I Was a German* (London, 1934), 57.

[14] Cited by Hans Kohn, *The Mind of Germany* (New York, 1955), 158 f.

[15] Heinrich Heine, "Why Did the Germans Take to the Romantic School?" Frederic Ewen, ed., *The Poetry and Prose of Heinrich Heine* (New York, 1948), 724.

[16] Alfred Kerr, cited by Tucholsky in his letter to Arnold Zweig (Zurich, December 15, 1935), Kurt Tucholsky, *Ausgewählte Briefe, 1913–1935* (Hamburg, 1962), 337. This will hereafter be referred to as *Ausgewählte Briefe.*

[17] Jakob Wassermann, *My Life as a German and Jew* (New York, 1933), 226 f. There is an enormous and generally excellent literature on the predicament of Germany's Jewish intellectuals. Besides the works of Jakob Wassermann, see also those of Arthur Schnitzler, Walther Rathenau, Arnold Zweig, Ernst Toller, Theodor Herzl. For a short and successful survey, see Solomon Liptzin, *Germany's Stepchildren* (New York, 1961).

[18] Zweig, *Bilanz der deutschen Judenheit,* 280. For a modern study on the political dilemma of the Jewish Germans, see Jakob Toury, *Die politischen Orientierungen der Juden in Deutschland von Jena bis Weimar* (Tübingen, 1966).

[19] These are the last lines from Tucholsky's last contribution to the *Weltbühne.* See Kaspar Hauser [Tucholsky], "Worauf man in Europa stolz ist," *WB,* November 8, 1932, p. 688. Also in *Gesammelte Werke,* III, 1096.

[20] In 1925 only 564,000 out of 62,400,000 Germans were Jewish by religion. See W. C. Woytinsky, *Zehn Jahre Neues Deutschland: Ein Gesamtüberblick in Zahlen* (Berlin, 1929), 25.

[21] Helmut Gruber, "The Politics of German Literature, 1914 to 1933" (unpublished Ph.D. dissertation, New York: Columbia University, 1962), 274.

[22] See, for instance, Koppel S. Pinson, *Modern Germany* (New York, 1954), 459.

Notes for Chapter II (pp. 30–61)

[1] Due to increasing interest in the culture of Weimar, *Die Weltbühne* has recently received some attention in Germany. The only comprehensive history today is Alf Enseling, *Die Weltbühne: Organ der "Intellektuellen Linken"* (Münster, Westf., 1962), 183 pp. Enseling argues that *Die Weltbühne* successfuly executed its role as a foremost representative of "individualistic journalism" (as opposed to collectivistic journalism aimed at a mass audience) but that it remained ineffective precisely because of the excessive individualism of its collaborators and their utopian program. Thoroughgoing as it is, this study makes difficult reading; it also seems mistaken in its assumption that the *Weltbühne's* "fundamental thesis" was *Logokratie,* that is, the rule of philosopher-kings. More entertaining and much more critical is Kurt Hiller, "Aufstieg, Glanz und Verfall der Weltbühne," *Konkret* (Hamburg), March–July, 1962. It points out that the editors of the *Weltbühne* in no way associated themselves with the philosophy of *Logokratie* which was the specialty of Hiller. E. W. Lunke's study, "Die deutsche Presse im eigenen Urteil, 1918 bis 1933: Eine fragmentarische Dartstellung der publizistischen Kritik—unter besonderer Berücksichtigung der radikaldemokratischen Zeitschrift 'Die Weltbühne'—an den geistigen, politischen und wirtschaftlichen Mangeln der Presse" (unpublished Ph.D. dissertation, University of Munich, 1952) is less formidable than its title. It is, in fact, quite informative although it suffers from the labored style inherent in *zeitungswissenschaftliche* dissertations.

There are several complete collections of the *Weltbühne* in Germany. In the United States the only complete collection is at the Library of the University of Michigan at Ann Arbor. There are nearly complete collections at the Library of Congress and the New York Public Library, and partial collections at the libraries of Princeton University (1905–1926), Columbia University (1922–1929), Stanford University (1931–1933), Brown University (1931–1932), and at the Library for Political Studies (Buttinger Library) in New York City (1925–1933, which has an almost complete collection of the exile *Weltbühne,* 1933–1939). The reader must be prepared to handle paper of extremely poor quality lest he becomes the last person to read the journal.

[2] The best succinct résumé of his life and works is in Enseling, 19 ff. See also, Wolfgang Steinke, "Der Publizist Siegfried Jacobsohn als Theaterkritiker" (unpublished Ph.D. dissertation, University of Berlin, 1960). For an homage to "an incomparable servant of truth," see Tucholsky, "Siegfried Jacobsohn," *WB*, December 7, 1926, p. 873. Also, Tucholsky's letters to Siegfried Jacobsohn in *Ausgewählte Briefe*, 89 ff.; Arthur Eloesser, "Siegfried Jacobsohn," *WB*, December 14, 1926, pp. 910–913, and Walther Victor, "Die Drei von der Weltbühne," in *Kehre wieder über die Berge* (New York, 1945), 229 ff. Jacobsohn's own published works include *Das Theater der Reichshauptstadt* (Munich, 1904); *Das Jahr der Bühne, 1911–1921* in ten volumes, a year-by-year collection of his theatrical reviews; *Max Reinhardt* (Berlin, 1910), and *Der Fall Jacobsohn* (Charlottenburg, 1913), a plaidoyer in connection with his plagiarism scandal.

[3] This and other information on Jacobsohn's early career has been culled mainly from *Der Fall Jacobsohn*; from Enseling, 19 ff., and Hiller, "Aufstieg, Glanz und Verfall der Weltbühne," *Konkret*.

[4] Siegfried Jacobsohn, *Das Theater der Reichshauptstadt.*

[5] Erwin Piscator, *Das politische Theater* (Berlin, 1929), 28.

[6] *Ibid.*

[7] Enseling, 24.

[8] Tucholsky, "Vormärz," *Die Schaubühne*, April 2, 1914, p. 382. Also in *Gesammelte Werke*, I, 169.

[9] *Ibid.*

[10] See Fritz Kortner, *Aller Tage Abend* (Munich, 1959), 221.

[11] Egon Friedell, "Die Westbarbaren," *Die Schaubühne*, October 29, 1914, pp. 318–323.

[12] *Ibid.*, 319.

[13] Alfred Polgar, "Der Krieg als Erzieher," *WB*, October 10, 1918, p. 337.

[14] Erwin R. Bergh, "Zehn Minuten mit S.J.," *WB*, November 29, 1927, p. 824.

[15] Victor, 222 f.

[16] Enseling, 23.

[17] Tucholsky, *Mit 5 PS* (Berlin, 1928), 14. Also in *Gesammelte Werke*, II, 1005.

[18] On the Stefan Grossmann bribery scandal, see "Berliner Theaterkritiker," *WB*, June 23, 1921, p. 692, and "An Rechtsanwalt Fritz Grünspan," *Ibid.*, July 7, 1921, pp. 22–26. A court of honor composed of journalists later found Jacobsohn's charges unfounded. *Ibid.*, May 4, 1922, p. 462. On the plagiarism accusation, see "Antworten," *ibid.*, March 31, 1925, p. 492.

[19] On the Wilhelm Herzog affair, see "Gerichtstag," *WB*, March 3, 1925, pp. 318–320, and "Antworten," *ibid.*, 334; also, "Antworten," *ibid.*, March 10, 1925, p. 375. It should be stated in Jacobsohn's defense that his charges against Herzog came from USPD sources, and that they were aired at the Reich conference of this party in 1920. On the Stresemann accusation, see "Litwin," *ibid.*, March 24, 1925, pp. 431–433, and *ibid.*, March 31, 1925, pp. 490–492. On Honnef and the German Nationalist Party, see Franz Reichwalden, "Ein deutschnationaler Schiebermagnat," *ibid.*, March 31, 1925, pp. 270–271; also "Antworten," *ibid.*, March 31, 1925, p. 490, and "Antworten," *ibid.*, April 7, 1925, p. 531.

[20] Arnold Zweig, *Bilanz des deutschen Judenheit*, 248.

[21] See Klaus-Peter Schulz, *Kurt Tucholsky in Selbstzeugnissen und Bilddokumenten* (Hamburg, 1959), 96 ff, and Enseling, 33 f.

[22] Tucholsky's popularity—and unpopularity—in the Weimar period, combined with his renaissance after World War II in both parts of Germany, produced a substantial literature. Practically all of Tucholsky's works were reprinted recently, including his pieces in the *Weltbühne*, scattered articles found in *Ulk*, *Die Welt am Montag*, *8 Uhr-Abendblatt*, *Uhu*, *Das andere Deutschland*, *Vossische Zeitung*, and at least twenty other periodicals. His *Gesammelte Werke* contains approximately 1800 of his articles, essays, poems, ballads, and short stories, all of which

(and some 700 more) had appeared in print previously. His *Ausgewählte Briefe* contains approximately 400 of his letters to friends. From the vast secondary literature, see especially, Schulz, *Kurt Tucholsky*, which contains, among others, a valuable bibliography; also, Hans Prescher, *Kurt Tucholsky* (Berlin, 1959), and Fritz J. Raddatz, *Tucholsky* (Munich, 1959), richly illustrated. For a critique of Tucholsky and the postwar Tucholsky vogue, see Hermann Kesten, "Kurt Tucholsky," *Der Monat* (Berlin), February, 1958, pp. 70–76, as well as the fascinating debate on the Kesten article in *Der Monat*, March–June, 1958. For an intelligent product of the hostile anti-Semitic literature, see Wilhelm Stapel, "Kurt Tucholsky," in *Forschungen zur Judenfrage* (Hamburg, 1937), II, 182 ff. Harold L. Poor, "Kurt Tucholsky" (unpublished Ph.D. dissertation, New York: Columbia University, 1965) is excellent, especially on Tucholsky and the Jews. A substantially revised version of this dissertation appeared recently as *Kurt Tucholsky and the Ordeal of Germany, 1914–1935* (New York, 1968). Harry Zohn, ed., *The World Is a Comedy* (Cambridge, Mass. 1957) and Kurt Tucholsky, *What If—?*, trans. Harry Zohn and Karl F. Ross (New York, 1967), contain some of Tucholsky's best writings. The Tucholsky Archives in Rottach-Egern, Bavaria, under the direction of Mary Gerold-Tucholsky, are extensive: manuscripts, published works, and recordings by Tucholsky, and a nearly complete collection of material published about him.

[23] Peter Panter [Tucholsky], "Ein Kind aus meiner Klasse," *WB*, March 3, 1925, p. 315. Also in *Gesammelte Werke*, II, 55. Translation by Zohn, 93 f.

[24] Tucholsky, "25 Jahre," *WB*, September 9, 1930, pp. 378. Also in *Gesammelte Werke*, III, 516.

[25] Tucholsky, letters to Mary Gerold-Tucholsky, *Ausgewählte Briefe*, 404 ff.

[26] *Ibid.*, 415.

[27] Peter Panter [Tucholsky], *Ein Pyrenäenbuch* (Berlin, 1927). There are several reprints of this work by Rowohlt (Hamburg). Also in *Gesammelte Werke*, II, 577–705.

[28] Tucholsky, *Rheinsberg: Ein Bilderbuch für Verliebte* (Charlottenburg, 1912), with many reprints. Also in *Gesammelte Werke*, I, 24–48. Tucholsky, *Schloss Gripsholm* (Berlin, 1931), with several reprints by the same publisher (Rowohlt). Also in *Gesammelte Werke*, III, 659–746.

[29] Cited by Zohn, 29.

[30] See Hans Sahl, "The Man with the Five Pseudonyms," *Politics* (New York City), V: 3 (Summer, 1948), 171.

[31] The descriptive quotations are from the Introduction to Tucholsky's *Mit 5 PS*.

[32] Tucholsky, letter to Maximilian Harden (Paris, October 12, 1924), *Ausgewählte Briefe*, 135.

[33] See, for instance, Raddatz, 66 ff.

[34] *Ibid.*, 70 ff.

[35] Stapel, 188.

[36] Tucholsky, "25 Jahre," *WB*, September 9, 1930, p. 380. Also in *Gesammelte Werke*, III, 519.

[37] *WB*, September 9, 1930, pp. 380 f.

[38] Tucholsky, letter to Franz Hammer (May 5, 1931), *Ausgewählte Briefe*, 213. Also cited by Schulz, 104.

[39] Tucholsky, "Wir Negativen," *WB*, March 13, 1919, pp. 279–285. Also in *Gesammelte Werke*, I, 372–377.

[40] *WB*, March 13, 1919, pp. 282, 284.

[41] Zohn, 16 f.

[42] Tucholsky, *Deutschland, Deutschland über alles* (Berlin, 1929), 226. There is a facsimile edition of this work published by Rowohlt (Hamburg) in 1964. Translation of this passage by Poor, "Kurt Tucholsky," 200 f.

[43] Tucholsky, letter to Walter Hasenclever (March 4, 1933), *Ausgewählte Briefe*, 248.

[44] Tucholsky, letter to Walter Hasenclever (October 7, 1934), *ibid.*, 288.

[45] Kaspar Hauser [Tucholsky], "Gesicht," *WB*, July 3, 1924, p. 33 f. Also in *Gesammelte Werke*, I, 1182 f. Translation by Zohn, 70 ff.

[46] Zohn, 17.

[47] Ignaz Wrobel [Tucholsky], "Die grossen Familien," *WB*, March 27, 1928, p. 473. Also in *Gesammelte Werke*, II, 1086. This passage was reproduced, characteristically, in the National Socialist *Deutsche Geschichte von 1918 bis 1938 in Dokumenten*, Ernst Forsthoff, ed. (Stuttgart, 1943), 442.

[48] Tucholsky, "Über den sogenannten 'Landesverrat,'" *Gesammelte Werke*, II, 496. This article was first printed in the pacifist *Das andere Deutschland*, September 11, 1926. Part of this passage was reproduced in the National Socialist theoretician Alfred Rosenberg's *Novemberköpfe* (2d ed.; Munich, 1939), 208.

[49] Tucholsky, letter to Mary Gerold-Tucholsky (December 19, 1935?), *Ausgewählte Briefe*, 501. Translation by Poor, "Kurt Tucholsky," 54 f.

[50] Schulz, 29.

[51] *Ibid.*

[52] Cited by Schulz, 109 f.

[53] Kaspar Hauser [Tucholsky], "Herr Wendriner lässt sich die Haare schneiden," *WB*, September 22, 1925, pp. 461 f.; also in *Gesammelte Werke*, II, 223 f.

[54] Kesten, *Der Monat*, February 1958, pp. 70–76.

[55] Stapel, 182 ff.

[56] *Ibid.*, 190.

[57] Kesten, *Der Monat*, February 1958, p. 70.

[58] *Ibid.*, 74.

[59] See, for instance, Hermann Budzislawski *et al.*, *Memorandum: Save Carl von Ossietzky*, n.p., n.d. [1935]; Felix Burger [Kurt R. Grossmann] and Kurt Singer, *Carl von Ossietzky* (Zurich, 1937); Berthold Jacob, *Weltbürger Ossietzky: Ein Abriss seines Lebens* (Paris, 1937).

[60] Alfred Kantorowicz, *Porträts* (Berlin, 1947), 5 f.

[61] Cited by Rühle, 186.

[62] Tucholsky, letter to Walter Hasenclever (March 4, 1933), *Ausgewählte Briefe*, 247 f.

[63] The most comprehensive study on Ossietzky is Raimund Koplin, *Carl von Ossietzky als politischer Publizist* (Berlin, 1964). Kurt R. Grossmann, *Ossietzky: Ein deutscher Patriot* (Munich, 1963), although enjoyable, is impressionistic, and deals mainly with the author's struggle side by side with Ossietzky against militarism and reactionary justice in Weimar Germany. It contains a dramatic account of Ossietzky's great trial and his martyrdom, and also a list of Ossietzky's published articles. Kurt Hiller, "Erinnerungen an Carl von Ossietzky," in *Koepfe und Troepfe*, 338 ff. is the best short account. It is frankly critical of Ossietzky the political writer and editor. For a sympathetic study in English, see Istvan Deak, "Weimar Germany's 'Homeless Left': The World of Carl von Ossietzky" (unpublished Ph.D. dissertation, New York: Columbia University, 1964). Maud von Ossietzky, *Maud v. Ossietzky erzählt: Ein Lebensbild* (Berlin [East], 1966) by the widow of Ossietzky is charming and straightforward but, of course, it tells more of her own life than that of Ossietzky. For an East-German interpretation of Ossietzky's politics, see Bruno Frei, *Carl v. Ossietzky: Ritter ohne Furcht und Tadel* (Berlin [East], 1966). It is complemented by a collection of Ossietzky's writings arranged topically: Bruno Frei and Hans Leonard, eds., *Carl v. Ossietzky: Schriften* (2 vols.; Berlin [East], 1966). This will hereafter be referred to as *Schriften;* Otto Stolz, ed., *Wenn Stalin katholisch würde* (Berlin [West], 1948), is an annotated collection of misleading anti-Communist quotations from the writings of Ossietzky and Tucholsky.

[64] Jacob, *Weltbürger Ossietzky*, 9. Also, Walter Mehring, "Carl von Ossietzky," *Deutsche Rundschau*, October, 1959, p. 900.

[65] Interview with Kurt R. Grossmann, New York City, May 22, 1962.

[66] See Maud von Ossietzky, 5 *et passim*.

[67] Walther Karsch, "Carl von Ossietzky," *Aufbau* (Berlin), November, 1945, pp. 222 f.

[68] See, for instance, Grossmann, *Ossietzky*, 17.

[69] *Schulthess' Europäischer Geschichtskalender*, 1908, p. 23 f.

[70] See "Delegiertentag der 'Demokratischen Vereinigung' " (Berlin, April 13, 1919), *Schulthess*,' 1909, p. 130.

[71] *Schulthess*,' 1912, p. 2 f.

[72] See, for instance, Ossietzky, "Militärdiktatur oder Bürgerrecht," *Das freie Volk*, January 31, 1914; also, "Auferstehung," *ibid.*, April 11, 1914.

[73] Ossietzky, "Sonnenwende," *Das freie Volk*, March 22, 1913. Also in *Schriften*, I, 11–15.

[74] There is an interesting discussion of German "monism" as an early and ethical (that is, not yet a racial) version of Social Darwinism in Hans-Günter Zmarzlik, "Der Sozialdarwinismus in Deutschland als geschichtliches Problem," *Vierteljahrshefte für Zeitgeschichte*, July, 1963, 246–273.

[75] Ossietzky, "Auferstehung," *Das freie Volk*, April 11, 1914.

[76] Ossietzky, "Der heilige Mars," *Das freie Volk*, May 31, 1913. Also in *Schriften*, I, 19–24.

[77] Ossietzky, "Der Prozess des Herrn Henrici," *Das freie Volk*, February 28, 1914.

[78] Ossietzky, "Militärdiktatur oder Bürgerrecht," address held on January 21, 1914, printed in *Das freie Volk*, January 31, 1914.

[79] Ossietzky, "Die Schüsse von Serajevo," *Das freie Volk*, July 4, 1914. Also in *Schriften*, I, 42–46.

[80] Ossietzky, "Deutschland im Weltkrieg," address held in Hamburg on March 25, 1915, printed in *Völker-Friede*, September, 1915, p. 101.

[81] Jacob, *Weltbürger Ossietzky*, 11, and Grossmann, *Ossietzky*, 42 f.

[82] Ossietzky, *Der Anmarsch der neuen Reformation* ("Flugschriften des deutschen Monistenbundes Ortsgruppe Hamburg. Neue Folge, 2"; Hamburg, 1919). Three articles in this pamphlet had been initially published in the *Monatsblätter des Deutschen Monistenbundes, Ortsgruppe Hamburg*, ed. Carl Riess. Also in *Schriften*, I, 50–82.

[83] Ossietzky, "Das werdende Deutschland: Ein Wort an alle Schwachmütigen" (December, 1918), *Der Anmarsch der neuen Reformation*, 21 ff. A shorter version of this article, entitled "Der Revolutionäre ringt mit seinem Popanz," appeared in Kurt Hiller's *Das Ziel: Viertes der Jahrbücher für geistige Politik* (Munich, 1920), 100 ff. *Das Ziel*, forum of the "Council of Intellectual Workers" was at that time well known to educated readers. Hiller undoubtedly did a favor to Ossietzky by publishing this article, a fact that Hiller later recalled with pride. (See Hiller, *Koepfe und Troepfe*, 344 f.)

[84] *Der Anmarsch . . .* , 25 f.

[85] Koplin, 45.

[86] See *Degener's Wer ist's?* (Berlin, 1928), 1610.

[87] "Der Weltkrieger als Weltversöhner: Ein Aufruf des 'Friedensbundes der Kriegsteilnehmer,' " *Berliner Volks-Zeitung*, October 19, 1919.

[88] Printed in *Nie wieder Krieg* (Berlin), February, 1921, p. 1.

[89] See *Nie wieder Krieg*, November, 1921.

[90] Ossietzky, "Ausverkauf," *Völker-Friede*, November, 1919, pp. 93 f.

[91] *Ibid.*, 94.

[92] Ossietzky, "Der Adlerknopf," *Berliner Volks-Zeitung*, January 3, 1920.

[93] Ossietzky, "Moskau und Potsdam," *ibid.*, June 24, 1920.

[94] See "Eine neue republikanische Partei," *Frankfurter Zeitung*, January 8, 1924; also, "Politische Tageschau," *Berliner Tageblatt*, January 7, 1924.

[95] Grossmann, *Ossietzky*, 99.

[96] See "Aufruf der Republikanischen Partei," *Berliner Tageblatt*, February 6, 1924; also, *Frankfurter Zeitung*, February 8, 1924.

[97] See *Die Welt am Montag*, March 24, 1924.

[98] *Vossische Zeitung*, March 23, 1924.

[99] Hiller, *Koepfe und Troepfe*, 346.

[100] See "Die Wahlen zum Reichstag am 4. Mai und am 7. Dezember 1924," *Statistik des Deutschen Reiches*, CCCXV, 1 (Berlin, 1928), 7, 86.

[101] See *Die Welt am Montag*, October 29, 1924.

[102] See Grossmann, *Ossietzky*, 99.

[103] *Das Tage-Buch*, May 31, 1924, and *ibid.*, August 31, 1924.

[104] Ossietzky, "Deutsche Linke," *Das Tage-Buch*, September 20, 1924, p. 1323.

[105] *Ibid.*

[106] Enseling, 32.

[107] Ossietzky, "Rechenschaft," *WB*, May 10, 1932, p. 708. Also in *Schriften*, II, 235.

[108] Hiller, *Koepfe und Troepfe*, 341.

[109] Hiller, *Konkret*, May, 1962, 21.

[110] Tucholsky, letter to Mary Gerold-Tucholsky (November 7, 1927), *Ausgewählte Briefe*, 480.

[111] Hiller, *Koepfe und Troepfe*, 339, *et passim*.

[112] *Ibid.*, 341.

[113] See Enseling, 149 ff.

[114] Hanns-Erich Kaminski, "Die neue Luft," *WB*, February 21, 1933, pp. 265–267.

[115] Interview with Manfred George in New York City, September 10, 1963.

Notes for Chapter III (*pp. 65–72*)

[1] Golo Mann, *Deutsche Geschichte des neunzehnten und zwanzigsten Jahrhunderts* (Frankfurt/M., 1959), 535.

[2] *Ibid.*

[3] There is a vast literature on the "Ideas of 1914." See especially, Kurt Sontheimer, *Antidemokratisches Denken in der Weimarer Republik* (Munich, 1962), 115 ff.; Klemens von Klemperer, *Germany's New Conservatism* (Princeton, N.J., 1957), 47 ff.; Friedrich C. Sell, *Die Tragödie des deutschen Liberalismus* (Stuttgart, 1953), 354 ff.; Ernst Troeltsch, "Die Ideen von 1914" (1916) in *Deutscher Geist und Westeuropa*, ed. Hans Baron (Tübingen, 1925); Hanna Hafkesbrink, *Unknown Germany* (New Haven, Conn., 1948); William K. Pfeiler, *War and the German Mind* (New York, 1941), and Werner Wirth, "Das Erlebnis des Krieges," in Moeller van den Bruck, H. V. Gleichen, and M. H. Boehm, eds., *Die Neue Front* (Berlin, 1922).

[4] Friedrich Meinecke, *The German Catastrophe* (Boston, 1963), 25.

[5] Ernst Troeltsch, "Die Ideen von 1914," in Hans Baron, ed., *Deutscher Geist und Westeuropa* (Tübingen, 1925), 35.

[6] Thomas Mann, *Doktor Faustus* (Frankfurt, 1956), 399.

[7] Thomas Mann, *Betrachtungen eines Unpolitischen* (1918) in *Gesammelte Werke* (Oldenburg, 1960), XII, 19.

[8] Fritz Stern, "The Political Consequences of the Unpolitical German," *History*, 3 (September 1960), p. 125.

[9] Golo Mann, *Deutsche Geschichte*, 573 f.

[10] *Die Fackel* (Vienna), December 5, 1914, p. 2.

[11] Lehmann-Russbüldt, *Der Kampf der Deutschen Liga für Menschenrechte*, 13 ff.

[12] Meinecke, 27.

[13] Gerlach, *Von rechts nach links*, 234 f.

[14] See Frank, *Heart on the Left*, 71 ff.

[15] On *Die weissen Blätter*, see H. Haase, "Die Antikriegsliteratur in der Zeitschrift 'Die weissen Blätter'" (unpublished Ph.D. dissertation, University of Berlin [East], 1956). Also, Lillian Schacherl, "Die Zeitschriften des Expressionismus" (unpublished Ph.D. dissertation, University of Munich, 1957–1958).

[16] René Schickele, "Der Mensch im Kampf," *Die weissen Blätter*, April, 1916, pp. 1 ff.

[17] Leonhard Frank, *Der Mensch ist gut* (Zurich, 1917), 16 f.

[18] Walter Hasenclever, "Antigone," in Kurt Pinthus, ed., *Gedichte, Dramen, Prosa* (Hamburg, 1963), 190. The drama "Antigone" was first published in book form in 1917 by Paul Cassirer in Berlin, and first presented on the stage in Leipzig on December 15, 1917. Translation of this passage is by H. F. Garten in his *Modern German Drama* (New York, 1959), 132.

[19] Frank, *Heart on the Left*, 81.

[20] Ossietzky, "Wandlungen der geistigen Atmosphäre," written in July, 1918 and printed in *Der Anmarsch der neuen Reformation*, 19 f. Also in *Schriften*, I, 65.

[21] Heinrich Mann, "Geist und Tat" (1910), in *Essays* (Berlin [East], 1954), I, 8 ff.

[22] Heinrich Mann, "Geist und Tat," *Das Ziel: Aufrufe zum tätigen Geist* (Munich, 1916), 8.

[23] Kurt Hiller, "Philosophie des Ziels," *Das Ziel* (1916), 187 ff.

[24] *Ibid.*, 217.

[25] Alfred Kerr, "Aufgaben für die Friedenszeit," *Das Ziel* (1916), 69.

Notes for Chapter IV (pp. 73–81)

[1] Ernst Troeltsch, *Spektator-Briefe* (Tübingen, 1924), 69.

[2] René Schickele, *Der neunte November* (Berlin, 1919), quoted in Karl Otten, ed., *Ahnung und Aufbruch* (Darmstadt, 1957), 24 f.

[3] René Schickele, "Nachwort," *Die weissen Blätter*, October, 1919, p. 433. This revealing passage can also be found in Sontheimer, *Antidemokratisches Denken in der Weimarer Republik*, 392.

[4] See, for instance, Georg Metzler, "Die Schuld am Kriege," *WB*, February 13, 1919, pp. 163–181.

[5] [Richard Grelling], *J'accuse: Von einem Deutschen* (Lausanne, 1915). See also, *I Accuse: By a German* (New York, 1915). On the use the French made of Grelling's book, see Gustav Fuchs, *Der deutsche Pazifismus* (Stuttgart, 1928), 29 f.

[6] See, for instance, Georg Metzler, "Die verruchte Lüge," *WB*, January 9, 1919, pp. 34–37.

[7] See, for instance, "Das Offiziercorps im Kriege," *WB*, January 8, 1920, pp. 38–42.

[8] Quoted in "Kurt Eisner," Franz Osterroth, ed., *Biographisches Lexikon des Sozialismus* (Hannover, 1960), I, 75. For a definitive analysis of Eisner's ethical socialist republic and the Bavarian events in general, see Allan Mitchell, *Revolution in Bavaria, 1918–1919* (Princeton, N.J., 1965).

[9] Toller, *I Was a German*, 153 ff.

[10] *Ibid.*, 275.

[11] See Louis Untermeyer's introduction to Ernst Toller, *Man and the Masses: A Play of the Social Revolution in Seven Scenes* (Garden City, N.Y., 1924), xiii ff.

[12] See "Rat Geistiger Arbeiter: Programm," *WB*, November 21, 1918, pp.

473–475, and *Ziel: Drittes der Jahrbücher für geistige Politik* (Munich, 1919), 219 ff.

[13] See Ziel (1919), 222 f.

[14] See Ziel, *Viertes der Jahr, bücher für geistige Politik* (Munich, 1920), 213 ff.

[15] *Ibid.*, 213.

[16] *Ibid.*

[17] Letter to Kurt Hiller (September 15, 1923), in Ernst Toller, *Prosa, Briefe, Dramen, Gedichte* (Hamburg, 1962), 231.

[18] Kurt Hiller, "Mussolini und unsereins," *WB*, January 12, 1926, pp. 45–48.

[19] Kurt Hiller, "Der Bund der Geistigen," *Die Schaubühne*, June 17, 1915, p. 562.

[20] See Kurt Hiller, *Geistige Grundlagen eines schöpferischen Deutschlands der Zukunft* (Hamburg, 1947).

[21] René Schickele, "Nachwort," *Die weissen Blätter*, October, 1919, p. 435.

[22] *Ibid.*, 437.

Notes for Chapter V (*pp. 82–92*)

[1] See Richard N. Hunt, *German Social Democracy, 1918–1933* (New Haven, Conn., 1964), 200 ff. Also, Ossip K. Flechtheim, *Die Kommunistische Partei Deutschlands in der Weimarer Republik* (Offenbach/M., 1948), 70 ff.

[2] See, for instance, Heinrich Ströbel, "Nach dem Putsch," *WB*, March 25, 1920, pp. 353–356.

[3] *Die Tat*, November, 1918, p. 561.

[4] Karl Rothammer, "Sechzig Millionen Deutsche," *WB*, August 11, 1921, pp. 137–138. See also, by the same author, "Deutschland als Weltmacht," *ibid.*, July 21, 1921, pp. 55–56.

[5] Heinrich Ströbel, "Der alte Wahn," *WB*, May 8, 1919, pp. 523 ff. See also, by the same author, "Die Entscheidung," *ibid.*, June 26, 1919, pp. 727–731, and "Friedenssabotage," *ibid.*, July 3, 1919, pp. 1–5.

[6] See especially the joint manifesto issued by the French and German Leagues for Human Rights, entitled, "Für eine Verständigung mit Frankreich," *WB*, June 1, 1922, pp. 546–547.

[7] Ossietzky, "Die Wiener Internationale," *Berliner Volks-Zeitung*, March 5, 1921.

[8] Ossietzky, "Reale Reparationspolitik," *Berliner Volks-Zeitung*, April 16, 1921.

[9] For an analysis of Count Kessler's projects, see Koplin, 62 ff.

[10] Flechtheim, 56.

[11] See Reimund Klinkhammer, *Die Aussenpolitik der Sozialdemokratischen Partei Deutschlands in der Zeit der Weimarer Republik* (Freiburg, 1955).

[12] Lilli Janasch, "Deutschland und Frankreich," *WB*, September 15, 1921, pp. 255–258.

[13] Egon Erwin Kisch, "Sears, Roebuck and Co.," *WB*, October 29, 1929, p. 669.

[14] Peter Panter [Tucholsky], "Babbitt," *WB*, May 5, 1925, pp. 665–669. Also in *Gesammelte Werke*, II, 111–117.

[15] Zohn, 42.

[16] Ignaz Wrobel [Tucholsky], "Zwischen zwei Kriegen," *WB*, February 10, 1925, pp. 185–189. Also in *Gesammelte Werke*, II, 38–43.

[17] *Ibid.*, 188.

[18] Eyck, I, 233.

[19] Flechtheim, 88 ff., and Eyck, I, 238.

[20] Flechtheim, 84.

[21] Carl Landauer, *European Socialism* (Berkeley and Los Angeles, 1959), I, 958.

[22] Morus [Richard Lewinsohn], "Die grosse Täuschung," *WB*, January 25, 1923, pp. 91–94.

[23] Morus, "Was ist das rechte Mittel," *WB*, February 15, 1923, pp. 173–175.

[24] "Der Dolchstoss," *WB*, April 5, 1923, pp. 379–381.

[25] Morus, "Waffenstillstand," *WB*, May 17, 1923, pp. 557–560.

[26] On Joseph Bloch, see Anna Siemens, *Ein Leben für Europa: In Memoriam Joseph Bloch* (Frankfurt/M., 1956).

[27] Felix Stössinger, "Gegen den Sicherheitspakt," *WB*, July 14, 1925, pp. 37–45.

Notes for Chapter VI (*pp. 93–101*)

[1] German-Soviet relations in the interwar period are the subject of an extensive literature. Some of the best general accounts are, Carr, *German-Soviet Relations Between the Two World Wars;* Gerald Freund, *Unholy Alliance* (New York, 1957), and Hans W. Gatzke, "Von Rapallo nach Berlin: Stresemann und die deutsche Russlandpolitik," *Vierteljahrshefte für Zeitgeschichte,* January, 1956, pp. 1–29.

[2] Paul Eltzbacher, "Die Rettung durch den Bolschewismus," *Die Tat,* June, 1919, pp. 171–175. See also, by the same author, *Der Bolschewismus und die deutsche Zukunft* (Jena, 1919).

[3] *Die Tat,* June, 1919, p. 175.

[4] E. Voigtländer, "Wer ist Wilson," *Der Türmer,* July, 1919, p. 288.

[5] J. E. Freiherr von Grotthuss, "Bolschewismus so oder so," *ibid.,* June, 1919, p. 278.

[6] See, for instance, Arthur Moeller van den Bruck, *Das Recht der jungen Völker* (Munich, 1919). German "National Bolshevism" has recently received scholarly attention somewhat in excess of its significance. The National Bolshevists (Ernst Niekisch, Karl Otto Paetel, August Winnig, and Otto Strasser), although intellectually stimulating, were leaders without followers and without political influence. They were not even astute political critics and observers. Divorced from political reality, they engaged in utopian schemes which collapsed when the National Socialists took power. Of the rich literature on the subject, see especially Otto-Ernst Schüddekopf, *Linke Leute von Rechts* (Stuttgart, 1960); Karl Otto Paetel, *Versuchung oder Chance?* (Göttingen, 1965), and the autobiographical Ernst Niekisch, *Gewagtes Leben* (Cologne, 1958).

[8] Carr (1966 ed.), 11. On Seeckt, see especially the heavily documented Friedrich von Rabenau, *Seeckt: Aus seinem Leben, 1918–1936* (2 vols.; Leipzig, 1940).

[9] Carr, 20 f. On Radek's early mission to Germany, see Otto-Ernst Schüddekopf, *Karl Radek in Berlin* (Hannover, 1962).

[10] On the Rapallo Treaty, see Alfred Anderle, *Die deutsche Rapallo-Politik: Deutsch-sowjetische Beziehungen, 1922–1929* (Berlin [East], 1962), and Herbert Helbig, *Die Träger der Rapallo-Politik* (Göttingen, 1958). Proof that the Rapallo treaty included no secret military clauses is provided by Seeckt in Rabenau, II, 313.

[11] Of the many studies on Russo-German military collaboration in the Weimar period, the following are particularly recommended: Helm Speidel, "Reichswehr und Rote Armee," *Vierteljahrshefte für Zeitgeschichte,* January, 1953, pp. 9–45; Gordon A. Craig, *The Politics of the Prussian Army, 1640–1945* (New York, 1956), 408 ff.; Hans W. Gatzke, "Russo-German Military Collaboration During the Weimar Republic," *The American Historical Review,* LXIII (1958), 565–597; F. L. Carsten, "The Reichswehr and the Red Army," *Survey* (London), October 1962, pp. 114–132, and Cecil F. Melville, *The Russian Face of Germany* (London, 1932). The last work contains a number of documents collected by the German Social Democratic Party.

[12] Eyck, I, 204, and 222 f. For an English translation of the Seeckt Memorandum, see John W. Wheeler-Bennett, *The Nemesis of Power* (London, 1954), 133 ff. For Seeckt's exclusively "Eastern" approach to foreign policy and for his plan to "take back everything we have lost," see Craig, 412 ff.

[13] See, for instance, Craig, 423 f.

[14] Kaspar Hauser [Tucholsky], "Herr Wendriner lässt sich die Haare schneiden," *WB*, September 22, 1925, p. 461. Also in *Gesammelte Werke*, II, 223.

[15] Tyrus, "Maltzans Verschwörung zu Genua," *WB*, May 4, 1922, pp. 450–452.

[16] Eyck, I, 205.

[17] There is no biography, known to this writer, of Joseph Wirth, one of the republic's outstanding politicians.

[18] Moritz Heimann, "Rapallo," *WB*, May 18, 1922, pp. 493–496.

[19] Morus [Ludwig Lewinsohn], "Katastrophenpolitik," *WB*, April 27, 1922, p. 427.

[20] Morus, "Das Ergebnis von Genua," *WB*, May 25, 1922, pp. 534–536.

[21] *Ibid.*, 535.

[22] Morus, "Filmzauber," *WB*, August 24, 1922, pp. 200–202.

[23] Flechtheim, 118 ff.

[24] Carr, 80.

[25] On the Locarno treaty, see especially Fritz Berber, ed., *Locarno: A Collection of Documents* (London, 1936); Gustav Stresemann, *Vermächtnis*, eds. Henry Bernhard *et al.* (Berlin, 1932), Vol. II, and K. D. Erdmann, "Das Problem der Ost- und Westorientierung in der Locarno-Politik Stresemanns," *Geschichte in Wissenschaft und Unterricht*, 6 (1955), 133–162.

[26] Carr, 86. See also S. William Halperin, *Germany Tried Democracy* (New York, 1965), 337 ff.

[27] Carr, 87.

[28] *Ibid.*

[29] *Ibid.*, 85, and 87.

[30] On the 1927 crisis in Russo-British relations and on the effect of the crisis on German foreign policy, see Harvey L. Dyck, "German Soviet Relations and the Anglo-Soviet Break, 1927," *Slavic Review*, March, 1966, pp. 67–83. On post-1926 Soviet-German relations, see *Weimar Germany and Soviet Russia, 1926–1933* (New York, 1966), by the same author.

[31] *Ibid.*, 70 f.

[32] Ignaz Wrobel [Tucholsky], "Brief an einem bessern Herrn," *WB*, March 24, 1925, pp. 426–430. Also in *Gesammelte Werke*, II, 67–72.

[33] *Gesammelte Werke*, 72.

[34] Felix Stössinger, "Gegen den Sicherheitspakt," *WB*, July 14, 1925, pp. 37–45.

[34a] Hans Schwann, "Fort mit Stresemann," *WB*, December 2, 1924, pp. 821–822.

[35] Morus, "Abfindungen," *WB*, October 6, 1925, pp. 545–547.

[36] Ossietzky, "Der plombierte Wagen," *WB*, April 20, 1926, pp. 599–605.

[37] *Ibid.*, 601.

[38] *Ibid.*, 604.

[39] Ossietzky, "Zwischen London und Moskau," *WB*, June 7, 1927, p. 888.

[40] Carr, 96.

[41] Wheeler-Bennett, 193.

[42] Eyck, II, 362, *et passim.*

Notes for Chapter VII (pp. 102–111)

[1] Theobald Tiger [Tucholsky], "Zehn Jahre deutsche 'Revolution,'" *Arbeiter Illustrierte Zeitung*, 44 (1928), 8. Also in *Gesammelte Werke*, II, 1304.

[2] For a detailed table of the German parliamentary elections between 1871 and 1933, see Pinson, 572 ff.

[3] For a verbatim record of the electoral platforms of the German political parties in January 1919, see Forsthoff, 20 ff.

[4] Evelyn Anderson, *Hammer or Anvil* (London, 1945), 62.

[5] *Ibid.*, 62 f.

[6] Hunt, 34.

[7] Carl E. Schorske, *German Social Democracy, 1905–1917* (New York, 1965), 322 ff.

[8] Poor, 91.

[9] Ossietzky, "Der Schatten der Paulskirche," *Berliner Volks-Zeitung*, August 11, 1921.

[10] *Ibid.*

[11] Pinson, 409.

[12] Ignaz Wrobel [Tucholsky], "Kapp-Lüttwitz," *WB*, March 25, 1920, pp. 357–363. Also in *Gesammelte Werke*, I, 614–621.

[13] *Gesammelte Werke*, I, 621.

[14] Ignaz Wrobel [Tucholsky], "Die zufällige Republik," *WB*, July 13, 1922, pp. 25–30. Also in *Gesammelte Werke*, I, 993–998.

[15] Eyck, I, 67.

[16] Leo Lania, "Die Sozialdemokratie," *WB*, October 11, 1923, p. 352. Also in Wolfgang Weyrauch, ed., *Ausnahmezustand: Eine Anthologie aus "Weltbühne" und "Tagebuch"* (Munich, 1966), 251.

[17] Eyck, I, 215 f.

[18] Cited by Eyck, I, 217.

[19] "Deutscher Balkan," *WB*, June 29, 1922, p. 642.

[20] Ignaz Wrobel [Tucholsky], "Das Opfer einer Republik," *Die Welt am Montag*, June 26, 1922. Also in *Gesammelte Werke*, I, 938 f.

[21] Richard Lewinsohn, "Die Zentrum-Krise," *WB*, July 14, 1921, pp. 27–32.

[22] Otto Flake, "Nach dem Mord," *WB*, July 6, 1922, pp. 1–3.

[23] *Ibid.*, 3.

[24] Ossietzky, "Von Kapp bis . . ." *WB*, March 11, 1930, pp. 376 f. Also in *Schriften*, I, 182.

[25] Lucius Schierling [Ossietzky], "Jubeljahr 1924," *Das Tage-Buch*, August 9, 1924, p. 1119.

[26] Ossietzky, "Lassalle," *Das Tage-Buch*, September 6, 1924, p. 1251.

[27] Ossietzky, "Rudolf Hilferding," *Das Tage-Buch*, 923.

[28] Ossietzky, "Schutz der Republik—die grosse Mode," *Das Tage-Buch*, September 13, 1924, p. 1291.

[29] *Ibid.*

[30] See Hunt, 52.

Notes for Chapter VIII (*pp. 112–121*)

[1] Richard Barkeley, *Die deutsche Friedensbewegung, 1870–1933* (Hamburg, 1948), 70.

[2] Norman Angell, "Peace Movements," *Encyclopedia of Social Sciences*, XII, 41 ff.

[3] Barkeley, 11.

[4] For an English translation, see *Lay Down Your Arms: The Autobiography of Martha von Tilling*, trans. T. Holmes (2d ed. rev.; London, 1894).

[5] Ossietzky, "Die Pazifisten," *Das Tage-Buch*, October 4, 1924, p. 1402. Also in *Schriften*, I, 119.

[6] Gerda Starker, "Die geschichtliche Entwicklung des deutschen Pazifismus seit 1900" (unpublished Ph.D. dissertation, University of Heidelberg, 1935), 13.

[7] Hans Wehberg, *Als Pazifist im Weltkriege* (Leipzig, 1919), 20.

[8] See Lehmann-Russbüldt, *Der Kampf der Deutschen Liga für Menschenrechte*, 82 f.

[9] Hiller, *Koepfe und Troepfe*, 345.

[10] See Hans Wehberg's critique of Hiller in "Kurt Hillers revolutionärer Pazifismus," *Die Friedenswarte*, April, 1930, pp. 97–99.

[11] Enseling, 110, and Hiller, *Koepfe und Troepfe*, 345.

[12] Ossietzky, "Die Pazifisten," *Schriften*, I, 118.

[13] *Schriften*, I, 120.

[14] Ossietzky, "Unselig sind die Friedfertigen," *WB*, February 19, 1929, p. 279. Also in *Schriften*, I, 127.

[15] Barkeley, 76 ff.

[16] Otto Gessler, *Reichswehrpolitik in der Weimarer Zeit* (Stuttgart, 1958), 171 *et passim*.

[17] Barkeley, 64.

[18] Ossietzky, "Die Pazifisten," *Schriften*, I, 120.

[19] Lehmann-Russbüldt, 124 ff.

[20] Enseling, 110 f; Barkeley, 100 f, and Lothar Persius, "A bas les canons?" *Das Tage-Buch*, October 8, 1927, pp. 1622–1625. This article has been reprinted in Weyrauch, 62–65.

[21] *Die Friedenswarte*, January, 1927.

[22] Barkeley, 102. See also, Paul Freiherr von Schoenaich, *Mein Finale* (Flensburg, 1947), 15 ff.

[23] Kurt Hiller, "An den Vorsitzenden der deutschen Friedensgesellschaft" (Freiherr von Schoenaich), *WB*, July 1, 1930, pp. 4–9.

[24] See "Die bürgerliche Linke in Deutschland," *Die Friedenswarte*, September, 1930, p. 280; also Barkeley, 111.

[25] Ignaz Wrobel [Tucholsky], "Über wirkungsvollen Pazifismus," *WB*, October 11, 1927, p. 557. Also in *Gesammelte Werke*, I, 337.

[26] Ignaz Wrobel [Tucholsky], "Militaria: Von grossen Requisitionen," *WB*, January 30, 1919, p. 112. Also in *Gesammelte Werke*, I, 337.

[27] "Militaria: Von kleinen Mädchen," *WB*, February 6, 1919, p. 134. Also in *Gesammelte Werke*, I, 338.

[28] "Militaria: Zur Erinnerung an den ersten August 1914," *WB*, August 14, 1919, p. 191. Also in *Gesammelte Werke*, I, 349.

[29] *Gesammelte Werke*, I, 358.

[30] On the activities of the Black Reichswehr, see, especially, Craig, 401 ff; Robert G. L. Waite, *Vanguard of Nazism* (Cambridge, Mass., 1952), 239 ff; Emil J. Gumbel, *Verräter verfallen der Feme*" (Berlin, 1929), 231 ff.

[31] The best account of the Küstrin putsch in English is in Waite, 247 ff. See also the other sources cited above. Further, Eyck, I, 262 ff, and Bruno Buchrucker, *Im Schatten Seeckts* (Berlin, 1928), 24 ff.

[32] [Carl Mertens], "Die vaterländischen Verbände: Erlebnisse und Erfahrungen," *WB*, August 18, 1925, pp. 239 ff *et passim*. His revelations were also published in book form: Carl Mertens, *Verschwörer und Fememörder* (Berlin-Charlottenburg, 1926). For extensive citations from Mertens' first article, see Grossmann, *Ossietzky*, 122 ff. Mertens himself later became a radical pacifist. See M. M. Gehrke, "Vaterländische Verbände," *WB*, October 25, 1932, pp. 630–631.

[33] See Emil J. Gumbel *et al.*, *Weissbuch über die Schwarze Reichswehr* (Berlin-Hessenwinkel, 1925); also, Otto Lehmann-Russbüldt, *Aggression* (London, 1942), 21 ff.

[34] See "Der Untersuchungsausschuss 'Fememorde' (SPD: 29. Januar 1925)," in Winfried Steffani, ed., *Die Untersuchungsausschüsse des Preussischen Landtages zur Zeit der Weimarer Republik* (Düsseldorf, 1960), 194 ff.

[35] Berthold Jacob, "Plaidoyer für Schulz," *WB*, March 22, 1927, pp. 446–450.

[36] On Jacob's and Ossietzky's *Feme*-trial, see Ossietzky, "Der Femeprozess," *WB*, December 27, 1927, pp. 951–955. Also in *Schriften*, I, 235–242. Further, Gumbel, "*Verräter verfallen der Feme,*" 350 ff; Grossmann, *Ossietzky*, 171 ff; Frei, 119 ff, and Alfred Apfel, *Behind the Scenes of German Justice* (London, 1935), 93 ff.

[37] See Gessler, 443 ff. Also Eyck, II, 189 f. On the *Lohmann-Skandal* see Richard Lewinsohn (Morus), *Das Geld in der Politik* (Berlin, 1930), 228 ff.

[38] See the well-documented account of Emil J. Gumbel, *Vom Fememord zur Reichskanzlei* (Heidelberg, 1962), 71; also, "Landesverrat," a special issue of *Die Menschenrechte*, November 15, 1927, and other issues of *Die Menschenrechte*, 1926–1933; also, *Acht Jahre politische Justiz* (Berlin, 1927), and Ernst Fraenkel, *Zur Soziologie der Klassenjustiz* (Berlin, 1930).

Notes for Chapter IX (*pp. 121–134*)

[1] Tucholsky, *Deutschland, Deutschland über alles*, 19.

[2] See, especially, Ossietzky, "Rechenschaft," *WB*, May 10, 1932, p. 701. Also in *Schriften*, II, 225 f.

[3] Ignaz Wrobel [Tucholsky], "Deutsche Richter," *WB*, April 12, 1927, p. 581. Also in *Gesammelte Werke*, II, 771.

[4] See the many contemporary references to German "class justice" in non-Communist writings. For instance, Fraenkel, 32 ff.

[5] There is more than adequate literature on political justice in the Weimar Republic but no significant study, known to this writer, on the administration of justice in general. For the most revealing contemporary account on political justice, see Emil J. Gumbel, *Vier Jahre politischer Mord* (Berlin, 1922), and by the same author, "*Verräter verfallen der Feme.*" See also, Emil J. Gumbel, ed., *Denkschrift des Reichsjustizministeriums* (Berlin, 1924); Ernst Fraenkel, *Zur Soziologie der Klassenjustiz;* Erich Kuttner, *Warum versagt die Justiz?* (Berlin, 1921); *Acht Jahre politische Justiz;* and Erich Eyck, *Die Krisis der deutschen Rechtspflege* (Berlin, 1926). Among the best modern studies are: Gumbel, *Vom Fememord zur Reichskanzlei;* Apfel, *Behind the Scenes of German Justice;* Karl D. Bracher, *Auflösung der Weimarer Republik* (Villingen, Schwarzwald, 1960), 191 ff; Wilhelm Hoegner, *Die verratene Republik* (Munich, 1958), 261 ff, and, finally, Heinrich Hannover and Elisabeth Hannover-Drück, *Politische Justiz 1918–1933* (Frankfurt/M., 1966). The contemporary issues of *Die Justiz* and *Die Menschenrechte* are mines of additional information.

[6] Gumbel, *Vom Fememord zur Reichskanzlei*, 46.

[7] *Ibid.*, 47.

[8] See Hannover and Hannover, 46 *et passim.*

[9] See Gumbel, *Vom Fememord zur Reichskanzlei*, 27 f.

[10] See, for instance, Hannover and Hannover, 62 f.

[11] *Ibid.*, 15.

[12] On the Jakubowski affair, see Grossmann, *Ossietzky*, 199 ff. Also, Bernard Düsing, *Die Geschichte der Abschaffung der Todesstrafe* (Offenbach, 1952), 169 ff, and Erich Mangold, "Strelitzer Figurinen," *WB*, June 18, 1929, pp. 931–934.

[13] *Die Menschenrechte*, July 25, 1929, pp. 1–7.

[14] See, for instance, Ignaz Wrobel [Tucholsky], "Deutsche Richter," *Gesammelte Werke*, II, 773.

[15] See Erich Kuttner, *Klassenjustiz* (Berlin, 1913), 16 f.

[16] See especially, Ignaz Wrobel, "Deutsche Richter," *WB*, April 12–26, 1927, pp. 581–584, 619–623, 663–666. Also in *Gesammelte Werke*, II, 771–783.

[17] *Gesammelte Werke*, II, 776.

[18] Alfred Polgar, "Von Verbrechern und Richtern," *Im Lauf der Zeit* (Hamburg, 1954), 39–46.

[19] *Ibid.*, 42.

[20] *Ibid.*, 43 ff.

[21] Hans Gathmann, "Ein Unschuldiger klagt an," *WB*, March 17, 1925, pp. 393–395.

[22] Ernst E. Schweitzer, "Die Lotterie der Schwurgerichte," *WB*, April 12, 1923, p. 413.

[23] *Ibid.*

[24] For more details on the Harden trial, see Gumbel, "*Verräter verfallen der Feme*," 56 ff, and Hannover and Hannover, 129 ff.

[25] Tucholsky, "Prozess Harden," *WB*, December 21, 1922, p. 645. Also in *Gesammelte Werke*, I, 1078.

[26] Rudolf Olden in *Das Zuchthaus—die politische Waffe*, 48 ff.

[27] Schweitzer, as quoted in Hannover and Hannover, 29.

[28] Schweitzer, *WB*, April 12, 1923, pp. 413 f.

[29] On the murderous students, see Hannover and Hannover, 98 ff.

[30] Schweitzer, *WB*, April 12, 1923, pp. 415 f.

[31] Manfred George, "Kontrolliert die Justiz," *WB*, September 29, 1925, pp. 493–494.

[32] Ignaz Wrobel, "Deutsche Richter," *Gesammelte Werke*, 772.

[33] See, for instance, Ignaz Wrobel [Tucholsky], "8 Uhr abends—Licht aus!" *WB*, December 10, 1929, pp. 866–871. Also in *Gesammelte Werke*, III, 269–274.

[34] See Ignaz Wrobel [Tucholsky], "Das schwarze Kreuz auf grünem Grunde," *WB*, April 21, 1931, pp. 577–581. Also in *Gesammelte Werke*, III, 836–840.

[35] See Ignaz Wrobel [Tucholsky], "Mit einem Zuchthäusler," *WB*, August 28, 1928, pp. 315–318. Also in *Gesammelte Werke*, II, 1207–1210.

[36] For a delightful description of *Wandervogel* practices, see Margarete Buber-Neumann, *Von Potsdam nach Moskau* (Stuttgart, 1957), 23 ff.

[37] *Ibid.*, 73.

[38] Walter Hasenclever, *Der Sohn: Ein Drama in fünf Akten* (Leipzig, 1917), 120 ff.

[39] Ossietzky, "The Revolt of German Women," *The Nation* (New York), November 7, 1928, pp. 478–480.

[40] See, for instance, Hans Ostwald, *Sittengeschichte der Inflation* (Berlin, 1931).

[41] See the charming illustrated account of Hermann Behr, *Die goldenen zwanziger Jahre*. See also Bruno E. Werner, *Die zwanziger Jahre* (Munich, 1962).

[42] See, for instance, Ossietzky, "Das lädierte Sakrament," *WB*, December 3, 1929, pp. 830–831.

[43] Heinrich Mann, *Der Untertan*, 478 f.

[44] See Hermann Hass, *Sitte und Kultur im Nachkriegsdeutschland* (Hamburg, 1932), 84.

[45] See Ossietzky's blasting of the new adultery law proposed by the Zentrum in "Das lädierte Sakrament."

[46] Ignaz Wrobel, "Deutsche Richter," *Gesammelte Werke*, II, 775.

[47] See "Rat Geistiger Arbeiter: Programm," *WB*, November 21, 1918, pp. 473–475, and *Ziel: Drittes der Jahrbücher für geistige Politik*, 219 ff.

[48] For a learned discussion of Hiller's sexual theories, see Enseling, 98 ff.

[49] Magnus Hirschfeld, "Der neue § 175: Ein Gesetz für Erpresser," *WB*, January 20, 1925, pp. 91–95. Also on the same subject, Ignaz Wrobel [Tucholsky], "Unzucht zwischen Männern," in "*§ 297 Unzucht zwischen Männern?*" *Ein Beitrag zum Strafgesetzreform*, ed. Richard Linsert (Berlin, 1929), 127 f. Also in *Gesammelte Werke*, III, 17–18.

[50] Erich Leisar, "§ 218," *WB*, March 31, 1925, pp. 465–467.

[51] Manfred George, "Das Recht auf Abtreibung," *WB*, January 5, 1922, pp. 7–9.

[52] *Ibid.*, 9.

[53] See, among others, Ossietzky, "Zum Falle Friedrich Wolf," *WB*, March 3, 1931, pp. 301–303; Friedrich Wolf, "Die Machtprobe," *ibid.*, March 24, 1931, pp. 413–418; and Else Kienle, "Der Fall Kienle," *ibid.*, April 14, 1931, pp. 535–539.

[54] Hannover and Hannover, 238 ff.

[55] *Ibid.*, 250 ff. For a verbatim rendering of the verdict of the court in 1929, see Ignaz Wrobel [Tucholsky], "Die Begründung," *WB*, March 19, 1929, pp. 435–438. Also in *Gesammelte Werke*, III, 52–56. See also, "Über die Berufsverhandlung in dem George Grosz Prozess," *Die Menschenrechte*, April 20, 1929, pp. 8–11.

[56] See, especially, "Der gelästerte Christus: das zweite Siegert-Urteil im Prozess George Grosz," *WB*, March 31, 1931, p. 310.

[57] Tucholsky, "Prozess Harden," *Gesammelte Werke*, I, 1078.

[58] Ignaz Wrobel [Tucholsky], "Die Unzüchtigen," *WB*, September 14, 1922, pp. 288–290. Also in *Gesammelte Werke*, I, 1057–1059.

Notes for Chapter X (*pp. 137–147*)

[1] Norbert Rosenberg, "Kapitalismus und Krieg," *WB*, August 24, 1922, pp. 183–186.

[2] Heinrich Ströbel, "Die geächtete Vernunft," *WB*, May 29, 1919, p. 616.

[3] Emil J. Gumbel, "Rede an Spartakus," *WB*, December 19, 1918, pp. 569–571.

[4] Heinrich Ströbel, "Führer," *WB*, May 1, 1919, pp. 491–495. See also Ludwig Jurisch, "Die Weimarer," *ibid.*, February 20, 1919, pp. 193–195.

[5] See Arnold Zweig, "Grabrede auf Spartakus," *WB*, January 23, 1919, pp. 75–78; Heinrich Ströbel, "Wie lange noch?," *ibid.*, May 22, 1919, pp. 581–585, and Kaspar Hauser [Tucholsky], "Zwei Erschlagene," *ibid.*, January 23, 1919, p. 97. Also in *Gesammelte Werke*, I, 361–362.

[6] Ströbel, "Die bedrohte Demokratie," *WB*, March 27, 1919, p. 338. See also "Herausforderung," *ibid.*, April 10, 1919, pp. 397–402, and "Die Rettung," *ibid.*, April 17, 1919, pp. 429–434.

[7] Ströbel, "Katastrophenpolitik," *WB*, July 10, 1919, pp. 30 f.

[8] *Ibid.*, 32 ff.

[9] Ströbel, "Das neue Reich," *WB*, August 7, 1919, p. 152.

[10] *Ibid.*, 151.

[11] Ströbel, "Radikale Tat," *WB*, July 17, 1919, pp. 59–63, and "Einigung," *ibid.*, September 25, 1919, pp. 369–374. See also Otto Lehmann-Russbüldt, "Der Bürgerschreck," *ibid.*, December 12, 1918, 545–547.

[12] Ströbel, "Sinowjews Verbündete," *WB*, October 21, 1920, pp. 443–445.

[13] Elias Hurwicz, "Der Maximalismus," *Die Schaubühne*, February 14, 1918, p. 148. See also Hurwicz, "Die Kinder in Sowjet-Russland," *WB*, July 7, 1921, pp. 4–5, and Lorarius, "Diktaturen," *Die Schaubühne*, January 10, 1918, p. 45.

[14] Elias Hurwicz, "Friede mit den Bolschewiki," *WB*, January 29, 1920, pp. 136–139; "Die jüngste Kundgebung der Menschewiki," *ibid.*, October 21, 1920, pp. 450–451; "Die Liquidation des Bolschewismus," *ibid.*, December 30, 1920, pp. 749–751.

[15] Ströbel, "Tatarischer und demokratischer Sozialismus," *WB*, June 24, 1920, pp. 737–740, and "Für den Völkerbund!" *ibid.*, July 29, 1920, pp. 129–132.

[16] Ströbel, "Warnung an Moskau," *WB*, September 16, 1920, p. 299.

[17] Ströbel, "Europas Selbstmord," *WB*, August 19, 1920, pp. 201–203; Elias Hurwicz, "Moskauer Kongress," *ibid.*, September 2, 1920, pp. 255–257.

[18] Ströbel, "Sozialistische Weltpolitik," *WB*, September 30, 1920, pp. 347–349.

[19] *Ibid.*, 349.

[20] *Ibid.*

[21] Ströbel, "Die geächtete Vernunft," *WB*, May 29, 1919, p. 615.

[22] Ströbel, "Tatarischer und demokratischer Sozialismus," *WB*, June 24, 1920, p. 740.

[23] Karl Rothammer, "Der Kommunistenputsch," *WB*, April 7, 1921, pp. 371–372.

[24] Ströbel, "Die Diktatur der Rechten," *WB*, January 29, 1920, pp. 129–132.

[25] Ströbel, "Das Kernproblem des Wiederaufbaus," *WB*, February 12, 1920, p. 198.

[26] *Ibid.*, 196 f.; also, "Sozialisierung und Wiederaufbau," *WB*, May 12, 1921, pp. 513–517.

[27] Eugen Lanz, "Der Hamburger Kongress," *WB*, June 7, 1923, pp. 653–656.

[28] Hans Bauer, "Das sächsische Gegengewicht," *WB*, September 20, 1923, pp. 283–286. On the Saxon "Workers' government," see Angress, 382 ff.

[29] Hermann Windschild, "Sachsen und die Folgen," *WB*, November 8, 1923, pp. 464 f.

[30] Arno Voigt, "Sachsen," *WB*, November 29, 1923, pp. 531–532.

[31] *Ibid.*, 533.

[32] Morus [Richard Lewinsohn], "Die Herren: Das Ende des Achtstundentages," *WB*, November 29, 1923, p. 536.

[33] Otto Flake, "Der Zug nach Rechts," *WB*, December 6, 1923, p. 552.

[34] *Ibid.*, 553.

[35] Ossietzky, "Der Adlerknopf," *Berliner Volks-Zeitung*, January 20, 1920.

[36] Karl Rothammer, "Der Parteitag in Görlitz, 1. Verstandskritik," *WB*, September 29, 191, pp. 310–312.

[37] Theobald Tiger [Tucholsky], "Der Parteitag in Görlitz, 2. Gefühlskritik," *WB*, September 29, 1921, p. 312. Also in *Gesammelte Werke*, I, 827–828.

Notes for Chapter XI *(pp. 148–164)*

[1] Leo Lania, "Das deutsche Hungergebiet," *WB*, May 26, 1925, p. 770.

[2] Morus [Richard Lewinsohn], "Die Aufgeklärten: Die Schwerindustrie treibt Menschenwirtschaft," *WB*, September 13, 1927, pp. 420–421.

[3] See pp. 99–101.

[4] Meridionalis, "Lenin und MacDonald," *WB*, February 4, 1924, pp. 187–188.

[5] Joseph Friedfeld, "Ein Monat Arbeiterregierung," *WB*, March 13, 1924, pp. 323–325; "MacDonalds Bewährung," *ibid.*, May 1, 1924, pp. 567–569; "England und Russland," *ibid.*, July 21, 1925, pp. 75–77; "Die neue Labour Party," *ibid.*, August 18, 1925, pp. 236–238.

[6] Hans Schwann, "Die Entwaffnungsfrage," *WB*, February 17, 1925, pp. 37–39.

[7] Ossietzky, "Vanity Fair," *WB*, September 14, 1926, pp. 399–402; "Völkerbund ohne Völker," *ibid.*, December 14, 1926, pp. 907–909.

[8] Jacob Altmeier, "Zeigner und Hitler," *WB*, April 10, 1924, p. 466.

[9] Ernst Toller, "Dokumente bayrischer Justiz," *WB*, 1924–1925.

[10] R. A. Siewers, "Der Maslow-Prozess," *WB*, September 22, 1925, pp. 451–452; Ronald Lechter, "Maslow," *ibid.*, September 15, 1925, pp. 426–427. See also Peter Kerdell, "Münchner Hungerstreik," *ibid.*, July 10, 1924, pp. 61–62; Erich Mühsam, "Der Stuttgarter Kommunistenprozess," *ibid.*, August 2, 1927, pp. 165–168.

[11] Emil Rabold, "Thüringen und Mecklenburg," *WB*, February 28, 1924, p. 257.

[12] Hans Schwann, "USPD," *WB*, May 22, 1924, pp. 683–684.

[13] Hans Bauer, "Zerfall der Sozialdemokratie?" *WB*, January 13, 1925, pp. 54–57; Alfons Steiniger, "Neu-Heidelberg," *ibid.*, July 28, 1925, pp. 483–488; Walter Fabian, "Die sächsische Sozialdemokratie," *ibid.*, November 22, 1927, pp. 777–779.

[14] Johannes Fischart [Erich Dombrowski], "Neue Politikerköpfe, IV, Ruth Fischer," *WB*, May 8, 1924, p. 620.

[15] Adolf Grabowsky, "Der kommunistische Orden," *WB*, January 6, 1925, p. 5.
[16] Kurt Kesten, "Das neue Russland," *WB*, March 27, 1924, pp. 399–401; "Leningrad," *ibid.*, June 5, 1924, pp. 763–765; Anker Kinkerby, "Der Winterpalast," *ibid.*, July 10, 1924, pp. 53–56; "Reise in Russland," *ibid.*, July 17, 1924, pp. 97–102; Axel Eggebrecht, "Die russische Wirklichkeit," *ibid.*, June 16, 1924, pp. 876–882.

[17] Adolf Grabowsky, "Der kommunistische Orden," *WB*, January 6, 1925, pp. 1–5; "Russischer Schein und Wirklichkeit," *ibid.*, June 23, 1925, pp. 919–922; "Die Freiheit in Sowjet Russland," *ibid.*, July 13, 1926, pp. 43–47.

[18] Ossietzky, "Stalin und Trotzki," *WB*, November 15, 1927, pp. 733–735.

[19] Morus [Richard Lewinsohn], "Alles in Ordnung: Kommunistenkongress," *WB*, July 21, 1925, p. 106.

[20] Alfons Steiniger, "An die deutschen Kommunisten," *WB*, September 11, 1924, pp. 369–372.

[21] Friedrich Schwag, "An die Amarxisten," *WB*, October 2, 1924, pp. 485–488.

[22] Kurt Hiller, "Wahlparole," *WB*, October 30, 1924, p. 649.

[23] Hiller, "Der landläufige Sozialismus, I, II," *WB*, July 10, and July 17, 1924, pp. 44–47, and 89–92.

[24] Hermann Wendel, "Von der Wissenschaft der Utopie," *WB*, September 4, 1924, pp. 345–348.

[25] *Ibid.*, 347.

[26] Kurt Hiller, "Wahlparole," *WB*, October 30, 1924, pp. 645–649.

[27] Hiller, "Der Reichspräsident," *WB*, March 3, 1925, pp. 290–304.

[28] Ignaz Wrobel [Tucholsky], "Was nun—?" *WB*, May 5, 1925, p. 648. Also in *Gesammelte Werke*, II, 111.

[29] *Gesammelte Werke*, II, 108 f.

[30] Leo Lania, "Eberts Erbe," *WB*, May 5, 1925, pp. 649–650.

[31] Alfons Steiniger, "Erwachende Kommunisten," *WB*, November 10, 1925, pp. 705–707.

[32] Ossietzky, "Krisen," *WB*, July 20, 1926, p. 721.

[33] Arthur Seehof, "Russlands Rüstungen," *WB*, May 24, 1927, pp. 837–838; Ossietzky, "Rache für Hankau," *ibid.*, May 24, 1927, pp. 805–808; "Feuer im Osten," *ibid.*, June 16, 1927, pp. 925–930.

[34] Alfons Steiniger, "Es lebe die Zweite Republik," *WB*, May 19, 1925, pp. 721–724.

[35] Kurt Hiller, "Politische Neugruppierung," *WB*, May 26, 1925, p. 762.

[36] Alfons Steiniger, "Ernstmachen!," *WB*, June 30, 1925, p. 947.

[37] Max Peters, "KPD, SPD, oder Deutsche Linke?," *WB*, October 6, 1925, pp. 513–514.

[38] Friedrich Schwag, "2½ te rediviva?," *WB*, October 13, 1925, pp. 551–552.

[39] Kurt Hiller, "Die Differenz mit der KPD," *WB*, October 20, 1925, pp. 588–591.

[40] Max Peters, "Lebendige Politik!" *WB*, December 15, 1925, p. 891.

[41] *Ibid.*

[42] Kurt Hiller, "Konzentration Links!" *WB*, February 15, 1927, pp. 248–252.

[43] Georg Ledebour, "Einigung und gemeinsame Aktion," *WB*, March 15, 1927, pp. 403–406; "Sind gemeinsame Aktionen möglich?" *ibid.*, April 19, 1927, pp. 617–619.

[44] Hans Bussman, "Vererbung," *WB*, January 5, 1926, pp. 35–36; Franz Leschnitzer, "Studenten Linksblock," *ibid.*, June 22, 1926, p. 986.

[45] Franz Leschnitzer, "Reichsbanner und Roter Frontkämpferbund," *WB*, March 30, 1926, pp. 513–515.

[46] On the "Settlement with the Princes" (*Fürstenabfindung*) and the campaign for the expropriation of their domains (*Fürstenenteignung*), see Schwarz, 125 ff;

Eyck, II, 62 ff, and Kurt Pritzkoleit, *Die neuen Herren* (Vienna, 1958), 68 ff. Heinz Karl, *Die deutsche Arbeiterklasse im Kampf um die Enteignung der Fürsten, 1925–1926* (Berlin [East], 1957), is not reliable.

[47] For a detailed but misleading account of the committee's actions, see Heinz Habedank, *Der Feind steht rechts* (Berlin [East], 1965), 23 ff.

[48] See, for instance, Eyck, II, 64 f.

[49] See *Das Tage-Buch*, April 3, 1926, pp. 520 f.

[50] Eyck, II, 64 f.

[51] Emil Rabold, "Die Stimme des Volkes," *WB*, January 26, 1926, p. 137.

[52] Ossietzky, "Fürstenabfindung und Russenvertrag," *WB*, May 14, 1926, pp. 679 f.

[53] Ossietzky, "Bürgerblock," *WB*, July 6, 1926, pp. 1–4.

[54] Ossietzky, ". . . à la Bratianu," *WB*, June 22, 1926, p. 951.

[55] Ossietzky, "Gastspiele," *WB*, June 26, 1926, pp. 991–994.

[56] Helmut Gruber, "Willi Münzenberg's German Communist Propaganda Empire, 1921–1933," *The Journal of Modern History*, September 1966, p. 284.

[57] Letter to Bernhard Wiedehöft (Le Vésinet, France, April 19, 1926), *Ausgewählte Briefe*, 177.

[58] Babette Gross, *Willi Münzenberg* (Stuttgart, 1967), 174.

[59] *Ibid.*, 234 f.

[60] Ossietzky, "Opposition?" *WB*, February 1, 1927, pp. 161–164, and "Der Kieler Parteitag," *ibid.*, May 31, 1927, pp. 845–850; Theobald Tiger [Tucholsky], "Opposition! Opposition!" *ibid.*, February 8, 1927, p. 213. Also in *Gesammelte Werke*, II, 721–722; Kurt Hiller, "Konzentration Links," *WB*, February 15, 1927, pp. 248–252.

[61] Ossietzky, "Noskes Schatten," *WB*, March 29, 1927, pp. 479–481. Also in *Schriften*, I, 305–309.

[62] Ossietzky, "Stahlhelm ante portas," *WB*, May 3, 1927, p. 687.

Notes for Chapter XII (pp. 165–185)

[1] See Henry A. Turner, *Stresemann and the Politics of the Weimar Republic* (Princeton, N.J., 1963), 220 ff. Also, Halperin, 358.

[2] "Die Brandenburgische Stahlhelmkundgebung am 1. und 2. September 1928, im Fürstenwalde," quoted in Johannes Hohlfeld, ed., *Deutsche Reichsgeschichte in Dokumenten, 1894–1934* (Berlin, 1934), III, 82.

[3] Halperin, 366.

[4] Kurt Hiller, "Wahlkampfforderung der linken SPD," *WB*, May 1, 1928, pp. 663–668.

[5] Ossietzky, "Die Stunde der Sozialdemokratie," *WB*, June 5, 1928, 851–854, and "Die Bahn, die uns geführt Lassalle," *ibid.*, July 17, 1928, 77–80. The latter also in *Schriften*, I, 310–315.

[6] On the "armored cruiser" or "pocket battleship" controversy, see Wolfgang Wacker, *Der Bau des Panzerschiffes "A" und der Reichstag* (Tübingen, 1959). Also, Halperin, 365 f., and Eyck, II, 153 *et passim*.

[7] Ossietzky, "Volksentscheid," *WB*, September 11, 1928, pp. 387–289.

[8] Ossietzky, "Groeners beinahe legaler Putsch," *WB*, November 20, 1928, p. 761. Also in *Schriften*, 176.

[9] "Deutscher Friedenstag in Nürnberg," *Die Friedenswarte*, December, 1928, p. 376.

[10] Ossietzky, "Zörgiebel ist schuld," *WB*, May 7, 1929, pp. 691–694; "Abdankung, Herr Polizeipräsident," *ibid.*, May 14, 1929, p. 729–736; "Genosse Z," *ibid.*, December 24, 1929, pp. 929–930; "Genosse Z. konfisziert," *ibid.*, January 21, 1930, pp. 148–149. Well before the May Day events, Ossietzky had strongly attacked

Zörgiebel for his anti-Communist tactics: "Wankende Despotien," *ibid.*, June 12, 1928, pp. 889–890. A number of these articles were reprinted in *Schriften*, I, 365–386.

11 See Grossmann, *Ossietzky*, 225 ff., Koplin, 128 ff., and Frei, 127 ff.

12 Ossietzky, "Kommunistengesetz?" *WB*, May 21, 1929, pp. 767–774.

13 Kurt Hiller, "Rundfrage über Rotfront," *WB*, November 12, 1929, pp. 722–724.

14 Hiller, "Rede vor roten Studenten," *WB*, January 1, 1929, pp. 1–4.

15 Hiller, "Attentat auf die Rote Hilfe," *WB*, April 16, 1929, pp. 586–589.

16 Wilhelm Pieck, "Die Überparteilichkeit der Roten Hilfe," *WB*, April 30, 1929, pp. 661–663.

17 There is considerable literature on the Sixth Congress of the Comintern and its effect on the policy of the KPD. See, for instance, Flechtheim, 150 ff., and Siegfried Bahne, "Die Kommunistische Partei Deutschlands," in Matthias and Morsey, 656 f.

18 Hans Conrad, "Arbeiter und Intellektuelle," *WB*, October 15, 1929, p. 585.

19 Richard Scheringer, "Entscheidung und Gründe," *Die Linkskurve*, June 1931, p. 55, and Ossietzky, "Leutnant Scheringer und die KPD," *WB*, June 23, 1931, pp. 900–902.

20 Heinz Pol, "Thälmann macht Revolution," *WB*, August 28, 1928, pp. 310–314.

21 Jakob Links [Heinz Pol], "Thälmann hält Linie," *WB*, June 18, 1929, pp. 919–922.

22 On the Young Plan controversy see, among others, Julius Curtius, *Der Young-Plan: Entstellung und Wahrheit* (Stuttgart, 1950), and Eyck, II, 188 ff *et passim*.

23 Morus [Richard Lewinsohn], "Unterschreiber," *WB*, July 2, 1929, pp. 29–31, and "Sachlieferungen," *ibid.*, September 3, 1929, pp. 370–372.

24 Ossietzky, "Vor der Frühjahrsoffensive," *WB*, January 29, 1929, p. 161. See also "Sklaven-Export," *ibid.*, October 22, 1929, pp. 609–610.

25 Ossietzky, "Der Kampf um den Youngplan," *WB*, July 23, 1929, p. 117.

26 Bracher, 293.

27 See the fine study of Helga Timm, *Die deutsche Sozialpolitik und der Bruch der Grossen Koalition in März 1930* (Düsseldorf, 1952). See also Rudolf Morsey, "Die deutsche Zentrumspartei," in Matthias and Morsey, 291 ff, and Bracher, 297 ff. For a more favorable view of Brüning's role in the crisis, see Werner Conze, "Die deutschen Parteien in der Staatsverfassung vor 1933," in Matthias and Morsey, 20 f., but also the critical reappraisal of Brüning's position and of Conze's defense of Brüning in Klaus Epstein, "The End of the German Parties in 1933," *Journal of Central European Affairs*, April, 1963, pp. 55 *et passim*.

28 Conze, 21.

29 Eyck, II, 278 ff.

30 See Erich Matthias, "Die Sozialdemokratische Partei Deutschlands," in Matthias and Morsey, 119 ff.; Wolfgang M. von Manowski, "Carlo Mierendorff and the Iron Front" (unpublished master's thesis, New York: Columbia University, 1967), and Karl Rohe, *Das Reichsbanner Schwarz Rot Gold* (Düsseldorf, 1966), 392 ff.

31 Kurt Hiller, "Sozialistenbund," *WB*, July 14, 1931, pp. 47–53.

32 See Hunt, 221 ff.

33 Trotsky's writings on the German situation are all contained in *Écrits, 1928–1940* (Paris, 1955–1959), III, 23–401. Written between September 1930 and June 1933, they number a total of sixteen articles. See, especially, "Le tournant de l'Internationale Communiste et la situation en Allemagne" (September 1930), 23–45; "Contre le national-socialisme: Les leçons du plébiscite 'rouge'" (August 1931), 59–84; "La clef de la situation internationale est en Allemagne" (Novem-

ber 1931), 85–105; "Et maintenant?" (January 1932), 107–230, "La seule voie" (September 1932), 259–319. On Trotsky's followers in Weimar Germany, see Siegfried Bahne, "Der Trotzkismus in Deutschland, 1931–1933: Ein Beitrag zur Geschichte der KPD und der Komintern" (unpublished Ph.D. dissertation, University of Heidelberg, 1958).

³⁴ See, for instance, K. L. Gerstorff [Fritz Sternberg], "Die Chancen des deutschen Fascismus," *WB*, August 26, and September 2, 1930, pp. 296–301 and 340–344; "Legaler Fascismus," *ibid.*, January 27, 1931, pp. 119–123; "Einheitsfront und Parteiapparat," *ibid.*, February 10, 1931, pp. 198–201; "Die Krisis der SPD," *ibid.*, April 14, 1931, pp. 522–525; "Ferdinand Fried und 'Die Tat,'" *ibid.*, May 26, 1931, pp. 751–756; "Das Toleranzedikt von Leipzig," *ibid.*, June 9, 1931, pp. 822–827; "Jugend, Staat und S.P.D." *ibid.*, June 23, 1931, pp. 903–906; "SPD gespalten!," *ibid.*, October 6, 1931, pp. 505–508, and "Illusionen über Hitler," *ibid.*, December 29, 1931, pp. 950–954.

³⁵ Trotsky, "Le tournant," *Écrits, 1928–1940*, III, 27.

³⁶ Trotsky, "Et maintenant?" *ibid.*, III, 228–230.

³⁷ Ossietzky, "Trotzki spricht aus Prinkipo," *WB*, December 22, 1931, pp. 911–913.

³⁸ Trotsky, "Diktatur Brüning," *WB*, March 1, 1932, pp. 319–326.

³⁹ Trotsky, "Das deutsche Rätsel," *WB*, November 8, 1932, pp. 673–678.

⁴⁰ See, for instance, Kurt Hiller, "Ist denn das in Deutschland unmöglich?" *WB*, September 10, 1929, pp. 386–389.

⁴¹ Besides Sternberg's above-mentioned articles, see Kurt Hiller, "Der Sprung ins Helle," *WB*, December 30, 1930, pp. 977–981; Ossietzky, "Wer gegen wen?" *ibid.*, November 24, 1931, pp. 767–770; and "Eiserne Front," *ibid.*, January 12, 1932, pp. 41–43. Also Erich Mühsam, "Aktive Abwehr," *ibid.*, December 15, 1931, pp. 880–881, and Wilhelm Stefan, "Antifaschistische Agitation auf dem Holzweg," *ibid.*, July 19, 1932, pp. 80–83.

⁴² Ossietzky, "Remarque-Film," *WB*, December 16, 1930, p. 891. Also in *Schriften*, II, 13.

⁴³ See Flechtheim, 175 f.

⁴⁴ Trotsky, "Contre le national-socialisme," *Écrits*, III, 59–84.

⁴⁵ Ossietzky, "Stillhalten und mitsingen: Kommunisten und Volksentscheid," *WB*, July 28, 1931, pp. 119–121, and "Volksentscheid," *ibid.*, August 11, 1931, pp. 199–201.

⁴⁶ Ossietzky, "Trotzkis Tragödie," *WB*, December 4, 1928, pp. 841–844.

⁴⁷ Jakob Links [Heinz Pol], "Thälmann hält Linie," *WB*, June 18, 1929, pp. 919–922.

⁴⁸ Ossietzky, "Trotzki spricht aus Prinkipo," *WB*, December 22, 1931, pp. 911–913.

⁴⁹ K. L. Gerstorff [Fritz Sternberg], "SPD gespalten!" *WB*, October 6, 1931, pp. 504–508.

⁵⁰ Trotsky, "La tragédie du prolétariat allemand," *Écrits*, III, 375–387.

⁵¹ See, for instance, "Antworten," February 12, 1929, p. 276, and Kurt Hiller, "Stalin und Trotzki," *ibid.*, November 29, 1932, pp. 786–791.

⁵² See, for instance, Hans Siemsen, "GPU," *WB*, May 19 and 26, 1931, pp. 718–722, and 758–763; Ossietzky, "Sowjet-Justiz," *ibid.*, December 2, 1930, pp. 811–812, and "Menschewiken," *ibid.*, March 10, 1931, pp. 348–350.

⁵³ Arnold Zweig, "Die Moskauer Hinrichtungen," *WB*, November 11, 1930, pp. 707–709.

⁵⁴ Ossietzky, "Gibt es noch eine Opposition?" *WB*, January 7, 1930, p. 40.

⁵⁵ Ossietzky, "Vor Sonnenaufgang," *WB*, September 16, 1930, p. 425.

⁵⁶ For an early example of the "disappearance theory," see Heinz Pol, "Das Ende der völkischen Bewegung," *WB*, March 17, 1925, pp. 386–387. For the period between 1930 and 1933, see, among others, Hanns-Erich Kaminski, "Überall

Linksruck," *ibid.*, October 4, 1932, pp. 489–491; Ossietzky, "Wintermärchen," *ibid.*, January 3, 1933, pp. 1–6, and [Anonymous], "Die grösste Firma," *ibid.*, January 17, 1933, pp. 91–94.

[57] Ossietzky, "Brutus schläft," *WB*, February 3, 1931, p. 157.

[58] Peter Panter [Tucholsky], "Schnipsel," *WB*, March 8, 1932, p. 378. Also in *Gesammelte Werke*, III, 1029.

[59] Quietus, "Die Zukunft des Nationalsozialismus," *WB*, September 23, 1930, pp. 477–480.

[60] Hanns-Erich Kaminski, "Die Rechte soll regieren," *WB*, September 23, 1930, pp. 470–473.

[61] Ossietzky, "Wir müssen durch," *WB*, June 16, 1931, p. 866.

[62] Ernst Toller, "Reichskanzler Hitler," *WB*, October 7, 1930, p. 538.

[63] *Ibid.*, 539.

[64] Ossietzky, "Einer von der Infanterie," *WB*, June 3, 1930, pp. 819–821.

[65] Ossietzky, "Brüning darf nicht bleiben," *WB*, September 23, 1930, p. 465. Pater Filucius is the main character of one of the cartoon books by the German satirist-artist Wilhelm Busch; the pater is shown as a hypocritical Jesuit.

[66] See Alfred Milatz, "Das Ende der Parteien im Spiegel der Wahlen 1930 bis 1933," in Matthias and Morsey, 764.

[67] Trotsky, "Et maintenant?" (January 1932), *Écrits*, III, 229.

[68] Kurt Hiller, "Der Präsident," *WB*, February 9, 1932, pp. 194–198. Reprinted in *Koepfe und Troepfe*, pp. 29–35.

[69] Letter to Adolf Wolffsky, Berlin (February 6, 1932), *Kurt Tucholsky Archiv* (Rottach-Egern/Obb.).

[70] Ossietzky, "Das Hindenburg-Syndikat," *WB*, February 2, 1932, pp. 151–153.

[71] Ossietzky, "Gang eins," *WB*, March 1, 1932, p. 315. Also in *Schriften*, II, 41.

[72] Ossietzky, "Duesterbergs düstere Rolle," *WB*, March 8, 1932, p. 353.

[73] Ossietzky, "Wer hat gesiegt?" *WB*, March 15, 1932, p. 390.

[74] K. L. Gerstorff [Fritz Sternberg], "Die Schlüsselstellung der KPD," *WB*, May 24, 1932, pp. 767–771.

[75] Kurt Hiller, "Zur Lage: Von N. Lenin," *WB*, May 24, 1932, pp. 771–774.

[76] Ossietzky, "Ein runder Tisch wartet," *WB*, May 3, 1932, p. 652. Also in *Schriften*, I, 355.

[77] *Ibid.*

Notes for Chapter XIII (pp. 189–198)

[1] Heinz Jäger [Walter Kreiser], "Windiges aus der deutschen Luftfahrt," *WB*, March 12, 1929, pp. 402–407.

[2] "Reich Finds Writer Betrayed Secrets," *The New York Times*, November 24, 1931, 8:2. In 1930, Kreiser spent eight months in Philadelphia working for the Pennsylvania Aircraft Syndicate.

[3] Jäger, *WB*, March 12, 1929, p. 407.

[4] Grossmann, *Ossietzky*, 261 ff, discusses the trial in detail. See also Walther Karsch, "Carl von Ossietzky," *Aufbau*, November, 1945, pp. 220 ff, Lunke, 25 ff, and Koplin, 184 ff.

[5] Ossietzky, "Der Prozess der Offiziere," *WB*, October 1, 1930, p. 501.

[6] André Pironneau, "Les révélations du procès de Leipzig," *L'écho de Paris*, February 23, 1932.

[7] Cited by Pironneau, *L'écho de Paris*, February 25, 1932.

[8] From a special note to the reader, attached to the *Weltbühne*, November 24, 1931.

[9] Groener in the Reichstag on March 19, 1931. *Stenographische Berichte der*

Verhandlungen des Reichstags: V. Wahlperiode, 1930, Vol. 445 (Berlin, 1931), 1727.

[10] Ossietzky, "Rechenschaft," *WB,* May 10, 1932, p. 689. For a transcript of Alsberg's personal memorandum to the Reich Ministry of Justice on the legal aspects of the case (February 13, 1932), see "Eingabe an den Herrn Justizminister," *WB,* May 17, 1932, pp. 736–740.

[11] Felix Burger [Kurt Grossmann] and Kurt Singer, *Carl von Ossietzky,* 34.

[12] See Walther Karsch, "33,000 für Ossietzky," *WB,* July 5, 1932, p. 11.

[13] See "Fragen und Meinungen," *WB,* December 1, 1931, p. 811, and "Weltecho des Leipziger Prozesses," *ibid.,* December 15, 1931, p. 884.

[14] *Berliner Tageblatt,* November 13, 1931. See also Koplin, 228.

[15] Quoted in *Berliner Tageblatt,* November 23, 1931, and December 1, 1931.

[16] *Interpellation Dr. Breitscheid und Genossen,* November 26, 1931. *Anlage Nr. 1240 zu den Stenographischen Berichten der Verhandlungen des Reichstags, V. Wahlperiode, 1930,* Vol. 451 (Berlin, 1932). See also Ossietzky, "Der Weltbühnen-Prozess," *WB,* December 1, 1931, pp. 809–810.

[17] Thomas Mann, "Brief an Rechtsanwalt Dr. Apfel" (January 10, 1932), *Gesammelte Werke,* XII, 670. Also in *WB,* May 17, 1932, pp. 741–742.

[18] *Hamburger Echo,* March 2, 1932, quoted in *WB,* March 8, 1932, p. 364.

[19] *Deutsche Allgemeine Zeitung* (Berlin), November 23, 1931.

[20] For a complete list of the signatories, see "Scheringer-Komitee," *WB,* April 12, 1932, p. 577.

[21] Ossietzky, "Der Weltbühnen-Prozess," *WB,* December 1, 1931, pp. 810 f.

[22] Groener, "Staatsverleumdung," *Deutsche Allgemeine Zeitung,* November 29, 1931.

[23] Ossietzky, "Offener Brief an Reichswehrminister Groener," *WB,* December 8, 1931, p. 839. Also in *Schriften,* II, 201–208.

[24] *WB,* December 8, 1931, p. 843.

[25] Ossietzky, "Rechenschaft," *WB,* May 10, 1932, pp. 689–709. Reprinted in *WB,* October 19, 1949. Special issue on Ossietzky. Also in *Schriften,* II, 209–237.

[26] Ossietzky, *WB,* May 10, 1932, p. 690.

[27] *Ibid.,* 691.

[28] *Ibid.,* 701.

[29] *Ibid.,* 706.

[30] *Ibid.,* 707. For a recent analysis of the pivotal role played by the Reichswehr in the politics of this era, see Thilo Vogelsang, *Reichswehr, Staat und NSDAP: Beiträge zur deutschen Geschichte, 1930–1932* (Stuttgart, 1962).

[31] Ossietzky, *WB,* May 10, 1932, p. 709.

[32] Alfred Polgar, "Ossietzky geht ins Gefängnis," *WB,* May 17, 1932, 742–744. Reprinted in *WB,* October 19, 1949. Special issue on Ossietzky.

Notes for Chapter XIV (*pp. 199–215*)

[1] See Hugo von Hofmannsthal, *Das Schrifttum als geistiger Raum der Nation* (Munich, 1927). For a masterly analysis of Hofmannsthal's address on the "legion of seekers," see Klemperer, 9 f.

[2] Hermann Rauschning, *The Conservative Revolution* (New York, 1941).

[3] For instance, Armin Mohler, *Die konservative Revolution in Deutschland, 1918–1932* (Stuttgart, 1950). It contains, among others, a bibliography of 6½ pages on the conservative revolution.

[4] *Ibid.,* 88 f.

[5] Stern, *The Politics of Cultural Despair,* pp. xvi and xviii.

[6] Ferdinand Fried [Friedrich Zimmermann], *Das Ende des Kapitalismus* (Jena, 1931), pp. 6 *et passim.*

[7] See, for instance, Hans Zehrer, "Achtung, junge Front! Draussenbleiben," *Die Tat*, April 1929, pp. 25–40, and "Rechts oder links?" *ibid.*, October 1931, pp. 505–559.

[8] K. L. Gerstorff [Fritz Sternberg], "Ferdinand Fried und 'Die Tat,'" *WB*, May 26, 1931, pp. 751–756.

[9] Rudolf Arnheim, "Lieber Herr von Ossietzky," *WB*, October 4, 1932, p. 519.

[10] Wilhelm Stapel, "Mein Kampf mit der NSDAP" (unpublished manuscript, n.d.; in the literary bequest of Wilhelm Stapel in Hamburg).

[11] Letter to Walter Hasenclever in Zurich (April, 1933). Tucholsky, *Ausgewählte Briefe*, 254.

[12] Ossietzky, "Die Antisemiten," *WB*, July 19, 1932, pp. 88–97. Also in *Schriften*, II, 275–289. What Ossietzky had particularly in mind was Blüher's *Erhebung gegen die christlichen Güter* (Hamburg, 1931). Ossietzky's commentary on the anti-Semitism of right-wing intellectuals was printed under his own name in the *Weltbühne*.

[13] "Die Antisemiten," *WB*, 91 ff.

[14] Thomas Murner [Ossietzky], "Otto Strassers 'deutscher Sozialismus,'" *WB*, August 16, 1932, pp. 230–234.

[15] *Ibid.*, 231.

[16] Ernst Jünger, *Der Arbeiter: Herrschaft und Gestalt* (Hamburg, 1932). See Thomas Murner [Ossietzky], "Der Jünger," *WB*, October 18, 1932, pp. 577–578.

[17] Thomas Murner [Ossietzky], "Zehrer und Fried," *WB*, November 22, 1932, pp. 771–775.

[18] *Ibid.*, 772.

[19] Stern, *The Politics of Cultural Despair*, 298.

[20] Ignaz Wrobel [Tucholsky], "Der bewachte Kriegschauplatz," *WB*, August 4, 1931, p. 191. Also in *Gesammelte Werke*, III, 905.

[21] Letters to Mary Gerold-Tucholsky (March 29 and May 13, 1932), Tucholsky, *Ausgewählte Briefe*, 494 f. and 497.

[22] See Ludwig Quidde, "Die beleidigte Reichswehr," *WB*, March 8, 1932, pp. 362–364; also, "Ein guter Tag für die Justiz," *ibid.*, July 5, 1932, pp. 5–8, and Grossmann, *Ossietzky*, 314 ff.

[23] See Walther Karsch, "Eine verworfene Revision," *WB*, November 22, 1932, pp. 776–777.

[23a] Theobald Tiger [Tucholsky], "Europa," *WB*, January 19, 1932, p. 74. English translation by Karl F. Ross in *What If —?*, 217.

[24] Tucholsky, "General-Quittung," *WB*, May 17, 1932, p. 736. Reprinted in the *Weltbühne*, October 19, 1949. Special issue on Ossietzky.

[25] For a dramatic account of Tucholsky's withdrawal from writing, see Schulz, 125 ff.

[26] Hanns-Erich Kaminski, "Militärdiktatur," *WB*, May 17, 1932, p. 725.

[27] Kaminski, "Brüning," *WB*, June 7, 1932, p. 846.

[28] K. L. Gerstorff [Sternberg], "Eiserne rote Front," *WB*, July 5, 1932, pp. 14–17.

[29] Gerstorff, "Die Zahlen vom 31. Juli," *WB*, August 9, 1932, pp. 199–201.

[30] Gerstorff, "Spaltungstendenzen bei den Nazis," *WB*, September 13, 1932, pp. 381–385.

[31] Hanns-Erich Kaminski, "Überall Linksruck," *WB*, October 4, 1932, pp. 489–490.

[32] See, for instance, Arthur Rosenberg, *A History of the German Republic*, trans. Ian F. D. Morrow and L. Marie Sieveking (London, 1936), 313.

[33] Kurt Hiller, "Über die Ursachen des nationalsozialistischen Erfolges," *WB*, August 23 and 30, 1932, pp. 270–274, and 309–314.

[34] *Ibid.*, 271.

[35] See Bracher, 645 ff.

[36] *Ibid.*, 658 ff, and Schwarz, 188.

[37] Bracher, 678.

[38] *Ibid.*, 682 ff.

[39] Zehrer, "An der Wende," *Die Tat*, September, 1932, p. 447.

[40] See "Der Weg der Tat," *Die Tat*, September, 1932, pp. 517–519.

[41] See Rolf Boelcke, "Die Spaltung des Nationalsozialismus," *Die Tat*, August, 1930, pp. 357–367, and Boelke [*sic*], "Die Krise der Nationalsozialisten," *Die Tat*, May 1931, pp. 127–132. For an attempt on the part of the *Tat* to couple National Socialists with the socialist trade unions, see Hans Zehrer, "Revolution oder Restauration," *Die Tat*, August 1932, pp. 353–393.

[42] Hanns-Erich Kaminski, "Der Säbel," *WB*, December 13, 1932, pp. 851–854.

[43] Kaminski, "Marschroute der Linken," *WB*, November 15, 1932, pp. 705–707.

[44] See Matthias in Matthias and Morsey, 176 f. For an expression of Social Democratic hostility toward Schleicher, see Otto Braun, *Von Weimar zu Hitler* (New York, 1940), 431 ff.

[45] See *Stenographische Berichte der Verhandlungen des Reichstags: VII. Wahlperiode, 1932.* Vol. 455. (Berlin, 1933), 112 ff.

[46] See *Mündlicher Bericht des 13. Ausschusses (Rechtspflege) über die von Dr. Breitscheid . . . Dr. Frick . . . Torgler . . . beantragten Gesetzentwürfe über Straffreiheit*, December 9, 1932. *Anlage Nr. 182 zu den Stenographischen Berichten der Verhandlungen des Reichstags, VII. Wahlperiode.* Vol. 455 (Berlin, 1933).

[47] See *B. Z. am Mittag* (December 21, 1932).

[48] Cited by Ossietzky in "*Rückkehr*," *WB*, December 27, 1932, p. 926.

[49] Walter Mehring, "Carl von Ossietzky," *Deutsche Rundschau*, October 1959, p. 902.

[50] Bracher, 686.

[51] *Ibid.*, 691.

[52] Ossietzky, "Der Flaschenteufel," *WB*, January 10, 1933, pp. 41–44.

[53] "Die grösste Firma," *WB*, January 17, 1933, p. 91.

[54] Ossietzky, "Wintermärchen," *WB*, January 3, 1933, pp. 1–6.

[55] *Ibid.*, 4.

[56] Hans Joachim Schoeps, "Das letzte Vierteljahr der Weimarer Republik im Zeitschriftenecho," *Geschichte in Wissenschaft und Unterricht*, August 1959, pp. 470 ff.

[57] See, for instance, Schwarz, 191.

[58] Hellmut von Gerlach, "Habebald und Eileleute," *WB*, February 7, 1933, pp. 197–198.

[59] Ossietzky, "Deutschland wartet," *WB*, February 14, 1933, pp. 233–236.

[60] Hanns-Erich Kaminski, "Nüchterne Betrachtung," *WB*, February 7, 1933, pp. 199–201.

[61] Kaminski, "Die neue Luft," *WB*, February 21, 1933, p. 265.

[62] Mehring, *Deutsche Rundschau*, October 1959, p. 903.

[63] Ossietzky, "Richard Wagner," *WB*, February 21, 1933, pp. 282–286, and "Herr Walter Bloem," *ibid.*, February 28, 1933, pp. 316–321.

[64] Kurt Hiller, "Heroismus und Pazifismus," *WB*, March 7, 1933, p. 350.

[65] Hiller, *Konkret*, March 1962, p. 7.

Notes for Epilogue (*pp. 216–221*)

[1] Willi Schlamm, "Einigung oder Untergang," *Die Wiener Weltbühne*, February 9, 1933, p. 157. Hereafter to be called *Wiener WB*.

[2] See, especially, Schlamm, "Fünf Minuten nach Zwölf," *Wiener WB*, February 2, 1933, pp. 125–126, and "Inventur," *ibid.*, March 23, 1933, pp. 345–348.

[3] *Resolution des Exekutivkomitees der Kommunistischen Internationale* (April 1, 1933). Cited by Bahne in Matthias and Morsey, 728.

[4] Paul Krey, "Sätze, die beurlaubt wurden," *Wiener WB*, March 30, 1933, p. 407.

[5] Leon Trotsky, "Porträt des Nationalsozialismus," *Die Neue Weltbühne*, July 13, 1933, p. 862. Hereafter to be called *NWB*. See also "Qu'est-ce que le national-socialisme?" *Écrits*, III, 398.

[6] Trotsky, "Die deutsche Katastrophe," *NWB*, June 8, 1933, p. 699. This article, written on May 28, 1933, at Prinkipo is not in *Écrits*.

[7] *Ibid.*, 702–703.

[8] See "Antworten," *NWB*, March 15, 1934, p. 347, and "Antworten," *ibid.*, March 22, 1934, p. 380. Also, Kurt Hiller, "Aufstieg, Glanz und Verfall der Weltbühne," *Konkret*, June 1962, p. 17.

[9] Information obtained from Heinz Pol, one of the owners of the *Neue Weltbühne* between 1934 and 1936. New York City, September 25, 1967.

[10] Hiller, *Konkret*, June 1962, p. 17, and July 1962, p. 20.

[11] See Louis Fischer's savage criticism of Trotsky in "Trotzkis Tragödie," *NWB*, April 12, 1934, pp. 449–454.

[12] Hermann Budzislawski, "Wer stürzt Hitler?" *NWB*, July 19, 1934, p. 895.

[13] On Social Democracy in exile, see Lewis J. Edinger, *German Exile Politics* (Berkeley and Los Angeles, 1956).

[14] Siegfried Aufhäuser, "Hauptfeind Fascismus," *NWB*, August 30, 1934, pp. 1088–1093. See also "Dennoch Einheitsfront," *NWB*, November 1, 1934, pp. 1383–1389.

[15] Walter [Walter Ulbricht], "Für die Aktionseinheit," *NWB*, October 25, 1934, p. 1354.

[16] Edinger, 145 ff.

[17] See, for instance, Max Seydewitz, "Die Illegalen entscheiden," *NWB*, December 19, 1935, pp. 1608–1611, and Walter [Ulbricht], "Die Gebot der Stunde," *ibid.*, November 7, 1935, pp. 1410–1414.

[18] Hermann Budzislawski, "Moskauer Abkommen," *NWB*, August 31, 1939, pp. 1081–1089.

[19] See *Neue Zürcher Zeitung*, January 26, 1936; Leopold Schwarzschild, "Literatur," *Das Neue Tage-Buch*, February 15, 1936, pp. 154–157, and "Briefe," *ibid.*, February 29, 1936, p. 215. For a list of the exiled German writers, containing 250 names, see Richard Drews and Alfred Kantorowicz, eds., *Verboten und verbrannt* (Berlin, 1947), 209 ff.

[20] On German exile literature in general, see Walter A. Berendsohn, *Die humanistische Front* (Zurich, 1946), and Wilhelm Sternfeld and Eva Tiedemann, eds., *Deutsche Exil-Literatur, 1933–1945* (Heidelberg, 1962) which contains at least 1500 names.

[21] Kurt Hiller, "Schutzhäftling 231," *NWB*, December 6, 1934, pp. 1547–1553 *et passim*. See, especially, *NWB*, January 17, 1935, p. 77.

[22] See Drews and Kantorowicz, 6.

[23] On Ossietzky's life and death under Hitler, and on the campaign for the Nobel Peace Prize, see the detailed account of Grossmann, *Ossietzky*, 335 ff, with several Gestapo documents on Ossietzky and other supporting material. See also Frei, 208 ff; Hilde Walter and Walther Kiaulehn, "Der Preis für einen Friedenspreis," *Deutsche Rundschau*, February 1961, pp. 136–147; Heinrich Mann, "Der Dulder Ossietzky," *WB*, May 4, 1948, pp. 449–456; "Im KZ Esterwegen," *WB*, October 19, 1949, pp. 29–30 (special issue on Ossietzky); "Dokumente der Gestapo," *WB*, October 19, 1949, pp. 34–40; Rolf Helm, "Der Betrug an Carl v. Ossietzky," *WB*, May 3 and 17, 1950, pp. 521–524 and 604–609: a

description of the shady dealings of Dr. Kurt Wannow, a Berlin lawyer who handled the transfer into Germany of the approximately 100,000 RM which constituted Ossietzky's Nobel Prize award. Wannow allegedly swindled Ossietzky and his family; they received very little of the money. Wannow was arrested by the Gestapo in June 1937 and sentenced to two years in prison for currency manipulation and—ironically—for perfidy toward Ossietzky. Of the flood of contemporary pamphlet literature, see especially, Felix Burger [Kurt R. Grossmann] and Kurt Singer, *Carl von Ossietzky* (1937) and Berthold Jacob, *Weltbürger Ossietzky* (1937).

Notes for Conclusion (pp. 222–228)

[1] Sontheimer, *Antidemokratisches Denken in der Weimarer Republik*, 395.

[2] Golo Mann, *Deutsche Geschichte*, 727.

[3] Golo Mann, *Encounter*, June 1955, p. 47.

[4] Gordon A. Craig, "Engagement and Neutrality in Weimar Germany," in Walter Laqueur and George L. Mosse, eds., *Literature and Politics in the Twentieth Century* (New York, 1967), 55.

[5] See, for instance, Habedank, 176 ff.

BIBLIOGRAPHY

BIBLIOGRAPHY

This list contains sources which seem particularly useful for a further study of Weimar Germany's left-wing intellectuals. Some of these have already been cited in the footnotes.

PERIODICALS

Communist Periodicals

Die Aktion (Berlin). Weekly (irregular). 1911–1932. Ed. Franz Pfemfert. ("Revolutionary communist.")
Berlin am Morgen (Berlin). Daily. 1929–1933. Ed. Bruno Frei [Benedikt Freistadt]. (Münzenberg press.)
Die Linkskurve (Berlin). Monthly. 1929–1932. Eds. Johannes R. Becher *et al.*
Der Rote Aufbau (Berlin). Monthly. 1928–1932. (Münzenberg press.)
Die Welt am Abend (Berlin). Daily. 1922–1933. Ed. Paul Friedländer. (Münzenberg press.)

Socialist Periodicals

Die Freiheit (Berlin). Daily. 1918–1923. Ed. Rudolf Hilferding. (Independent Socialist.)
Die Gesellschaft (Berlin). Monthly. 1924–1933. Ed. Rudolf Hilferding.
ISK. Mitteilungsblatt des Internationalen Sozialistischen Kampf-Bundes (Göttingen; later Berlin). 1926–1932. Ed. Willi Eichler. (Organ of the Nelson League.)
Klassenkampf (until 1928: *Sozialistische Politik und Wirtschaft*). Bi-weekly. 1923–1933. Eds. Paul Levi (till 1930), Kurt Rosenfeld, Max Seydewitz, Heinrich Ströbel, Max Adler. (Left-wing Social Democrat.)
Neue Blätter für den Sozialismus (Potsdam). Monthly. 1930–1933. Eds. Eduard Heinemann, Fritz Klatt, Paul Tillich. (Christian socialist.)
Sächsisches Volksblatt (Zwickau). Daily. Ed. Max Seydewitz. (Left-wing Social Democrat.)

321

Sozialistische Monatshefte (Berlin). Monthly. 1897–1933. Ed. Joseph Bloch.

Radical Democratic Periodicals

8 Uhr-Abendblatt (formerly: *Nationalzeitung*, Berlin). Daily. 1910–1933. Ed. Victor Hahn.
Das Forum (Munich; later Berlin). Monthly. 1914–1915; 1918–1924. Ed. Wilhelm Herzog.
Montag Morgen (Berlin). Weekly. 1923–? Ed. Stefan Grossmann.
Das Tage-Buch (Berlin). Weekly. 1920–1933. Eds. Stefan Grossmann, Leopold Schwarzschild, and Carl von Ossietzky (1924–1926).
Die Welt am Montag (Berlin). Weekly. 1895–1933. Ed. Hellmut von Gerlach.
Die Weltbühne (until 1918: *Die Schaubühne*, Berlin). Weekly. 1905–1933. Eds. Siegfried Jacobsohn (till 1926); Kurt Tucholsky (1926–1927); Carl von Ossietzky (1927–1933); Walther Karsch (1933).
Das Ziel (Leipzig and Munich). Yearly. 1915–1920. Ed. Kurt Hiller (Activist, Logocratic.)

Pacifist Periodicals

Das andere Deutschland (until 1925: *Der Pazifist*, Hagen, Westphalia). Weekly. 1920–1933. Ed. Friedrich Küster. (Revolutionary pacifist.)
Die Friedenswarte (Berlin). Monthly. 1899–? Eds. Alfred Fried (till 1921); Hans Wehberg (1921–?).
Die Menschheit (Bern; later Wiesbaden). 1914–1931. Eds. Friedrich Wilhelm Foerster and Fritz Röttcher. (Changed in 1930 to *Chronik der Menschheit.*)
Die Menschenrechte (Berlin). Monthly. 1926–1933. Ed. Kurt R. Grossmann. (Organ of the German League for Human Rights.)
Der Völkerfriede (Esslingen; later Leipzig). Monthly. 1915–1919. Ed. Carl von Ossietzky (1919). (Organ of the German Peace League.)
Die weissen Blätter (Leipzig; Bern; Berlin). Monthly. 1913–1920. Ed. René Schickele.

Democratic Periodicals

Berliner Tageblatt (Berlin: Mosse Verlag). Daily. 1871–1939. Ed. Theodor Wolff.
Berliner Volks-Zeitung (Berlin). Daily. 1853–1939. Ed. Otto Nuschke.
Deutsche Republik (Frankfurt/M.). Weekly. 1926–1933. Eds. Joseph Wirth and Heinrich Teipel.
Der Deutsche Volkswirt (Berlin). Weekly. 1926–1943. Ed. Gustav Stolper.
März (Munich). Weekly. 1907–1917. Eds. Ludwig Thoma, Hermann Hesse, Kurt Aram (till 1913); Wilhelm Herzog and Theodor Heuss (1913–1917).

Liberal-Republican Periodicals

Frankfurter Zeitung (Frankfurt/M.). Daily. 1856 to present. (After World War II known as *Frankfurter Allgemeine Zeitung.*) Ed. H. Simon *et al.*
Die Hilfe (Berlin). Bi-weekly. 1895–1943. Eds. Friedrich Naumann (till

1919); Anton Erkelenz and Gertrud Bäumer (1919–1933); Theodor Heuss *et al.* (1933–1943).
Die Neue Rundschau (Berlin: S. Fischer Verlag). Monthly. 1890–1942; 1945 to present. Ed. Rudolf Kayser.
Vossische Zeitung (originally: *Berlinische privilegierte Zeitung*, Berlin). Daily. 1704–1934. Eds. Georg Bernhard (1920–1929); Julius Elbau (1929–1933).

Confessional Periodicals
Hochland (Munich). Monthly. 1903–1941; 1946 to present. Ed. Karl Muth. (Catholic.)
Stimmen der Zeit (Freiburg). Monthly. 1871–1935; 1936–1941; 1946 to present. Ed. Josef Kreitmaier. (Society of Jesus.)
Zeitwende (today: *Die neue Furche*). 1924–1941; 1946 to present. Eds. Tim Klein, Otto Gründler, and Friedrich Langenfass. (Lutheran.)

Conservative Periodicals
Die Kunstwart (Munich). Monthly. 1887–1932. Eds. Ferdinand Avenarius (1887–1923); Wolfgang Schumann (1923–1926); Hermann Rinn (1926–1932).
Preussische Jahrbücher (Berlin). Monthly. 1858–1935. Eds. Hans Delbrück (till 1920); Walter Schotte, Walter Heynen and Emil Daniels (1920–1935).
Süddeutsche Monatshefte (Munich). Monthly. 1904–1936. Ed. P. N. Cossmann.
Der Türmer (Berlin). Monthly. 1898–1943. Eds. Jeannot E. Freiherr von Grotthuss (till 1919); Friedrich Lienhard (1920–1928); K. A. Walther (1928–?).

Conservative Revolutionary, Young Conservative, etc., Periodicals
Deutsche Rundschau (Berlin). Monthly. 1874–1942; 1946 to present. Ed. Rudolf Pechel.
Deutsches Volkstum (Hamburg). Monthly. 1898–1941. Eds. Wilhelm Stapel and A. E. Günther.
Das Gewissen (Berlin). Weekly. 1919–? Eds. Moeller van den Bruck (till 1925) and Heinrich Freiherr von Gleichen. (Organ of the "June Club.")
Die Tat (Jena). Monthly. 1909–1938. Eds. Eugen Diederichs (till 1927); Adam Kuckhoff (1927–1928); Hans Zehrer (1928–1933).
Widerstand (Dresden). 1926–1934. Eds. Ernst Niekisch and August Winnig. (National Bolshevist.)

National Socialist Periodicals
Der Reichswart. Weekly. 1920–?. Ed. Count Ernst von Reventlow.

Other Periodicals
Die Fackel (Vienna). Irregular. 1899–1936. Ed. Karl Kraus.
Die Zukunft (Berlin). Weekly. 1892–1922. Eds. Maximilian Harden and Max Krell (the latter after 1921).

Books and Articles

Abrams, Irwin. "Bertha von Suttner and the Nobel Peace Prize," *Journal of Central European Affairs*, October 1962, pp. 286–307.

Adling, Wilfried, *et al.*, eds. *Lexikon sozialistischer deutscher Literatur von den Anfängen bis 1945: Monographisch-biographische Darstellungen.* Halle: VEB Verlag Sprache und Literatur, 1963.

Acht Jahre politische Justiz: Das Zuchthaus—die politischen Rechte. Berlin: Deutsche Liga für Menschenrechte, 1927.

Anderson, Evelyn. *Hammer or Anvil: The Story of the German Working-Class Movement.* London: Victor Gollancz, 1945.

Angress, Werner T. "Pegasus and Insurrection: *Die Linkskurve* and Its Heritage," *Central European History*, March 1968, pp. 35–55.

———. *Stillborn Revolution: The Communist Bid for Power in Germany, 1921–1923.* Princeton, N.J.: Princeton University Press, 1963.

Apfel, Alfred. *Behind the Scenes of German Justice: Reminiscences of a German Barrister, 1882–1933.* London: John Lane, 1935.

Assmus, Erhard. "Die publizistische Diskussion um den Militarismus, 1850–1950." Unpublished Ph.D. Dissertation, University of Erlangen, 1951.

Bab, Julius. *Das Theater der Gegenwart.* Leipzig: J. J. Weber, 1928.

———. *Die deutsche Kriegslyrik 1914–1918: Eine kritische Bibliographie.* Stettin: Norddeutscher Verlag, 1920.

Barkeley, Richard. *Die deutsche Friedensbewegung, 1870–1933.* Hamburg: Hammerich und Lesser, 1948.

Behr, Hermann. *Die goldenen zwanziger Jahre: Das fesselnde Panorama einer entfesselten Zeit.* Hamburg: Hammerich und Lesser, 1964.

Benda, Julien. *The Betrayal of the Intellectuals.* Trans. Richard Aldington. Introduction by Herbert Read. Boston: Beacon Press, 1955.

Berendsohn, Walter A. *Die humanistische Front: Einführung in die deutsche Emigranten-Literatur. I. Teil: von 1933 bis zum Kriegsausbruch.* Zurich: Europa Verlag, 1946.

Borkenau, Franz. *The Communist International.* London: Faber and Faber, 1938.

Bracher, Karl D. *Die Auflösung der Weimarer Republik.* Villingen, Schwarzwald: Ring Verlag, 1960.

———. "Die Weimarer Republik im Spiegel der Memoiren-Literatur," *Politische Literatur*, January 1953, pp. 339–350.

Braun, Otto. *Von Weimar zu Hitler.* 2d ed. New York: Europa Verlag, 1940.

Brunzel, H. P. "Die Tat, 1918–1933." Unpublished Ph.D. Dissertation, University of Bonn, 1952.

Buber-Neumann, Margarete. *Von Potsdam nach Moskau: Stationen eines Irrweges.* Stuttgart: Deutsche Verlags-Anstalt, 1957.

Buchheim, Karl. *Leidensgeschichte des zivilen Geistes oder die Demokratie in Deutschland.* Munich: Kösel-Verlag, 1951.

Buchrucker, Bruno. *Im Schatten Seeckts: Die Geschichte der "Schwarzen Reichswehr."* Berlin: Kampf-Verlag, 1928.

Carr, H. *German-Soviet Relations Between the Two World Wars,*

1919–1939. Baltimore, Md.: The Johns Hopkins Press, 1951. New ed. New York: Harper and Row, 1966.

Craig, Gordon A. *The Politics of the Prussian Army, 1640–1945.* New York: Oxford University Press, 1956.

Diederichs, Eugen. *Aus meinem Leben.* 3d ed. Leipzig: Felix Meiner, 1942.

————. *Leben und Werk.* Ed. Lulu von Strauss und Torney-Diederichs. Jena: E. Diederichs Verlag, 1936.

Dormandi, Mario. "The German Youth Movement." Unpublished Ph.D. Dissertation, New York: Columbia University, 1960.

Dovifat, Emil. "Die Presse," *Zehn Jahre Deutsche Geschichte, 1918–1928.* Berlin, 1928, pp. 501–512.

Drechsler, Hanno. *Die Sozialistische Arbeiterpartei Deutschlands (SAPD): Ein Beitrag zur Geschichte der deutschen Arbeiterbewegung am Ende der Weimarer Republik.* ("Marburger Abhandlungen zur politischen Wissenschaft," Vol. II.) Meisenheim/Glan: Anton Hain, 1965.

Drews, Richard, and Kantorowicz, Alfred, eds. *Verboten und verbrannt: Deutsche Literatur 12 Jahre unterdrückt.* Berlin: Heinz Ullstein-Hellmut Kindler Verlag, 1947.

Dyck, Harvey L. *Weimar Germany and Soviet Russia, 1926–1933: A Study in Diplomatic Instability.* New York: Columbia University Press, 1966.

Edinger, Lewis. *German Exile Politics: The Social Democratic Executive Committee in the Nazi Era.* Berkeley and Los Angeles: University of California Press, 1956.

Ein Jahrhundert "Frankfurter Zeitung." Frankfurt/M.: Sonderheft der "Gegenwart," 1956.

Enseling, Alf. *Die Weltbühne: Organ der "Intellektuellen Linken."* ("Studien zur Publizistik," Vol. II.) Münster, Westf.: Verlag C. J. Fahle, 1962.

Erdmann, Karl D. "Die Geschichte der Weimarer Republik als Problem der Wissenschaft," *Vierteljahrshefte für Zeitgeschichte,* January 1955, pp. 1–19.

Eschenburg, Theodor *et al.,* eds. *The Path to Dictatorship 1918–1933: Ten Essays.* Trans. John Conway. Introduction by Fritz Stern. Garden City, N.Y.: Doubleday and Co., 1966.

Ewen, Frederic. *The Poetry and Prose of Heinrich Heine.* New York: The Citadel Press, 1948.

Eyck, Erich. *A History of the Weimar Republic.* Trans. H. P. Hanson and R. G. L. Waite. 2 vols. Cambridge, Mass.: Harvard University Press, 1962–1963.

————. *Die Krisis der deutschen Rechtspflege.* Berlin: Verlag für Kulturpolitik, 1926.

Fechter, Paul. *An der Wende der Zeit.* Gütersloh: L. Bertelsmann Verlag, 1949.

————, ed. *Geschichte der deutschen Literatur.* Vol II. *Die Literatur des zwanzigsten Jahrhunderts.* Gütersloh: Siegbert Mohn Verlag, 1960.

Fischer, Ruth. *Stalin and German Communism.* Cambridge, Mass.: Harvard University Press, 1948.

Flake, Otto. *Es wird Abend: Bericht aus einem langen Leben.* Gütersloh: Siegbert Mohn Verlag, 1960.

Flechtheim, Ossip K. *Die Kommunistische Partei Deutschlands in der Weimarer Republik*. Offenbach/M.: Bollwerk-Verlag Karl Drott, 1948.

Fliess, Peter J. *Freedom of the Press in the German Republic, 1918–1933*. Baton Rouge, La.: Louisiana State University Press, 1955.

Foerster, Friedrich W. *Erlebte Weltgeschichte 1869–1953: Memoiren*. Nürnberg: Glock und Lutz, 1953.

Forsthoff, Ernst, ed. *Deutsche Geschichte von 1918 bis 1938 in Dokumenten*. 3d ed. Stuttgart: A. Kröner Verlag, 1943.

Fraenkel, Ernst. *Zur Soziologie der Klassenjustiz*. Berlin: E. Laub Verlag, 1930.

Frank, Leonhard. *Der Mensch ist gut*. Zurich: Max Rascher Verlag, 1917.

———. *Heart on the Left*. Trans. Cyrus Brooks. London: Arthur Barker, 1954.

Frei, Bruno. *Carl v. Ossietzky: Ritter ohne Furcht und Tadel*. Berlin [East]: Aufbau-Verlag, 1966.

Freund, Gerald. *Unholy Alliance: Russian-German Relations from the Treaty of Brest-Litovsk to the Treaty of Berlin*. New York: Harcourt, Brace and Co., 1957.

Fried, Ferdinand [Friedrich Zimmermann]. *Das Ende des Kapitalismus*. Jena: E. Diederichs Verlag, 1931.

Fuchs, Gustav. *Der deutsche Pazifismus*. Stuttgart: Verlag von W. Kohlhammer, 1928.

Fuller, Leon W. "The War of 1914 as Interpreted by German Intellectuals," *The Journal of Modern History*, June 1942, pp. 145–160.

Garten, H. F. *Modern German Drama*. New York: Grove Press, 1959.

Gay, Peter. *The Dilemma of Democratic Socialism: Eduard Bernstein's Challenge to Marx*. New York: Collier Books, 1962.

Gerlach, Hellmut von. *Erinnerungen eines Junkers*. Berlin: Verlag Die Welt am Montag, n.d.

———. *Von Rechts nach Links*. Ed. Emil Ludwig. Zurich: Europa Verlag, 1937.

Gessler, Otto. *Reichswehrpolitik in der Weimarer Zeit*. Stuttgart: Deutsche Verlags-Anstalt, 1958.

Glaeser, Ernst. *Jahrgang 1902*. Berlin: Gustav Kiepenheuer Verlag, 1931. 1st ed. 1928.

———, ed. *Fazit: Ein Querschnitt durch die deutsche Publizistik*. Hamburg: Gebrüder Enoch Verlag, 1929.

[Grelling, Richard.] *I Accuse: By a German*. Trans. Alexander Gray. New York: George H. Duran Co., 1915.

Greuner, Ruth and Reinhart. *Ich stehe links . . . Carl von Ossietzky über Geist und Ungeist der Weimarer Republik*. Berlin [East]: Buchverlag der Morgen, 1963.

Gross, Babette. *Willi Münzenberg: Eine politische Biographie*. Introduction by Arthur Koestler. ("Schriftenreihe der Vierteljahrshefte für Zeitgeschichte," No. 14/15.) Stuttgart: Deutsche Verlags-Anstalt, 1967.

Grossmann, Kurt R. *Ossietzky: Ein deutscher Patriot*. Munich: Kindler Verlag, 1963.

Grossmann, Stefan. *Der Hochverräter Ernst Toller: Die Geschichte eines Prozesses*. Berlin: Rowohlt, 1919.

————. *Ich war begeistert: Eine Lebensgeschichte.* Berlin: S. Fischer Verlag, 1931.

Gruber, Helmut. "The Politics of German Literature, 1914–1933: A Study of the Expressionist and Objectivist Movements." Unpublished Ph.D. Dissertation, New York: Columbia University, 1962.

————. "Willi Münzenberg's German Communist Propaganda Empire, 1921–1933." *The Journal of Modern History,* September 1966, pp. 278–297.

————, ed. *International Communism in the Era of Lenin.* Greenwich, Conn.: Fawcett Publications, 1967.

Gumbel, Emil J. *"Verräter verfallen der Feme": Opfer, Mörder, Richter, 1919–1929.* Berlin: Malik Verlag, 1929.

————. *Vier Jahre politischer Mord.* Berlin: Malik Verlag, 1922.

————. *Vom Fememord zur Reichskanzlei.* Heidelberg: L. Schneider, 1962.

———— *et al.,* eds. *Weissbuch über die Schwarze Reichswehr.* Berlin: Verlag der Neuen Gesellschaft, 1925.

Haas, Willi. *Die literarische Welt.* 2 vols. Berlin: Rowohlt, 1961.

Haase, H. "Die Antikriegsliteratur in der Zeitschrift 'Die weissen Blätter.'" Unpublished Ph.D. Dissertation, University of Berlin [East], 1956.

Habedank, Heinz. *Der Feind steht rechts: Bürgerliche Linke im Kampf gegen den deutschen Militarismus, 1925–1933.* Berlin [East]: Buchverlag der Morgen, 1965.

Hafkesbrink, Hanna. *Unknown Germany: An Inner Chronicle of the First World War Based on Letters and Diaries.* New Haven, Conn.: Yale University Press, 1948.

Halperin, S. William. *Germany Tried Democracy: A Political History of the Reich from 1918 to 1933.* New York: W. W. Norton, 1965.

Handbuch der deutschen Tagespresse (Deutscher Institut für Zeitungskunde.") Berlin: Carl Duncker Verlag, 1932.

Hannover, Heinrich, and Hannover-Drück, Elisabeth. *Politische Justiz 1918–1933.* Introduction by Karl D. Bracher. Frankfurt/M.: Fischer Bücherei, 1966.

Hasenclever, Walter. *Gedichte, Dramen, Prosa.* Ed. Kurt Pinthus. Hamburg: Rowohlt, 1963.

Hass, Hermann. *Sitte und Kultur im Nachkriegsdeutschland.* Hamburg: Hanseatische Verlagsanstalt, 1932.

Hauser, Otto. *Die Juden und Halbjuden der deutschen Literatur.* Leipzig: Verlag "Der Mensch," 1933.

Heine, Heinrich. *Religion and Philosophy in Germany.* Trans. John Snodgrass. Introduction by Ludwig Marcuse. Boston: Beacon Press, 1959.

Herzfelde, Wieland, ed. *Der Malik-Verlag, 1916–1947: Ausstellungskatalog.* Berlin [East]: Deutsche Akademie der Künste, 1967.

Herzog, Wilhelm. *Menschen, denen ich begegnete.* Bern: Francke Verlag, 1959.

Hiller, Kurt. "Aufstieg, Glanz und Verfall der Weltbühne," *Konkret* (Hamburg), March–July 1962.

————. *Der Sprung ins Helle: Reden, offne Briefe, Zwiegespräche, Essays, Thesen, Pamphlete.* Leipzig: W. R. Lindner Verlag, 1932.

———. *Geist werde Herr: Kundgebungen eines Aktivisten vor, in und nach dem Kriege.* Berlin: Erich Reiss Verlag, 1920.

———. *Geistige Grundlagen eines schöpferischen Deutschlands der Zukunft.* Hamburg: Rowohlt, 1947.

———. *Koepfe und Troepfe: Profile aus einem Vierteljahrhundert.* Hamburg: Rowohlt, 1950.

———. *Logokratie oder ein Weltbund des Geistes.* Leipzig: Verlag der Neue Geist, 1921.

Hoegner, Wilhelm. *Die verratene Republik.* Munich: Isar Verlag, 1958.

Hofmannsthal, Hugo von. *Das Schrifttum als geistiger Raum der Nation.* Munich: Bremer Presse, 1927.

Hohlfeld, Johannes, ed. *Deutsche Reichsgeschichte in Dokumenten, 1894–1934.* Berlin: Vertrieb amtlicher Veröffentlichungen, 1934. Vols. III and IV.

Horkenbach, Cuno, ed. *Das Deutsche Reich von 1918 bis heute.* Berlin: Verlag für Presse, Wirtschaft und Politik, 1930.

Hüttig, Helmut. *Die politischen Zeitschriften der Nachkriegszeit in Deutschland.* Leipzig, 1928. (Printed Ph.D. Dissertation.)

Hughes, H. Stuart. *Consciousness and Society: The Reorientation of European Social Thought, 1890–1930.* New York: Alfred A. Knopf, 1958.

Hunt, Richard N. *German Social Democracy, 1918–1933.* New Haven, Conn.: Yale University Press, 1964.

[Jacobsohn, Siegfried] S. J. *Der Fall Jacobsohn.* Charlottenburg: Verlag der Schaubühne, 1913.

Kantorowicz, Alfred. *Deutsches Tagebuch.* 2 vols. Munich: Kindler Verlag, 1959.

———. *Porträts: Deutsche Schicksale.* Berlin: Chronos Verlag, 1947.

Karl, Heinz. *Die deutsche Arbeiterklasse im Kampf um die Enteignung der Fürsten, 1925–1926.* Berlin [East]: Buchverlag der Morgen, 1957.

Kaznelson, Siegmund, ed. *Juden im deutschen Kulturbereich: Ein Sammelwerk.* 3d ed. Berlin: Jüdischer Verlag, 1962.

Kessler, Harry Graf. *Tagebücher, 1918–1937.* Ed. Wolfgang Pfeiffer-Belli. Frankfurt/M.: Insel Verlag, 1961.

Kesten, Hermann. *Der Geist der Unruhe.* Cologne: Kiepenheuer und Witsch, 1959.

Klemperer, Klemens von. *Germany's New Conservatism: Its History and Dilemma in the Twentieth Century.* Princeton, N.J.: Princeton University Press, 1957.

Koestler, Arthur. *Arrow in the Blue.* 2 vols. New York: Macmillan, 1952–1954.

———. *The Invisible Writing: An Autobiography.* Boston: Beacon Press, 1954.

Kohn, Hans. *The Mind of Germany.* New York: Charles Scribner's Sons, 1955.

Kollman, Eric C. "Reinterpreting Modern German History: The Weimar Republic," *Journal of Central European Affairs,* January 1962, pp. 434–451.

Koplin, Raimund. *Carl von Ossietzky als politischer Publizist.* Berlin: Verlag Annedore Leber, 1964.

Kortner, Fritz. *Aller Tage Abend.* Munich: Kindler Verlag, 1959.

Koszyk, Kurt. *Zwischen Kaiserreich und Diktatur: Die sozialdemokratische Presse von 1914 bis 1933.* Heidelberg: Quelle und Meyer, 1958.
Kraus, Karl. *Gesammelte Werke.* Ed. Heinrich Fischer. 12 vols. Munich: Kösel-Verlag, 1952 ff.
Krell, Max. *Das alles gab es einmal.* Frankfurt/M.: Heinrich Scheffler, 1961.
Krieger, Leonard. *The German Idea of Freedom.* Boston: Beacon Press, 1957.
Kunisch, Hermann, ed. *Handbuch der deutschen Gegenwartsliteratur.* Munich: Nymphenburger Verlagshandlung, 1965.
Kuttner, Erich. *Warum versagt die Justiz?* Berlin: Verlag für Sozialwissenschaft, 1921.
Landauer, Carl. *European Socialism.* 2 vols. Berkeley and Los Angeles: University of California Press, 1959.
Laqueur, Walter Z. *Young Germany: A History of the German Youth Movement.* New York: Basic Books, 1962.
————, and Mosse, George L., eds. *The Left-wing Intellectuals Between the Wars, 1919–1939.* New York: Harper Torchbooks, 1966.
Lehmann-Russbüldt, Otto. *Aggression: The Origin of Germany's War Machine.* London: Hutchinson and Co., 1942.
————. *Der Kampf der Deutschen Liga für Menschenrechte vormals Bund Neues Vaterland für den Weltfrieden, 1914–1927.* Berlin: Hensel und Co., 1927.
Lewinsohn, Richard [Morus]. *Das Geld in der Politik.* Berlin: S. Fischer Verlag, 1930.
Link, Werner. *Die Geschichte des Internationalen Jugend-Bundes (IJB) und des Internationalen Sozialistischen Kampf-Bundes (ISK).* ("Marburger Abhandlungen zur politischen Wissenschaft," Vol. I.) Meisenheim/Glan: Anton Hain, 1964.
Liptzin, Solomon. *Germany's Stepchildren.* New York: World Publishing Co., 1961.
Lunke, E. W. "Die deutsche Presse im eigenen Urteil, 1918 bis 1933." Unpublished Ph.D. Dissertation, University of Munich, 1952.
Mann, Erika, and Mann, Klaus. *The Other Germany.* New York: Modern Age Books, 1940.
Mann, Golo. *Deutsche Geschichte des neunzehnten und zwanzigsten Jahrhunderts.* Frankfurt/M.: S. Fischer Verlag, 1961.
————. "The Intellectuals," *Encounter,* June 1955, pp. 42–49.
Mann, Heinrich. *Essays.* 2 vols. Berlin [East]: Aufbau-Verlag, 1954.
Mann, Klaus. *The Turning Point: Thirty-Five Years in This Century.* New York: L. B. Fischer, 1942.
Mann, Thomas. *Betrachtungen eines Unpolitischen.* Berlin: S. Fischer Verlag, 1920.
————. *Briefe.* Ed. Erika Mann. Frankfurt/M.: S. Fischer Verlag, 1961.
————. *Gesammelte Werke.* 12 vols. Oldenburg: S. Fischer Verlag, 1960.
Manowski, Wolfgang M. von. "Carlo Mierendorff and the Iron Front." Unpublished Master's Thesis, New York: Columbia University, 1967.
Marcuse, Ludwig. *Mein zwanzigstes Jahrhundert: Auf dem Weg zu einer Autobiographie.* Munich: Paul List Verlag, 1960.
Matthias, Erich, and Morsey, Rudolf, eds. *Das Ende der Parteien 1933.*

Düsseldorf: Droste Verlag, 1960.

Meinecke, Friedrich. *Politische Schriften und Reden.* Ed. Georg Kotowski. Darmstadt: Siegfried Toeche-Mittler Verlag, 1958.

————. *The German Catastrophe: Reflections and Recollections.* Trans. Sidney B. Fay. Boston: Beacon Press, 1963. 1st ed. in German, 1946.

Mendelssohn, Peter de. *Zeitungsstadt Berlin.* Berlin: Ullstein, 1959.

Mertens, Carl. *Verschwörer und Fememörder.* Berlin-Charlottenburg: Verlag der Weltbühne, 1926.

Mitchell, Allan. *Revolution in Bavaria, 1918–1919: The Eisner Regime and the Soviet Republic.* Princeton, N.J.: Princeton University Press, 1965.

Mohler, Armin. *Die konservative Revolution in Deutschland, 1918–1932: Grundriss ihrer Weltanschauung.* Stuttgart: Friedrich Vorwerk Verlag, 1950. (With a detailed list of the conservative revolutionary periodicals.)

Mommsen, Wolfgang J. *Max Weber und die deutsche Politik, 1890–1920.* Tübingen: J. C. B. Mohr, 1959.

Mosse, George. *The Culture of Western Europe.* Chicago: Rand McNally and Co., 1961.

Mühsam, Erich. *Auswahl: Gedichte, Drama, Prosa.* Berlin: Verlag Volk und Welt, 1961.

————. *Unpolitische Erinnerungen.* Notes by Dieter Schiller. Düsseldorf: Brücken Verlag, 1961.

Müller-Jabusch, Maximilian, ed. *Handbuch des öffentlichen Lebens.* Leipzig: K. F. Koehler, 1931.

Neue Deutsche Biographie. Berlin: Duncker and Humboldt, 1952 ff. (As of 1967 in seven vols.: *A-Har.*)

Neurohr, Jean. *Der Mythos vom Dritten Reich.* Stuttgart: J. G. Cottasche Buchhandlung, 1957.

Niekisch, Ernst. *Gewagtes Leben: Begegnungen und Begebnisse.* Cologne: Kiepenheuer und Witsch, 1958.

Osborn, Max, ed. *50 Jahre Ullstein, 1877–1927.* Berlin: Ullstein, 1927.

[Ossietzky, Carl von] *Carl von Ossietzky: Schriften.* Eds. Bruno Frei and Hans Leonard. 2 vols. Berlin [East]: Aufbau-Verlag, 1966.

Ossietzky, Maud. *Maud v. Ossietzky erzählt: Ein Lebensbild.* Berlin [East]: Buchverlag der Morgen, 1966.

Osterroth, Franz, ed. *Biographisches Lexikon des Sozialismus.* Vol. I. Hannover: J. H. W. Dietz Nachf., 1960.

————, and Dieter Schuster, eds. *Chronik der deutschen Sozialdemokratie.* Hannover: J. H. W. Dietz Nachf., 1963.

Ostwald, Hans. *Sittengeschichte der Inflation: Ein Kulturdokument aus den Jahren des Marksturzes.* Berlin: Neufeld und Henius, 1931.

Otten, Karl, ed. *Ahnung und Aufbruch: Expressionistische Prosa.* Darmstadt: Hermann Luchterhand Verlag, 1957.

Paetel, Karl Otto. *Versuchung oder Chance? Zur Geschichte des deutschen Nationalbolschewismus.* Göttingen: Musterschmidt Verlag, 1965.

Paulsen, Wolfgang. *Aktivismus und Expressionismus: Eine typologische Untersuchung.* Bern: Gotthelf, 1935.

Pechel, Rudolf. *Die Deutsche Rundschau.* Hamburg: Rütten und Loening Verlag, 1961.

Pfeiler, William K. *War and the German Mind: The Testimony of Men of*

Fiction Who Fought at the Front. New York: Columbia University Press, 1941.

Pinson, Koppel S. *Modern Germany: Its History and Civilization.* New York: The Macmillan Co., 1954.

Piscator, Erwin. *Das politische Theater.* Berlin: Adalbert Schultz Verlag, 1929.

Polgar, Alfred. *Im Lauf der Zeit.* Hamburg: Rowohlt, 1954.

Poliakov, Léon, and Wulf, Josef, eds. *Das Dritte Reich und seine Denker: Dokumente.* Berlin: Arani Verlag, 1959.

Poor, Harold L. "Kurt Tucholsky: A Leftist Intellectual Views the Weimar Republic." Unpublished Ph.D. Dissertation, New York: Columbia University, 1965.

――――. *Kurt Tucholsky and the Ordeal of Germany, 1914–1935.* New York: Charles Scribner's Sons, 1968.

Prescher, Hans. *Kurt Tucholsky.* Berlin: Colloquium Verlag, 1959.

Pritzkoleit, Kurt. *Die neuen Herren: Die Mächtigen in Staat und Wirtschaft.* Vienna: Verlag Kurt Desch, 1958.

Pross, Harry. *Literatur und Politik: Geschichte und Programme der politisch-literarischen Zeitschriften im deutschen Sprachgebiet seit 1870.* Olten: Walter Verlag, 1963.

――――, ed. *Die Zerstörung der deutschen Politik: Dokumente, 1871–1933.* Frankfurt/M.: Fischer Bücherei, 1959.

Raddatz, Fritz J. *Tucholsky: Eine Bildbiographie.* Munich: Kindler Verlag, 1959.

Rauschning, Hermann. *The Conservative Revolution.* New York: Putnam, 1941.

Reichel, Karl Ferdinand. *Die pazifistische Presse.* Würzburg: Konrad Triltsch Verlag, 1938.

Reichshandbuch der deutschen Gesellschaft. 2 vols. Berlin: Deutscher Wirtschaftsverlag, 1931.

Reut-Nicolussi, E. "Drei österreichische Rufer zum Frieden," *Gemeinschaft des Geistes: Ein Symposium.* ("Schriftenreihe der Oesterreichischen Unesco-Kommission," No. 14.)

Rogge, Helmuth. "Aus Maximilian Hardens politischer Publizistik, 1912–1922," *Publizistik,* September–October 1961, pp. 301–337.

Rohe, Karl. *Das Reichsbanner Schwarz Rot Gold: Ein Beitrag zur Geschichte und Struktur der politischen Kampfverbände zur Zeit der Weimarer Republik.* ("Beiträge zur Geschichte des Parlamentarismus und der politischen Parteien," 34.) Düsseldorf: Droste Verlag, 1966.

Rosenberg, Arthur. *A History of the German Republic.* Trans. Ian F. D. Morrow and L. Marie Sieveking. London: Methuen and Co., 1936.

Rühle, Günther. *Theater für die Republik 1917–1933—Im Spiegel der Kritik.* Frankfurt/M.: S. Fischer Verlag, 1967.

Rühle, Jürgen. *Literatur und Revolution: Die Schriftsteller und der Kommunismus.* Cologne: Kiepenheuer und Witsch, 1960.

Schacherl, Lillian. "Die Zeitschriften des Expressionismus." Unpublished Ph.D. Dissertation, University of Munich, 1957–1958.

Schay, Rudolf. *Juden in der deutschen Politik.* Berlin: Welt-Verlag, 1929.

Schlawe, Fritz. *Literarische Zeitschriften, 1910–1933.* Stuttgart: J. B. Metzler, 1962.

Schoenaich, Paul Freiherr von. *Mein Finale.* Flensburg: Verlagshaus Christian Wolff, 1947.

Schoeps, Hans Joachim. "Das letze Vierteljahr der Weimarer Republik im Zeitschriftenecho," *Geschichte in Wissenschaft und Unterricht,* August 1959.

Schorske, Carl E. *German Social Democracy, 1905–1917: The Development of the Great Schism.* New York: John Wiley, 1965.

Schüddekopf, Otto-Ernst. *Linke Leute von Rechts: Die nationalrevolutionären Minderheiten und der Kommunismus in der Weimarer Republik.* Stuttgart: W. Kohlhammer Verlag, 1960.

———, ed. *Das Heer und die Republik: Quellen zur Politik der Reichswehrführung, 1918 bis 1933.* Hannover: Norddeutsche Verlagsanstalt O. Goedel, 1955.

Schulz, Klaus-Peter. *Kurt Tucholsky in Selbstzeugnissen und Bilddokumenten.* Hamburg: Rowohlt, 1959. (With a bibliography.)

Schwarz, Albert. *Die Weimarer Republik.* Konstanz: Akademische Verlagsgesellschaft Athenaion, 1958.

Schwarzschild, Leopold. *Die letzten Jahre vor Hitler: Aus dem "Tagebuch" 1929–1933.* Ed. Valerie Schwarzschild. Hamburg: Christian Wegner Verlag, 1966.

———. *Von Krieg zu Krieg.* Amsterdam: Querido Verlag, 1947.

Schwerin, Christoph, ed. *Der goldene Schnitt: Essayisten der Neuen Rundschau, 1890–1960.* Frankfurt/M.: S. Fischer Verlag, 1960.

Sechzig Jahre Eugen Diederichs Verlag: Ein Almanach. Düsseldorf: E. Diederichs Verlag, 1956.

Seeckt, Hans v. *Aus seinem Leben, 1918–1936.* Ed. Friedrich von Rabenau. Leipzig: von Hase und Koehler Verlag, 1940.

Sell, Friedrich C. *Die Tragödie des deutschen Liberalismus.* Stuttgart: Deutsche Verlags-Anstalt, 1953.

Sokel, Walter H. *The Writer in Extremis: Expressionism in Twentieth-Century German Literature.* Stanford, Calif.: Stanford University Press, 1959.

———, ed. *An Anthology of German Expressionist Drama: A Prelude to the Absurd.* Garden City, N.J.: Doubleday and Co., 1963.

Sontheimer, Kurt. *Antidemokratisches Denken in der Weimarer Republik: Die politischen Ideen des deutschen Nationalismus zwischen 1918 und 1933.* Munich: Nymphenburger Verlagshandlung, 1962.

———. "Der Tatkreis," *Vierteljahrshefte für Zeitgeschichte,* July 1959, pp. 229–260.

———. *Thomas Mann und die Deutschen.* Munich: Nymphenburger Verlagshandlung, 1961.

Sperlings Zeitschriften- und Zeitungs-Adressbuch: Handbuch der deutschen Presse. Leipzig: Verlag des Börsenvereins der deutschen Buchhändler, 1929 ff.

Stampfer, Friedrich. *Die ersten 14 Jahre der deutschen Republik.* 2d ed. Offenbach/M.: Bollwerk Verlag, 1947.

Stapel, Wilhelm. *Die literarische Vorherrschaft der Juden, 1918–1933.* Hamburg: Hanseatische Verlagsanstalt, 1937.

———. "Kurt Tucholsky," *Forschungen zur Judenfrage.* ("Sitzungsberichte der Forschungsabteilung Judenfrage des Reichsinstituts für Geschichte des neuen Deutschlands vom 12. bis 14. Mai 1937," Vol. II.) Hamburg: Hanseatische Verlagsanstalt, 1937, pp. 182–215.

―――. *Literatenwäsche.* Berlin: Widerstands-Verlag, 1930.

Starker, Gerda. "Die geschichtliche Entwicklung des deutschen Pazifismus seit 1900: Ein Beitrag zum Zusammenbruch Deutschlands im Weltkrieg." Unpublished Ph.D. Dissertation, University of Heidelberg, 1935.

Steffani, Winfried, ed. *Die Untersuchungsausschüsse des Preussischen Landtages zur Zeit der Weimarer Republik.* ("Kommission für Geschichte des Parlamentarismus und der politischen Parteien.") Düsseldorf: Droste Verlag, 1960.

Stern, Fritz. "The Political Consequences of the Unpolitical German," *History*, 3. September 1960, pp. 104–134.

―――. *The Politics of Cultural Despair: A Study in the Rise of the Germanic Ideology.* Berkeley and Los Angeles: University of California Press, 1961.

Sternfeld, Wilhelm, and Tiedemann, Eva, eds. *Deutsche Exil-Literatur 1933–1945: Eine Bio-Bibliographie.* ("Veröffentlichungen der Deutschen Akademie für Sprache und Dichtung," No. 29.) Heidelberg: Verlag Lambert Schneider, 1962.

Stolper, Toni. *Ein Leben in Brennpunkten unserer Zeit, Wien, Berlin, New York: Gustav Stolper, 1888–1947.* Tübingen: Rainer Wunderlich Verlag, 1960.

Ströbel, Heinrich. *The German Revolution and After.* Trans. H. J. Stenning. New York: Thomas Seltzer, n.d.

Taube, Utz-Friedebert. *Ludwig Quidde: Ein Beitrag zur Geschichte des demokratischen Gedankens in Deutschland.* ("Münchener Historische Studien. Abteilung Neuere Geschichte," Vol. V.) Kallmünz, Opf.: Verlag Michael Lassleben, 1963.

Toller, Ernst. *Ausgewählte Schriften.* Notes by Bodo Uhse and Bruno Kaiser. Berlin [East]: Verlag Volk und Welt, 1961.

―――. *I Was a German: An Autobiography.* Trans. Edward Crankshaw. London: John Lane, 1934.

―――. *Prosa, Briefe, Dramen, Gedichte.* Introduction by Kurt Hiller. Hamburg: Rowohlt, 1962.

Toury, Jakob. *Die politischen Orientierungen der Juden in Deutschland von Jena bis Weimar.* Tübingen: J. C. B. Mohr (Paul Siebeck), 1966.

Treue, Wolfgang. *Deutsche Parteiprogramme 1861–1956.* Vol. III. Göttingen: Musterschmidt Verlag, 1956.

Troeltsch, Ernst. *Deutscher Geist und Westeuropa.* Ed. Hans Baron. Tübingen: Verlag J. C. B. Mohr, 1925.

―――. *Spektator-Briefe: Aufsätze über die deutsche Revolution und die Weltpolitik, 1918–1922.* Ed. Hans Baron. Tübingen: Verlag J. C. B. Mohr, 1924.

Trotsky, Leon. *Écrits, 1928–1940.* Paris: Quatrième Internationale, 1955–1959. Vol. III.

Tucholsky, Kurt. *Ausgewählte Briefe, 1913–1935.* Eds. Mary Gerold-Tucholsky and Fritz J. Raddatz. Hamburg: Rowohlt, 1962.

―――. *Deutschland, Deutschland über alles: Ein Bilderbuch von Kurt Tucholsky und vielen Fotografen. Montiert von John Heartfield.* Berlin: Neuer Deutscher Verlag, 1929. Also, Hamburg: Rowohlt, 1964.

Weimar Germany's Left-Wing Intellectuals

————. *Gesammelte Werke.* Eds. Mary Gerold-Tucholsky and Fritz J. Raddatz. 3 vols. Hamburg: Rowohlt, 1960–1961.

————. *What If—? Satirical Writings of Kurt Tucholsky.* Trans. Harry Zohn and Karl F. Ross. New York: Funk and Wagnalls, 1967.

Turner, Henry A. *Stresemann and the Politics of the Weimar Republic.* Princeton, N.J.: Princeton University Press, 1963.

Ullstein, Heinz. *Spielplatz meines Lebens: Erinnerungen.* Munich: Kindler Verlag, 1961.

Ullstein, Hermann. *The Rise and Fall of the House of Ullstein.* New York: Simon and Schuster, 1943.

Unruh, Fritz von. *Mächtig seid Ihr nicht in Waffen: Reden.* Nürnberg: Verlag Hans Carl, 1957.

Utitz, Emil. *Egon Erwin Kisch: Der klassische Journalist.* Berlin [East]: Aufbau-Verlag, 1965.

Victor, Walther. *Kehre wieder über die Berge: Eine Autobiographie.* New York: Willard Publishing Co., 1945.

Vogelsang, Thilo. "Neuere Literatur zur Geschichte der Weimarer Republik," *Vierteljahrshefte für Zeitgeschichte,* April 1961, pp. 211–224.

Wacker, Wolfgang. *Der Bau des Panzerschiffes "A" und der Reichstag.* Tübingen: J. C. B. Mohr, 1959.

Wagner, Walter. "Politische Justiz in der Weimarer Republik," *Politische Meinung,* March 1961, pp. 50–63, and May 1961, pp. 48–61.

Waite, Robert G. L. *Vanguard of Nazism: The Free Corps Movement in Postwar Germany, 1918–1923.* Cambridge, Mass.: Harvard University Press, 1952.

Wassermann, Jakob. *My Life as a German and a Jew.* Trans. N. S. Brainin. New York: Coward-McCann, 1933.

Wehberg, Hans. *Als Pazifist im Weltkriege.* Leipzig: Der Neue Geist Verlag, 1919.

————. *Die Führer der deutschen Friedensbewegung, 1890 bis 1933.*

Werner, Bruno E. *Die zwanziger Jahre: Von Morgens bis Mitternachts.* Munich: Bruckmann, 1962.

Weyrauch, Wolfgang, ed. *Ausnahmezustand: Eine Anthologie aus "Weltbühne" und "Tagebuch."* Munich: Verlag Kurt Desch, 1966.

Wheeler-Bennett, John W. *The Nemesis of Power: The German Army in Politics, 1918–1945.* London: Macmillan, 1954.

Wilde, Harry. *Theodor Plievier: Nullpunkt der Freiheit. Biographie.* Munich: Verlag Kurt Desch, 1965.

Young, Harry F. *Maximilian Harden: Censor Germaniae.* The Hague: Nijhoff, 1959.

Zahn, Manfred. "Die öffentliche Meinung und die Presse." Unpublished Ph.D. Dissertation, University of Münster, 1953.

Zohn, Harry, ed. *The World Is a Comedy: A Tucholsky Anthology.* Cambridge, Mass.: Sci-Art Publishers, 1957.

Zweig, Arnold. *Bilanz der deutschen Judenheit, 1933.* Amsterdam: Querido Verlag, 1934.

Zwoch, Gerhard. "Die Erfüllungs- und Verständigungspolitik der Weimarer Republik und die deutsche öffentliche Meinung." Unpublished Ph.D. Dissertation, University of Kiel, 1950.

INDEX

335